COLONIAL COMICS

New England, 1620-1750

Library of Congress Cataloging-in-Publication Data

Colonial comics / edited by Jason Rodriguez.
     pages cm
   ISBN 978-1-938486-30-2
1. United States--History--Colonial period, ca. 1600-1775--Comic books, strips, etc. 2. United States--History--Colonial period, ca. 1600-1775--Juvenile literature. 3. Graphic novels. I. Rodriguez, Jason (Comic book author)
   E188.C723 2014
   973.2--dc23

                                    2014031715

Printed in the United States
0 9 8 7 6 5 4 3 2 1

Design by Jason Rodriguez
Cover image © Scott White

Fulcrum Publishing
4690 Table Mountain Dr., Ste. 100
Golden, CO 80403
800-992-2908 • 303-277-1623
www.fulcrumbooks.com

COLONIAL COMICS

New England, 1620-1750

Edited by Jason Rodriguez

Assistant Editors A. David Lewis and J.L. Bell

FULCRUM

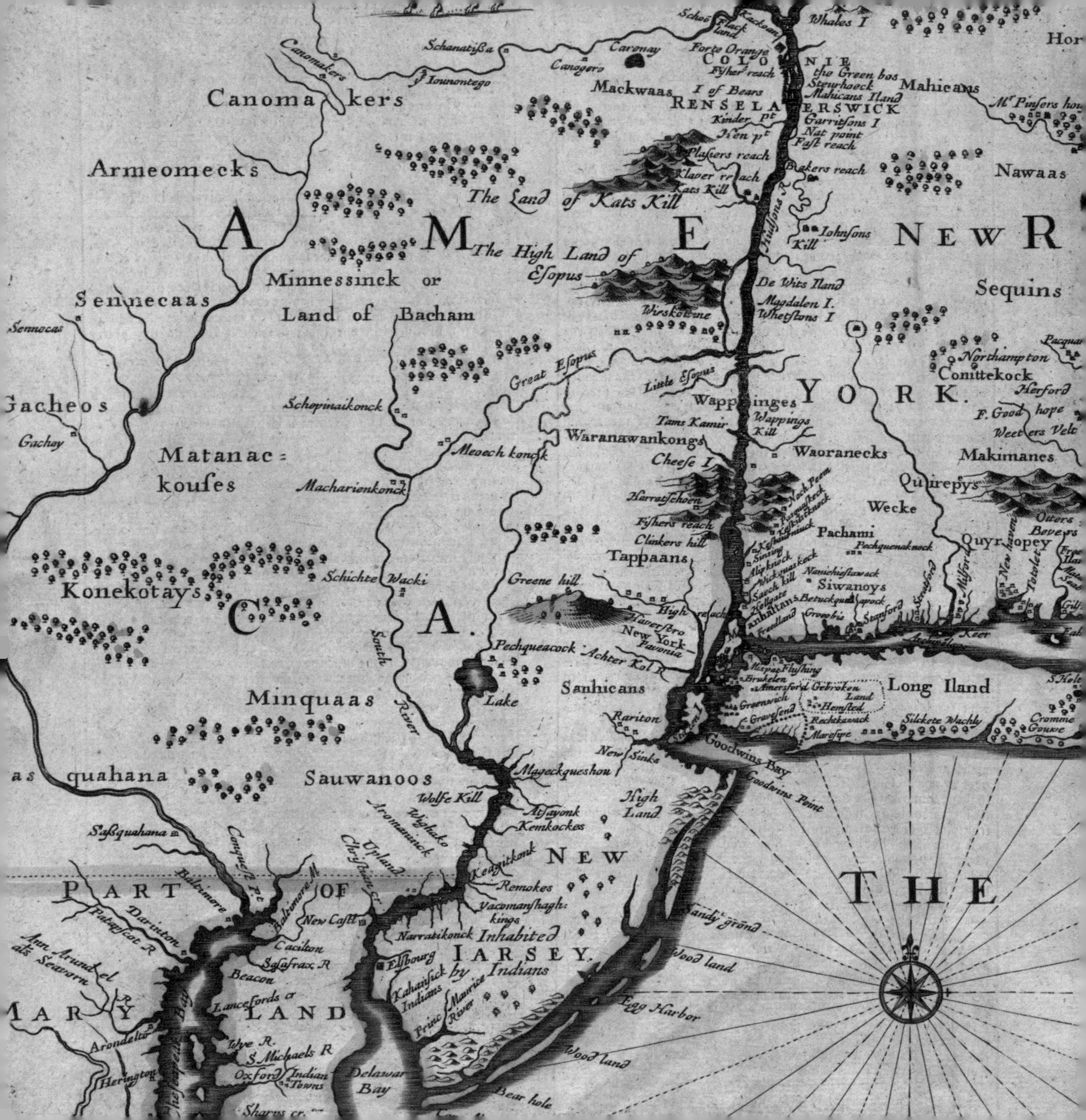

Canomakers
Schanatissa
Caronay
Canogero
Iounontego
Canomakers
Mackwaas
Forte Orange
COLONIE
Fishers reach
I of Bears
RENSELAERSWICK
the Green bos
Steurhoeck
Mahicans Iland
Mahicans
Garritsons I
Nat point
Fast reach
Kinder pt
Hen pt
Plasiers reach
Klaver reach
Kats Kill
Bakers reach
Nawaas
Armeomecks
The Land of Kats Kill
A M E
Hudsons R
Johnsons Kill
NEW R
The High Land of Esopus
Minnessinck or
Land of Bacham
Sennecaas
Sennecas
De Wits Iland
Magdalen I.
Whetstons I
Sequins
Wirskonne
Great Esopus
Little Esopus
Northampton
Conittekock
YORK.
Herford
F. Good hope
Weeters Velt
Gacheos
Gachay
Schepinaikonck
Wappinges
Wappings Kill
Tans Kamir
Waranawankongs
Meoech konck
Matanackouses
Machatienkonck
Cheese I
Waoranecks
Makimanes
Quirepys
Harratschoen
Wecke
Pachami
Fishers reach
Clinkers hill
Tappaans
Quyrnopey
New haven
Milford
Stratford
Konekotays
Schichte Wacki
Greene hill
Siwanoys
C A.
High reach
Haverstro
New York
Pavonia
Stanford
South River
Pechqueacock
Achter Kol R
Lake
Sanhicans
Long Iland
Minquaas
Rariton
Gravesend
Greenwich
Hemsted
Flushing
Breukelen
Amersford
Gebroken Land
Rechkawack
Silckete Wachly
Cromme Gouwe
Goodwins Bay
Goodwins Point
New Sinks
quahana
Sauwanoos
Mageckqueshou
Wolfe Kill
High Land
Sasquahana
Aromaminck
Wighako
Atsayonk
Kemkockes
Upland
Christina cr
Conquest Pt
Baltimore
NEW
PART OF
Keagitkonk
Remokes
Yacomanshagh:kings
THE
Darinton
Patapsco R
New Castl
Cacilton
Sasafrax R
Narratikonck
Inhabited
IARSEY.
by Indians
Ann Arundel als Seavorn
Beacon
Elsbourg
Kahatisick Indians
Maurice River
Sandy grond
Wood land
MARYLAND
Lancefords cr
Arondelto
Wye R.
S. Michaels R
Oxford
Indian Towns
Herington
Chesapeake Bay
Delawar Bay
Egg Harbor
Wood land
Bear hole
Sharps cr

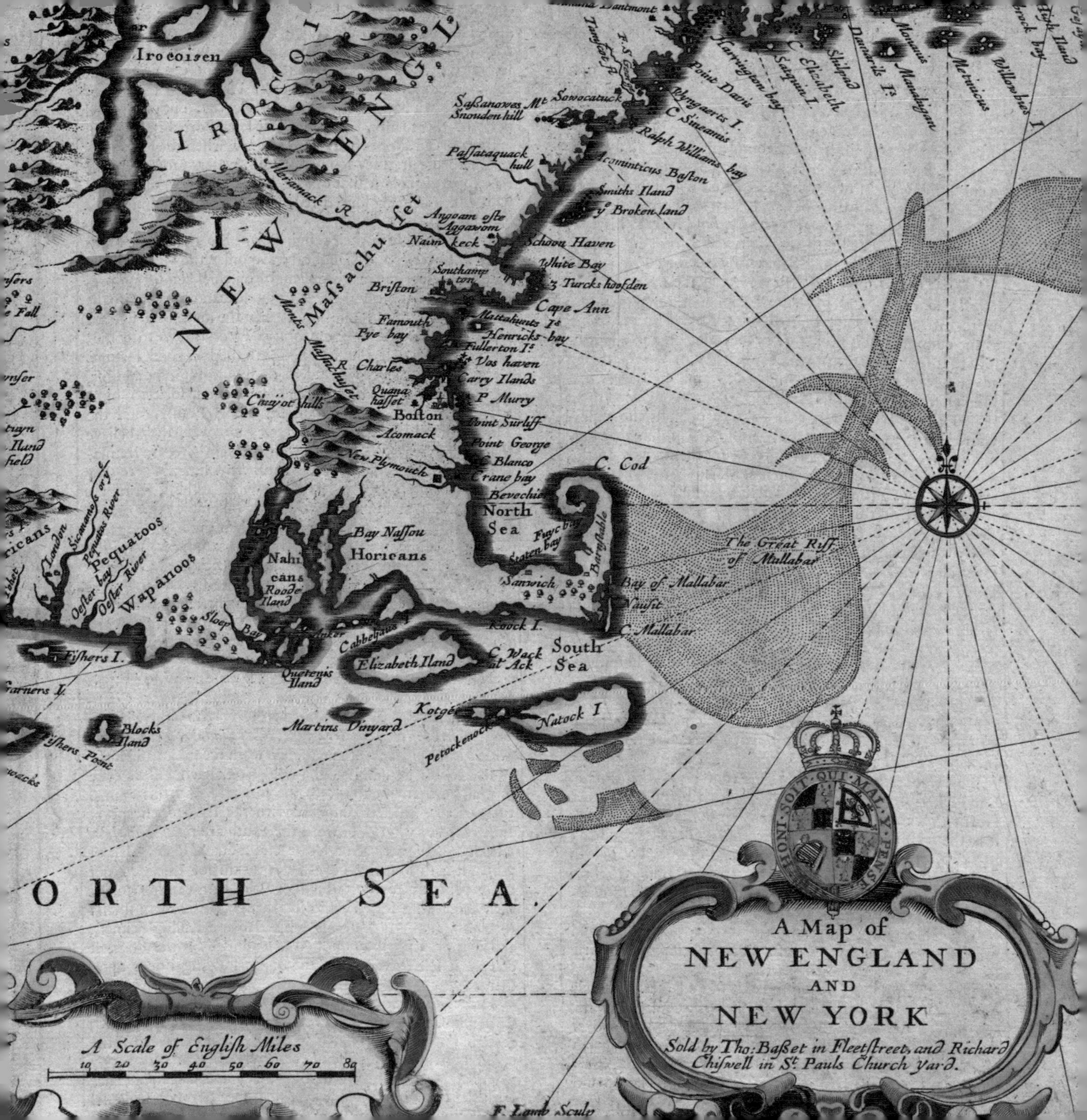
A Map of
NEW ENGLAND
AND
NEW YORK
Sold by Tho: Baßet in Fleetstreet, and Richard
Chiswell in St. Pauls Church yard.
A Scale of English Miles
10 20 30 40 50 60 70 80
F. Lamb Sculp
HONI SOIT QUI MAL Y PENSE
NEW ENGL
IROQUOI
Irocoisen
Merimack R
Massachuset
Monts
Sassanowes Mt Snouden hill
Sowocatuck
Passataquack hull
Acominticus Baston
Smiths Iland
ye Broken land
Angoam oste Aggawom
Naimkeck
Schoon Haven
White Bay
Southampton
Briston
3 Turcks hoofden
Cape Ann
Famouth
Pye bay
Mattahunts Is
Henricks bay
Fullerton Is
Vos haven
R Charles
Carry Ilands
P Murry
Quanahasset
Chaujot hills
Massachuset
Boston
Acomack
Point Surliff
Point George
C Blanco
New Plymouth
Crane bay
C. Cod
Bevechier
North Sea
Fuyc bay
Staten bay
Barnstable
Bay Nassou
Horicans
Nahicans
Roode Iland
Pequatoos
Wapanoos
Pequatoos River
Oester bay
Oester River
Sanwich
Bay of Mallabar
Nausit
C. Mallabar
The Great Riff of Mallabar
Roock I.
Cabbelgaus
Anker
Sloep Bay
Fishers I.
Quetenis Iland
Elizabeth Iland
C. Wack at Ack
South Sea
Martins Vinyard
Kotgé
Petockenock
Natock I
Blocks Iland
Fishers Point
London
Point Davis
Harrington bay
C Elizabeth
Sutquin I.
Shipland
Damarils Is
Monanis
Mandagan
Metinicus
Willowbies I.
Wyngaerts I.
C Sineamis
Ralph Williams bay
NORTH SEA.

Contents

From the Editor

For most of my childhood, my knowledge of New England history between the years 1620 and 1750 consisted of the following three topics:

1. Plimoth (or Plymouth) and Boston
2. Tisquantum (or Squanto) and the Pilgrims
3. Something about witches

It was 130 years of history reduced to (mainly) nameless people who ate turkey and occasionally burned suspected witches. The country where I was born and raised, a country that was once inhabited by other nations, reduced to several cities, a single Native American, a group of people who weren't happy in England, and some charred bodies.

But that's not this book. This is the book I wish I had back then. This is a book about the people who came to America, people who were more than turkey aficionados, interacting with a collection of native people and not this one Native American who was really friendly to them before he mysteriously disappeared.

This book is about the people who came over from England (and the people they sometimes brought with them), the communities they created, and the people they pushed westward. John Winthrop,

Cotton Mather, and Tisquantum were not the only people living in America over those 130 years. There were also women, lots of them. There were kids. Free thinkers and philosophers. Teachers. Doctors and business owners. People with good intentions along with the people who wanted everything, even if it meant taking it from the people who didn't have the means to fight back. I want to tell those stories—the good and the bad.

This period of American history, for me, represents a period where we were finding our footing. Where some people were committing atrocities, but where there were also some truly revolutionary people who were testing the boundaries of the society that they lived in and who were beginning to form the basis of what would eventually become an American identity.

And, not surprisingly, these people did more than eat turkey and burn suspected witches.

I hope you enjoy this collection of stories. They're stories about people, which are oftentimes more interesting than stories about caricatures.

Jason Rodriguez
Arlington, Virginia

Harried Out of The Land

Story by Nick Bunker, Art by Chris Piers,
Colors by Jason Axtell, and Letters by Jason Hanley

England, early in the year 1603: a nation in suspense, anxiously awaiting the end of an era. For more than a century, the dynasty known as the Tudors have reigned supreme.

But now, as a long, hard winter draws to an end, the last of the dynasty lies close to death. Henry's daughter Elizabeth is 69, an exhausted old woman, lonely and depressed. She has been Queen for 45 years, but her best days are far behind her. Even so, she will leave a gap that will be very hard to fill.

On March 26, 1603, King James of Scotland learns the Crown of England is his for the taking. He knows the danger of a nation divided, and he wants to bring peace and harmony to his domain. To do that, he needs to deal with the troublemakers. Irish rebels, Roman Catholics... and a small, vocal group known as the Puritans.

8

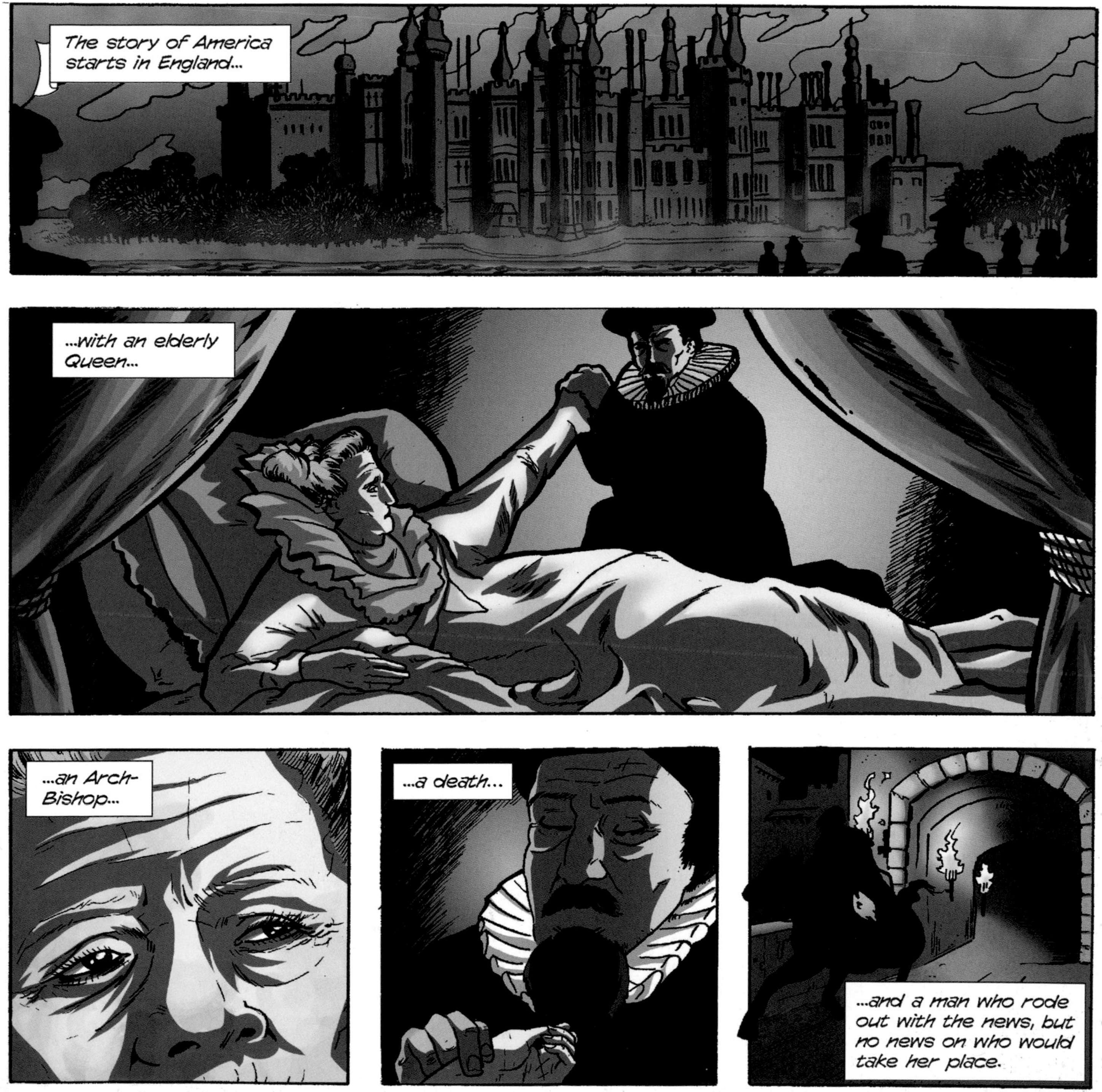
The story of America starts in England...
...with an elderly Queen...
...an Arch-Bishop...
...a death...
...and a man who rode out with the news, but no news on who would take her place.

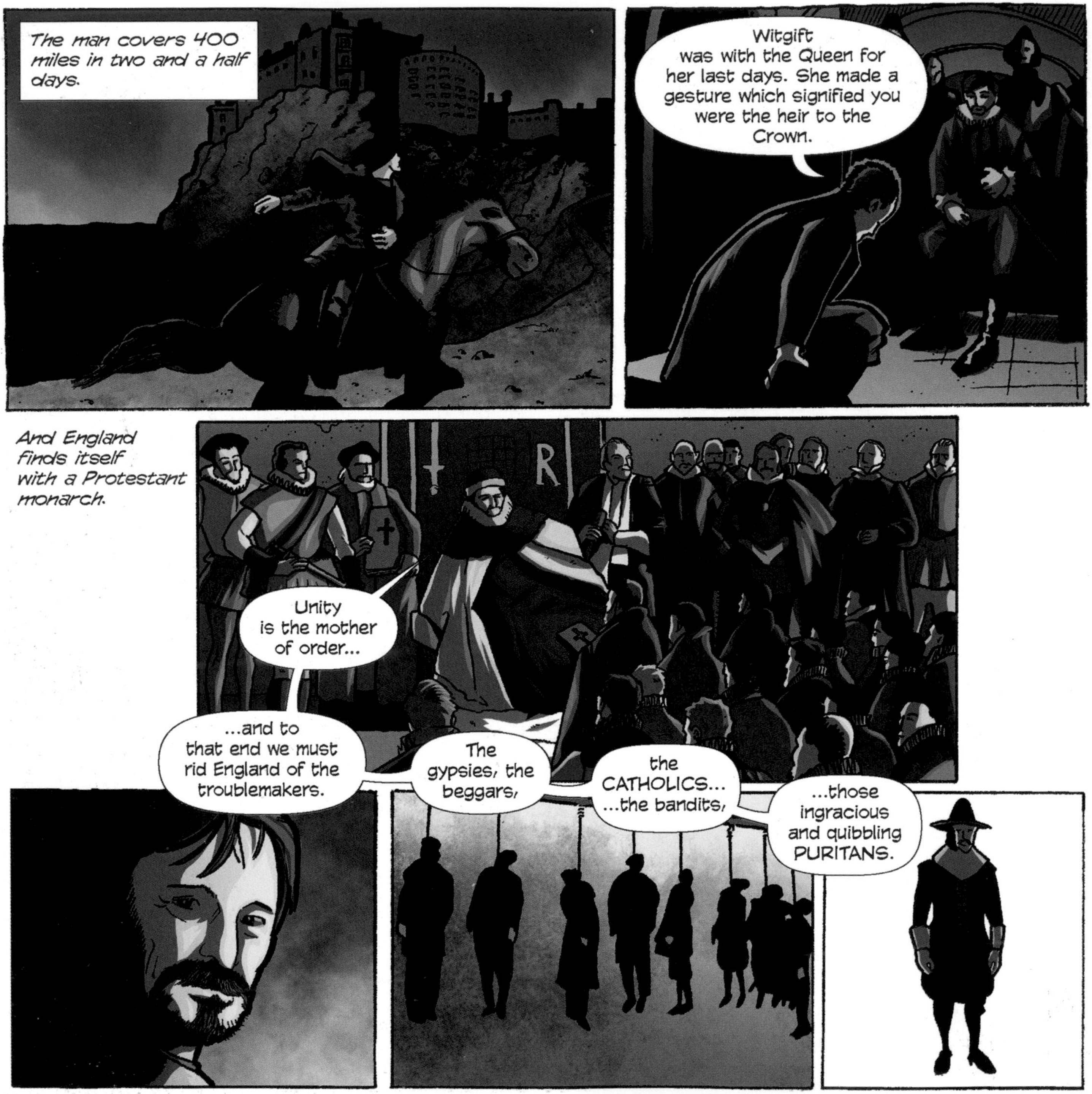
The man covers 400 miles in two and a half days.
Witgift was with the Queen for her last days. She made a gesture which signified you were the heir to the Crown.
And England finds itself with a Protestant monarch.
R
Unity is the mother of order...
...and to that end we must rid England of the troublemakers.
The gypsies, the beggars,
the CATHOLICS... ...the bandits,
...those ingracious and quibbling PURITANS.

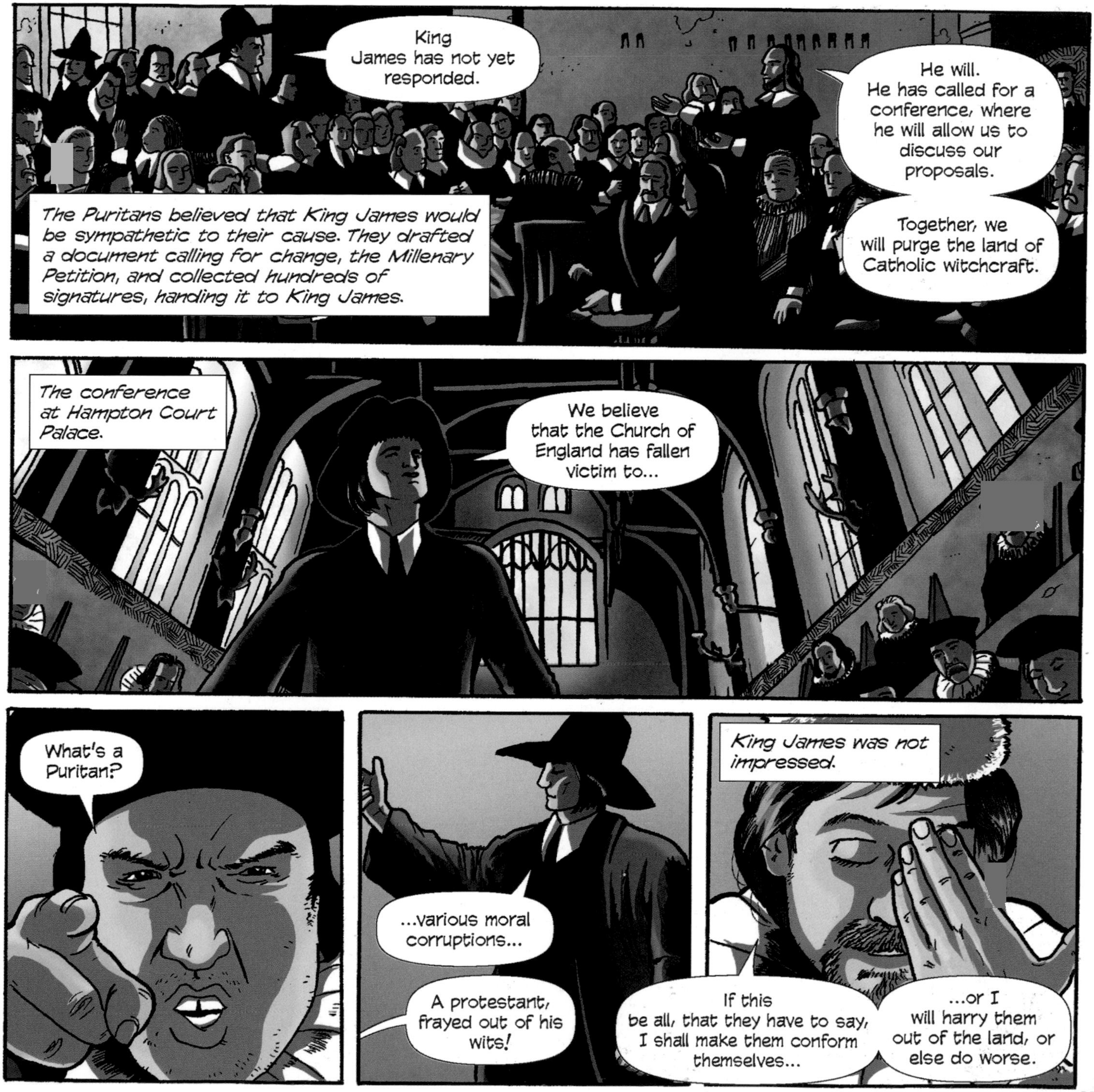
King James has not yet responded.
He will. He has called for a conference, where he will allow us to discuss our proposals.
The Puritans believed that King James would be sympathetic to their cause. They drafted a document calling for change, the Millenary Petition, and collected hundreds of signatures, handing it to King James.
Together, we will purge the land of Catholic witchcraft.
The conference at Hampton Court Palace.
We believe that the Church of England has fallen victim to...
What's a Puritan?
...various moral corruptions...
A protestant, frayed out of his wits!
King James was not impressed.
If this be all, that they have to say, I shall make them conform themselves...
...or I will harry them out of the land, or else do worse.

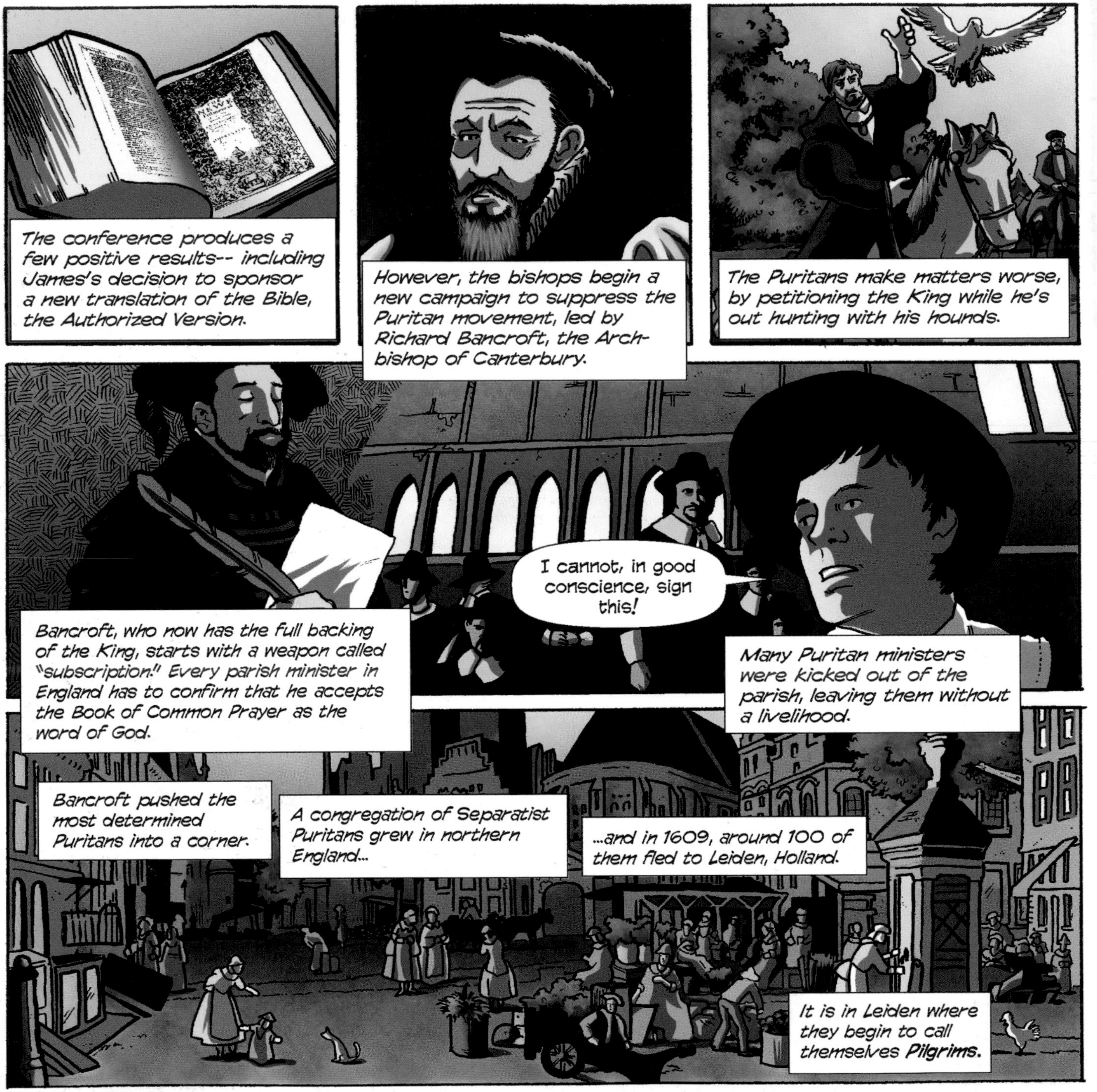

The conference produces a few positive results-- including James's decision to sponsor a new translation of the Bible, the Authorized Version.
However, the bishops begin a new campaign to suppress the Puritan movement, led by Richard Bancroft, the Arch-bishop of Canterbury.
The Puritans make matters worse, by petitioning the King while he's out hunting with his hounds.
Bancroft, who now has the full backing of the King, starts with a weapon called "subscription." Every parish minister in England has to confirm that he accepts the Book of Common Prayer as the word of God.
I cannot, in good conscience, sign this!
Many Puritan ministers were kicked out of the parish, leaving them without a livelihood.
Bancroft pushed the most determined Puritans into a corner.
A congregation of Separatist Puritans grew in northern England...
...and in 1609, around 100 of them fled to Leiden, Holland.
It is in Leiden where they begin to call themselves **Pilgrims**.

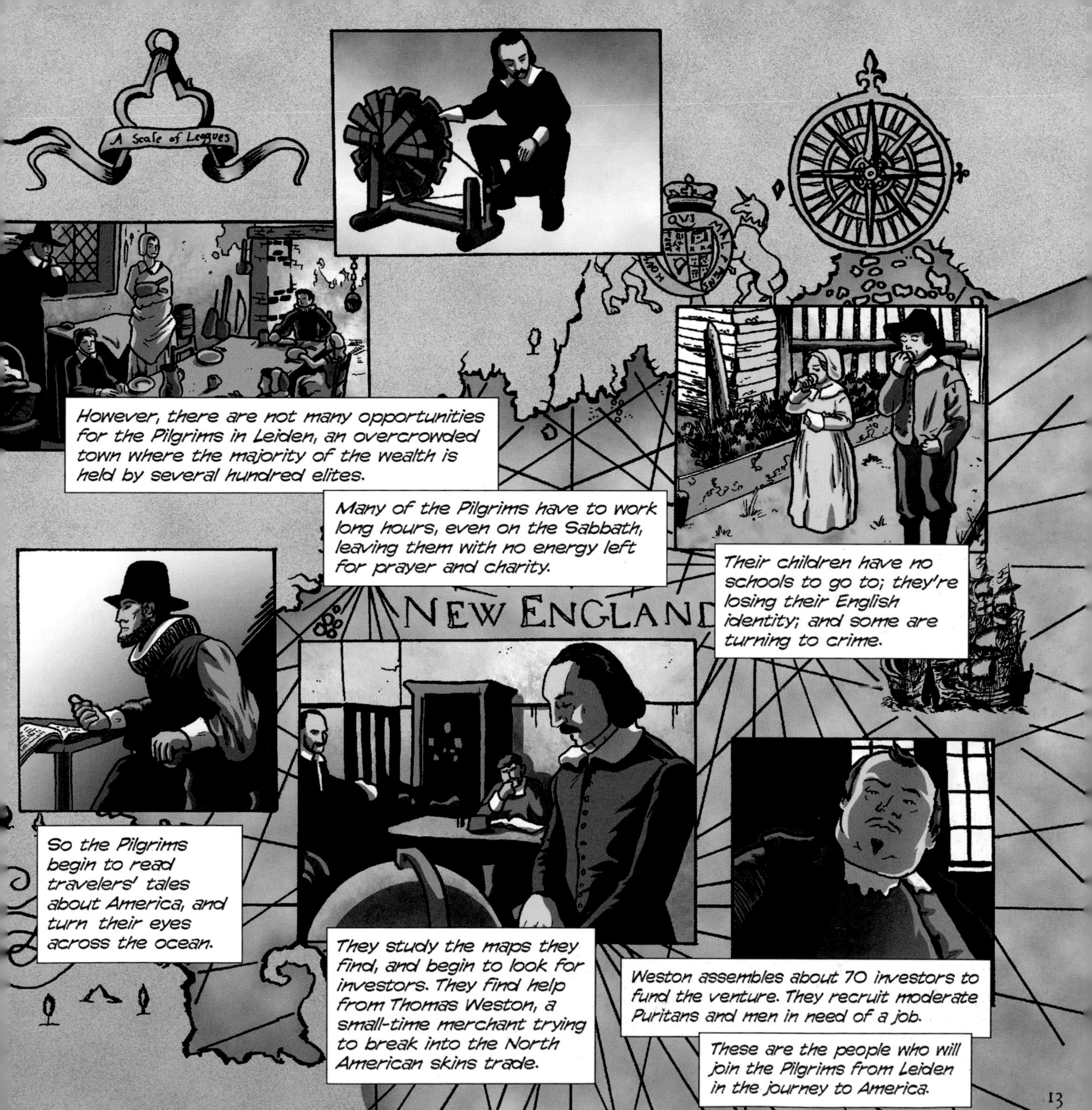
A Scale of Leagues
However, there are not many opportunities for the Pilgrims in Leiden, an overcrowded town where the majority of the wealth is held by several hundred elites.
Many of the Pilgrims have to work long hours, even on the Sabbath, leaving them with no energy left for prayer and charity.
Their children have no schools to go to; they're losing their English identity; and some are turning to crime.
NEW ENGLAND
So the Pilgrims begin to read travelers' tales about America, and turn their eyes across the ocean.
They study the maps they find, and begin to look for investors. They find help from Thomas Weston, a small-time merchant trying to break into the North American skins trade.
Weston assembles about 70 investors to fund the venture. They recruit moderate Puritans and men in need of a job.
These are the people who will join the Pilgrims from Leiden in the journey to America.

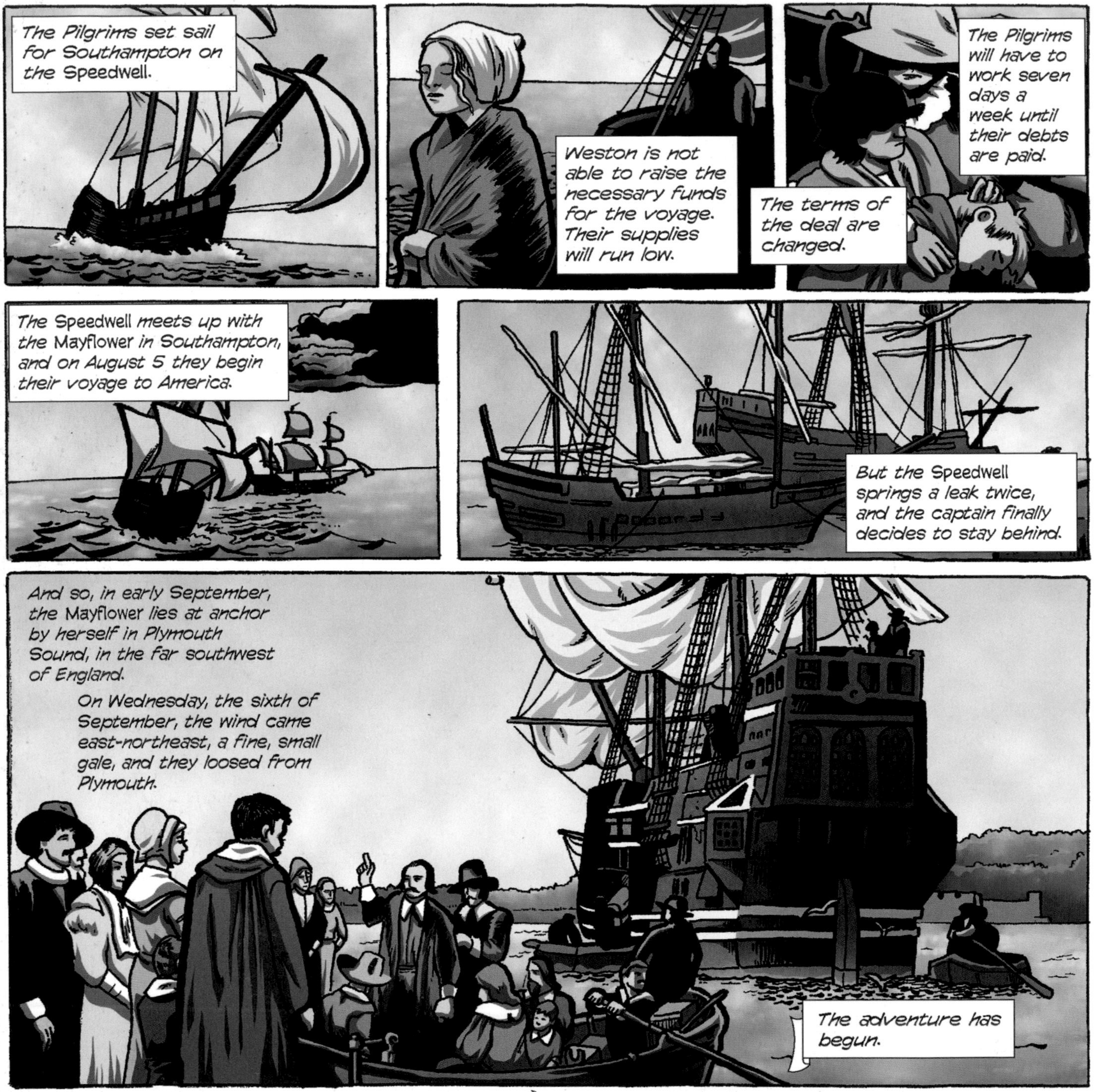
The Pilgrims set sail for Southampton on the Speedwell.
Weston is not able to raise the necessary funds for the voyage. Their supplies will run low.
The Pilgrims will have to work seven days a week until their debts are paid.
The terms of the deal are changed.
The Speedwell meets up with the Mayflower in Southampton, and on August 5 they begin their voyage to America.
But the Speedwell springs a leak twice, and the captain finally decides to stay behind.
And so, in early September, the Mayflower lies at anchor by herself in Plymouth Sound, in the far southwest of England.
On Wednesday, the sixth of September, the wind came east-northeast, a fine, small gale, and they loosed from Plymouth.
The adventure has begun.

Cut out and fold your very own *Mayflower*! Just cut along the dotted line and follow the directions to the right. You don't want to cut a page out of this book? Then go to http://www.colonialcomics.com for a print-out of this page and a video tutorial on how to fold it!

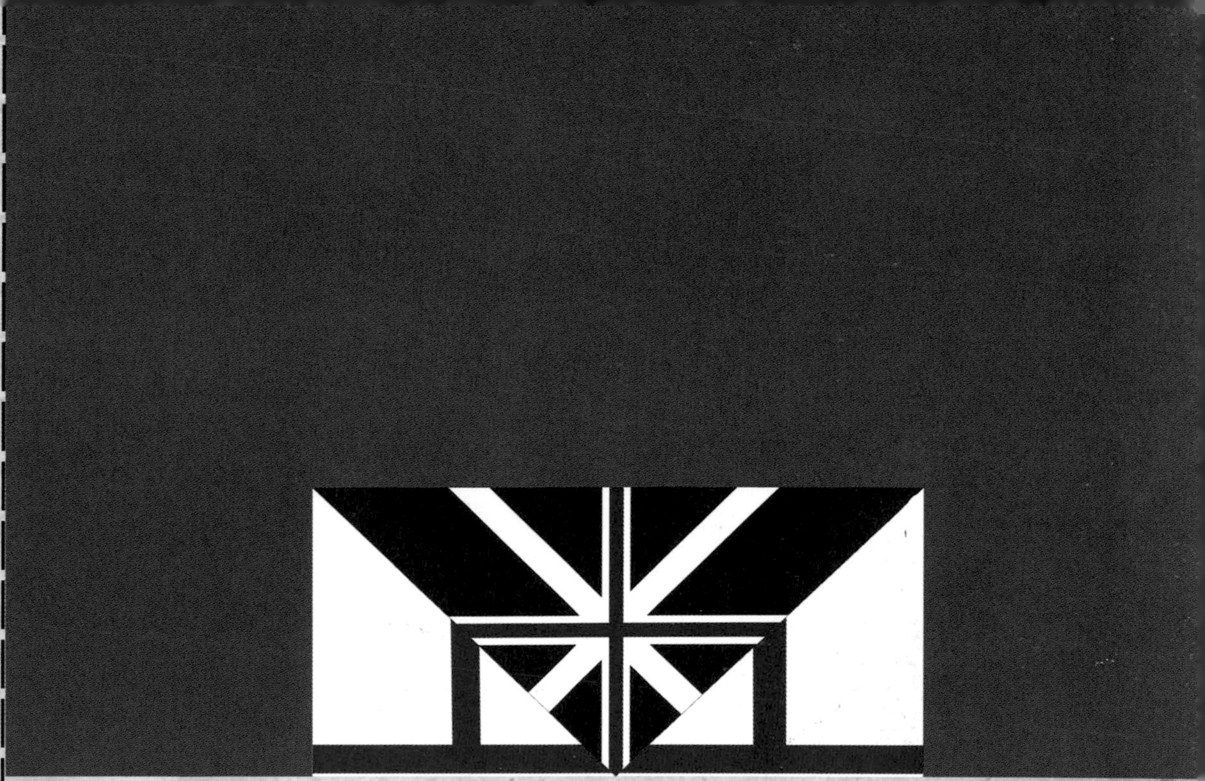

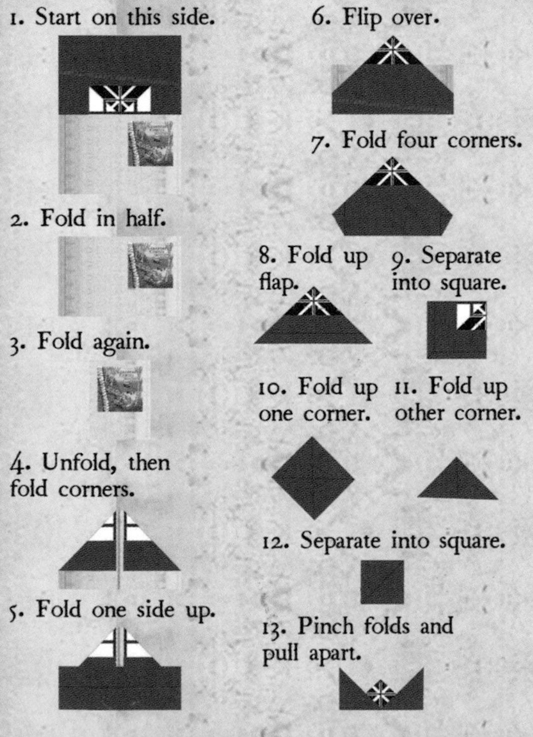

1. Start on this side.
2. Fold in half.
3. Fold again.
4. Unfold, then fold corners.
5. Fold one side up.
6. Flip over.
7. Fold four corners.
8. Fold up flap.
9. Separate into square.
10. Fold up one corner.
11. Fold up other corner.
12. Separate into square.
13. Pinch folds and pull apart.

The *Mayflower* set sail with two flags. The first flag was branded with the St. George Cross. St. George had been the patron saint of England since the late 1200s. The second flag was the Union Flag, which was a combination of the St. George Cross and the cross of St. Andrew, the patron saint of Scotland. The Union Flag was first introduced in 1606 to celebrate the union of England and Scotland.

The *Mayflower* set sail on September 16, 1620, and anchored in Cape Cod in mid-November. There were 102 passengers on the *Mayflower*, composed of Separatist Puritans, Merchant Adventurers, and their servants. In addition to the passengers, there were at least thirty crew members, a couple of dogs, and possibly some goats, pigs, and chickens.

Did you know?
  - The *Mayflower* was supposed to be one of two ships making the voyage across the Atlantic Ocean. The other ship (the *Speedwell*) sprung a leak and had to head back.
  - Only one passenger died before the *Mayflower* anchored in Cape Cod, a member of the crew who was making fun of the other passengers' sea sickness!
  - However, more than fifty passengers died less than a year after anchoring in Cape Cod, most of them during the first winter.

Squanto

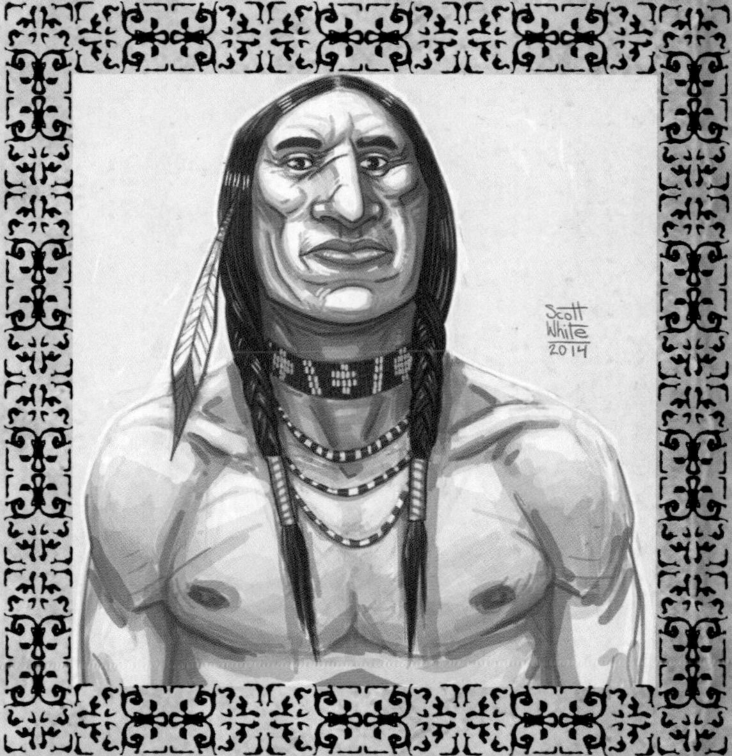
Scott
White
2014

Real Name: Tisquantum
Occupation: Diplomatic liaison
Legal Status: Member of the Patuxet tribe
Place of Birth: Patuxet (Plymouth)
Bio: In 1605, Squanto was one of six young Native American men kidnapped by English explorer George Weymouth. After learning English, Squanto returned to North America in 1614. A captain on that expedition kidnapped him again and sailed for Spain, planning to sell him into slavery. With the help of Catholic friars, Squanto escaped back to England. Working as an interpreter, he crossed the Atlantic three more times before finally reaching home in 1619, only to find his Patuxet people devastated by unfamiliar diseases.

The following year, the Pilgrims arrived at what they called Plymouth. Squanto met them in March, 1621, after their first hard winter. He taught them valuable farming and trapping skills, and was a liaison between them and the Wampanoag leader Massasoit—who may have felt that Squanto was too much of a free agent. After a diplomatic mission in 1622 Squanto died suddenly, perhaps from poison, and was buried in Plymouth Colony.

J.L. Bell, Scott White, and Jason Rodriguez

Thomas Morton, Merry Mount's Lord of Misrule

Story and Art by E.J. Barnes

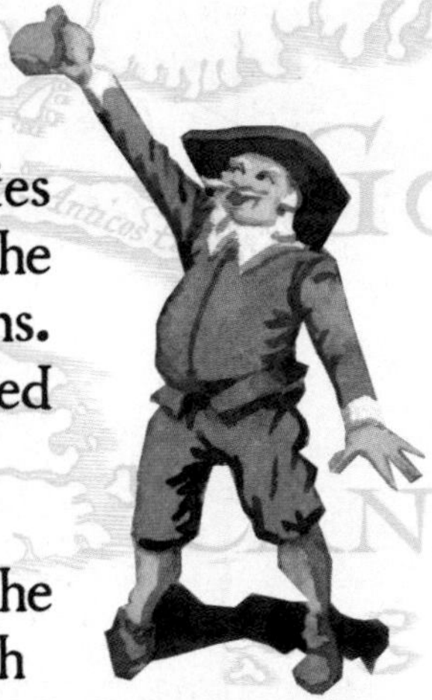

Not all the English colonists arriving in the territories of the Massachusett and Wampanoag nations in the 1620s and 1630s were either Pilgrims or Puritans. Many colonists were followers of the established Church of England, also known as Anglicans.

Anglicans were different from the Pilgrims and the Puritans in several ways. They looked to the Church of England's Book of Common Prayer as the proper source for readings on the Sabbath and other solemn occasions, instead of the Bible. Also, the Anglican clergy's attitude toward music, games, and other entertainment on Sundays was more nuanced than that of the Puritans, restricting the type, time, and place instead of outright prohibition.

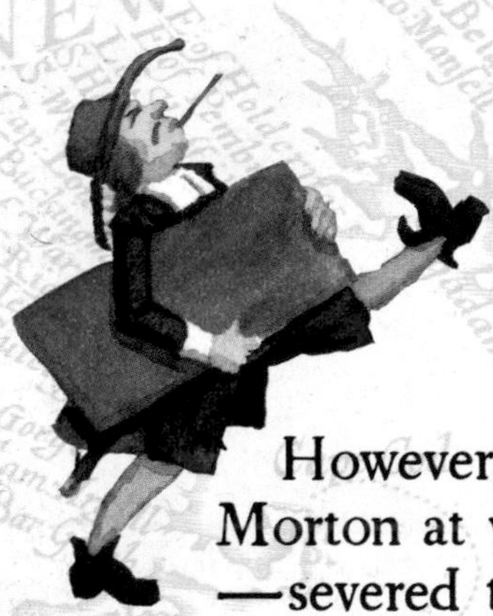

As was the case with Plymouth Colony, independent plantations in New England often had investors back in England who hoped to make back their money through various schemes. Most of these independent settlements sought help from Plymouth Colony when food ran low or trouble erupted between them and the Native people.

However, one settlement—founded by the Anglican Thomas Morton at what is now Mount Wollaston in Quincy, Massachusetts—severed ties with all but one of its investors, and went feral.

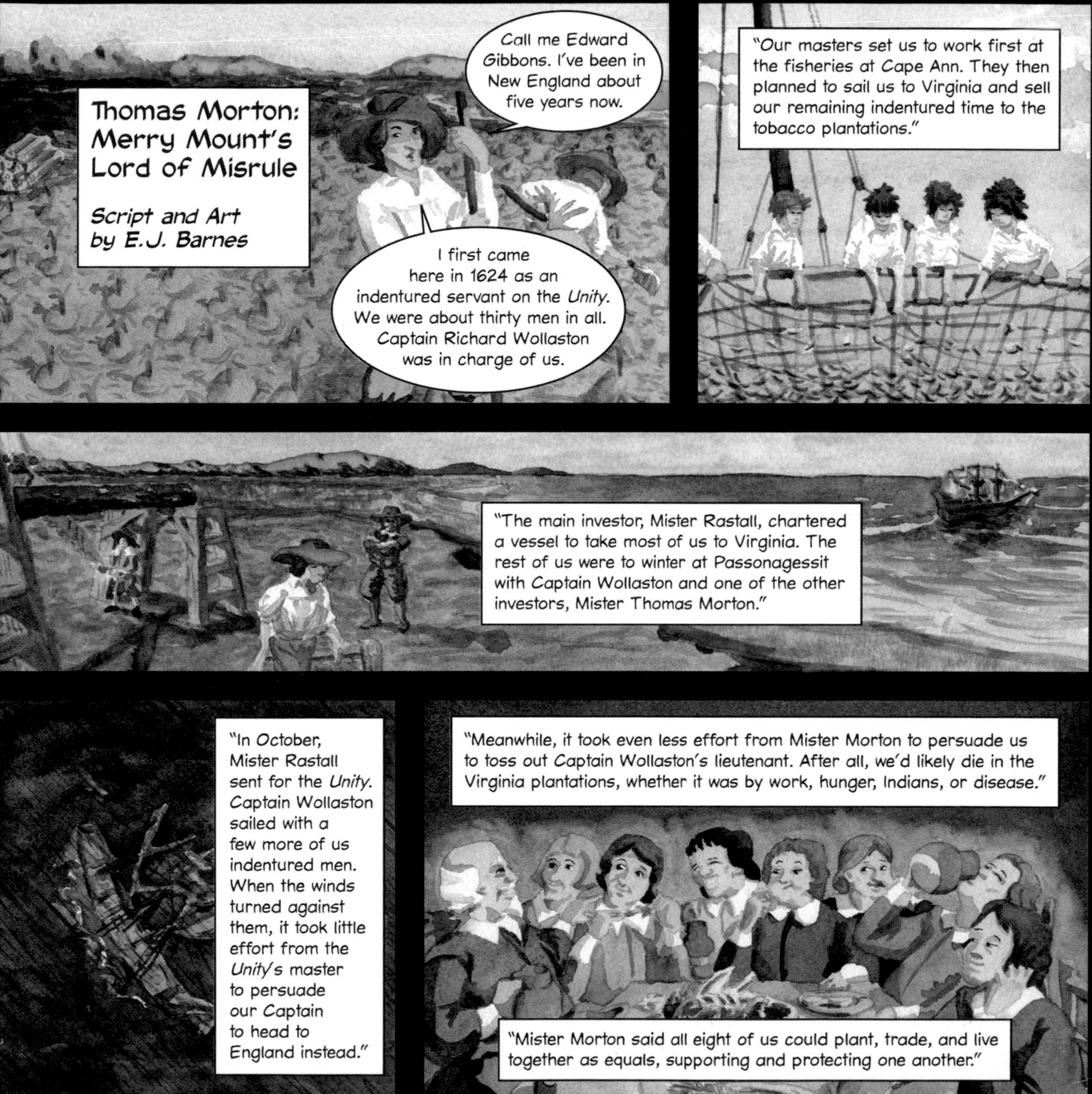
Thomas Morton: Merry Mount's Lord of Misrule
Script and Art by E.J. Barnes
Call me Edward Gibbons. I've been in New England about five years now.
I first came here in 1624 as an indentured servant on the *Unity*. We were about thirty men in all. Captain Richard Wollaston was in charge of us.
"Our masters set us to work first at the fisheries at Cape Ann. They then planned to sail us to Virginia and sell our remaining indentured time to the tobacco plantations."
"The main investor, Mister Rastall, chartered a vessel to take most of us to Virginia. The rest of us were to winter at Passonagessit with Captain Wollaston and one of the other investors, Mister Thomas Morton."
"In *October*, Mister Rastall sent for the *Unity*. Captain Wollaston sailed with a few more of us indentured men. When the winds turned against them, it took little effort from the *Unity's* master to persuade our Captain to head to England instead."
"Meanwhile, it took even less effort from Mister Morton to persuade us to toss out Captain Wollaston's lieutenant. After all, we'd likely die in the Virginia plantations, whether it was by work, hunger, Indians, or disease."
"Mister Morton said all eight of us could plant, trade, and live together as equals, supporting and protecting one another."

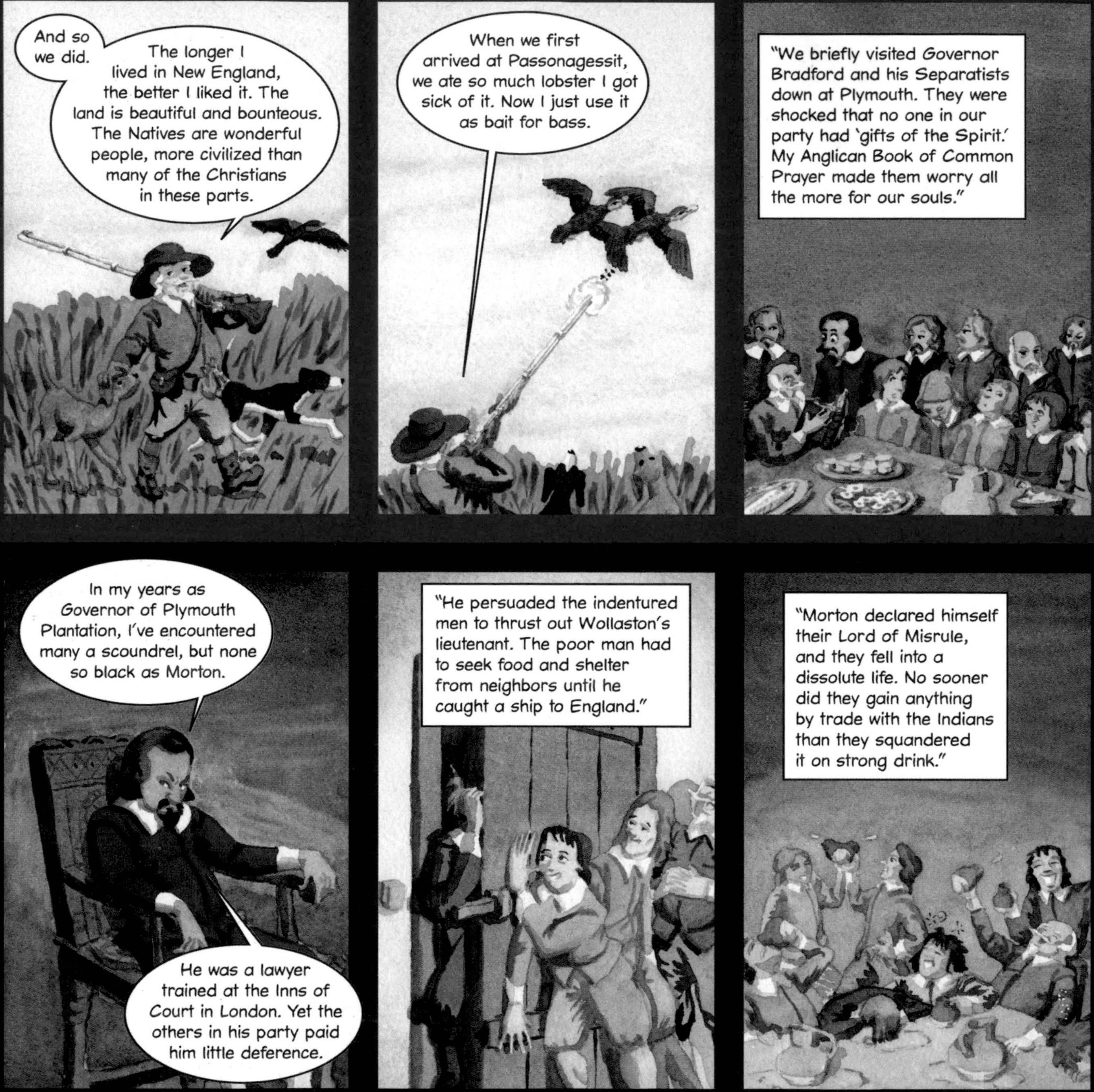
And so we did.
The longer I lived in New England, the better I liked it. The land is beautiful and bounteous. The Natives are wonderful people, more civilized than many of the Christians in these parts.
When we first arrived at Passonagessit, we ate so much lobster I got sick of it. Now I just use it as bait for bass.
"We briefly visited Governor Bradford and his Separatists down at Plymouth. They were shocked that no one in our party had 'gifts of the Spirit.' My Anglican Book of Common Prayer made them worry all the more for our souls."
In my years as Governor of Plymouth Plantation, I've encountered many a scoundrel, but none so black as Morton.
He was a lawyer trained at the Inns of Court in London. Yet the others in his party paid him little deference.
"He persuaded the indentured men to thrust out Wollaston's lieutenant. The poor man had to seek food and shelter from neighbors until he caught a ship to England."
"Morton declared himself their Lord of Misrule, and they fell into a dissolute life. No sooner did they gain anything by trade with the Indians than they squandered it on strong drink."

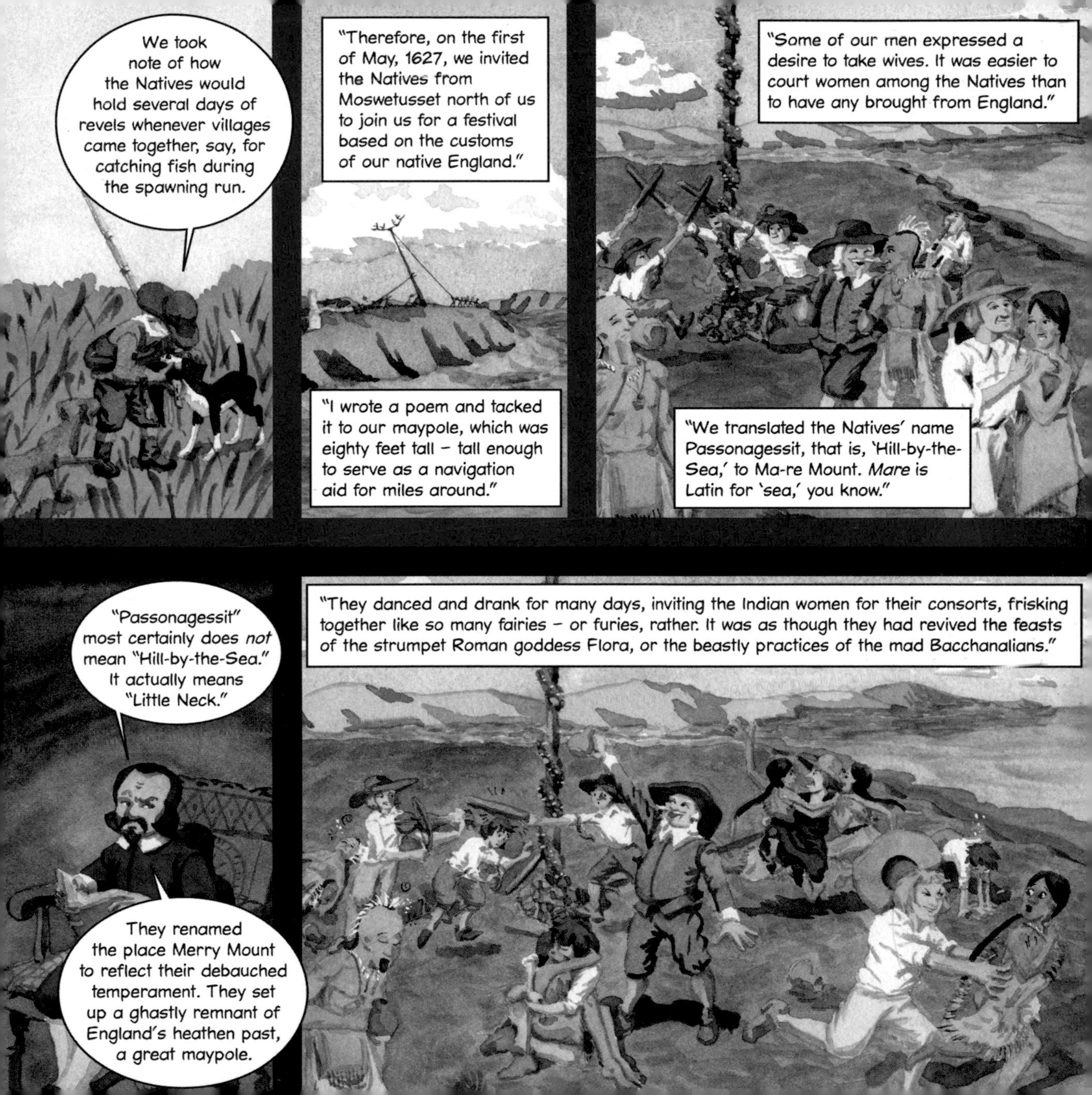
We took note of how the Natives would hold several days of revels whenever villages came together, say, for catching fish during the spawning run.
"Therefore, on the first of May, 1627, we invited the Natives from Moswetusset north of us to join us for a festival based on the customs of our native England."
"I wrote a poem and tacked it to our maypole, which was eighty feet tall – tall enough to serve as a navigation aid for miles around."
"Some of our men expressed a desire to take wives. It was easier to court women among the Natives than to have any brought from England."
"We translated the Natives' name Passonagessit, that is, 'Hill-by-the-Sea,' to Ma-re Mount. *Mare* is Latin for 'sea,' you know."
"Passonagessit" most certainly does *not* mean "Hill-by-the-Sea." It actually means "Little Neck."
They renamed the place Merry Mount to reflect their debauched temperament. They set up a ghastly remnant of England's heathen past, a great maypole.
"They danced and drank for many days, inviting the Indian women for their consorts, frisking together like so many fairies – or furies, rather. It was as though they had revived the feasts of the strumpet Roman goddess Flora, or the beastly practices of the mad Bacchanalians."

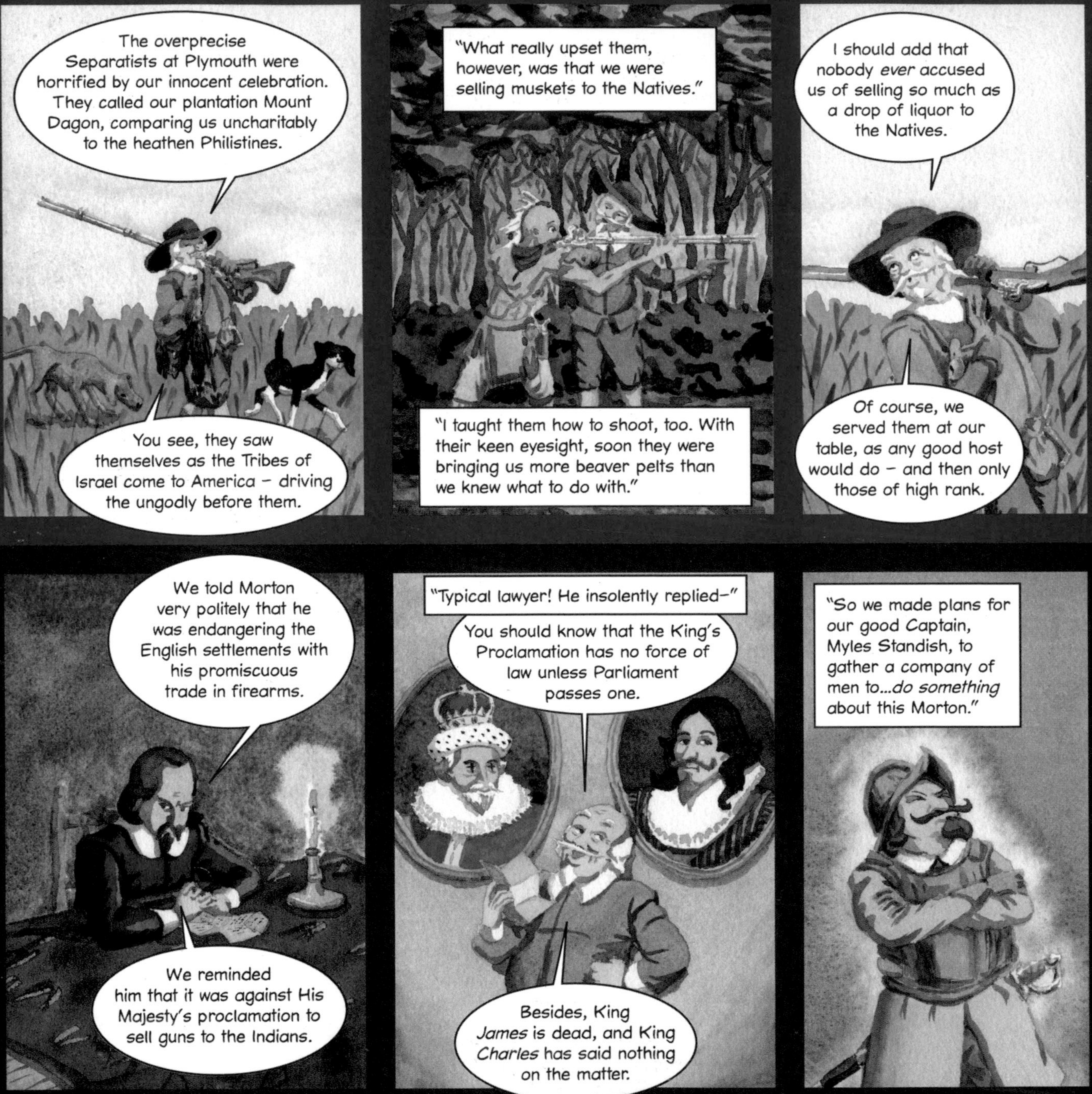
The overprecise Separatists at Plymouth were horrified by our innocent celebration. They called our plantation Mount Dagon, comparing us uncharitably to the heathen Philistines.
You see, they saw themselves as the Tribes of Israel come to America – driving the ungodly before them.
"What really upset them, however, was that we were selling muskets to the Natives."
"I taught them how to shoot, too. With their keen eyesight, soon they were bringing us more beaver pelts than we knew what to do with."
I should add that nobody *ever* accused us of selling so much as a drop of liquor to the Natives.
Of course, we served them at our table, as any good host would do – and then only those of high rank.
We told Morton very politely that he was endangering the English settlements with his promiscuous trade in firearms.
We reminded him that it was against His Majesty's proclamation to sell guns to the Indians.
"Typical lawyer! He insolently replied–"
You should know that the King's Proclamation has no force of law unless Parliament passes one.
Besides, King *James* is dead, and King *Charles* has said nothing on the matter.
"So we made plans for our good Captain, Myles Standish, to gather a company of men to...*do something* about this Morton."

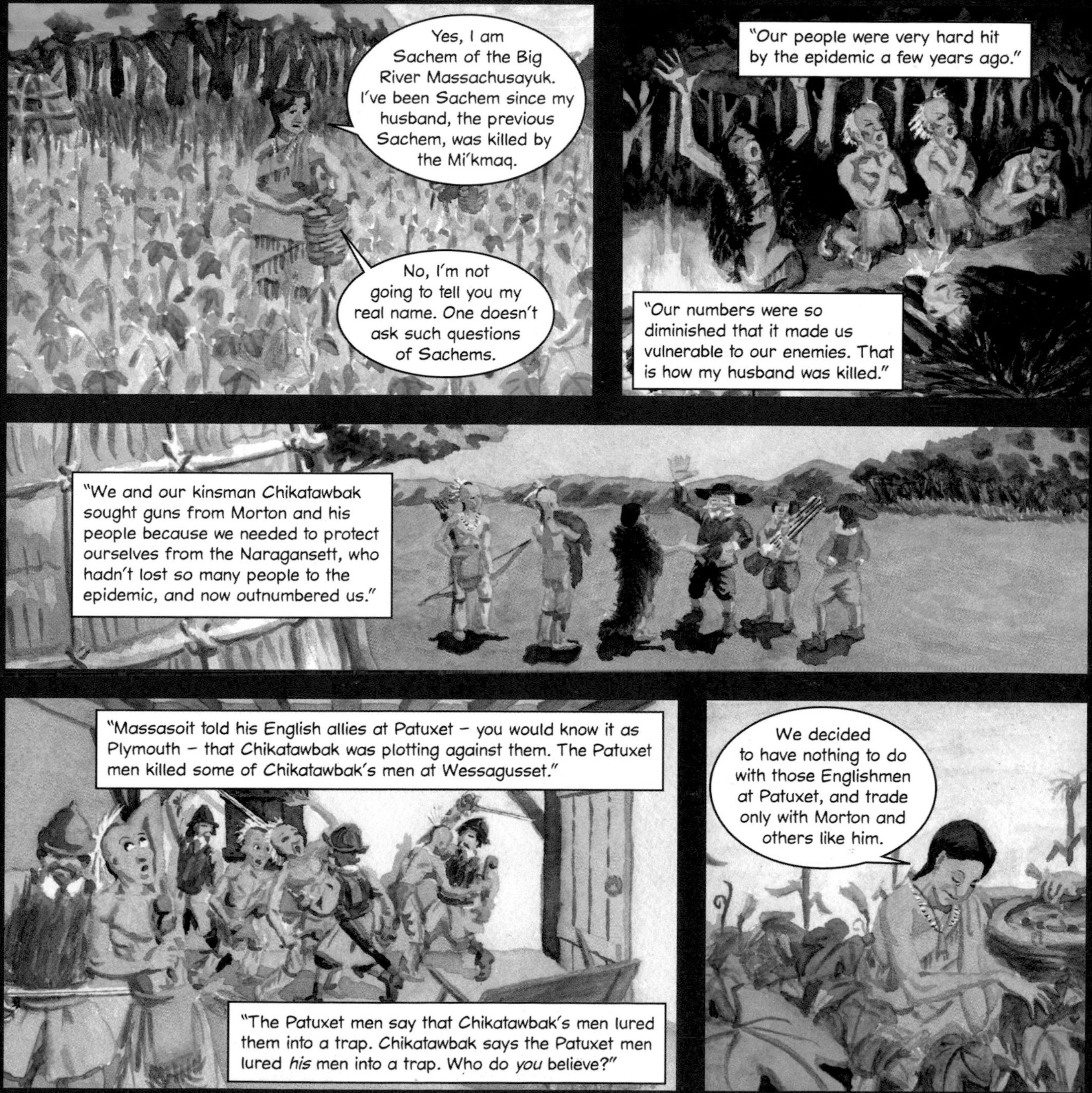
Yes, I am Sachem of the Big River Massachusayuk. I've been Sachem since my husband, the previous Sachem, was killed by the Mi'kmaq.
No, I'm not going to tell you my real name. One doesn't ask such questions of Sachems.
"Our people were very hard hit by the epidemic a few years ago."
"Our numbers were so diminished that it made us vulnerable to our enemies. That is how my husband was killed."
"We and our kinsman Chikatawbak sought guns from Morton and his people because we needed to protect ourselves from the Naragansett, who hadn't lost so many people to the epidemic, and now outnumbered us."
"Massasoit told his English allies at Patuxet – you would know it as Plymouth – that Chikatawbak was plotting against them. The Patuxet men killed some of Chikatawbak's men at Wessagusset."
"The Patuxet men say that Chikatawbak's men lured them into a trap. Chikatawbak says the Patuxet men lured *his* men into a trap. Who do *you* believe?"
We decided to have nothing to do with those Englishmen at Patuxet, and trade only with Morton and others like him.

"About a year after our first May Day celebrations, the Separatists sent their Captain Shrimp and his Nine Worthies against us."

"They came on a day when most of our party was off trading with the Natives. Only two of my consociates were home, but the three of us armed ourselves and took our stand."

"Captain Shrimp offered us parley, and said he would give us quarter, promising no harm would come to my person."

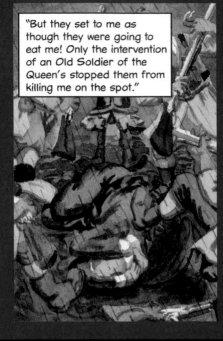

"But they set to me as though they were going to eat me! Only the intervention of an Old Soldier of the Queen's stopped them from killing me on the spot."

Several other plantations in the area had asked us to send Captain Standish to shut down Morton's gun trade.

"Morton and his men shut themselves in his house, armed to the teeth. When Captain Standish summoned him to yield, he only scoffed."

Come and get me if you dare, Shrimp!

"Morton and his men came out, not to yield but to shoot."

Ow.

"But they were so drunk that their guns were too heavy for them. No one was hurt except one man, and he not gravely."

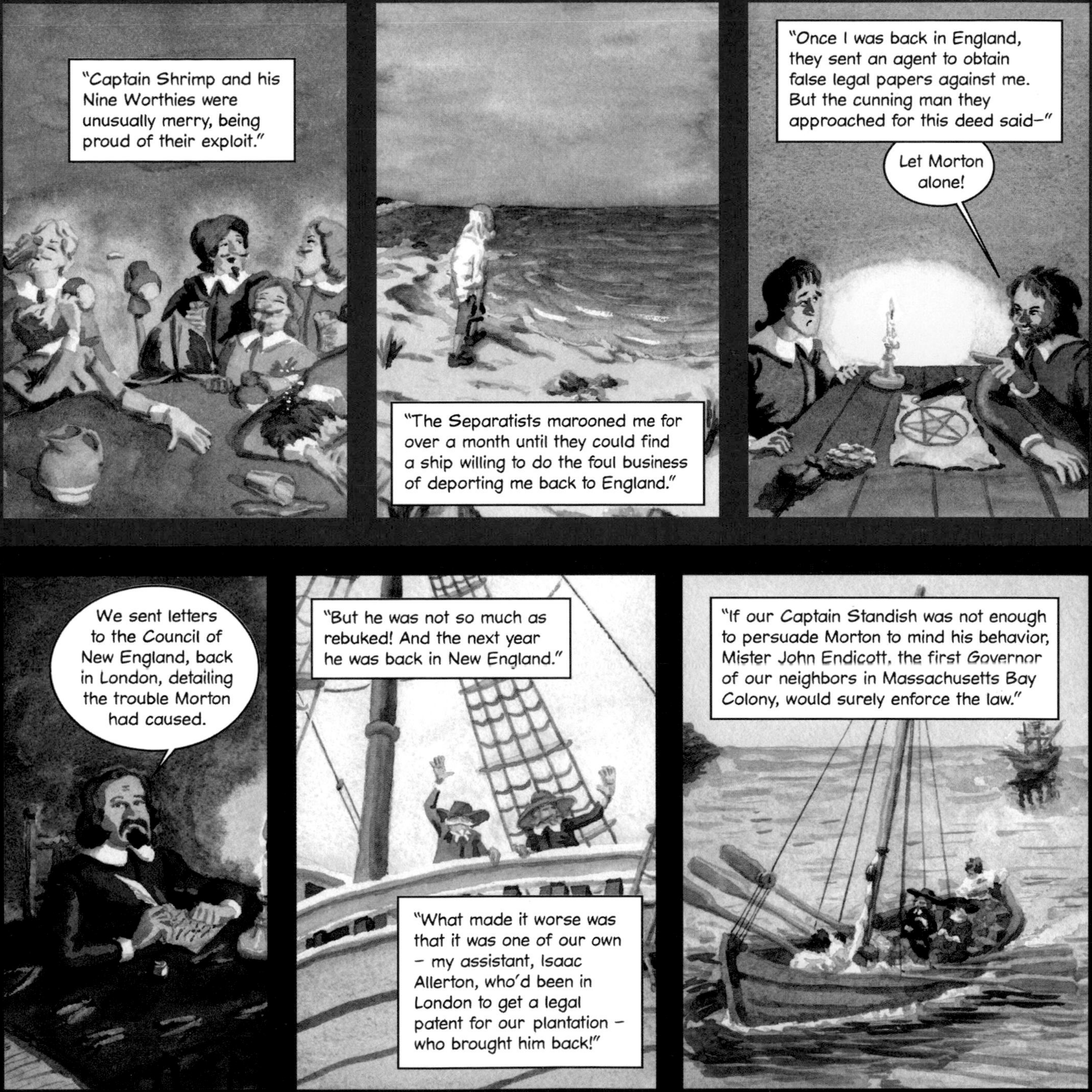
"Captain Shrimp and his Nine Worthies were unusually merry, being proud of their exploit."
"The Separatists marooned me for over a month until they could find a ship willing to do the foul business of deporting me back to England."
"Once I was back in England, they sent an agent to obtain false legal papers against me. But the cunning man they approached for this deed said–"
Let Morton alone!
We sent letters to the Council of New England, back in London, detailing the trouble Morton had caused.
"But he was not so much as rebuked! And the next year he was back in New England."
"What made it worse was that it was one of our own – my assistant, Isaac Allerton, who'd been in London to get a legal patent for our plantation – who brought him back!"
"If our Captain Standish was not enough to persuade Morton to mind his behavior, Mister John Endicott, the first Governor of our neighbors in Massachusetts Bay Colony, would surely enforce the law."

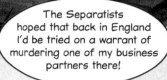

The Separatists hoped that back in England I'd be tried on a warrant of murdering one of my business partners there!

They didn't know that this was nothing more than a nuisance charge brought by my idiot stepson. He'd been hounding me in and out of court from the day I married his mother.

"Meanwhile, one Endicott, or as I prefer to call him, Captain Littleworth, arrived in Salem with a new Patent for the Massachusetts Bay Colony. This he carried everywhere as an emblem of his authority."

"Most people took him for a fiddler."

"Not long after my return to Ma-re Mount, this Captain Littleworth hatched a plot to have me brought before the Court of his successor as Governor of Massachusetts Bay Colony – one Winthrop, whom I will call Joshua Temperwell."

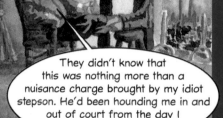

By 1629, Morton had returned to his old nest in the Massachusett Indians' territory.

"Mister Endicott of Massachusetts Bay Colony cut down his maypole, and rebuked Morton's men for their profaneness, praying that they would see the light of God."

"He put out a new warrant for Morton's arrest, after some Indians complained to us that he had shot at them in an attempt to steal a canoe."

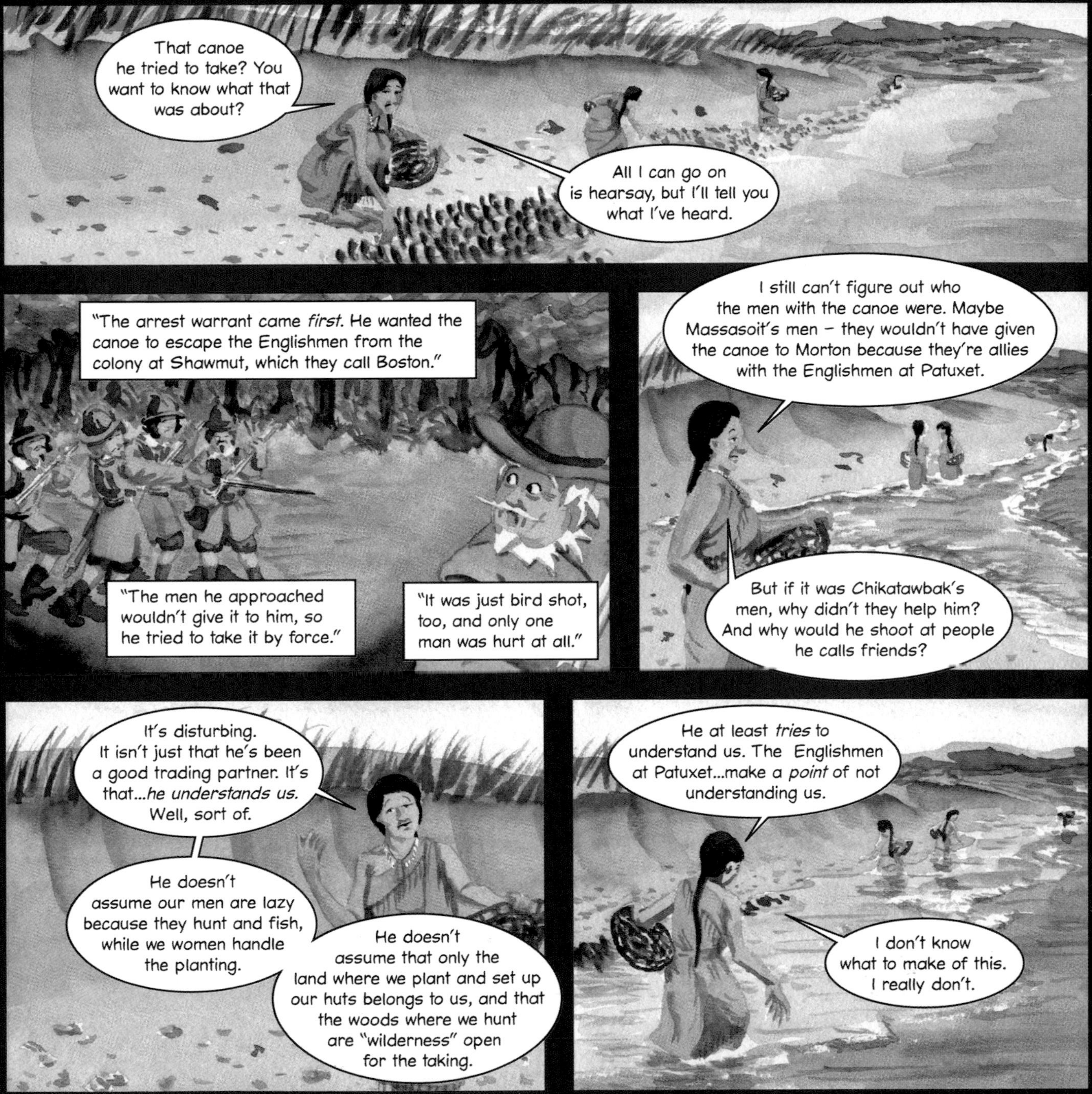
That canoe he tried to take? You want to know what that was about?
All I can go on is hearsay, but I'll tell you what I've heard.
"The arrest warrant came *first*. He wanted the canoe to escape the Englishmen from the colony at Shawmut, which they call Boston."
"The men he approached wouldn't give it to him, so he tried to take it by force."
"It was just bird shot, too, and only one man was hurt at all."
I still *can't* figure out who the men with the canoe were. Maybe Massasoit's men – they wouldn't have given the canoe to Morton because they're allies with the Englishmen at Patuxet.
But if it was Chikatawbak's men, why didn't they help him? And why would he shoot at people he calls friends?
It's disturbing. It isn't just that he's been a good trading partner. It's that...*he understands us.* Well, sort of.
He doesn't assume our men are lazy because they hunt and fish, while we women handle the planting.
He doesn't assume that only the land where we plant and set up our huts belongs to us, and that the woods where we hunt are "wilderness" open for the taking.
He at least *tries* to understand us. The Englishmen at Patuxet...make a *point* of not understanding us.
I don't know what to make of this. I really don't.

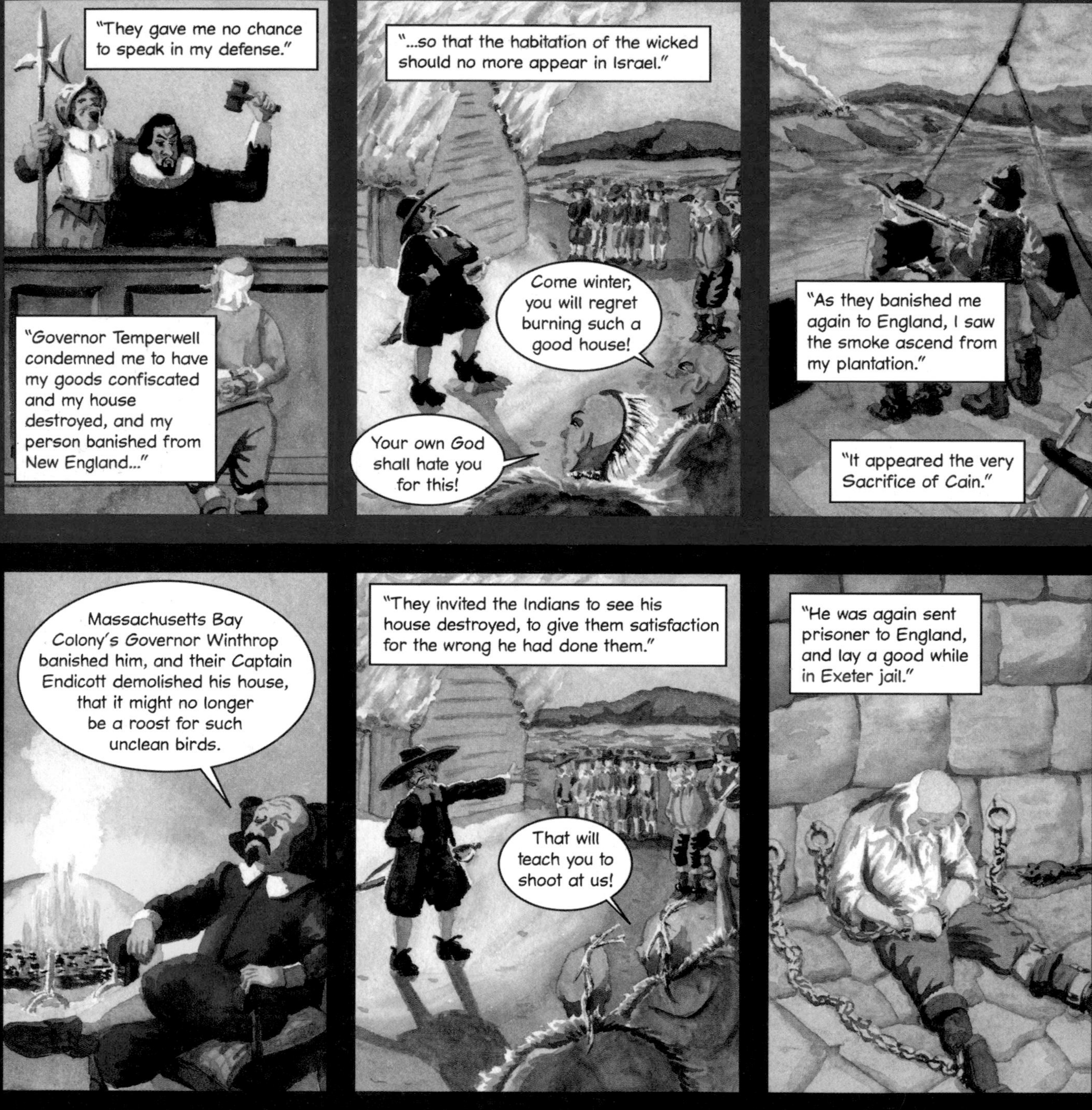
"They gave me no chance to speak in my defense."
"Governor Temperwell condemned me to have my goods confiscated and my house destroyed, and my person banished from New England..."
"...so that the habitation of the wicked should no more appear in Israel."
Come winter, you will regret burning such a good house!
Your own God shall hate you for this!
"As they banished me again to England, I saw the smoke ascend from my plantation."
"It appeared the very Sacrifice of Cain."
Massachusetts Bay Colony's Governor Winthrop banished him, and their Captain Endicott demolished his house, that it might no longer be a roost for such unclean birds.
"They invited the Indians to see his house destroyed, to give them satisfaction for the wrong he had done them."
That will teach you to shoot at us!
"He was again sent prisoner to England, and lay a good while in Exeter jail."

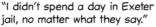

"I didn't spend a day in Exeter jail, no matter what they say."

"I did, however, spend thrice the usual time at sea, the Separatists having paid the captain to take the long route – via the Canaries and Azores – and undersupply the ship on every leg of the journey. So if I should 'happen' to starve, I would not be missed."

"In 1632, my patron, Sir Ferdinando Gorges, petitioned the Council of New England to invalidate the Massachusetts Bay Colony's charter, and replace it with his own."

"I was happy to testify to the illegal maneuvers of the Separatists, as did others who had been unjustly treated by them."

"I also wrote a book of my experiences in America, regarding the land and its people...and the Separatists I met there."

"It is called *The New English Canaan*, as New England is a land of milk and honey, and the Separatists claim it as their own from the pagan peoples already dwelling there."

That unworthy man wrote a most infamous and scurrilous book, full of lies and slanders against many godly men.

"My successor as Governor at Plymouth, Edward Winslow, answered the Council's questions to their satisfaction."

"But, doubtless at Morton's instigation, the Archbishop of Canterbury questioned poor Mister Winslow on church matters in the Colony, and he wound up spending four months in Fleet Prison."

"The Church of England sent us the bill for feeding him while in jail."

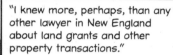
"I knew more, perhaps, than any other lawyer in New England about land grants and other property transactions."

Remember Captain Shrimp? He lives over there, now, right here in Duxbury. He knows I'm hunting on his property, and he can't do a thing about it.

"My patron, Sir Ferdinando, was an ardent Royalist, so when he lost to the Roundheads on the battlefield around 1642, I thought it best to return to the land I loved."

He keeps turning up, like a bad penny. The wars in England made it too hot for him, so now he's back.

Winslow tells me he's poor as a hermit...reduced to drinking *water*.

"Our spies say he may be a Royalist agitator, working with the King's Party underground in these parts, promising them our land should they triumph."

"O happy news! Massachusetts Bay Colony's Captain Endicott has caught up with him, and brought him before Governor Winthrop. Finally, this rogue will know justice."

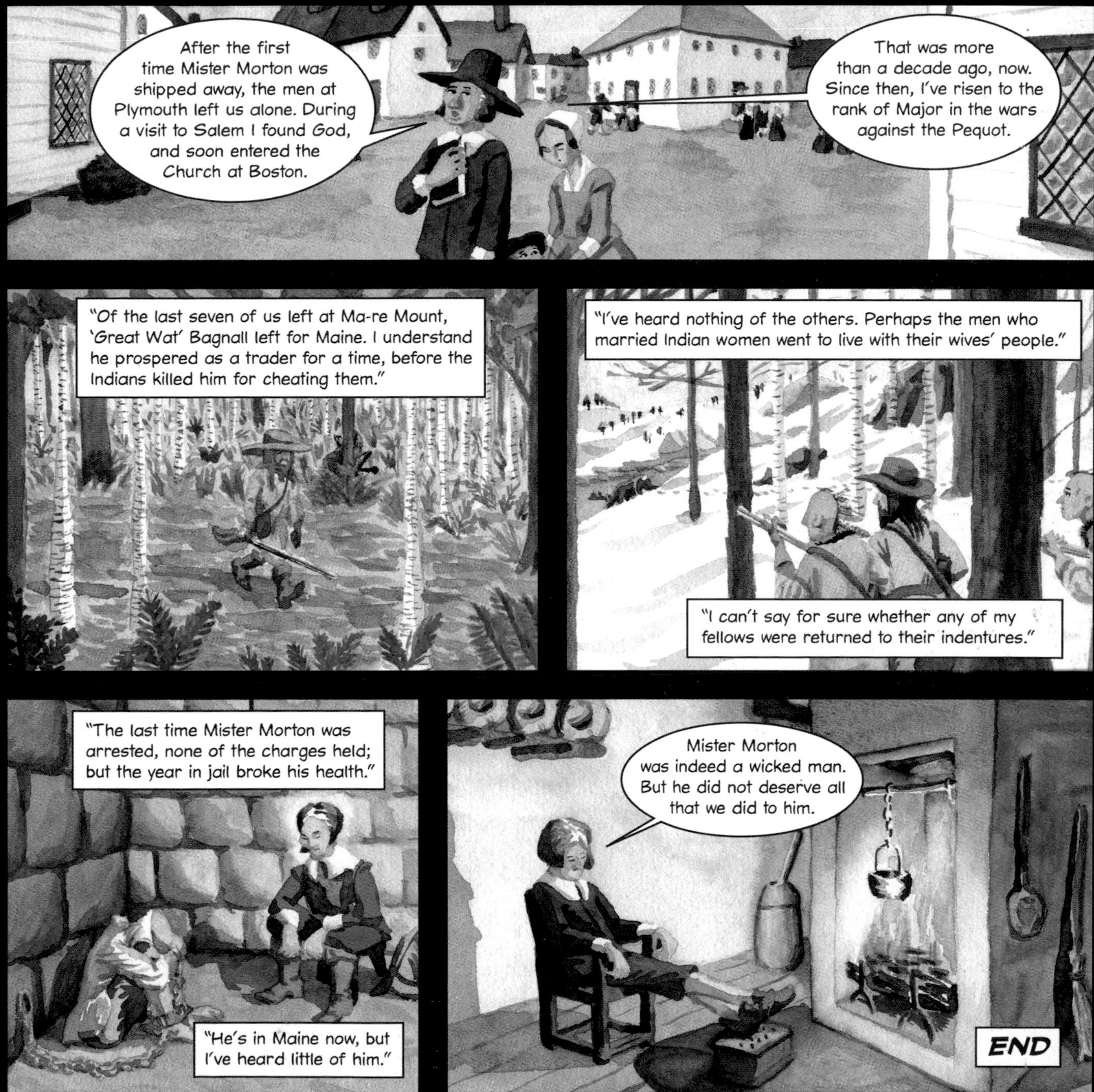
After the first time Mister Morton was shipped away, the men at Plymouth left us alone. During a visit to Salem I found God, and soon entered the Church at Boston.
That was more than a decade ago, now. Since then, I've risen to the rank of Major in the wars against the Pequot.
"Of the last seven of us left at Ma-re Mount, 'Great Wat' Bagnall left for Maine. I understand he prospered as a trader for a time, before the Indians killed him for cheating them."
"I've heard nothing of the others. Perhaps the men who married Indian women went to live with their wives' people."
"I can't say for sure whether any of my fellows were returned to their indentures."
"The last time Mister Morton was arrested, none of the charges held; but the year in jail broke his health."
"He's in Maine now, but I've heard little of him."
Mister Morton was indeed a wicked man. But he did not deserve all that we did to him.
END

TROUBLESOME SOWS

Story by Virginia DeJohn Anderson and Art by Michæl Sgier

As ships came to the New World, they unloaded more than just human colonists; they also brought their livestock with them. Importing livestock was a revolutionary development for the area, as Native Americans did not domesticate animals the way European settlers did.

The problem with livestock was that it needed space to graze, and it was difficult and expensive for the colonists to allow the livestock to do so on their farmland. So they began to practice free-range animal husbandry, allowing livestock to roam freely outside of their farms to feed and mate.

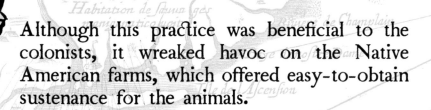

Although this practice was beneficial to the colonists, it wreaked havoc on the Native American farms, which offered easy-to-obtain sustenance for the animals.

This tale represents a collage of stories resulting from tensions arising from the practice of free-range animal husbandry, but the result was the same in all cases. Native American land was continuously encroached upon, straining relations between the colonists and the Native Americans and moving the tribes further westward.

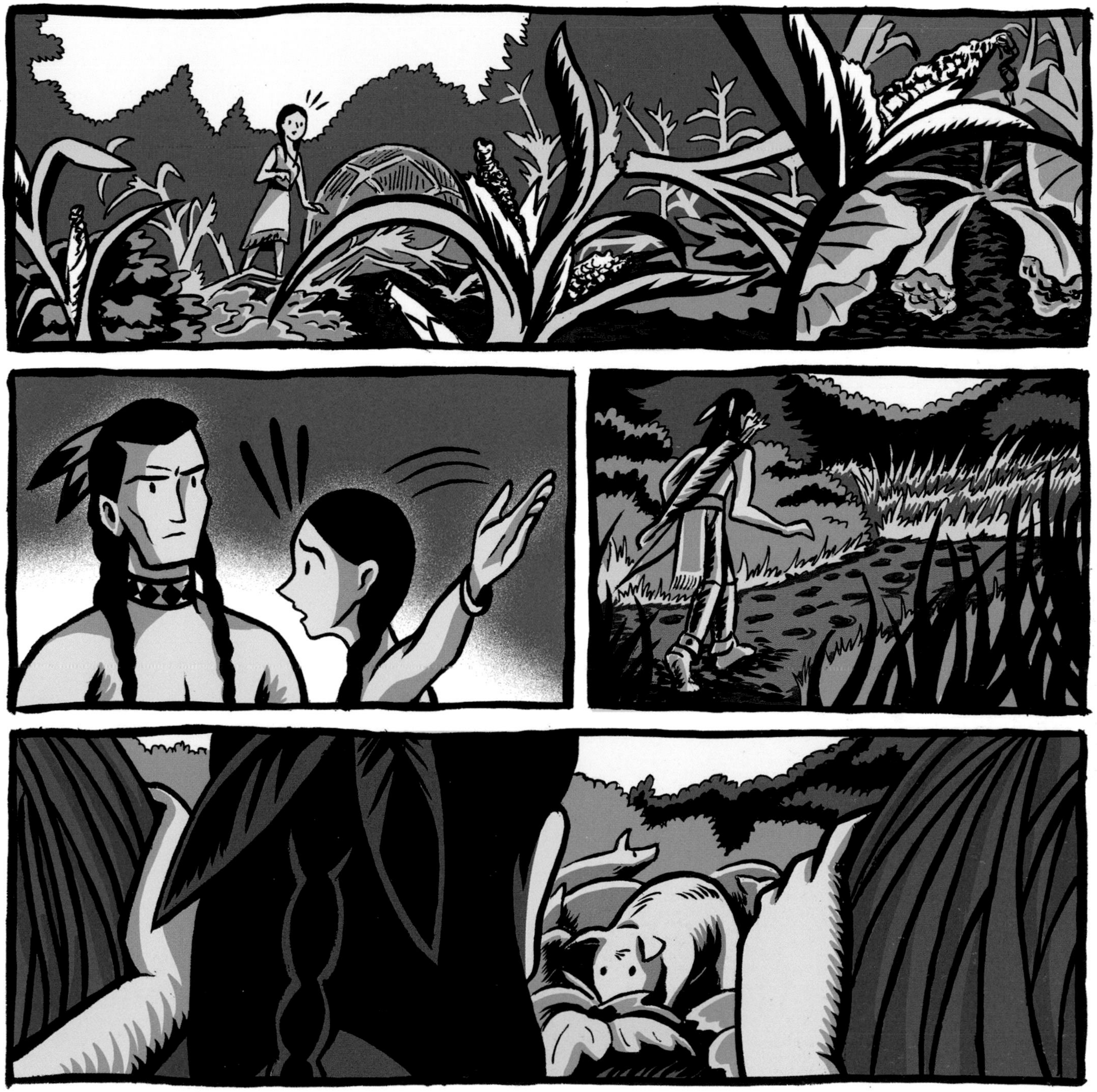

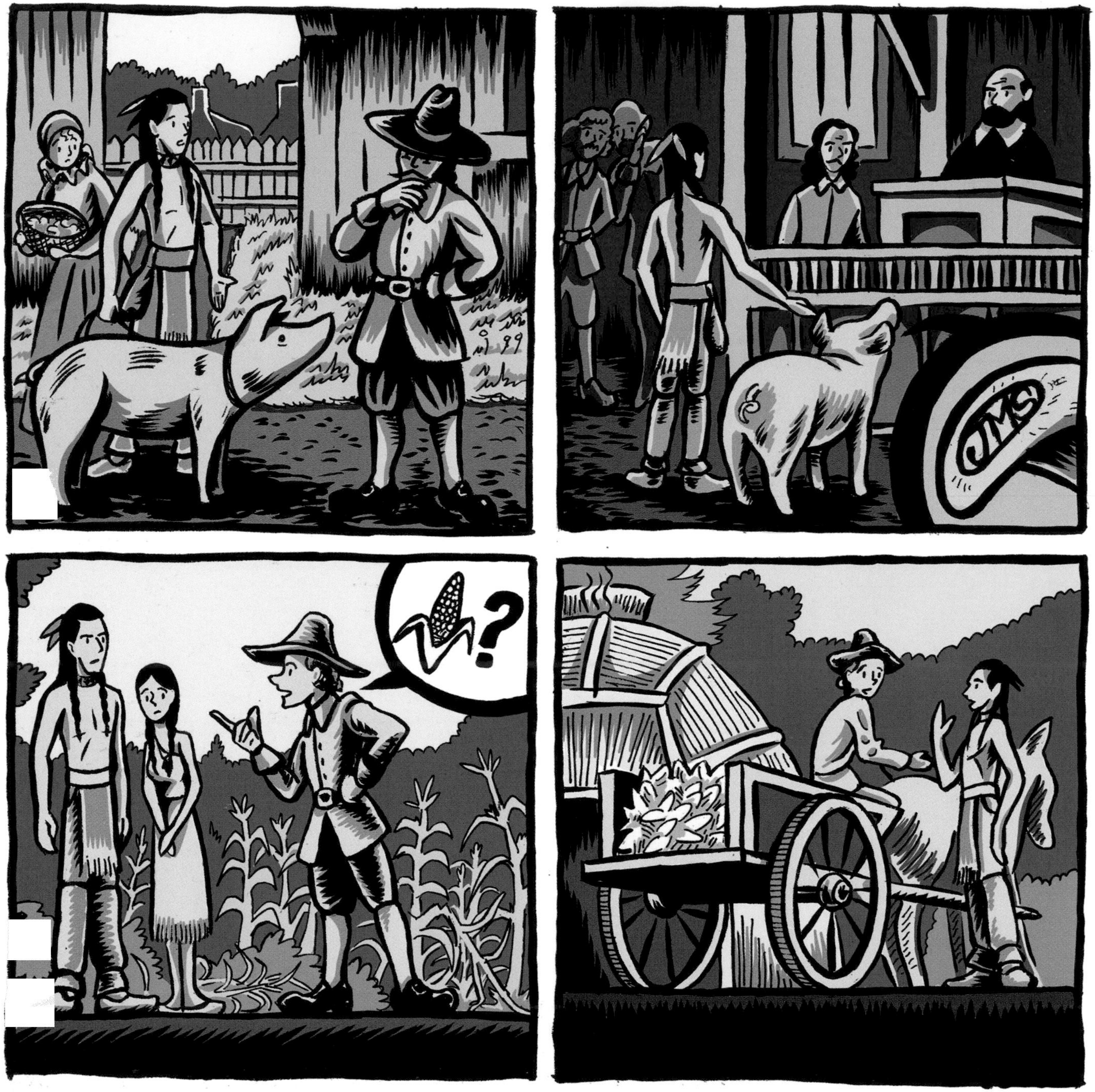
JMS
?

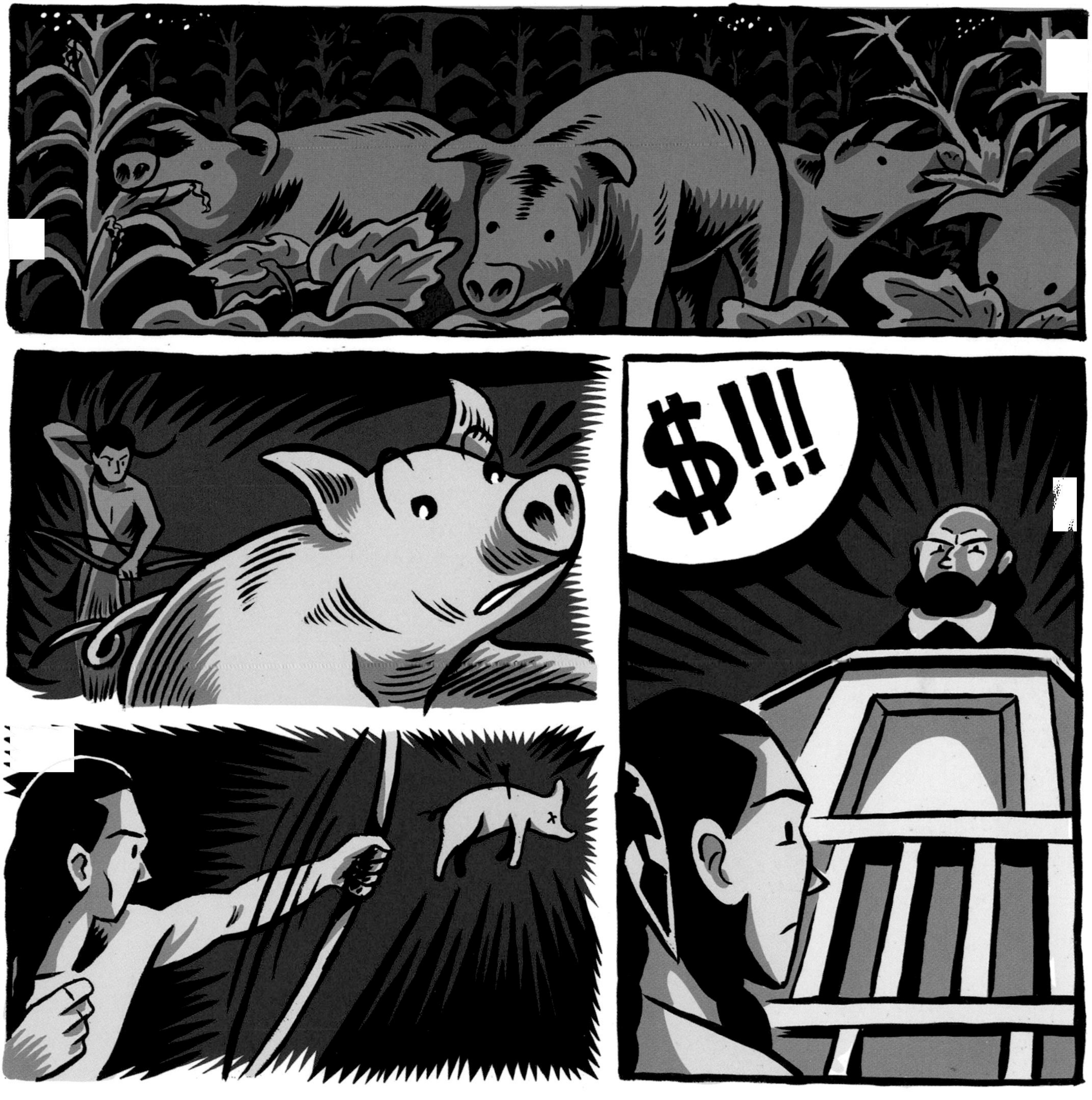
$!!!

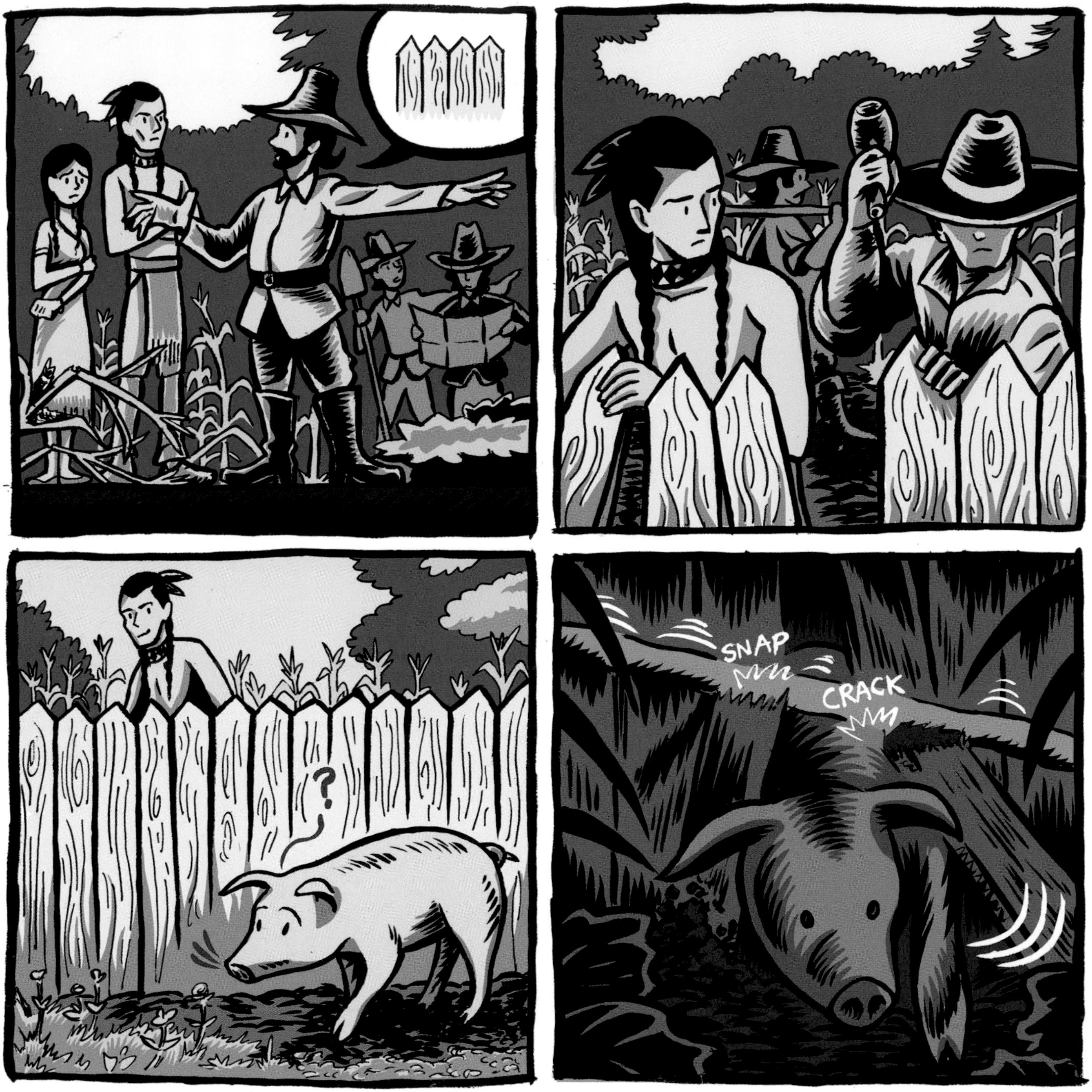
?
SNAP
CRACK

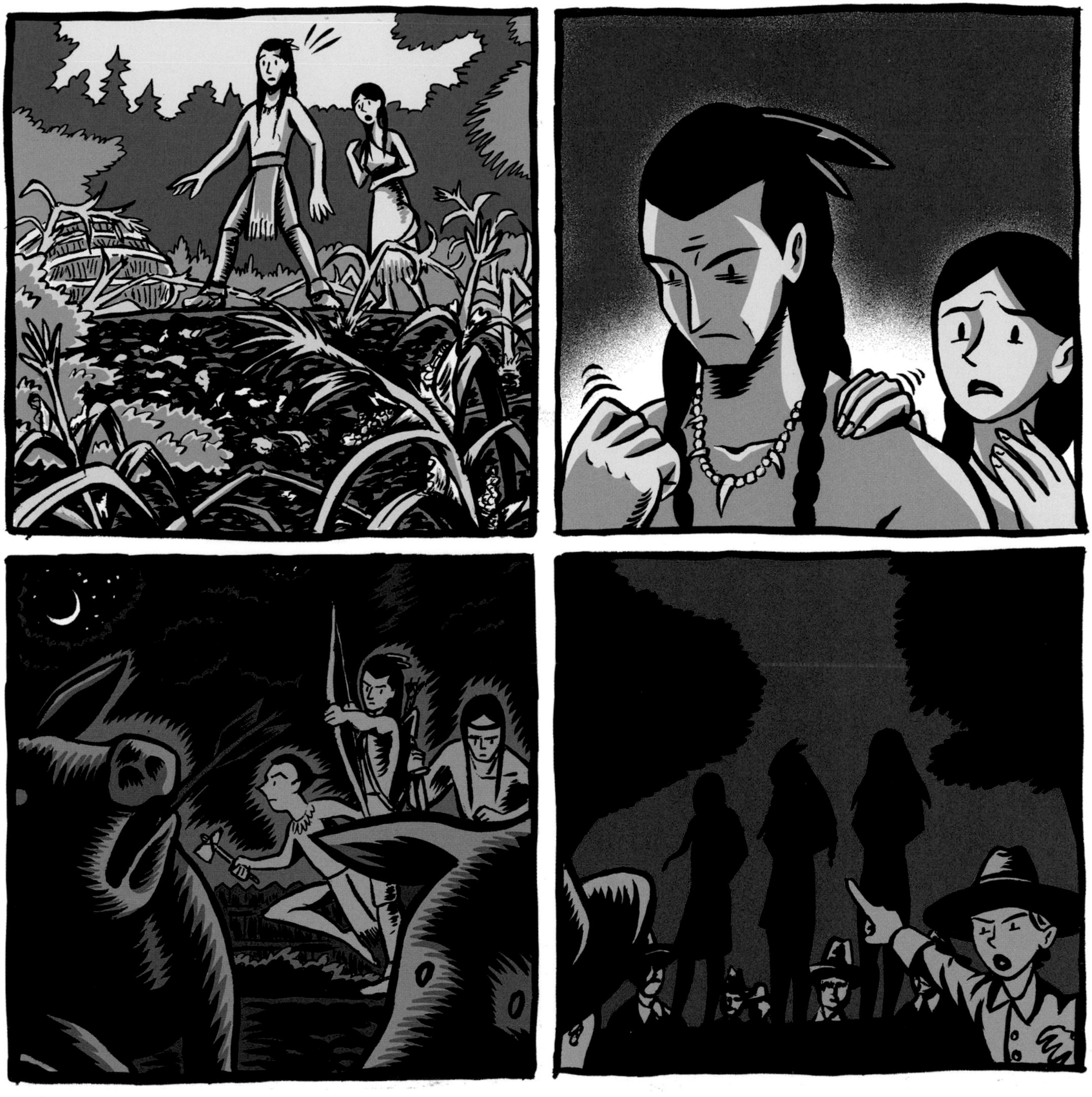

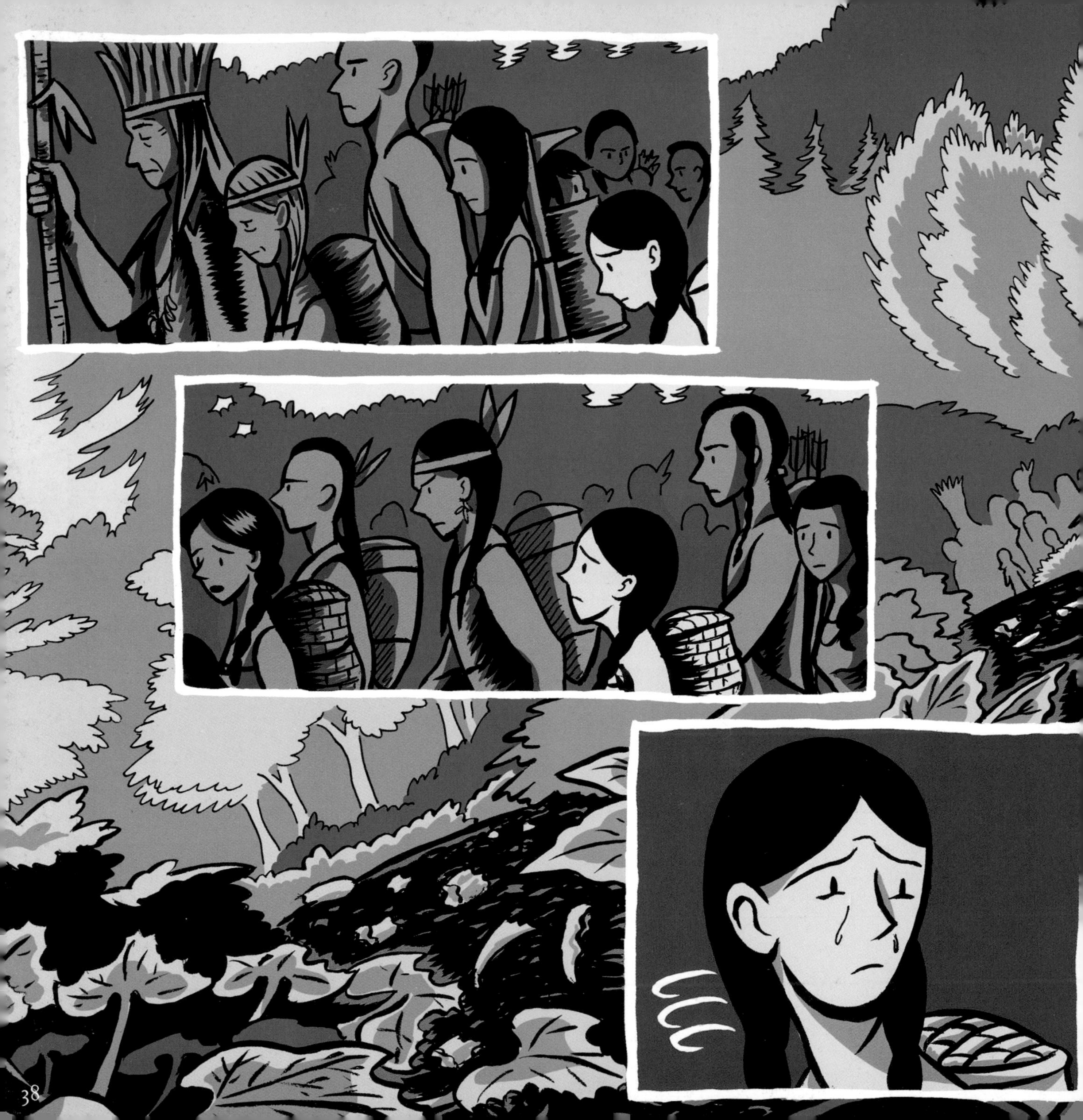

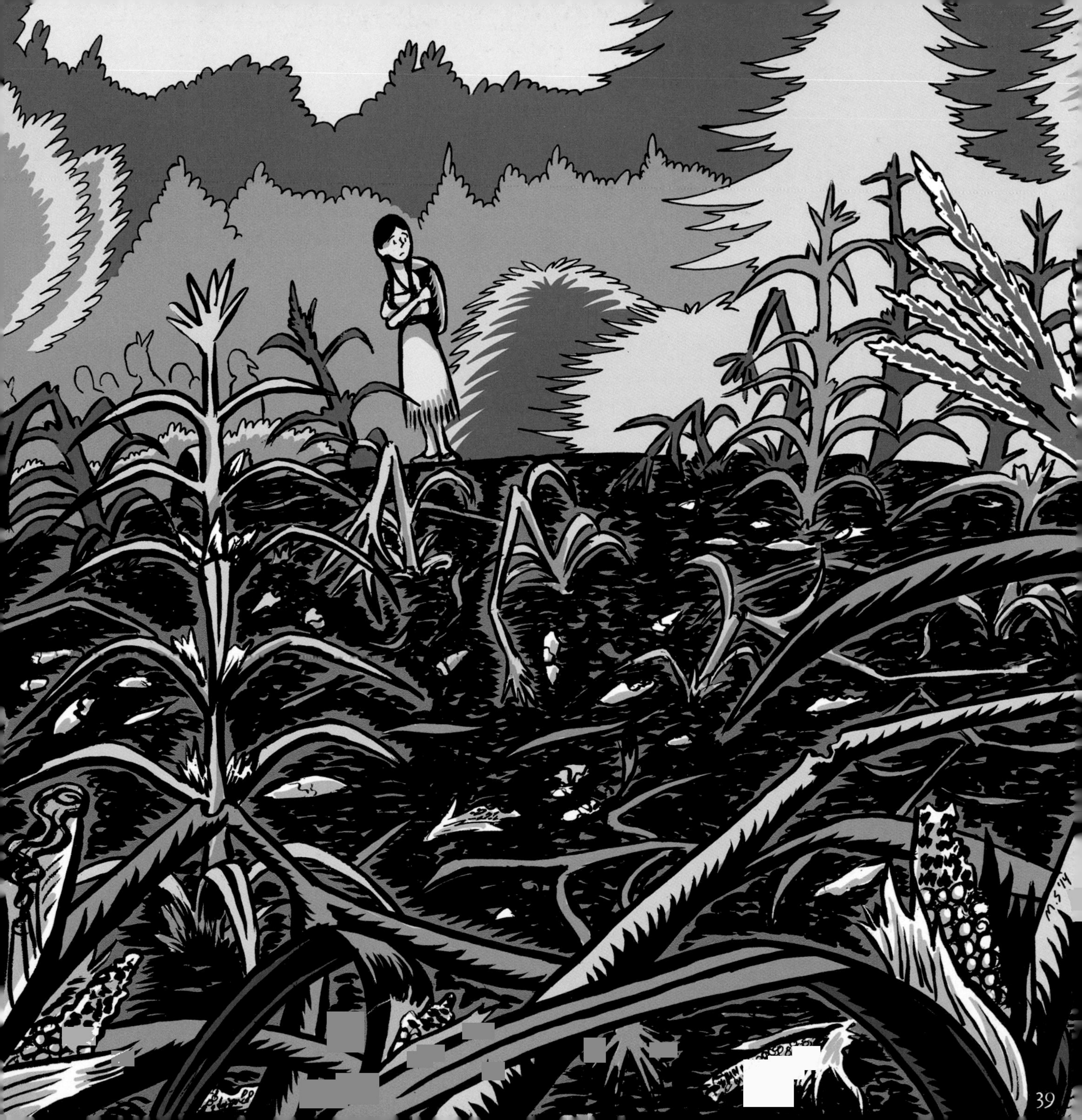

The Governor

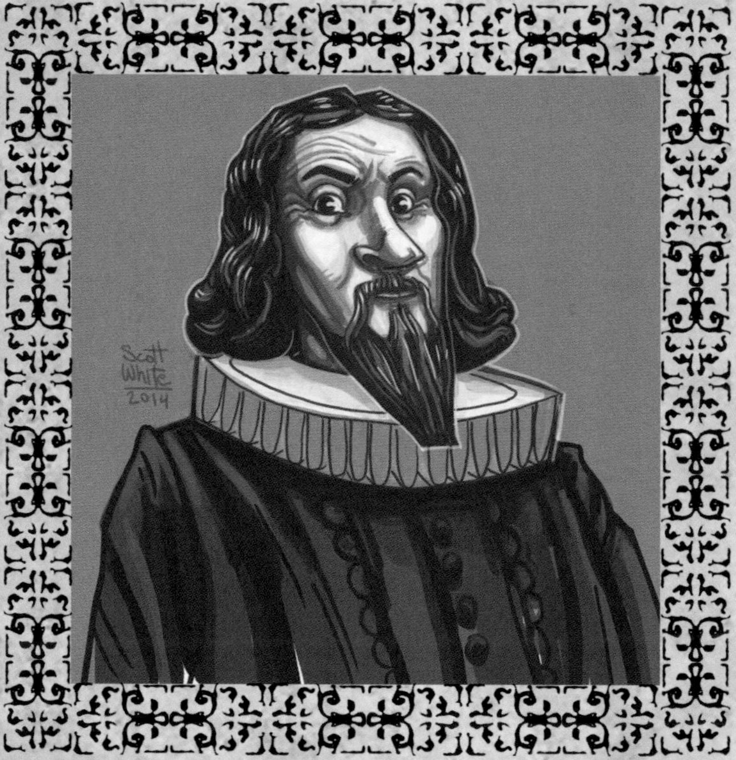
Scott
White
2014

Real Name: John Winthrop
Occupation: Lawyer
Legal Status: Lord of Groton Manor; Governor of Massachusetts
Place of Birth: Suffolk, England
Bio: Born into wealth in 1588, John Winthrop attended college at Cambridge. A Puritan, he opposed many traditional practices of the Church of England. King Charles I's dissolution of Parliament in 1629 convinced Winthrop to join the Massachusetts Bay Company to found a religious colony in America. The company directors made him governor.

Winthrop arrived in Massachusetts on the *Arbella* in 1630, and his third wife followed in 1631. In a sermon for his fellow travelers, he spoke of making their new home a "City upon a Hill," an example to other Christians. The company fleet landed at Salem, but Winthrop soon led efforts to found Boston, one of many new towns to follow.

Winthrop served four stints as governor, totaling twelve years. He was a moderate, but only by Puritan standards—he still banished religious dissenters. He preferred to keep power in a few leaders' hands, especially his own.

His daily journals, published long after his death in 1649, put his name at the center of early Massachusetts history.

J.L. Bell, Scott White, and Jason Rodriguez

Garden in the Wilderness

Story by Matt Bœhm and Art by Ellen T. Crenshaw

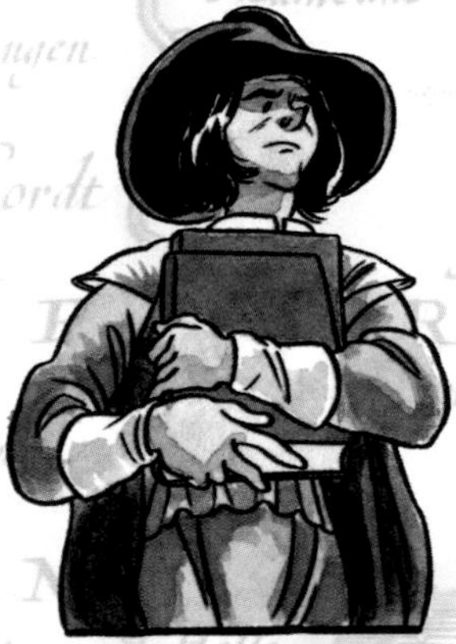

It has been seven years since Roger Williams was forced out of Massachusetts Bay Colony, convicted of spreading "diverse, new, and dangerous opinions." Since his exile, he has settled on Narragansett land, a land he calls *Providence.*

Now, in 1643, Williams's experiment in creating his free colony faces threats from its neighbors. Lacking an official charter leaves *Providence Plantations* vulnerable. Though England is in the middle of a civil war, Roger Williams must return to London and petition Parliament to grant a charter.

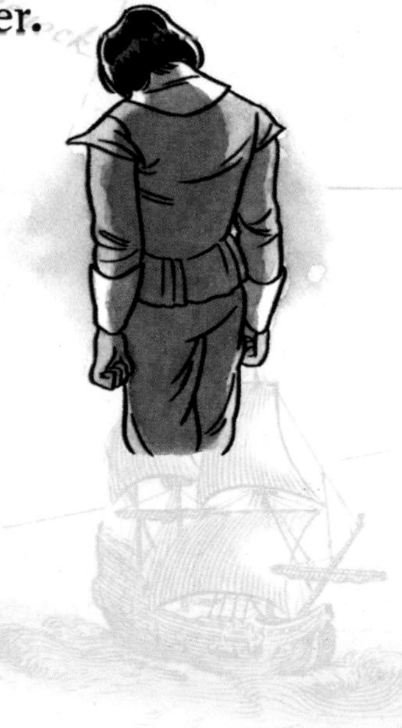

Ex-Massachusetts Governor *Sir Henry Vane*—"Harry" to his friends—is on Williams's side, but agents for the Bay colony have also arrived in London and are actively moving against him.

Obtaining a charter will be no easy task.

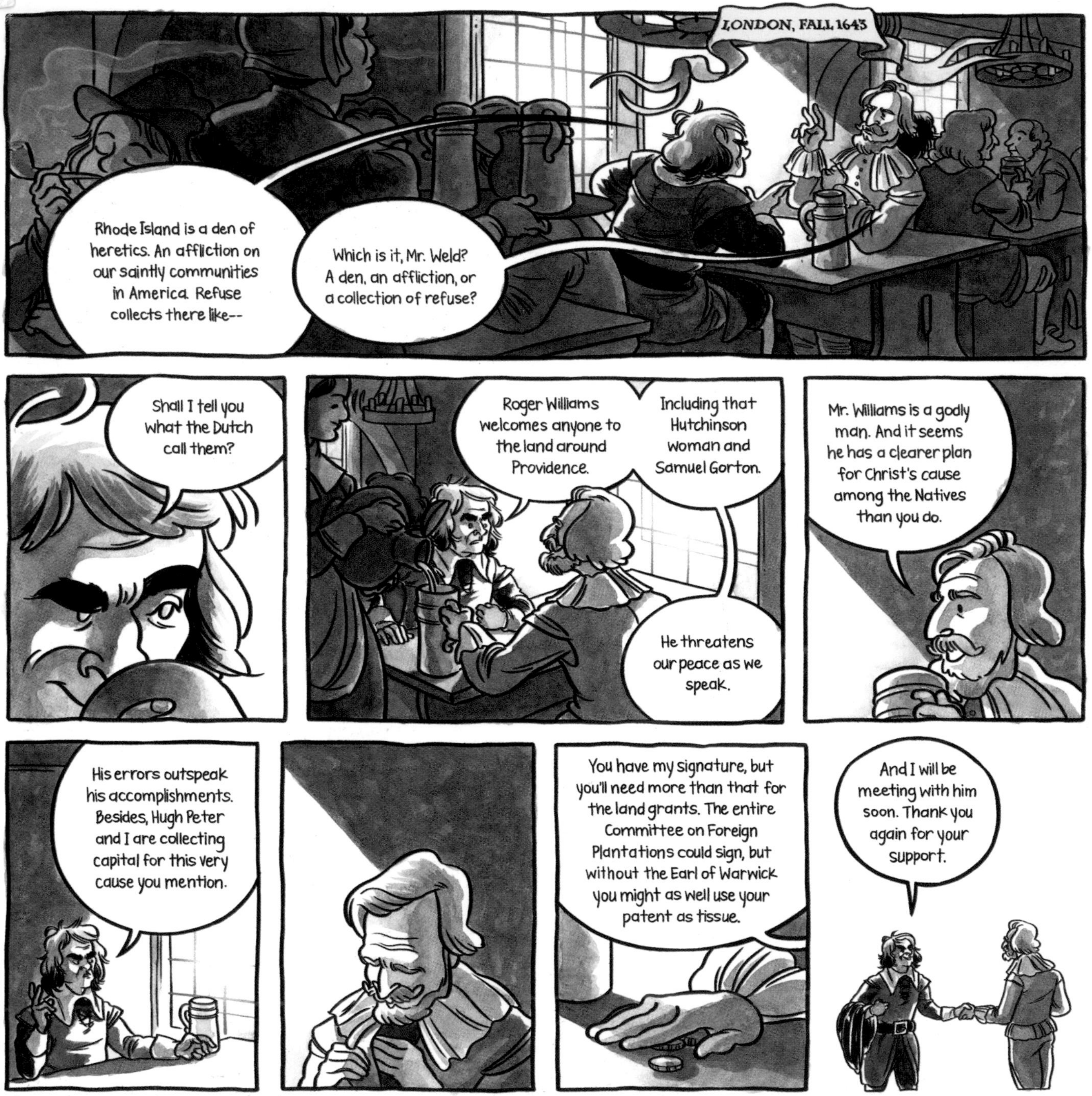
LONDON, FALL 1643
Rhode Island is a den of heretics. An affliction on our saintly communities in America. Refuse collects there like--
Which is it, Mr. Weld? A den, an affliction, or a collection of refuse?
Shall I tell you what the Dutch call them?
Roger Williams welcomes anyone to the land around Providence.
Including that Hutchinson woman and Samuel Gorton.
He threatens our peace as we speak.
Mr. Williams is a godly man. And it seems he has a clearer plan for Christ's cause among the Natives than you do.
His errors outspeak his accomplishments. Besides, Hugh Peter and I are collecting capital for this very cause you mention.
You have my signature, but you'll need more than that for the land grants. The entire Committee on Foreign Plantations could sign, but without the Earl of Warwick you might as well use your patent as tissue.
And I will be meeting with him soon. Thank you again for your support.

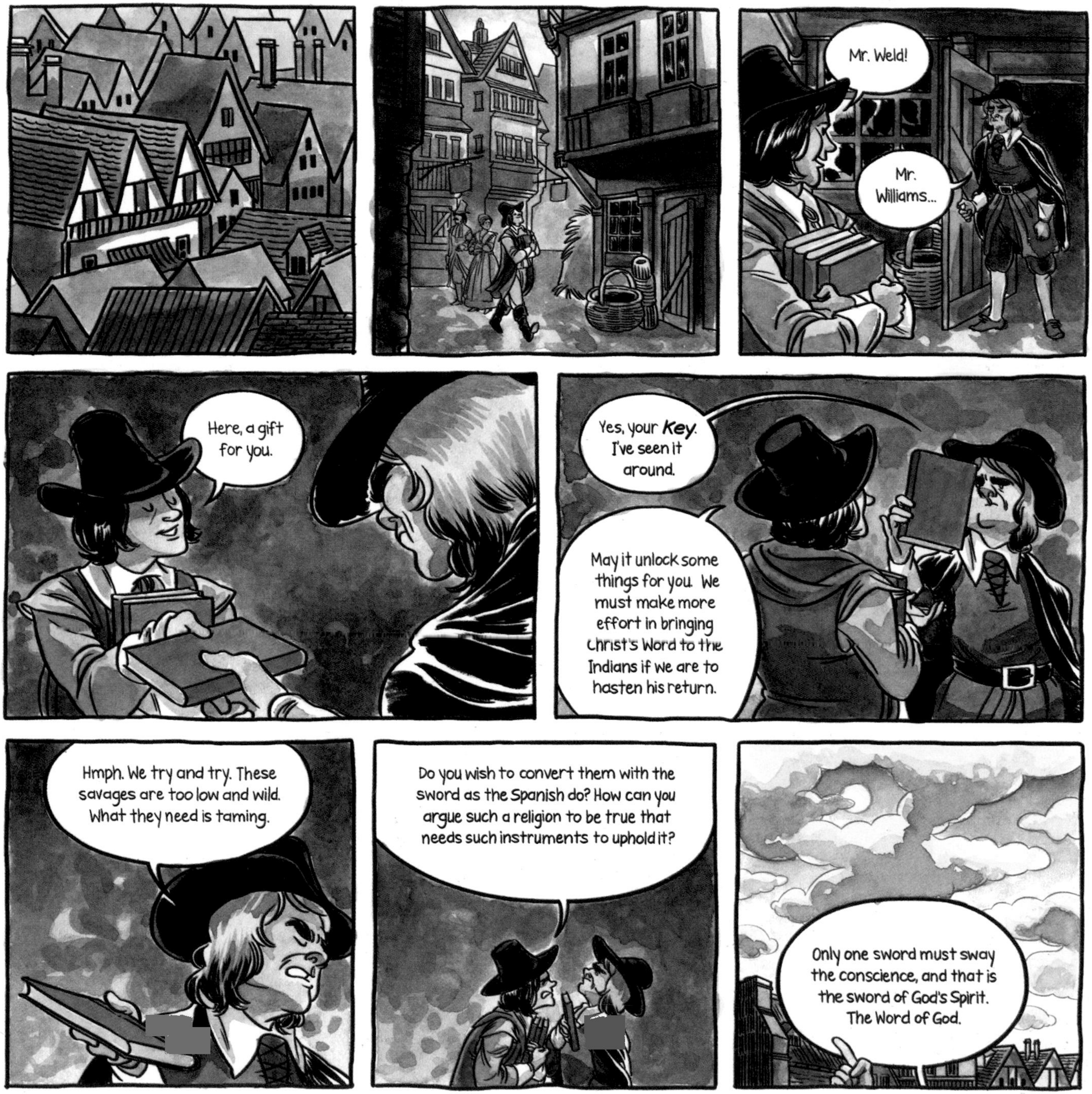
Mr. Weld!
Mr. Williams...
Here, a gift for you.
Yes, your *Key*. I've seen it around.
May it unlock some things for you. We must make more effort in bringing Christ's Word to the Indians if we are to hasten his return.
Hmph. We try and try. These savages are too low and wild. What they need is taming.
Do you wish to convert them with the sword as the Spanish do? How can you argue such a religion to be true that needs such instruments to uphold it?
Only one sword must sway the conscience, and that is the sword of God's Spirit. The Word of God.

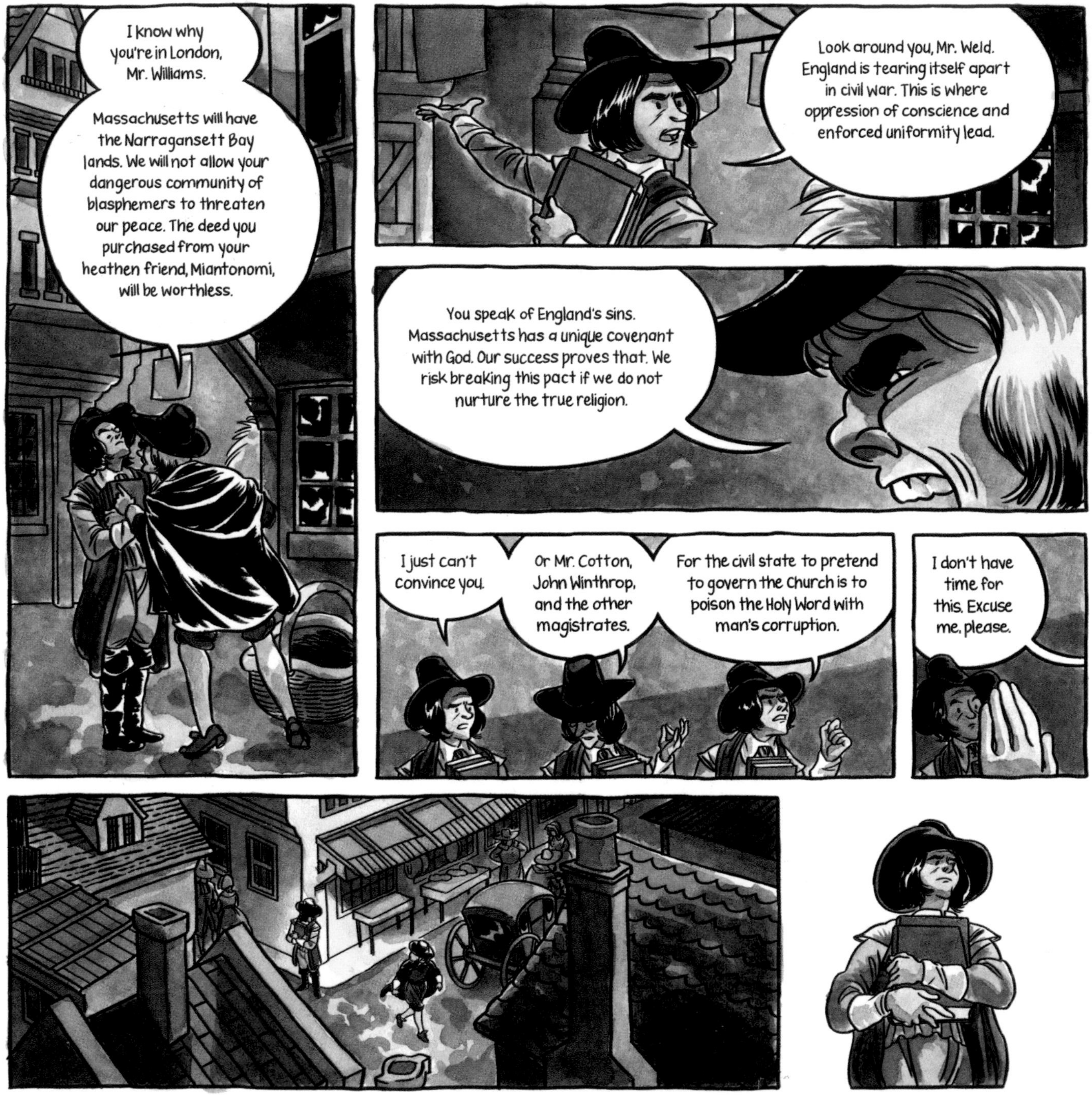

I know why you're in London, Mr. Williams.
Massachusetts will have the Narragansett Bay lands. We will not allow your dangerous community of blasphemers to threaten our peace. The deed you purchased from your heathen friend, Miantonomi, will be worthless.
Look around you, Mr. Weld. England is tearing itself apart in civil war. This is where oppression of conscience and enforced uniformity lead.
You speak of England's sins. Massachusetts has a unique covenant with God. Our success proves that. We risk breaking this pact if we do not nurture the true religion.
I just can't convince you.
Or Mr. Cotton, John Winthrop, and the other magistrates.
For the civil state to pretend to govern the Church is to poison the Holy Word with man's corruption.
I don't have time for this. Excuse me, please.

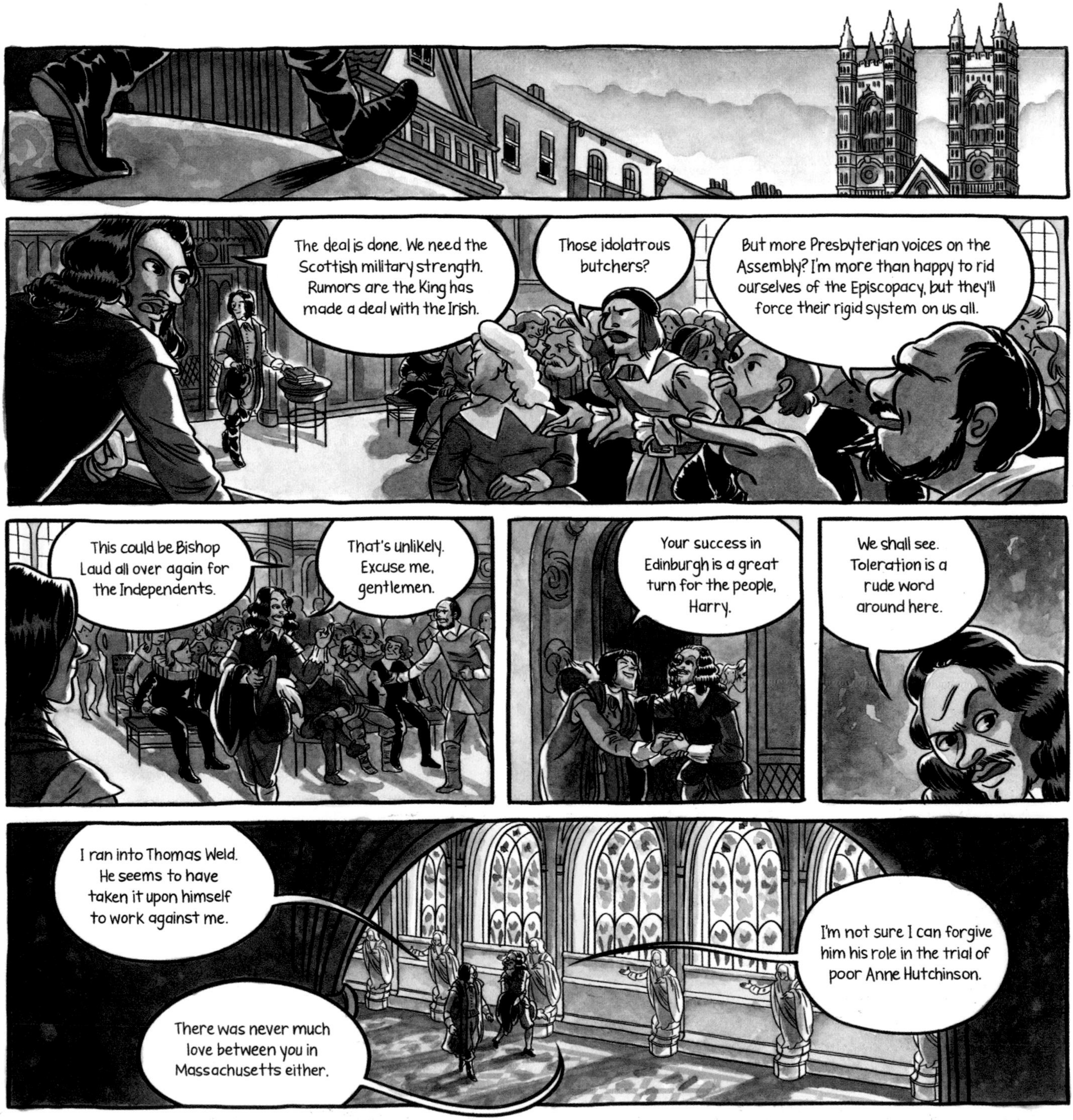

The deal is done. We need the Scottish military strength. Rumors are the King has made a deal with the Irish.
Those idolatrous butchers?
But more Presbyterian voices on the Assembly? I'm more than happy to rid ourselves of the Episcopacy, but they'll force their rigid system on us all.
This could be Bishop Laud all over again for the Independents.
That's unlikely. Excuse me, gentlemen.
Your success in Edinburgh is a great turn for the people, Harry.
We shall see. Toleration is a rude word around here.
I ran into Thomas Weld. He seems to have taken it upon himself to work against me.
There was never much love between you in Massachusetts either.
I'm not sure I can forgive him his role in the trial of poor Anne Hutchinson.

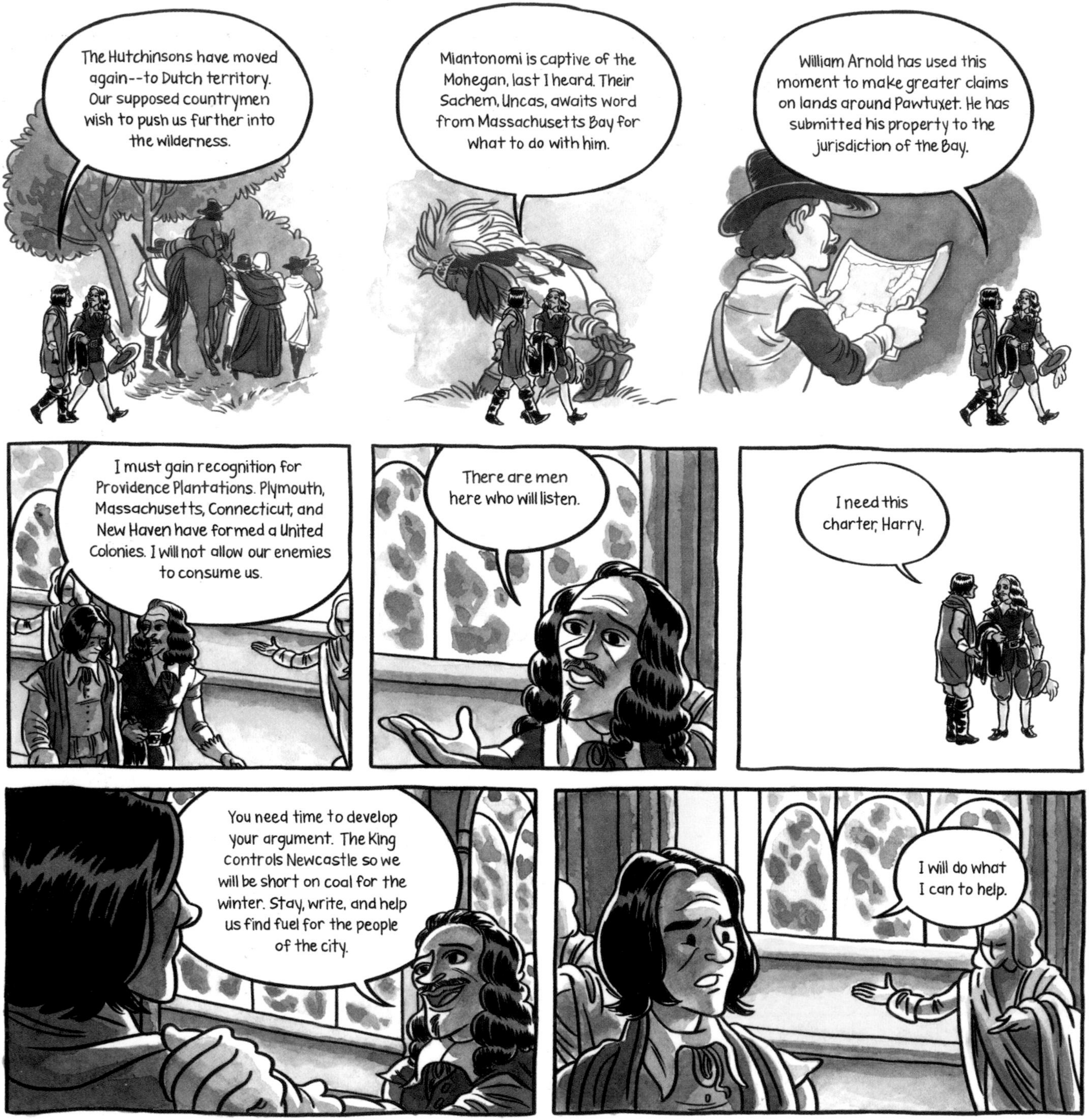
The Hutchinsons have moved again--to Dutch territory. Our supposed countrymen wish to push us further into the wilderness.
Miantonomi is captive of the Mohegan, last I heard. Their Sachem, Uncas, awaits word from Massachusetts Bay for what to do with him.
William Arnold has used this moment to make greater claims on lands around Pawtuxet. He has submitted his property to the jurisdiction of the Bay.
I must gain recognition for Providence Plantations. Plymouth, Massachusetts, Connecticut, and New Haven have formed a United Colonies. I will not allow our enemies to consume us.
There are men here who will listen.
I need this charter, Harry.
You need time to develop your argument. The King controls Newcastle so we will be short on coal for the winter. Stay, write, and help us find fuel for the people of the city.
I will do what I can to help.

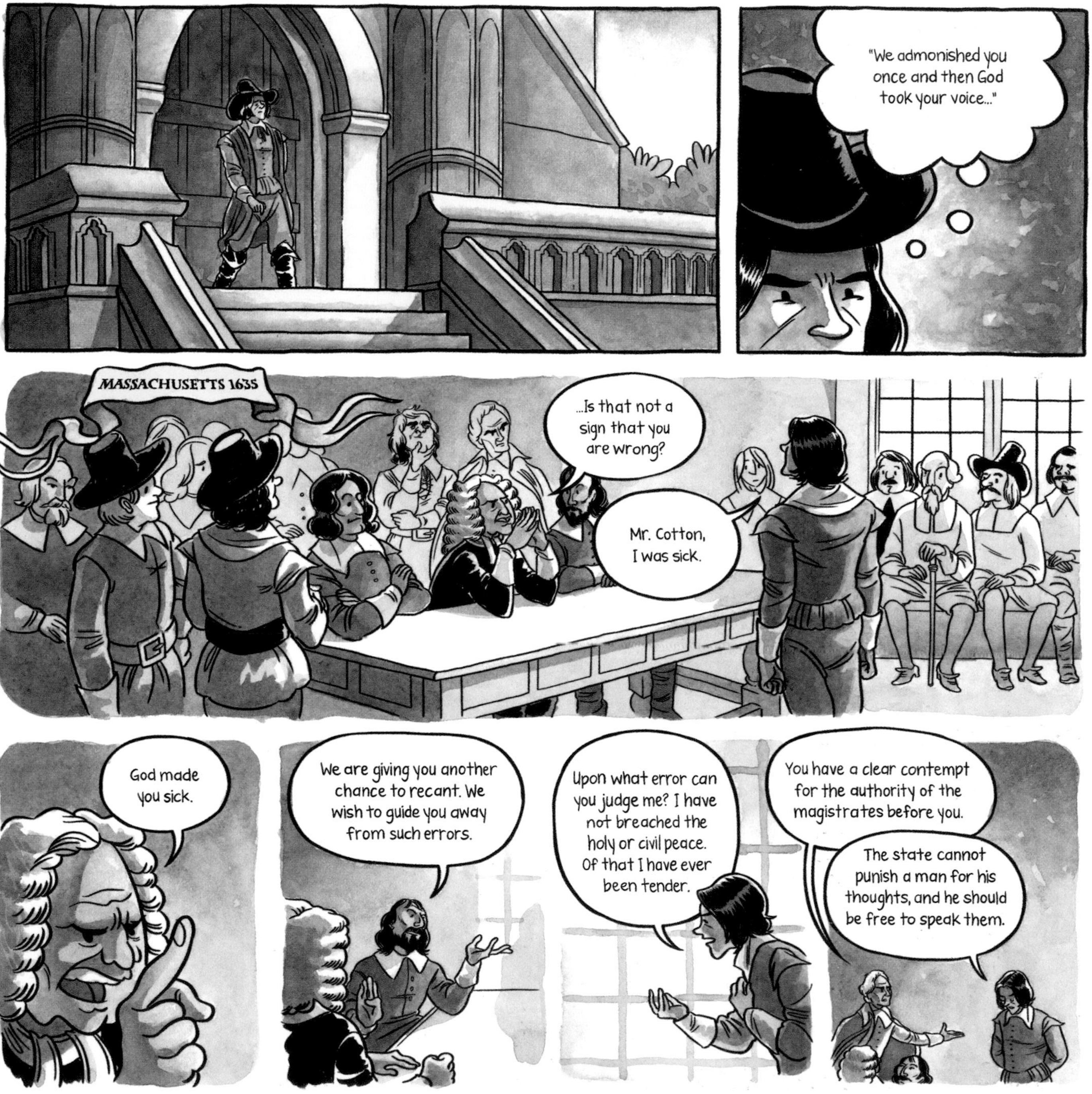
"We admonished you once and then God took your voice..."
MASSACHUSETTS 1635
...Is that not a sign that you are wrong?
Mr. Cotton, I was sick.
God made you sick.
We are giving you another chance to recant. We wish to guide you away from such errors.
Upon what error can you judge me? I have not breached the holy or civil peace. Of that I have ever been tender.
You have a clear contempt for the authority of the magistrates before you.
The state cannot punish a man for his thoughts, and he should be free to speak them.

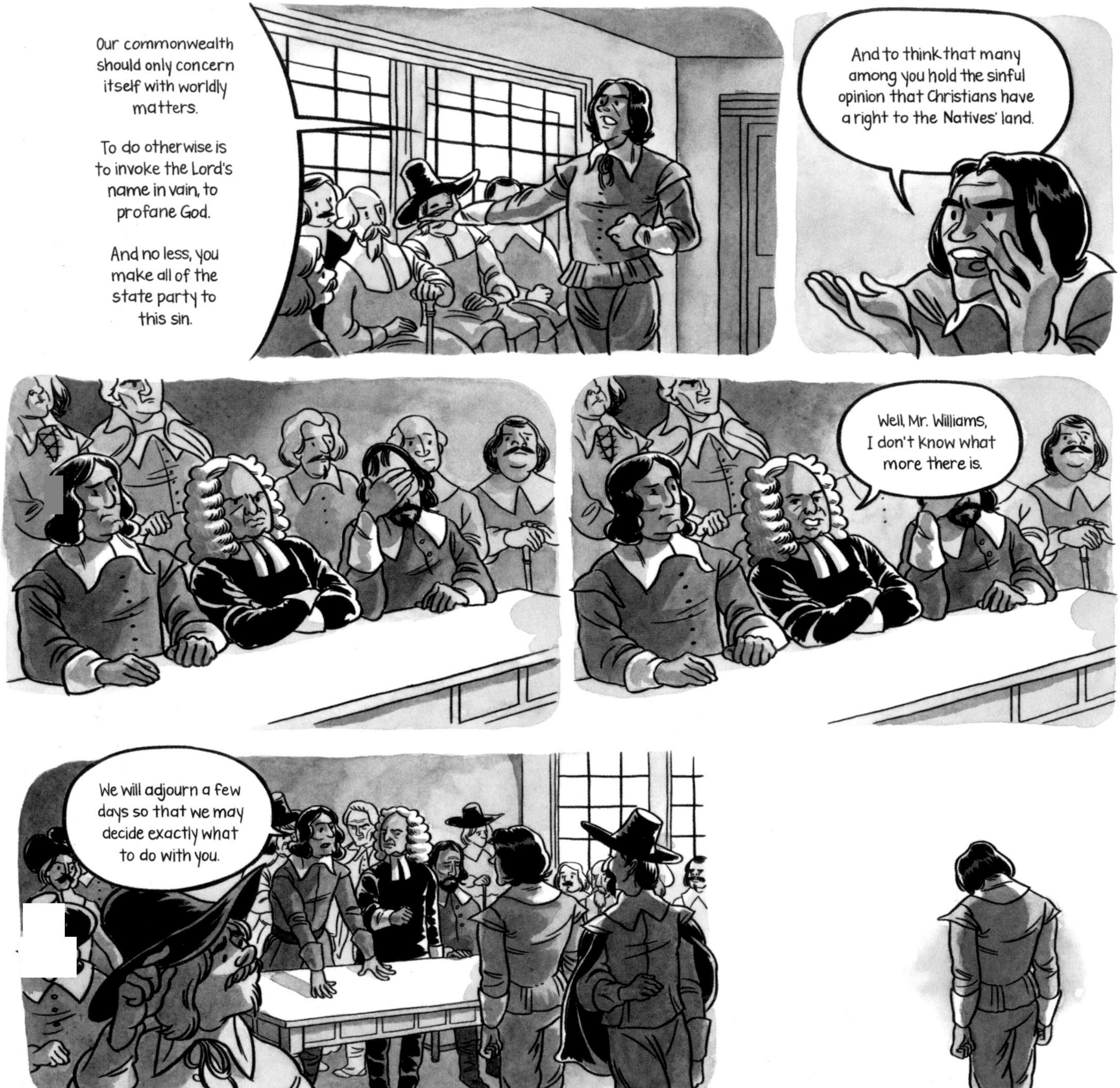

Our commonwealth should only concern itself with worldly matters.
To do otherwise is to invoke the Lord's name in vain, to profane God.
And no less, you make all of the state party to this sin.
And to think that many among you hold the sinful opinion that Christians have a right to the Natives' land.
Well, Mr. Williams, I don't know what more there is.
We will adjourn a few days so that we may decide exactly what to do with you.

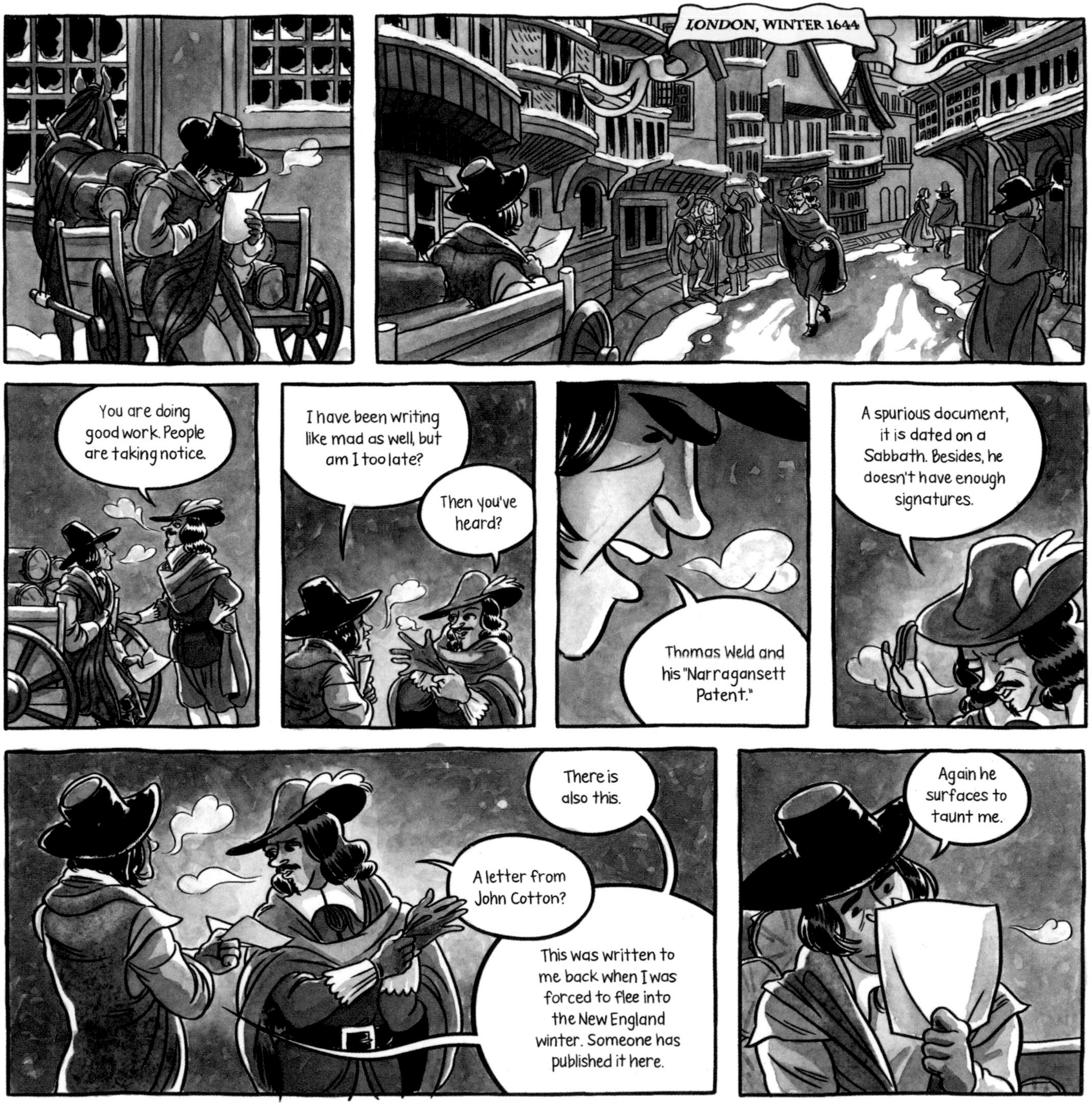
LONDON, WINTER 1644
You are doing good work. People are taking notice.
I have been writing like mad as well, but am I too late?
Then you've heard?
Thomas Weld and his "Narragansett Patent."
A spurious document, it is dated on a Sabbath. Besides, he doesn't have enough signatures.
There is also this.
A letter from John Cotton?
This was written to me back when I was forced to flee into the New England winter. Someone has published it here.
Again he surfaces to taunt me.

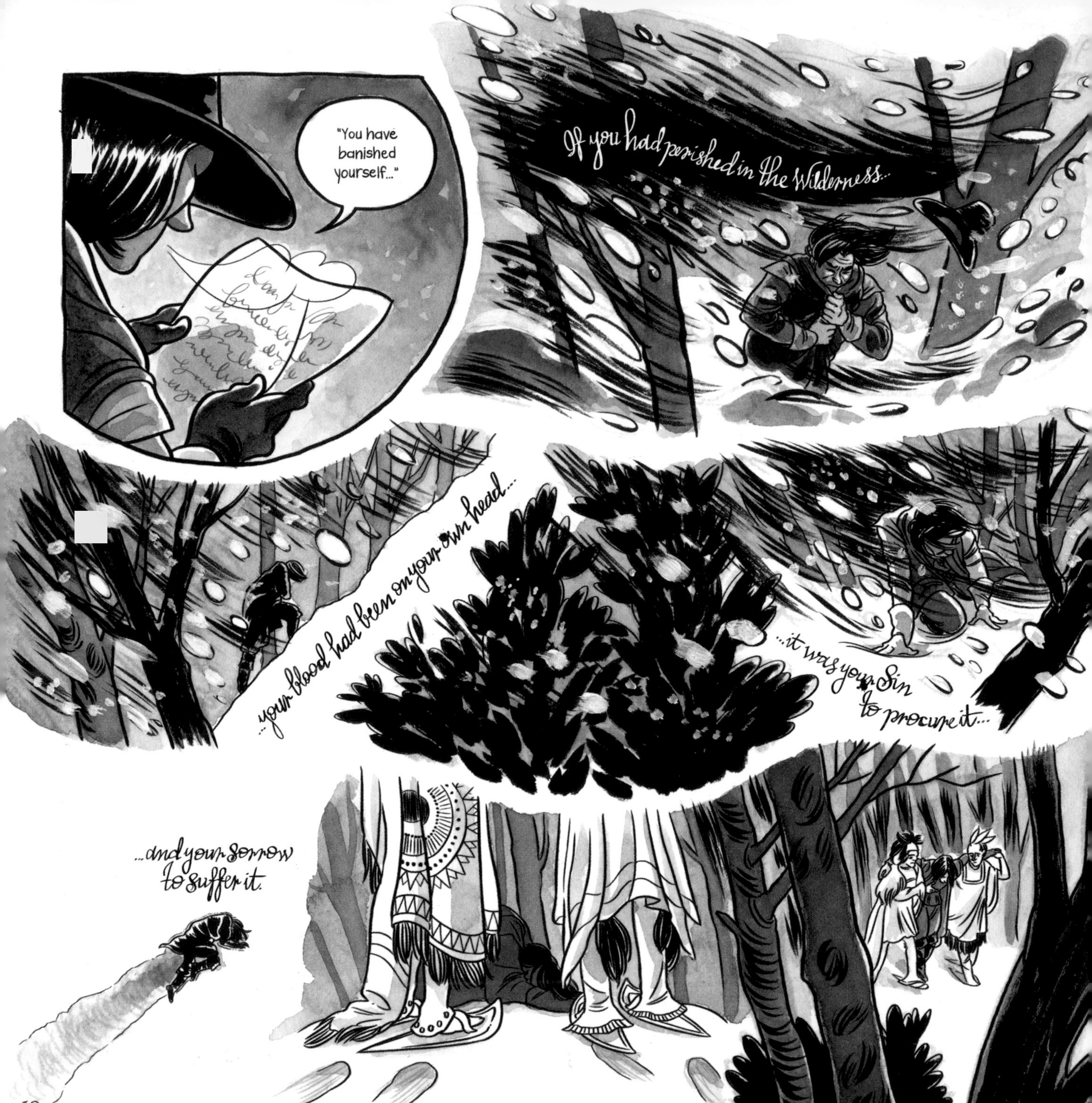
"You have banished yourself..."
If you had perished in the Wilderness...
...your blood had been on your own head...
...it was your Sin to procure it...
...and your sorrow to suffer it.

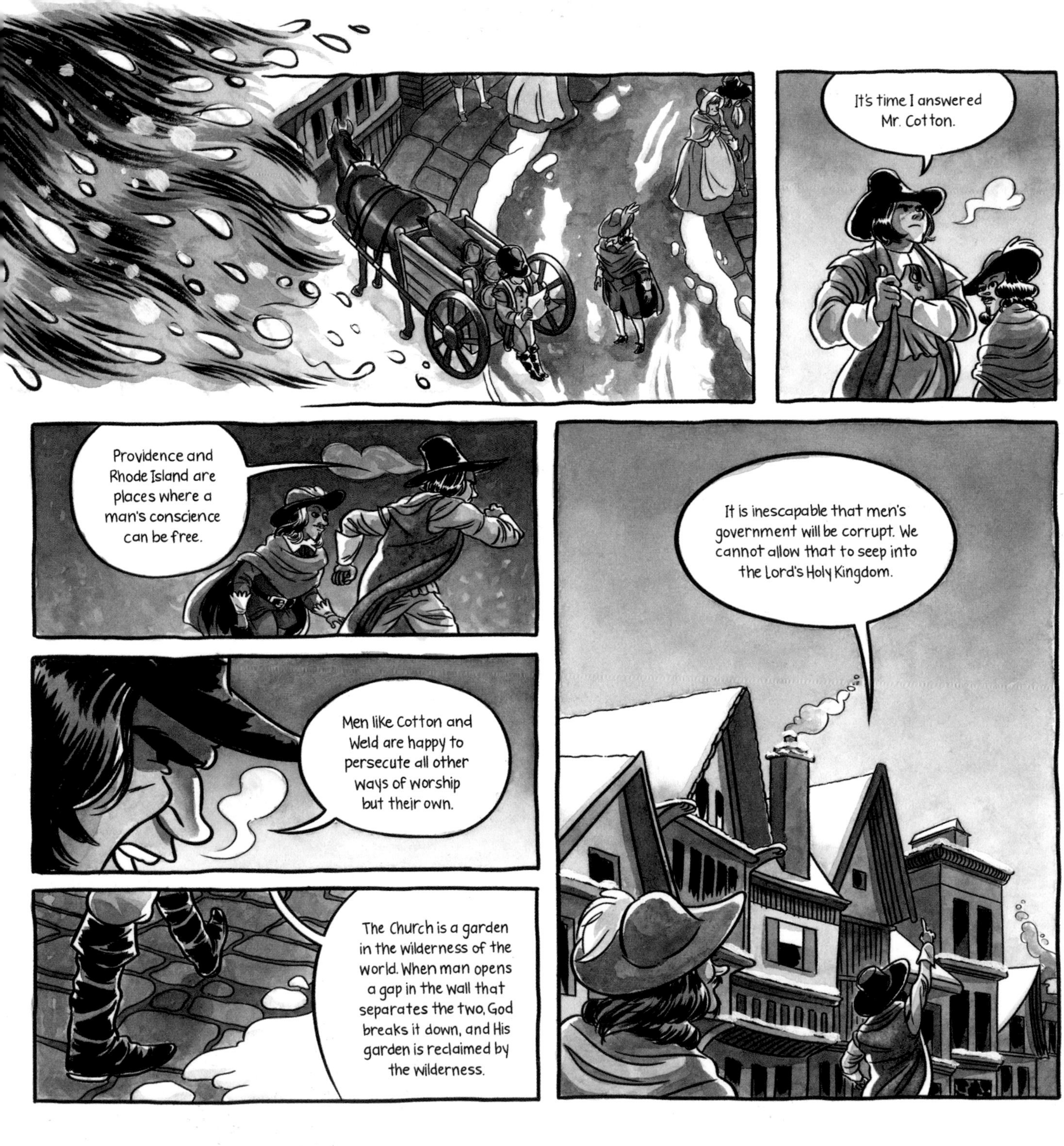
It's time I answered Mr. Cotton.
Providence and Rhode Island are places where a man's conscience can be free.
It is inescapable that men's government will be corrupt. We cannot allow that to seep into the Lord's Holy Kingdom.
Men like Cotton and Weld are happy to persecute all other ways of worship but their own.
The Church is a garden in the wilderness of the world. When man opens a gap in the wall that separates the two, God breaks it down, and His garden is reclaimed by the wilderness.

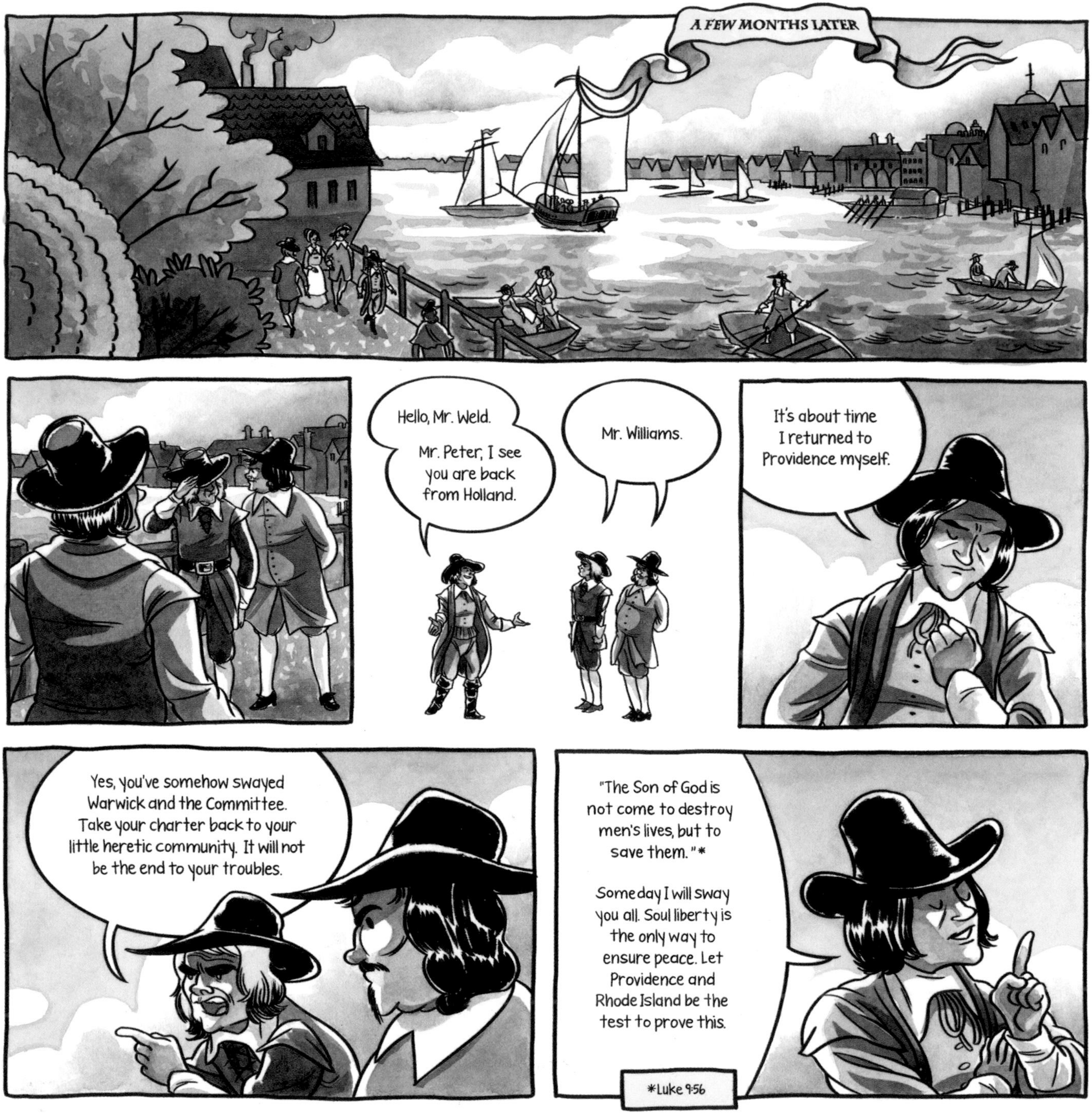
A FEW MONTHS LATER
Hello, Mr. Weld.
Mr. Peter, I see you are back from Holland.
Mr. Williams.
It's about time I returned to Providence myself.
Yes, you've somehow swayed Warwick and the Committee. Take your charter back to your little heretic community. It will not be the end to your troubles.
"The Son of God is not come to destroy men's lives, but to save them."*
Someday I will sway you all. Soul liberty is the only way to ensure peace. Let Providence and Rhode Island be the test to prove this.
*Luke 9:56

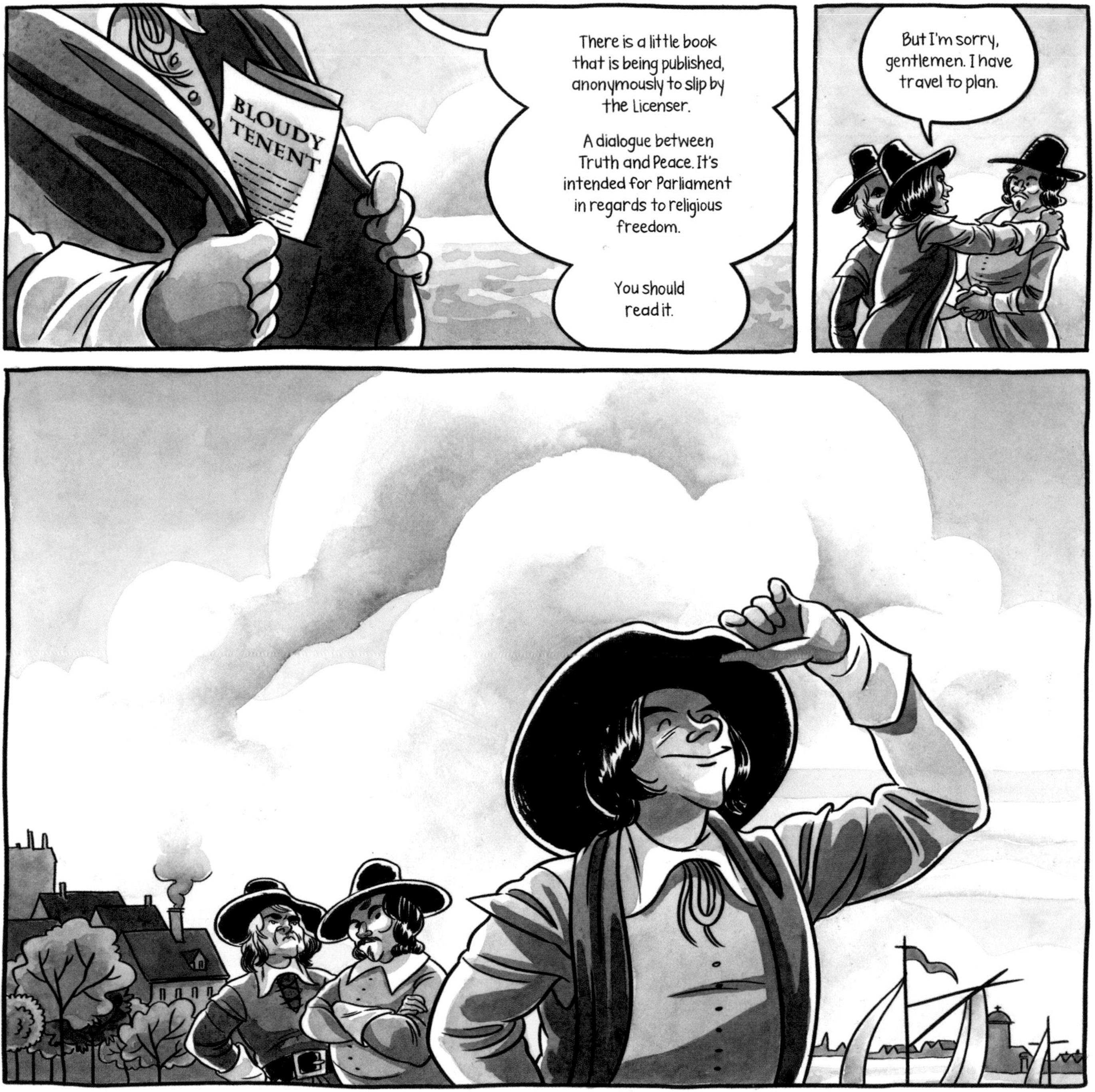
BLOUDY TENENT
There is a little book that is being published, anonymously to slip by the Licenser.
A dialogue between Truth and Peace. It's intended for Parliament in regards to religious freedom.
You should read it.
But I'm sorry, gentlemen. I have travel to plan.
ETC'13

THE TRIAL OF ANNE HUTCHINSON
Story by Alexander Danner and Art by Matt Rawson

Roger Williams wasn't the only resident of the Massachusetts Bay Colony whose beliefs put him at odds with the Puritan establishment. Anne Hutchinson, who arrived in Boston in 1634 with her eleven children, quickly began hosting Sunday discussion groups for women during which participants would discuss the weekly sermon and Hutchinson would often give her own interpretations of the weekly readings.

These meetings became very popular, and she eventually began to attract the attention of the more orthodox ministers in the colony. These men were displeased with her teachings, as Anne Hutchinson encouraged people to ignore church authority.

Instead of being silenced, Hutchinson openly challenged her detractors. She was eventually put on trial in November of 1637.

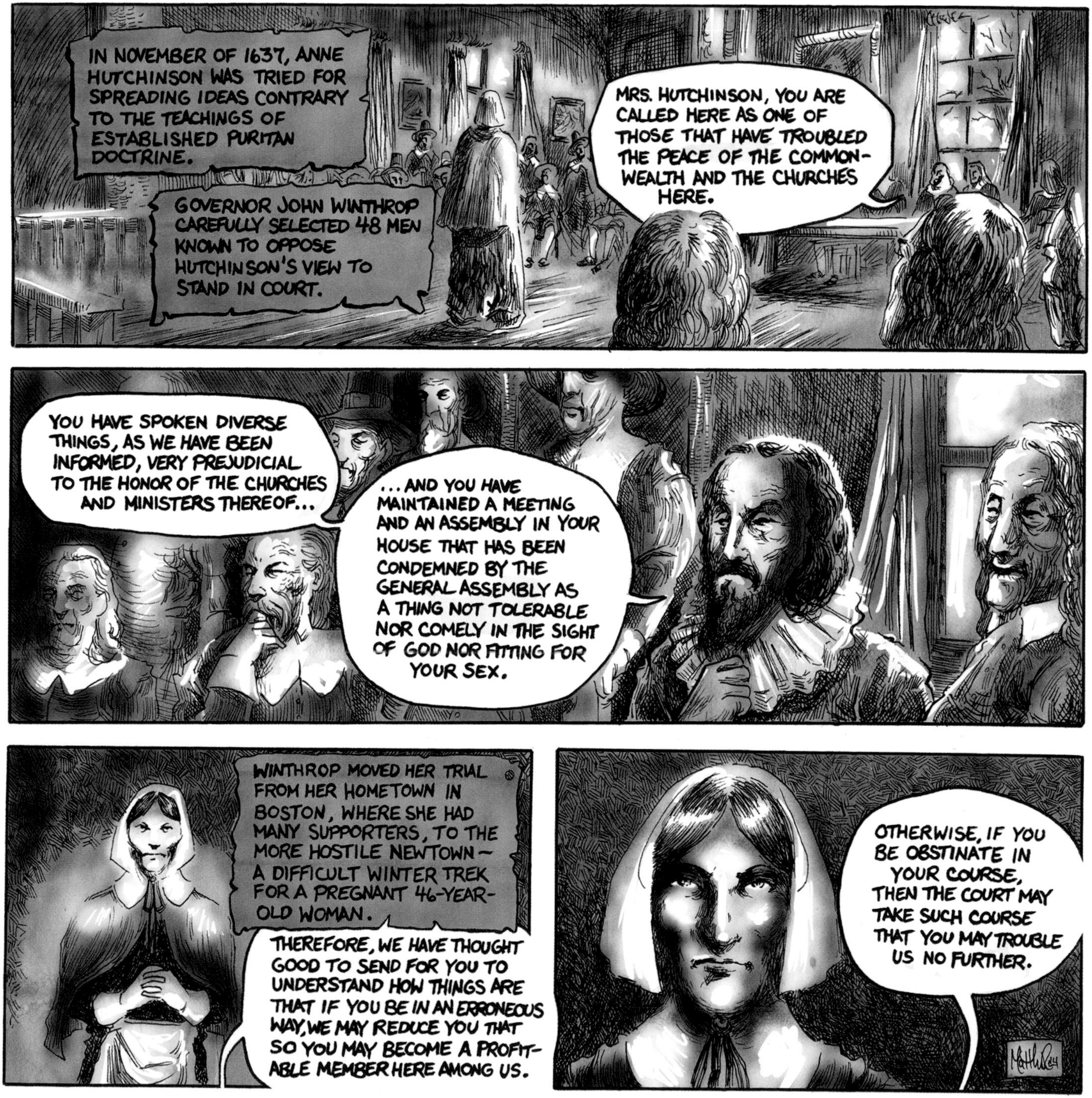
IN NOVEMBER OF 1637, ANNE HUTCHINSON WAS TRIED FOR SPREADING IDEAS CONTRARY TO THE TEACHINGS OF ESTABLISHED PURITAN DOCTRINE.
GOVERNOR JOHN WINTHROP CAREFULLY SELECTED 48 MEN KNOWN TO OPPOSE HUTCHINSON'S VIEW TO STAND IN COURT.
MRS. HUTCHINSON, YOU ARE CALLED HERE AS ONE OF THOSE THAT HAVE TROUBLED THE PEACE OF THE COMMONWEALTH AND THE CHURCHES HERE.
YOU HAVE SPOKEN DIVERSE THINGS, AS WE HAVE BEEN INFORMED, VERY PREJUDICIAL TO THE HONOR OF THE CHURCHES AND MINISTERS THEREOF...
...AND YOU HAVE MAINTAINED A MEETING AND AN ASSEMBLY IN YOUR HOUSE THAT HAS BEEN CONDEMNED BY THE GENERAL ASSEMBLY AS A THING NOT TOLERABLE NOR COMELY IN THE SIGHT OF GOD NOR FITTING FOR YOUR SEX.
WINTHROP MOVED HER TRIAL FROM HER HOMETOWN IN BOSTON, WHERE SHE HAD MANY SUPPORTERS, TO THE MORE HOSTILE NEWTOWN — A DIFFICULT WINTER TREK FOR A PREGNANT 46-YEAR-OLD WOMAN.
THEREFORE, WE HAVE THOUGHT GOOD TO SEND FOR YOU TO UNDERSTAND HOW THINGS ARE THAT IF YOU BE IN AN ERRONEOUS WAY, WE MAY REDUCE YOU THAT SO YOU MAY BECOME A PROFITABLE MEMBER HERE AMONG US.
OTHERWISE, IF YOU BE OBSTINATE IN YOUR COURSE, THEN THE COURT MAY TAKE SUCH COURSE THAT YOU MAY TROUBLE US NO FURTHER.

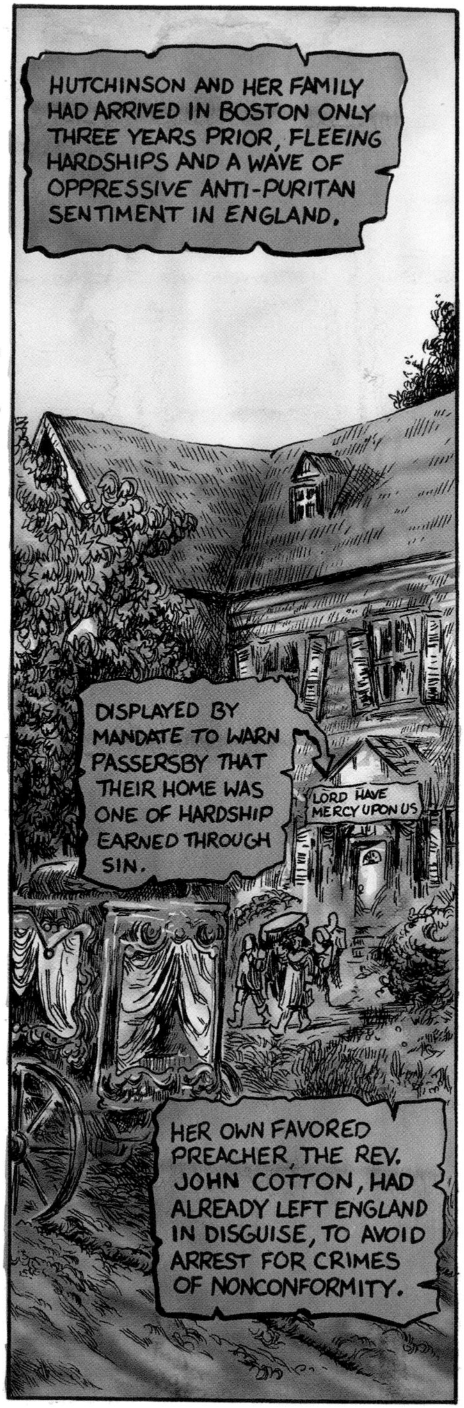
HUTCHINSON AND HER FAMILY HAD ARRIVED IN BOSTON ONLY THREE YEARS PRIOR, FLEEING HARDSHIPS AND A WAVE OF OPPRESSIVE ANTI-PURITAN SENTIMENT IN ENGLAND.
DISPLAYED BY MANDATE TO WARN PASSERSBY THAT THEIR HOME WAS ONE OF HARDSHIP EARNED THROUGH SIN.
LORD HAVE MERCY UPON US
HER OWN FAVORED PREACHER, THE REV. JOHN COTTON, HAD ALREADY LEFT ENGLAND IN DISGUISE, TO AVOID ARREST FOR CRIMES OF NONCONFORMITY.

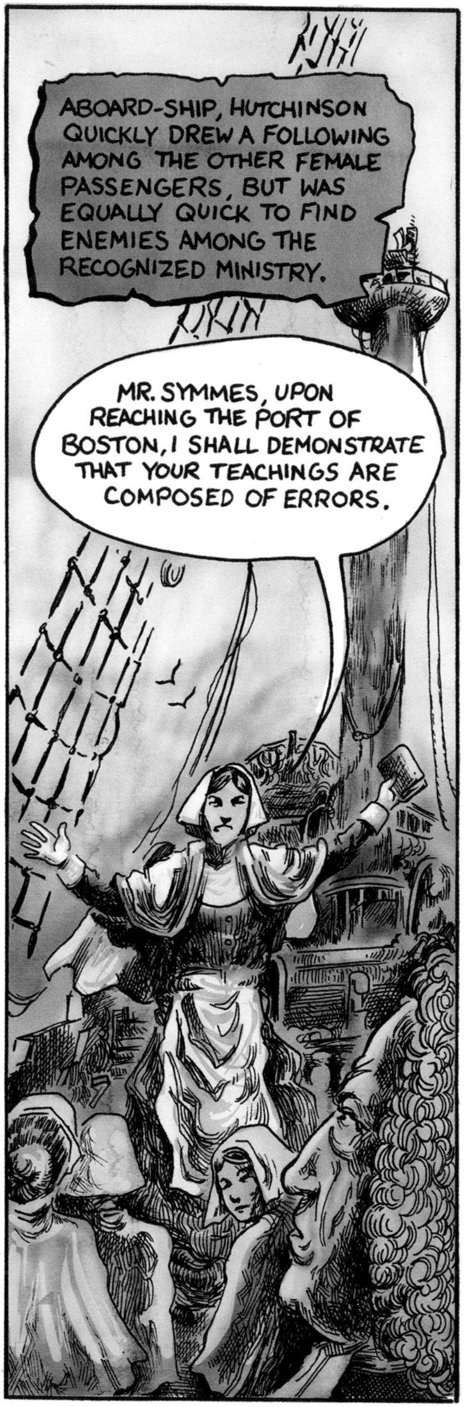
ABOARD-SHIP, HUTCHINSON QUICKLY DREW A FOLLOWING AMONG THE OTHER FEMALE PASSENGERS, BUT WAS EQUALLY QUICK TO FIND ENEMIES AMONG THE RECOGNIZED MINISTRY.
MR. SYMMES, UPON REACHING THE PORT OF BOSTON, I SHALL DEMONSTRATE THAT YOUR TEACHINGS ARE COMPOSED OF ERRORS.

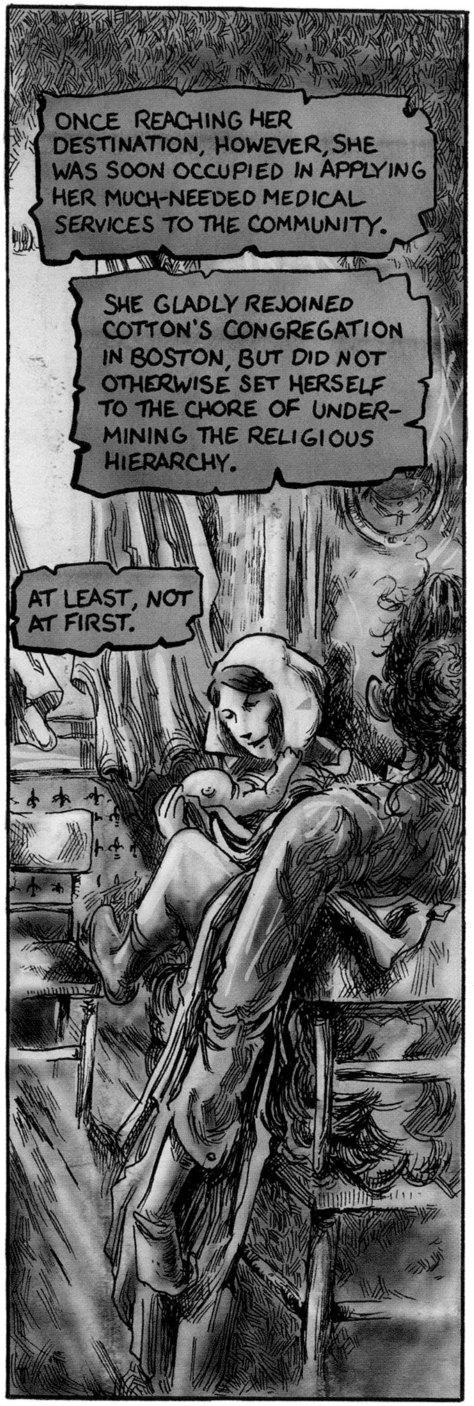
ONCE REACHING HER DESTINATION, HOWEVER, SHE WAS SOON OCCUPIED IN APPLYING HER MUCH-NEEDED MEDICAL SERVICES TO THE COMMUNITY.
SHE GLADLY REJOINED COTTON'S CONGREGATION IN BOSTON, BUT DID NOT OTHERWISE SET HERSELF TO THE CHORE OF UNDERMINING THE RELIGIOUS HIERARCHY.
AT LEAST, NOT AT FIRST.

IT WAS CUSTOM IN BOSTON AT THE TIME FOR WOMEN TO JOIN IN WEEKLY PRAYER CIRCLES. IN FACT, HUTCHINSON HAD BEEN INDIRECTLY RE-BUKED FOR NOT JOINING ONE IMMEDIATELY UPON HER ARRIVAL IN BOSTON.

SHE WAS ALLOWED TO SIT, DUE TO HER OBVIOUS PHYSICAL CONDITION.

WHY DO YOU KEEP SUCH A MEETING AT YOUR HOUSE AS YOU DO EVERY WEEK UPON A SET DAY?

IT IS LAWFUL FOR ME TO DO SO, AS IT IS ALL YOUR PRACTICES. CAN YOU FIND A WARRANT FOR YOURSELF AND CONDEMN ME FOR THE SAME THING?

BEING EXPERIENCED IN LEADING WOMEN'S RELIGIOUS MEETINGS, HUTCHINSON CHOSE TO START HER OWN CIRCLE RATHER THAN TAKE TUTELAGE UNDER OTHER WOMEN.

BECAUSE I DID NOT GO TO SUCH MEETINGS IT WAS REPORTED THAT I DID NOT ALLOW OF SUCH MEETINGS BUT HELD THEM UNLAWFUL. THEREFORE, IN THAT REGARD THEY SAID I WAS PROUD AND DESPISED ALL ORDINANCES.

UPON THAT A FRIEND TOLD ME OF IT, AND I, TO PREVENT SUCH ASPERSIONS, TOOK IT UP. BUT IT WAS IN PRACTICE BEFORE I CAME.

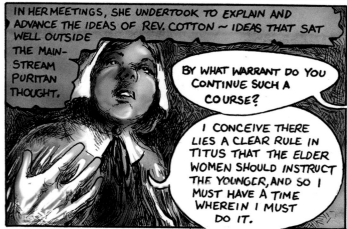

IN HER MEETINGS, SHE UNDERTOOK TO EXPLAIN AND ADVANCE THE IDEAS OF REV. COTTON ~ IDEAS THAT SAT WELL OUTSIDE THE MAINSTREAM PURITAN THOUGHT.

BY WHAT WARRANT DO YOU CONTINUE SUCH A COURSE?

I CONCEIVE THERE LIES A CLEAR RULE IN TITUS THAT THE ELDER WOMEN SHOULD INSTRUCT THE YOUNGER, AND SO I MUST HAVE A TIME WHEREIN I MUST DO IT.

A CHARISMATIC SPEAKER WITH UNUSUAL IDEAS, HUTCHINSON QUICKLY DREW LARGE NUMBERS TO HER CIRCLE, WHICH WORRIED TOWN LEADERS, WHO RESPONDED WITH NEW ORDINANCES AGAINST LARGE GATHERINGS OF WOMEN...

ALL THIS I GRANT YOU, I GRANT YOU A TIME FOR IT...

BUT YOU MUST TAKE IT IN THIS SENSE: THAT ELDER WOMEN MUST INSTRUCT THE YOUNGER ABOUT THEIR BUSINESS, AND TO LOVE THEIR HUSBANDS, AND NOT TO MAKE THEM CLASH, MRS. HUTCHINSON ...

...THE VERY SAME GATHERINGS HUTCHINSON HAD EARLIER BEEN CHIDED FOR NOT JOINING!

WILL IT PLEASE YOU TO ANSWER ME THIS AND TO GIVE ME A RULE, FOR THEN I WILL WILLINGLY SUBMIT TO ANY TRUTH.

IF ANY COME TO MY HOUSE TO BE INSTRUCTED IN THE WAYS OF GOD, WHAT RULE HAVE I TO PUT THEM AWAY?

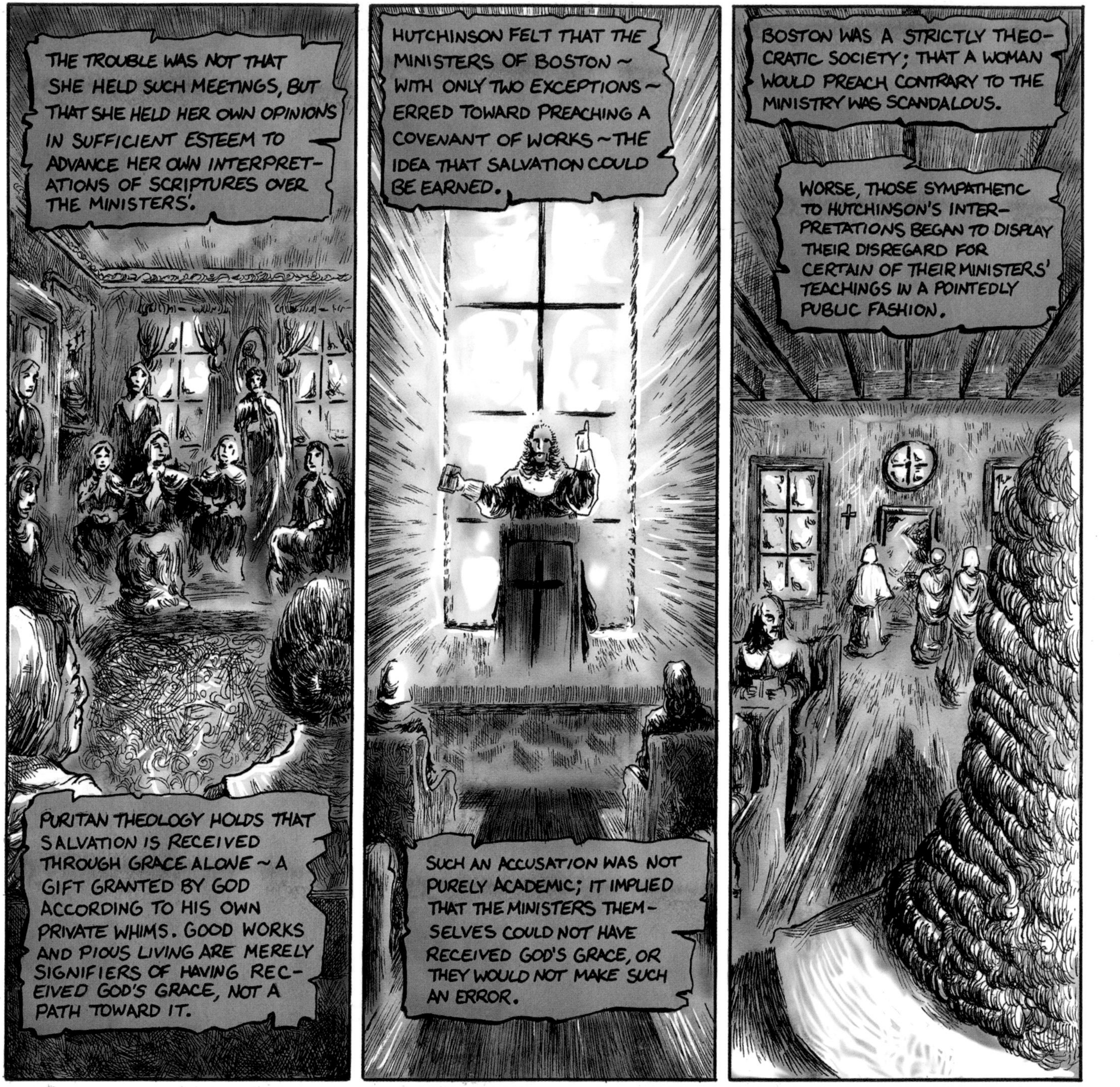
THE TROUBLE WAS NOT THAT SHE HELD SUCH MEETINGS, BUT THAT SHE HELD HER OWN OPINIONS IN SUFFICIENT ESTEEM TO ADVANCE HER OWN INTERPRETATIONS OF SCRIPTURES OVER THE MINISTERS'.
PURITAN THEOLOGY HOLDS THAT SALVATION IS RECEIVED THROUGH GRACE ALONE ~ A GIFT GRANTED BY GOD ACCORDING TO HIS OWN PRIVATE WHIMS. GOOD WORKS AND PIOUS LIVING ARE MERELY SIGNIFIERS OF HAVING RECEIVED GOD'S GRACE, NOT A PATH TOWARD IT.
HUTCHINSON FELT THAT THE MINISTERS OF BOSTON ~ WITH ONLY TWO EXCEPTIONS ~ ERRED TOWARD PREACHING A COVENANT OF WORKS ~ THE IDEA THAT SALVATION COULD BE EARNED.
SUCH AN ACCUSATION WAS NOT PURELY ACADEMIC; IT IMPLIED THAT THE MINISTERS THEMSELVES COULD NOT HAVE RECEIVED GOD'S GRACE, OR THEY WOULD NOT MAKE SUCH AN ERROR.
BOSTON WAS A STRICTLY THEOCRATIC SOCIETY; THAT A WOMAN WOULD PREACH CONTRARY TO THE MINISTRY WAS SCANDALOUS.
WORSE, THOSE SYMPATHETIC TO HUTCHINSON'S INTERPRETATIONS BEGAN TO DISPLAY THEIR DISREGARD FOR CERTAIN OF THEIR MINISTERS' TEACHINGS IN A POINTEDLY PUBLIC FASHION.

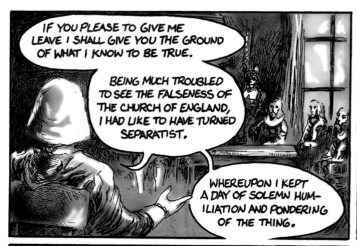

IF YOU PLEASE TO GIVE ME LEAVE I SHALL GIVE YOU THE GROUND OF WHAT I KNOW TO BE TRUE.

BEING MUCH TROUBLED TO SEE THE FALSENESS OF THE CHURCH OF ENGLAND, I HAD LIKE TO HAVE TURNED SEPARATIST.

WHEREUPON I KEPT A DAY OF SOLEMN HUMILIATION AND PONDERING OF THE THING.

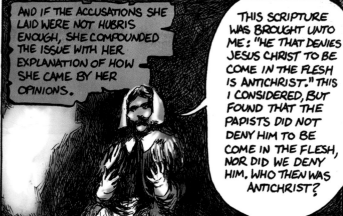

AND IF THE ACCUSATIONS SHE LAID WERE NOT HUBRIS ENOUGH, SHE COMPOUNDED THE ISSUE WITH HER EXPLANATION OF HOW SHE CAME BY HER OPINIONS.

THIS SCRIPTURE WAS BROUGHT UNTO ME: "HE THAT DENIES JESUS CHRIST TO BE COME IN THE FLESH IS ANTICHRIST." THIS I CONSIDERED, BUT FOUND THAT THE PAPISTS DID NOT DENY HIM TO BE COME IN THE FLESH, NOR DID WE DENY HIM. WHO THEN WAS ANTICHRIST?

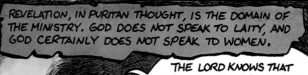

REVELATION, IN PURITAN THOUGHT, IS THE DOMAIN OF THE MINISTRY. GOD DOES NOT SPEAK TO LAITY, AND GOD CERTAINLY DOES NOT SPEAK TO WOMEN.

THE LORD KNOWS THAT I COULD NOT OPEN SCRIPTURE; HE MUST BY HIS PROPHETICAL OFFICE OPEN IT TO ME ... AND THE LORD WAS PLEASED TO BRING THIS SCRIPTURE OUT OF THE HEBREWS: "HE THAT DENIES THE TESTAMENT DENIES THE TESTATOR." I SAW THAT THOSE WHICH DID NOT TEACH THE NEW COVENANT HAD THE SPIRIT OF ANTICHRIST. UPON THIS HE REVEALED THE MINISTRY TO ME.

HUTCHINSON'S CLAIM OF DIVINE INSIGHT CHALLENGED MORE THAN JUST THE SOCIAL NORMS OF HER GENDER AND CLASS.

EVER SINCE, I BLESS THE LORD, HE HATH LET ME SEE WHICH WAS THE CLEAR MINISTRY AND WHICH THE WRONG.

HOW DO YOU KNOW THAT WAS THE SPIRIT?

SHE WAS DEMOCRATIZING ACCESS TO GOD HIMSELF!

DEP. GOV. THOMAS DUDLEY

HOW DID ABRAHAM KNOW THAT IT WAS GOD THAT BID HIM OFFER HIS SON, BEING A BREACH OF THE SIXTH COMMANDMENT?

BY AN IMMEDIATE VOICE.

SO TO ME BY AN IMMEDIATE REVELATION, BY THE VOICE OF HIS OWN SPIRIT TO MY SOUL.

59

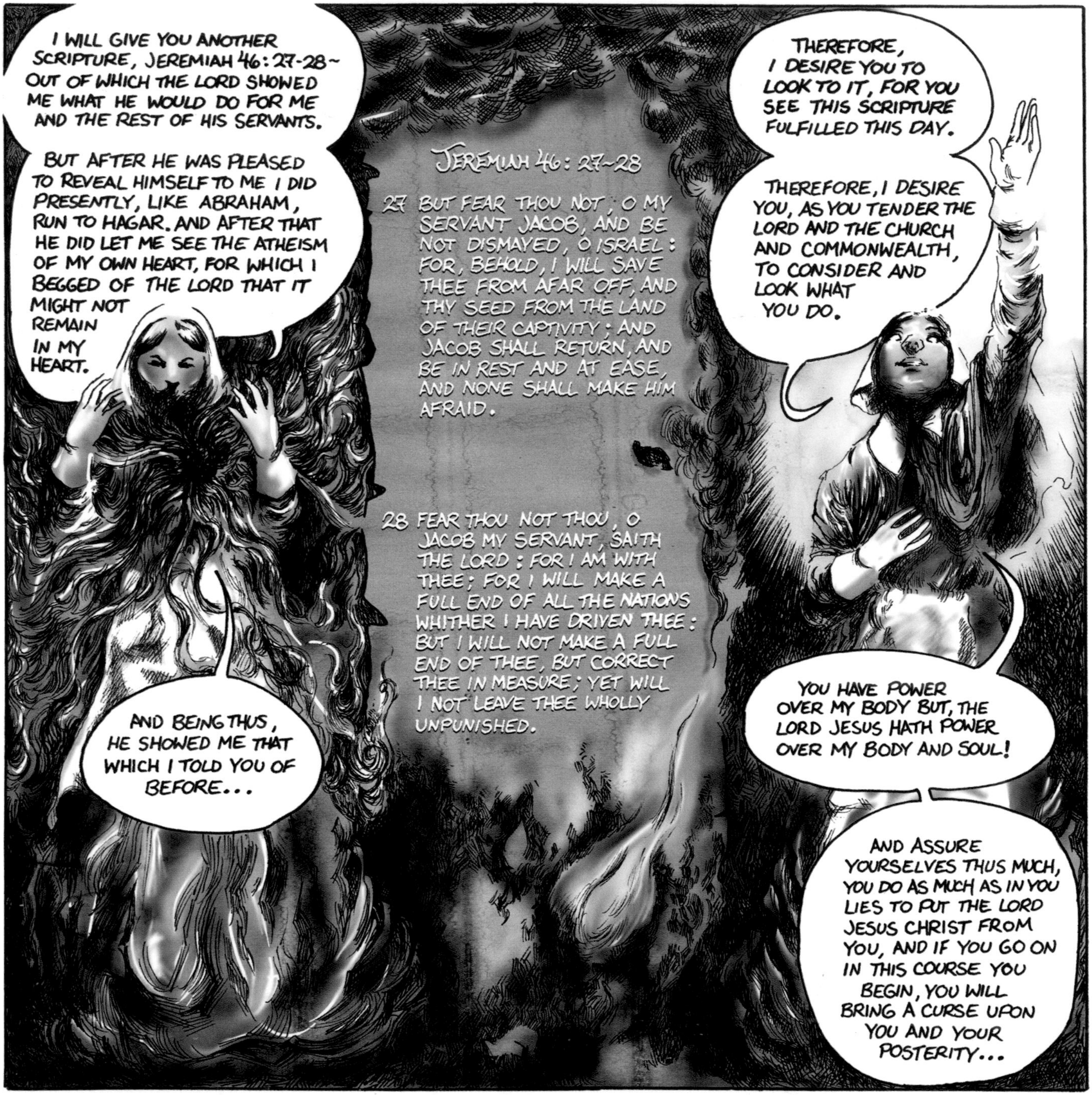
I WILL GIVE YOU ANOTHER SCRIPTURE, JEREMIAH 46:27-28~ OUT OF WHICH THE LORD SHOWED ME WHAT HE WOULD DO FOR ME AND THE REST OF HIS SERVANTS.
BUT AFTER HE WAS PLEASED TO REVEAL HIMSELF TO ME I DID PRESENTLY, LIKE ABRAHAM, RUN TO HAGAR. AND AFTER THAT HE DID LET ME SEE THE ATHEISM OF MY OWN HEART, FOR WHICH I BEGGED OF THE LORD THAT IT MIGHT NOT REMAIN IN MY HEART.
AND BEING THUS, HE SHOWED ME THAT WHICH I TOLD YOU OF BEFORE...
JEREMIAH 46: 27~28
27 BUT FEAR THOU NOT, O MY SERVANT JACOB, AND BE NOT DISMAYED, O ISRAEL: FOR, BEHOLD, I WILL SAVE THEE FROM AFAR OFF, AND THY SEED FROM THE LAND OF THEIR CAPTIVITY; AND JACOB SHALL RETURN, AND BE IN REST AND AT EASE, AND NONE SHALL MAKE HIM AFRAID.
28 FEAR THOU NOT THOU, O JACOB MY SERVANT, SAITH THE LORD: FOR I AM WITH THEE; FOR I WILL MAKE A FULL END OF ALL THE NATIONS WHITHER I HAVE DRIVEN THEE: BUT I WILL NOT MAKE A FULL END OF THEE, BUT CORRECT THEE IN MEASURE; YET WILL I NOT LEAVE THEE WHOLLY UNPUNISHED.
THEREFORE, I DESIRE YOU TO LOOK TO IT, FOR YOU SEE THIS SCRIPTURE FULFILLED THIS DAY.
THEREFORE, I DESIRE YOU, AS YOU TENDER THE LORD AND THE CHURCH AND COMMONWEALTH, TO CONSIDER AND LOOK WHAT YOU DO.
YOU HAVE POWER OVER MY BODY BUT, THE LORD JESUS HATH POWER OVER MY BODY AND SOUL!
AND ASSURE YOURSELVES THUS MUCH, YOU DO AS MUCH AS IN YOU LIES TO PUT THE LORD JESUS CHRIST FROM YOU, AND IF YOU GO ON IN THIS COURSE YOU BEGIN, YOU WILL BRING A CURSE UPON YOU AND YOUR POSTERITY...

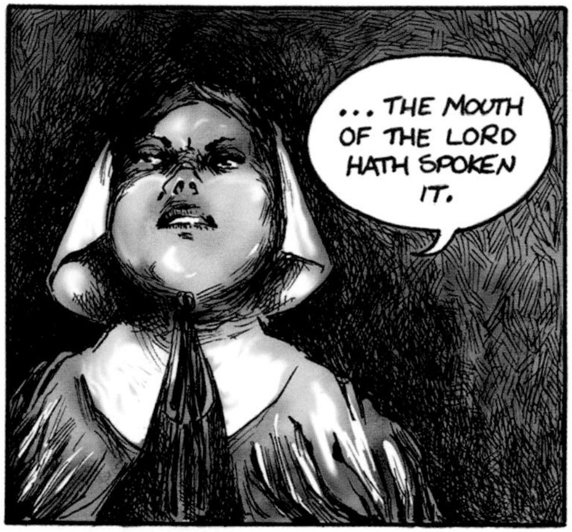
...THE MOUTH OF THE LORD HATH SPOKEN IT.

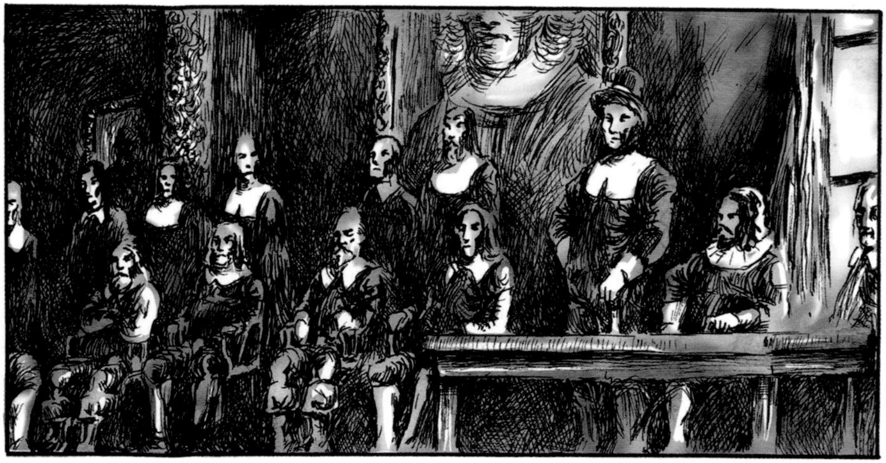

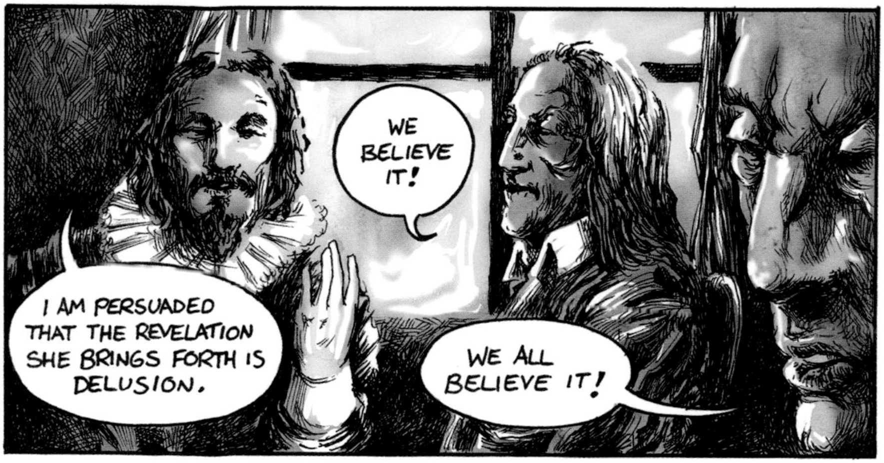
I AM PERSUADED THAT THE REVELATION SHE BRINGS FORTH IS DELUSION.
WE BELIEVE IT!
WE ALL BELIEVE IT!

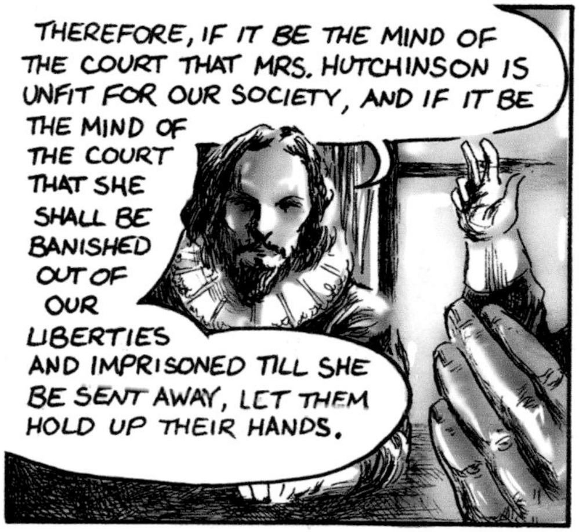
THEREFORE, IF IT BE THE MIND OF THE COURT THAT MRS. HUTCHINSON IS UNFIT FOR OUR SOCIETY, AND IF IT BE THE MIND OF THE COURT THAT SHE SHALL BE BANISHED OUT OF OUR LIBERTIES AND IMPRISONED TILL SHE BE SENT AWAY, LET THEM HOLD UP THEIR HANDS.

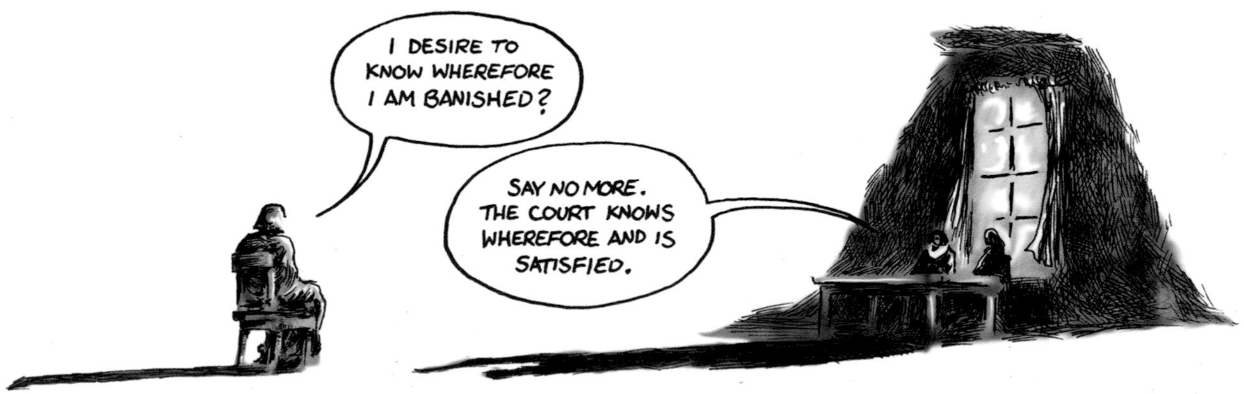
I DESIRE TO KNOW WHEREFORE I AM BANISHED?
SAY NO MORE. THE COURT KNOWS WHEREFORE AND IS SATISFIED.

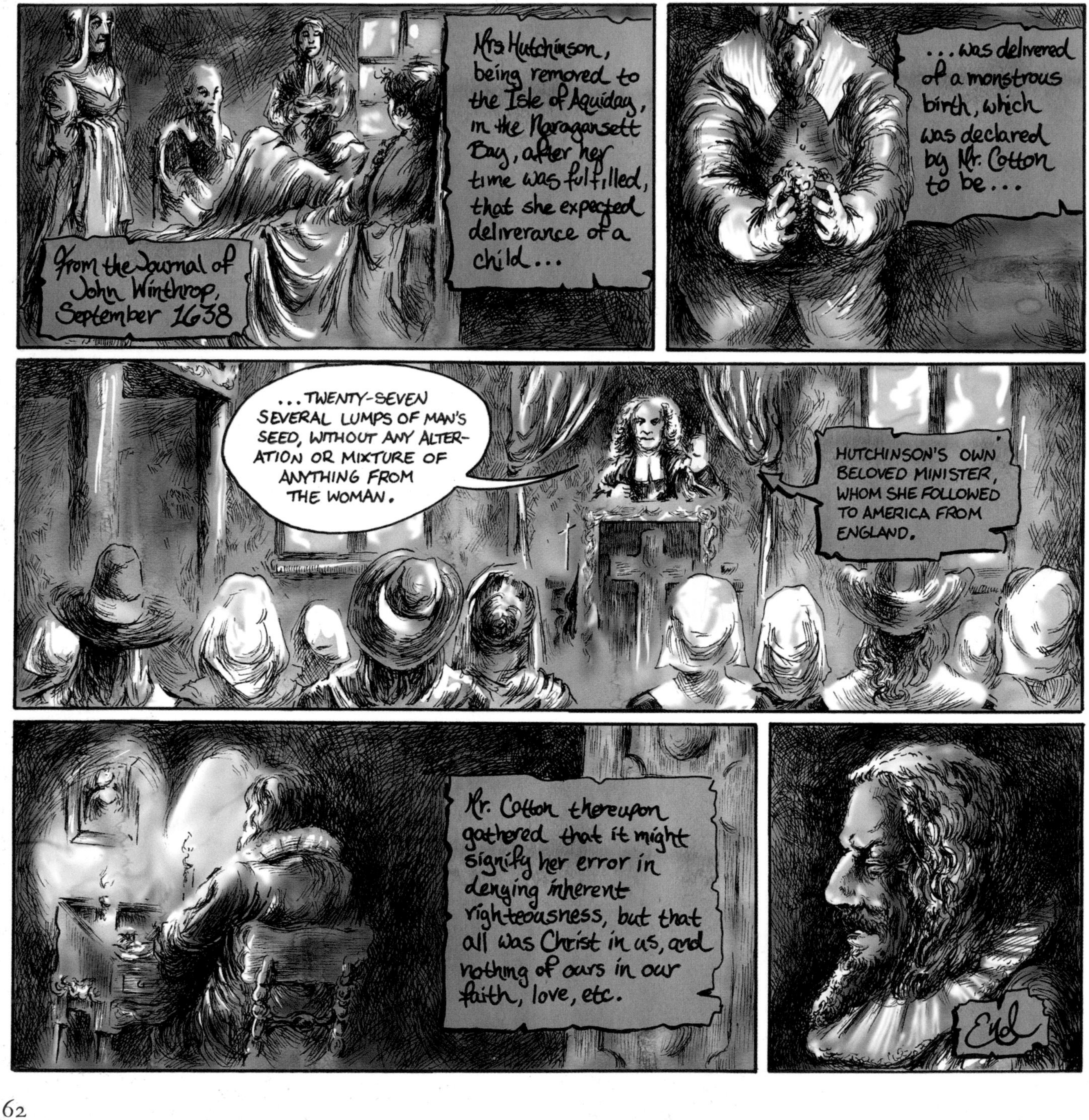
From the Journal of John Winthrop, September 1638
Mrs. Hutchinson, being removed to the Isle of Aquiday, in the Naragansett Bay, after her time was fulfilled, that she expected deliverance of a child...
...was delivered of a monstrous birth, which was declared by Mr. Cotton to be...
...TWENTY-SEVEN SEVERAL LUMPS OF MAN'S SEED, WITHOUT ANY ALTERATION OR MIXTURE OF ANYTHING FROM THE WOMAN.
HUTCHINSON'S OWN BELOVED MINISTER, WHOM SHE FOLLOWED TO AMERICA FROM ENGLAND.
Mr. Cotton thereupon gathered that it might signify her error in denying inherent righteousness, but that all was Christ in us, and nothing of ours in our faith, love, etc.
End

THE HOLY MAN

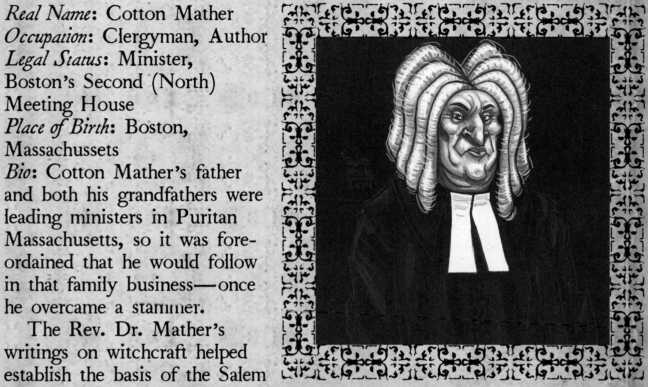

Real Name: Cotton Mather
Occupation: Clergyman, Author
Legal Status: Minister,
Boston's Second (North)
Meeting House
Place of Birth: Boston,
Massachussets
Bio: Cotton Mather's father
and both his grandfathers were
leading ministers in Puritan
Massachusetts, so it was fore-
ordained that he would follow
in that family business—once
he overcame a stammer.

The Rev. Dr. Mather's
writings on witchcraft helped
establish the basis of the Salem
Witch Trials of 1692, and witnesses reported that he attended the Rev.
George Burroughs's execution. Mather wrote about many more topics,
however, producing more than 400 books and pamphlets. He argued for
inoculation to curb smallpox epidemics when most doctors found that idea
dangerous. He recorded some of the first observations of plant hybridiza-
tion and even theorized that microscopic organisms could make people sick.

Though still respected at the time of his death in 1728, Mather had
watched his father's world erode: their church held less influence over civic
affairs, and Massachusetts enjoyed less political autonomy.

Jason Rodriguez, Scott White, and J.L. Bell

The Press's Widow: Elizabeth Glover

Story by Erika Swyler, Art by Noël Tuazon, and Letters by Jason Hanley

If you read Sarah Vowell's *The Wordy Shipmates*, you'll learn that the colonists who came over from England wrote down practically every thought they ever had. It stands to reason, then, that they would want a printing press in the Massachusetts Bay Colony, and Reverend Joseph Glover was happy to bring his over.

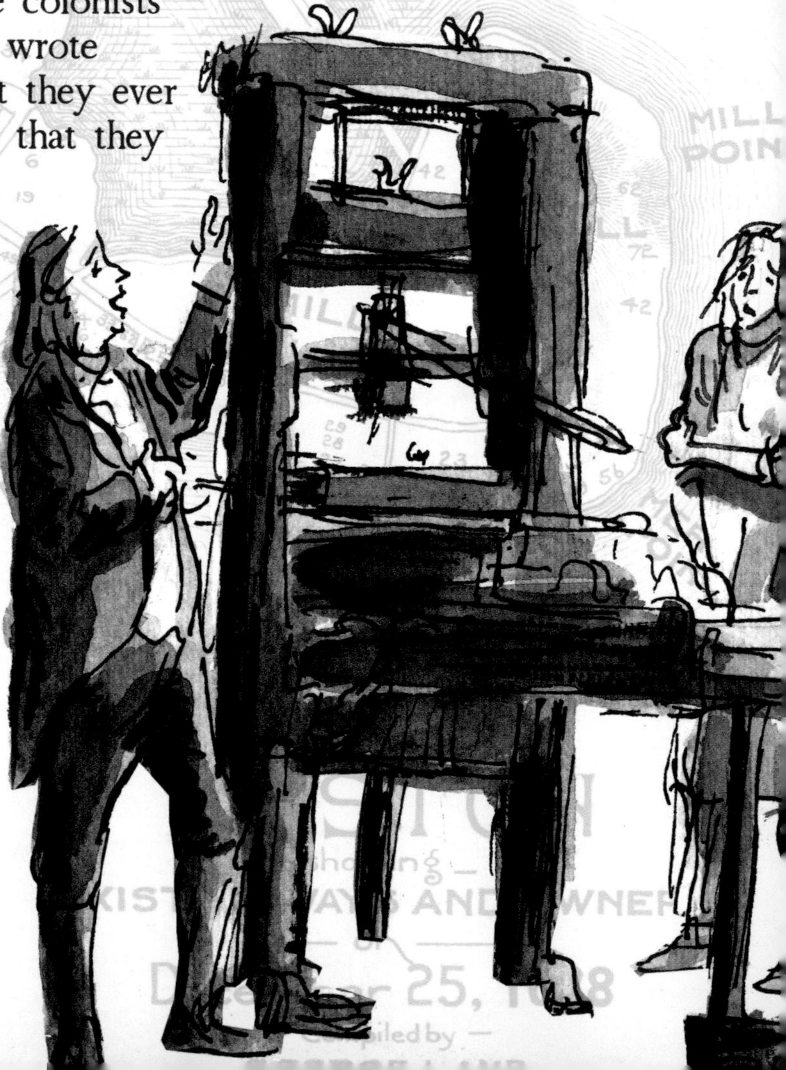

The voyages across the Atlantic were long, however, and people often died during the trip. And this was the case with Joseph Glover, who left behind his wife, children, debtors, and a printing press... but no way for his wife to start a business that would have provided for any of the people who were counting on her.

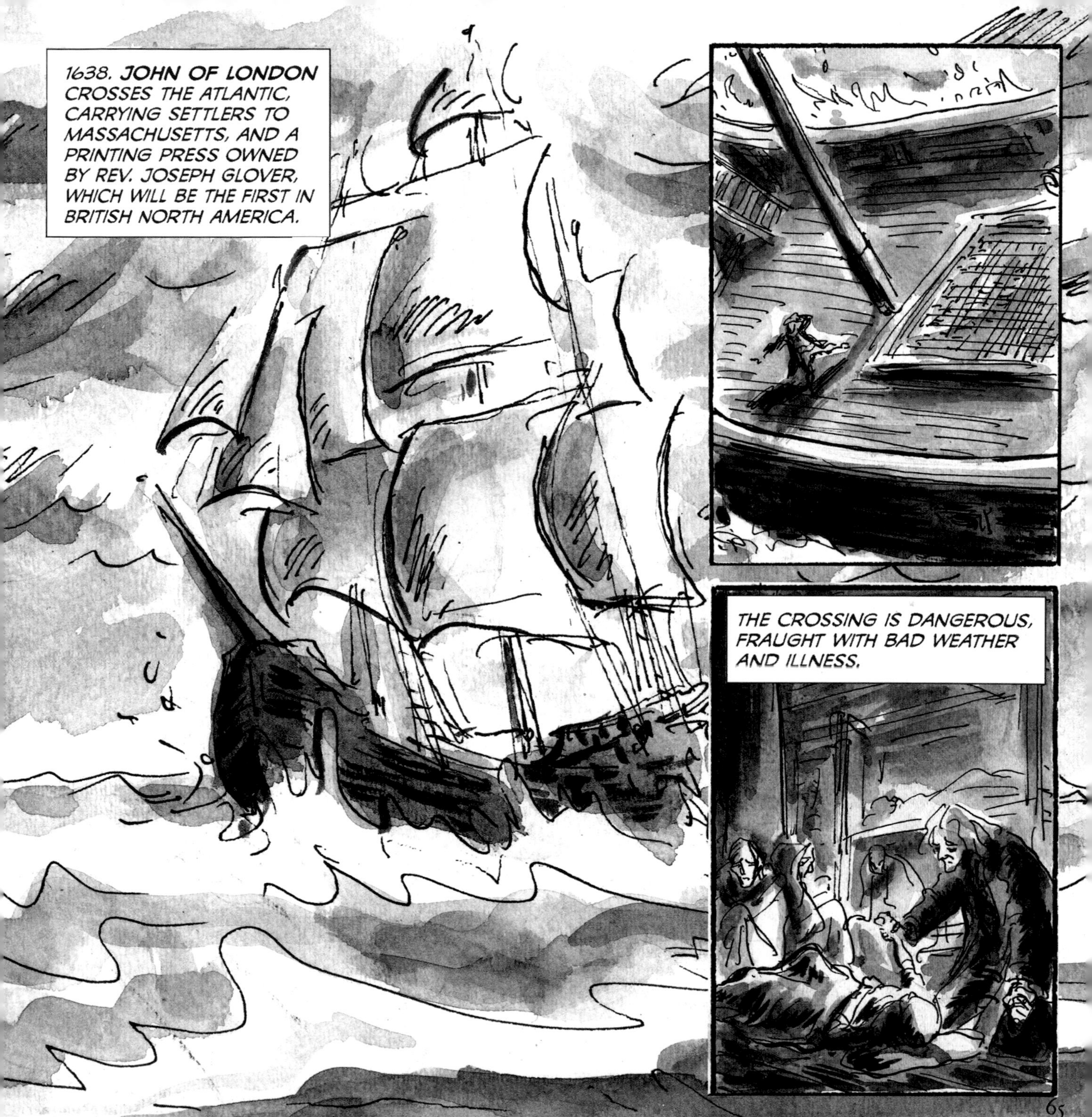
1638. JOHN OF LONDON CROSSES THE ATLANTIC, CARRYING SETTLERS TO MASSACHUSETTS, AND A PRINTING PRESS OWNED BY REV. JOSEPH GLOVER, WHICH WILL BE THE FIRST IN BRITISH NORTH AMERICA.
THE CROSSING IS DANGEROUS, FRAUGHT WITH BAD WEATHER AND ILLNESS.

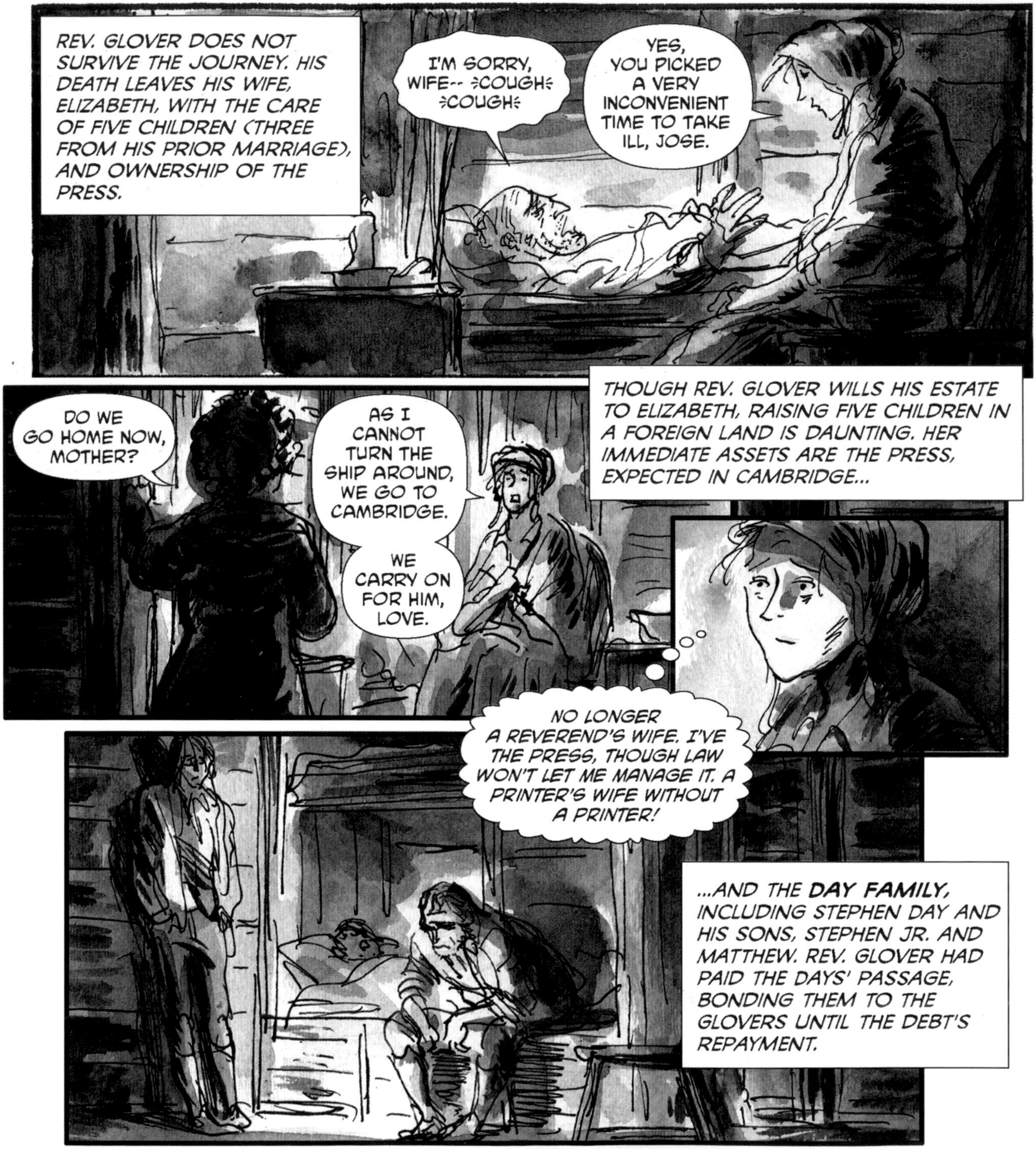
REV. GLOVER DOES NOT SURVIVE THE JOURNEY. HIS DEATH LEAVES HIS WIFE, ELIZABETH, WITH THE CARE OF FIVE CHILDREN (THREE FROM HIS PRIOR MARRIAGE), AND OWNERSHIP OF THE PRESS.
I'M SORRY, WIFE-- *COUGH* *COUGH*
YES, YOU PICKED A VERY INCONVENIENT TIME TO TAKE ILL, JOSE.
THOUGH REV. GLOVER WILLS HIS ESTATE TO ELIZABETH, RAISING FIVE CHILDREN IN A FOREIGN LAND IS DAUNTING. HER IMMEDIATE ASSETS ARE THE PRESS, EXPECTED IN CAMBRIDGE...
DO WE GO HOME NOW, MOTHER?
AS I CANNOT TURN THE SHIP AROUND, WE GO TO CAMBRIDGE.
WE CARRY ON FOR HIM, LOVE.
NO LONGER A REVEREND'S WIFE. I'VE THE PRESS, THOUGH LAW WON'T LET ME MANAGE IT. A PRINTER'S WIFE WITHOUT A PRINTER!
...AND THE DAY FAMILY, INCLUDING STEPHEN DAY AND HIS SONS, STEPHEN JR. AND MATTHEW. REV. GLOVER HAD PAID THE DAYS' PASSAGE, BONDING THEM TO THE GLOVERS UNTIL THE DEBT'S REPAYMENT.

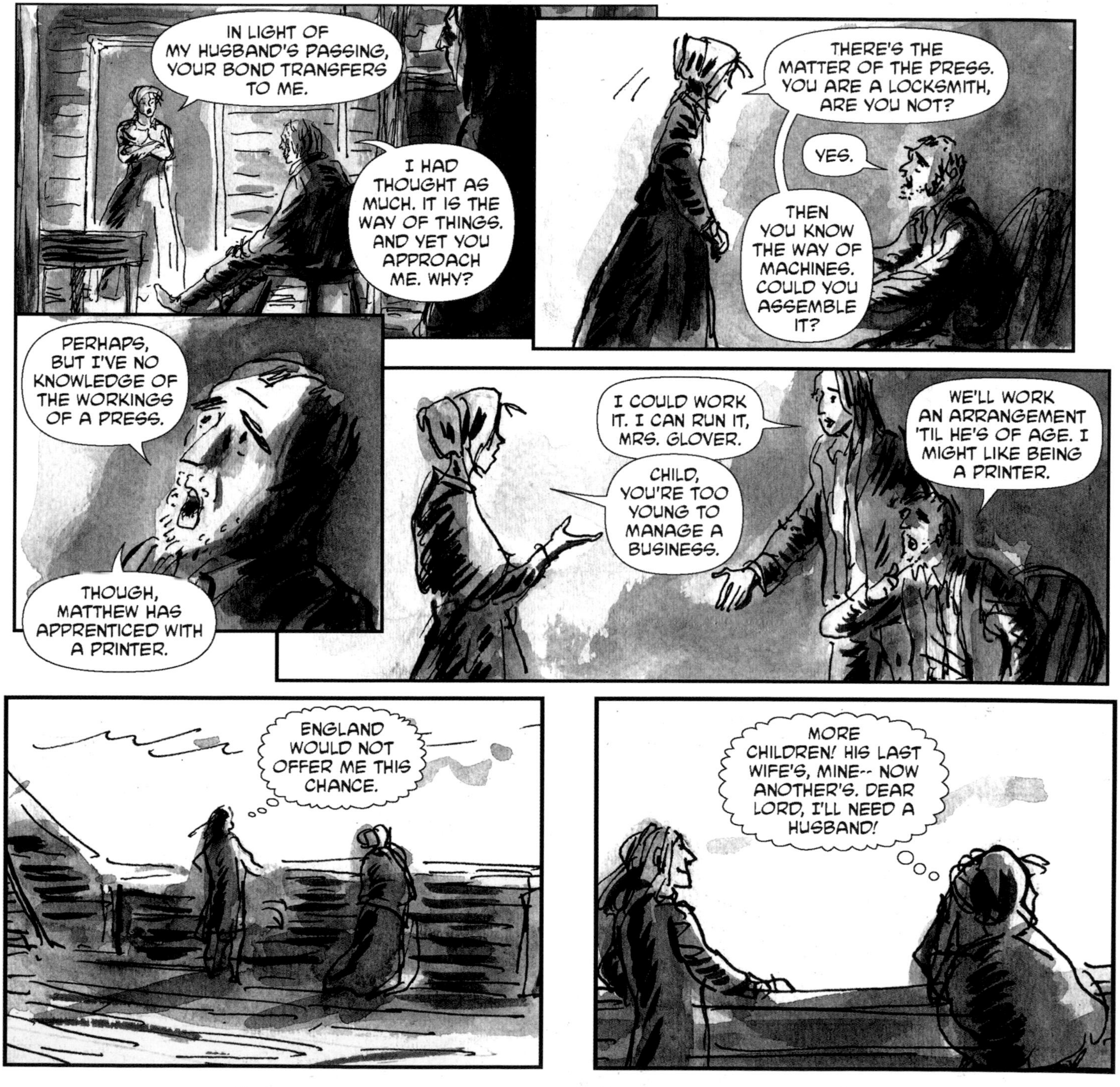
IN LIGHT OF MY HUSBAND'S PASSING, YOUR BOND TRANSFERS TO ME.
I HAD THOUGHT AS MUCH. IT IS THE WAY OF THINGS. AND YET YOU APPROACH ME. WHY?
THERE'S THE MATTER OF THE PRESS. YOU ARE A LOCKSMITH, ARE YOU NOT?
YES.
THEN YOU KNOW THE WAY OF MACHINES. COULD YOU ASSEMBLE IT?
PERHAPS, BUT I'VE NO KNOWLEDGE OF THE WORKINGS OF A PRESS.
THOUGH, MATTHEW HAS APPRENTICED WITH A PRINTER.
I COULD WORK IT. I CAN RUN IT, MRS. GLOVER.
CHILD, YOU'RE TOO YOUNG TO MANAGE A BUSINESS.
WE'LL WORK AN ARRANGEMENT 'TIL HE'S OF AGE. I MIGHT LIKE BEING A PRINTER.
ENGLAND WOULD NOT OFFER ME THIS CHANCE.
MORE CHILDREN! HIS LAST WIFE'S, MINE-- NOW ANOTHER'S. DEAR LORD, I'LL NEED A HUSBAND!

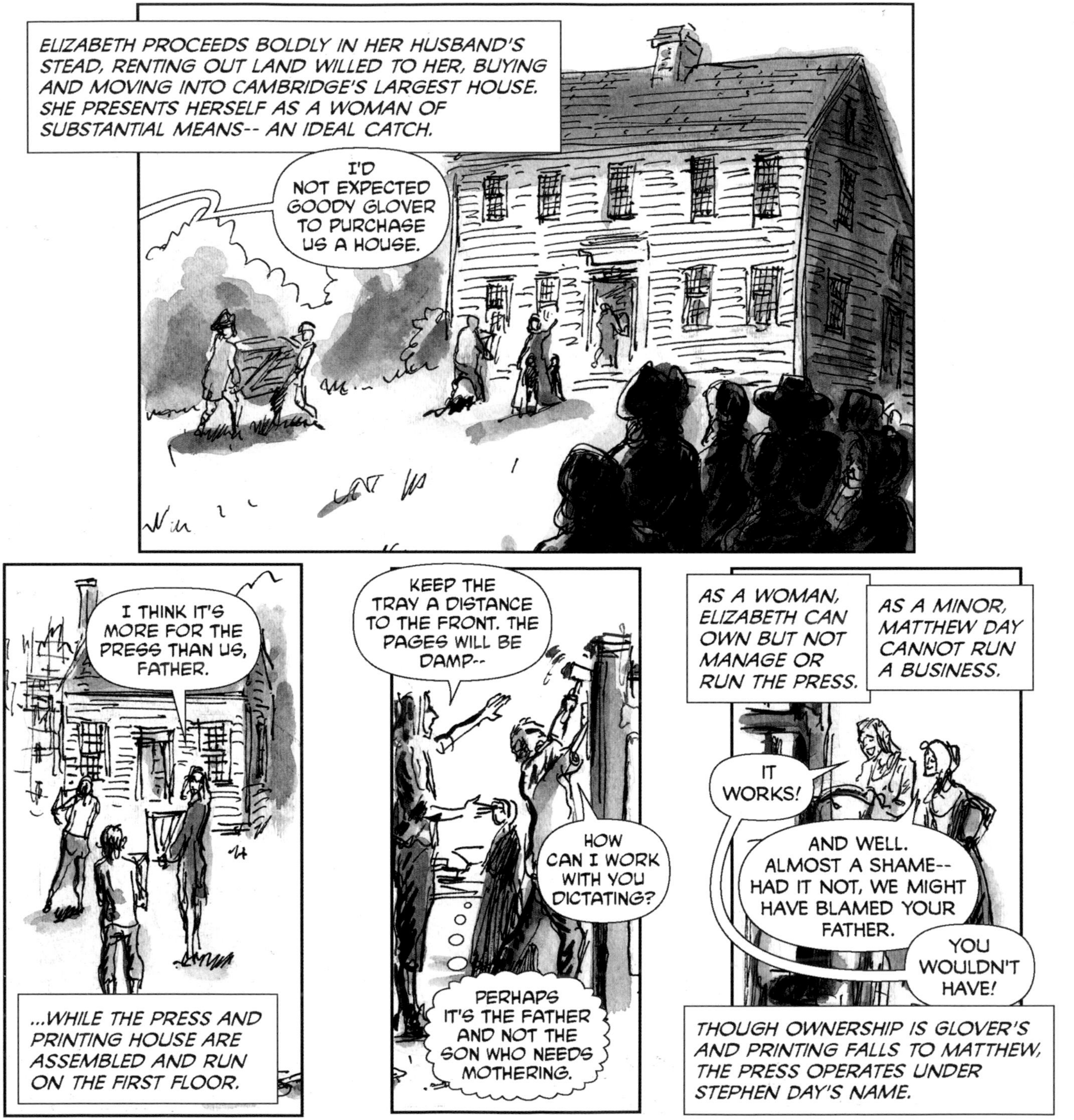
ELIZABETH PROCEEDS BOLDLY IN HER HUSBAND'S STEAD, RENTING OUT LAND WILLED TO HER, BUYING AND MOVING INTO CAMBRIDGE'S LARGEST HOUSE. SHE PRESENTS HERSELF AS A WOMAN OF SUBSTANTIAL MEANS-- AN IDEAL CATCH.
I'D NOT EXPECTED GOODY GLOVER TO PURCHASE US A HOUSE.
I THINK IT'S MORE FOR THE PRESS THAN US, FATHER.
...WHILE THE PRESS AND PRINTING HOUSE ARE ASSEMBLED AND RUN ON THE FIRST FLOOR.
KEEP THE TRAY A DISTANCE TO THE FRONT. THE PAGES WILL BE DAMP--
HOW CAN I WORK WITH YOU DICTATING?
PERHAPS IT'S THE FATHER AND NOT THE SON WHO NEEDS MOTHERING.
AS A WOMAN, ELIZABETH CAN OWN BUT NOT MANAGE OR RUN THE PRESS.
AS A MINOR, MATTHEW DAY CANNOT RUN A BUSINESS.
IT WORKS!
AND WELL. ALMOST A SHAME-- HAD IT NOT, WE MIGHT HAVE BLAMED YOUR FATHER.
YOU WOULDN'T HAVE!
THOUGH OWNERSHIP IS GLOVER'S AND PRINTING FALLS TO MATTHEW, THE PRESS OPERATES UNDER STEPHEN DAY'S NAME.

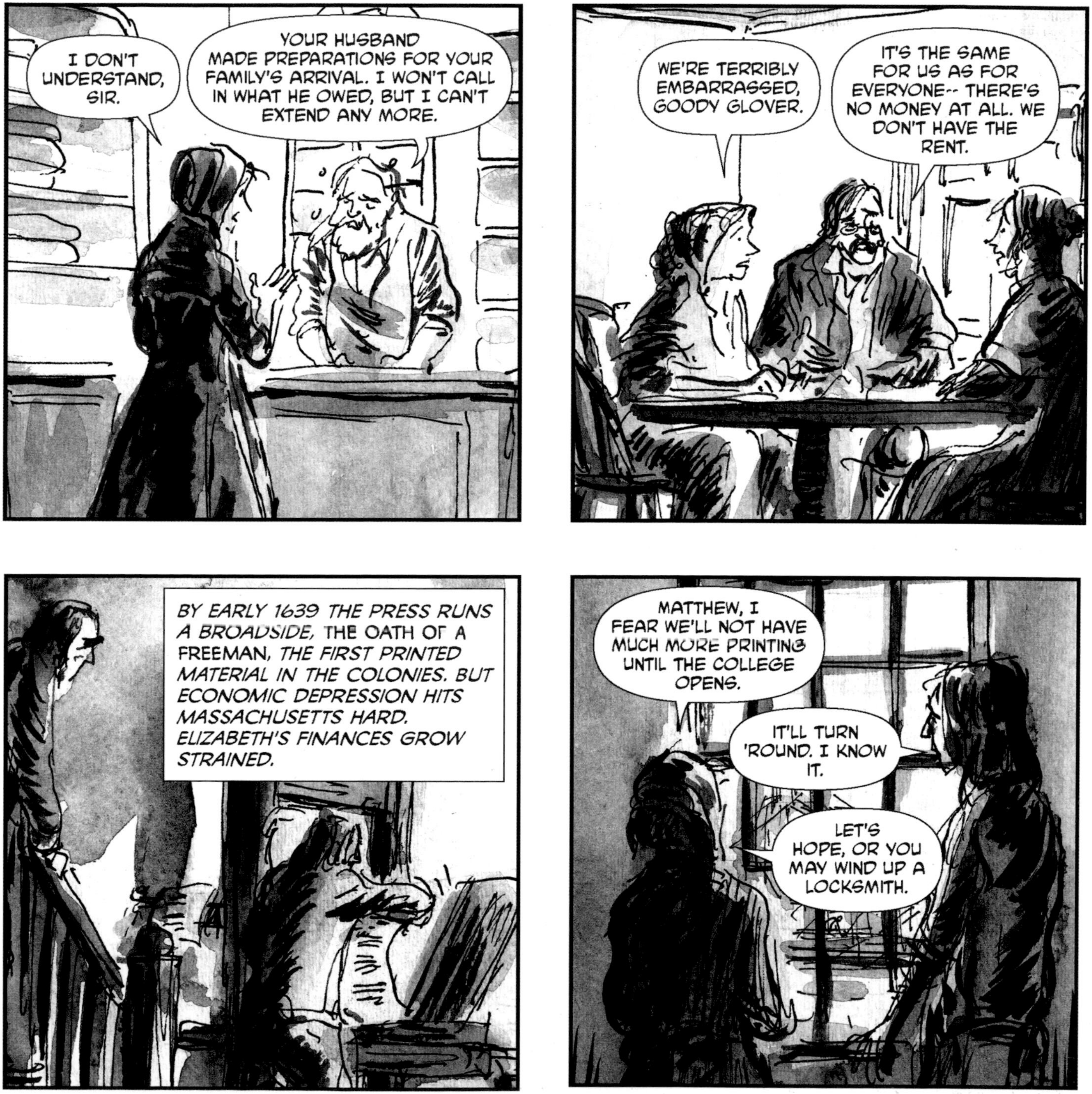
I DON'T UNDERSTAND, SIR.
YOUR HUSBAND MADE PREPARATIONS FOR YOUR FAMILY'S ARRIVAL. I WON'T CALL IN WHAT HE OWED, BUT I CAN'T EXTEND ANY MORE.
WE'RE TERRIBLY EMBARRASSED, GOODY GLOVER.
IT'S THE SAME FOR US AS FOR EVERYONE-- THERE'S NO MONEY AT ALL. WE DON'T HAVE THE RENT.
BY EARLY 1639 THE PRESS RUNS A BROADSIDE, THE OATH OF A FREEMAN, *THE FIRST PRINTED MATERIAL IN THE COLONIES. BUT ECONOMIC DEPRESSION HITS MASSACHUSETTS HARD. ELIZABETH'S FINANCES GROW STRAINED.*
MATTHEW, I FEAR WE'LL NOT HAVE MUCH MORE PRINTING UNTIL THE COLLEGE OPENS.
IT'LL TURN 'ROUND. I KNOW IT.
LET'S HOPE, OR YOU MAY WIND UP A LOCKSMITH.

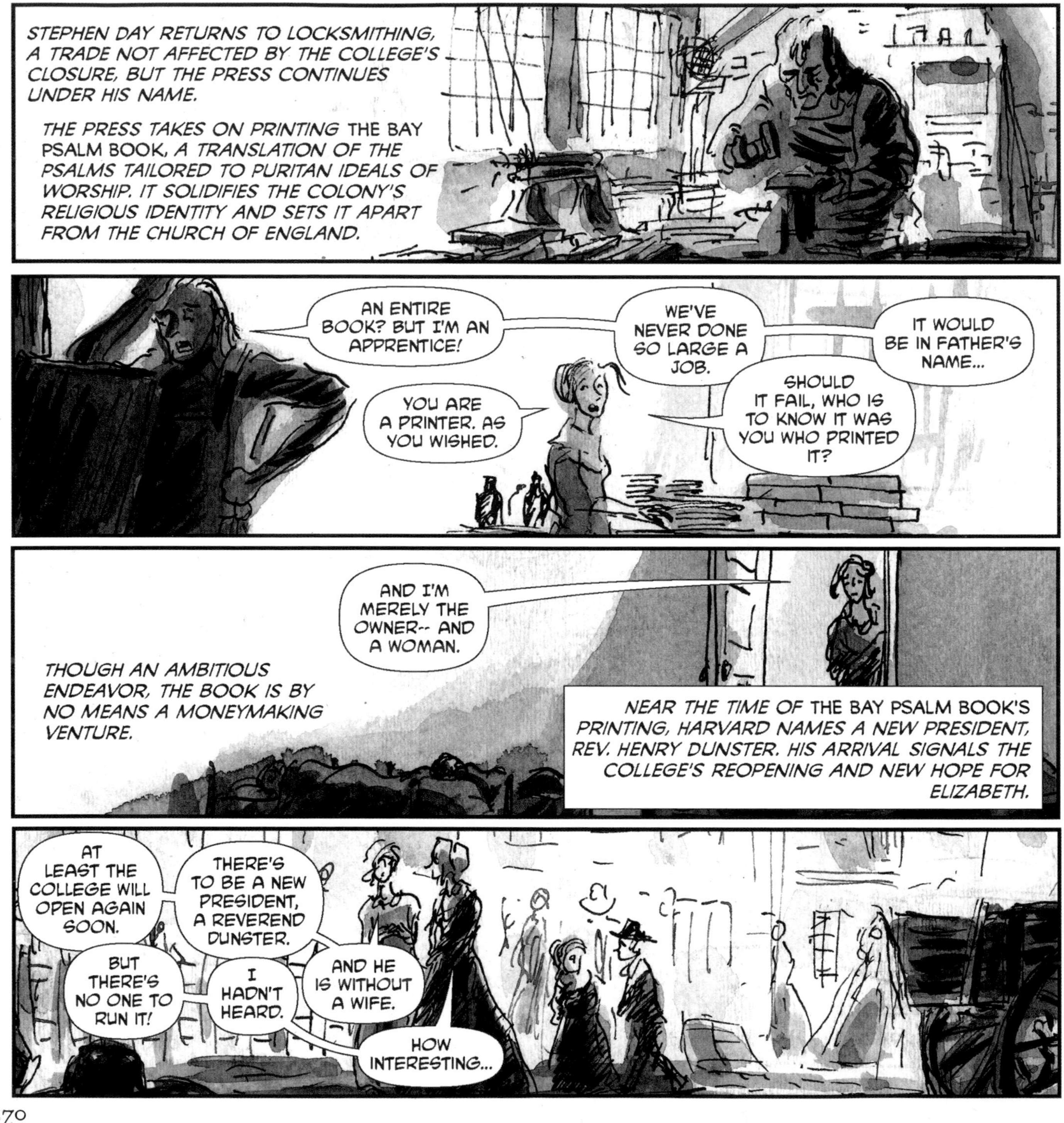
STEPHEN DAY RETURNS TO LOCKSMITHING, A TRADE NOT AFFECTED BY THE COLLEGE'S CLOSURE, BUT THE PRESS CONTINUES UNDER HIS NAME.
THE PRESS TAKES ON PRINTING THE BAY PSALM BOOK, A TRANSLATION OF THE PSALMS TAILORED TO PURITAN IDEALS OF WORSHIP. IT SOLIDIFIES THE COLONY'S RELIGIOUS IDENTITY AND SETS IT APART FROM THE CHURCH OF ENGLAND.
AN ENTIRE BOOK? BUT I'M AN APPRENTICE!
YOU ARE A PRINTER. AS YOU WISHED.
WE'VE NEVER DONE SO LARGE A JOB.
IT WOULD BE IN FATHER'S NAME...
SHOULD IT FAIL, WHO IS TO KNOW IT WAS YOU WHO PRINTED IT?
AND I'M MERELY THE OWNER-- AND A WOMAN.
THOUGH AN AMBITIOUS ENDEAVOR, THE BOOK IS BY NO MEANS A MONEYMAKING VENTURE.
NEAR THE TIME OF THE BAY PSALM BOOK'S PRINTING, HARVARD NAMES A NEW PRESIDENT, REV. HENRY DUNSTER. HIS ARRIVAL SIGNALS THE COLLEGE'S REOPENING AND NEW HOPE FOR ELIZABETH.
AT LEAST THE COLLEGE WILL OPEN AGAIN SOON.
THERE'S TO BE A NEW PRESIDENT, A REVEREND DUNSTER.
BUT THERE'S NO ONE TO RUN IT!
I HADN'T HEARD.
AND HE IS WITHOUT A WIFE.
HOW INTERESTING...

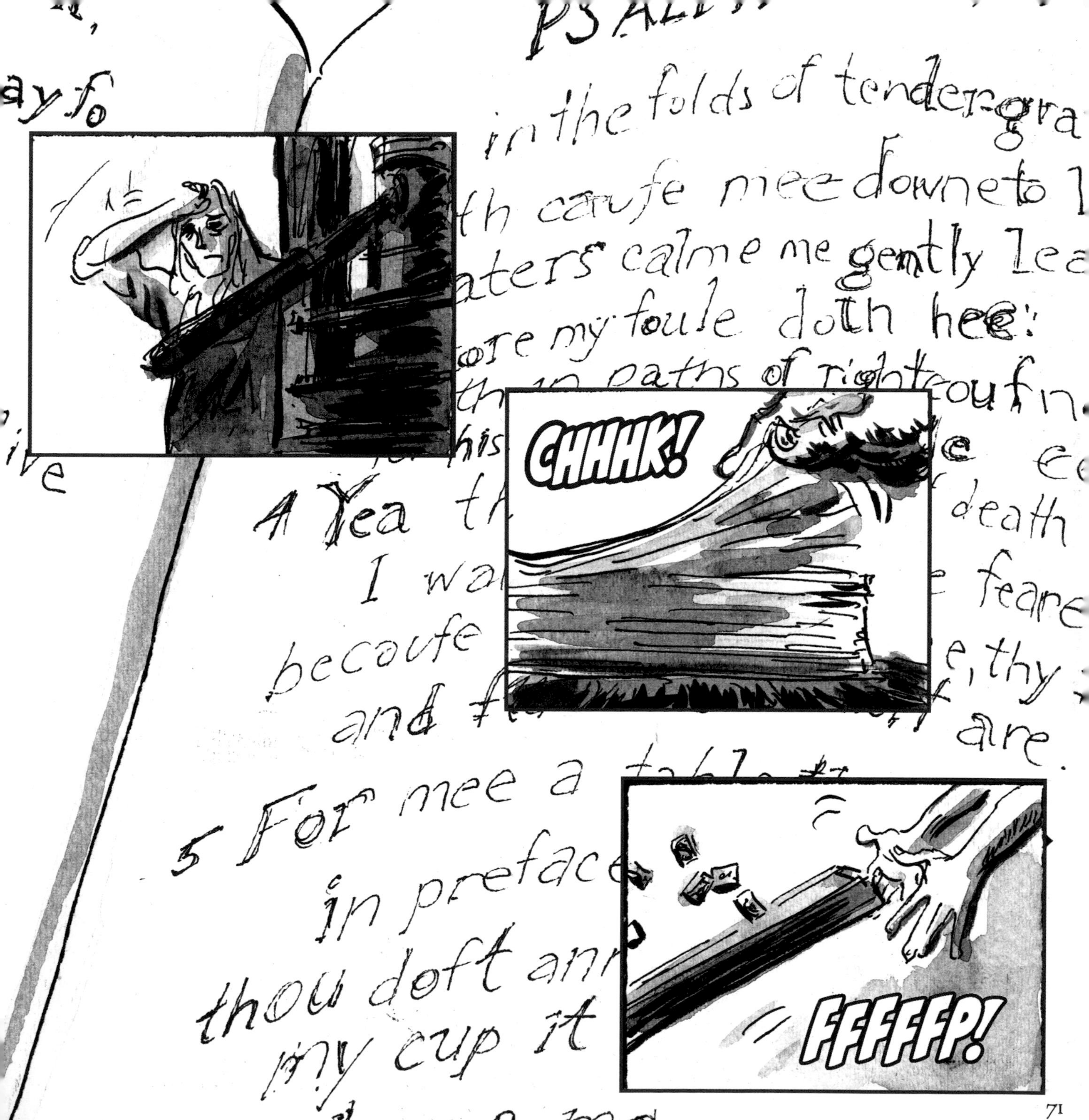

in the folds of tender-gra

...th caufe mee downe to l

...aters calme me gently lea

...ore my foule doth hee:

...paths of righteoufn...

A Yea th...

I wa...

becaufe...

and fl...

CHHHK!

5 For mee a table...

in preface...

thou doft ann...

my cup it...

FFFFFP!

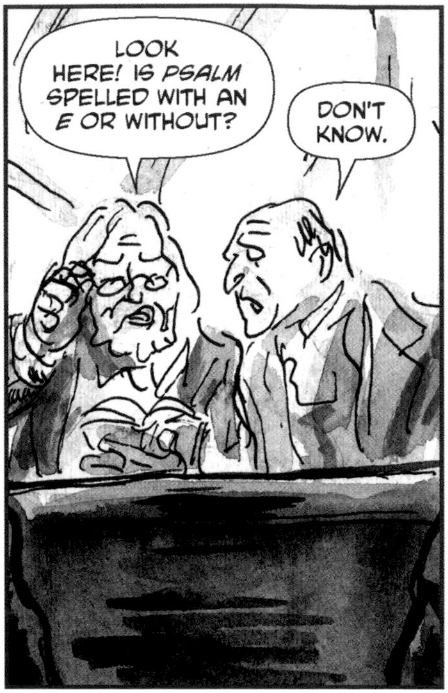
LOOK HERE! IS *PSALM* SPELLED WITH AN *E* OR WITHOUT?
DON'T KNOW.

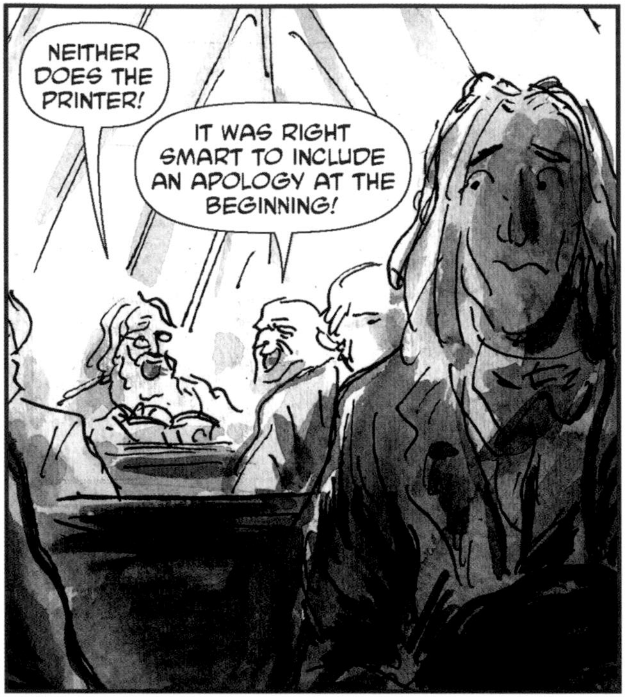
NEITHER DOES THE PRINTER!
IT WAS RIGHT SMART TO INCLUDE AN APOLOGY AT THE BEGINNING!

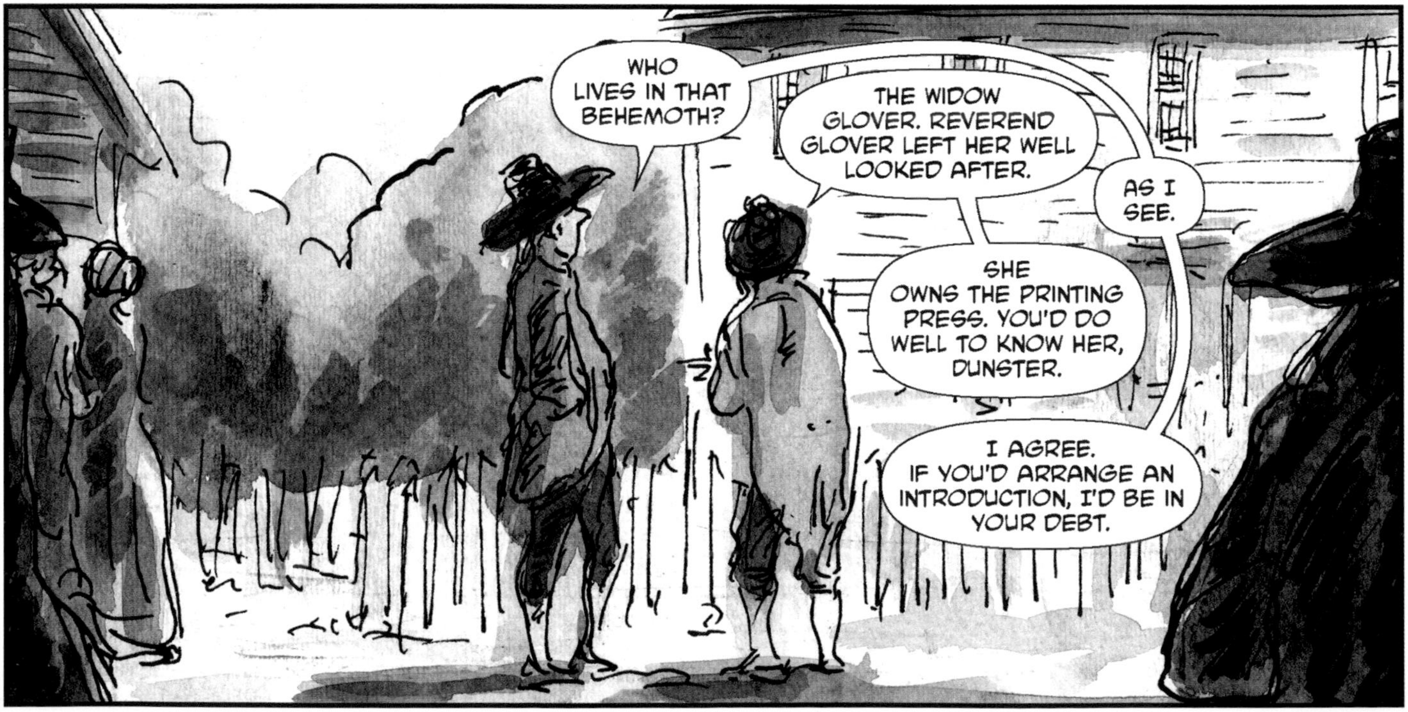
WHO LIVES IN THAT BEHEMOTH?
THE WIDOW GLOVER. REVEREND GLOVER LEFT HER WELL LOOKED AFTER.
AS I SEE.
SHE OWNS THE PRINTING PRESS. YOU'D DO WELL TO KNOW HER, DUNSTER.
I AGREE. IF YOU'D ARRANGE AN INTRODUCTION, I'D BE IN YOUR DEBT.

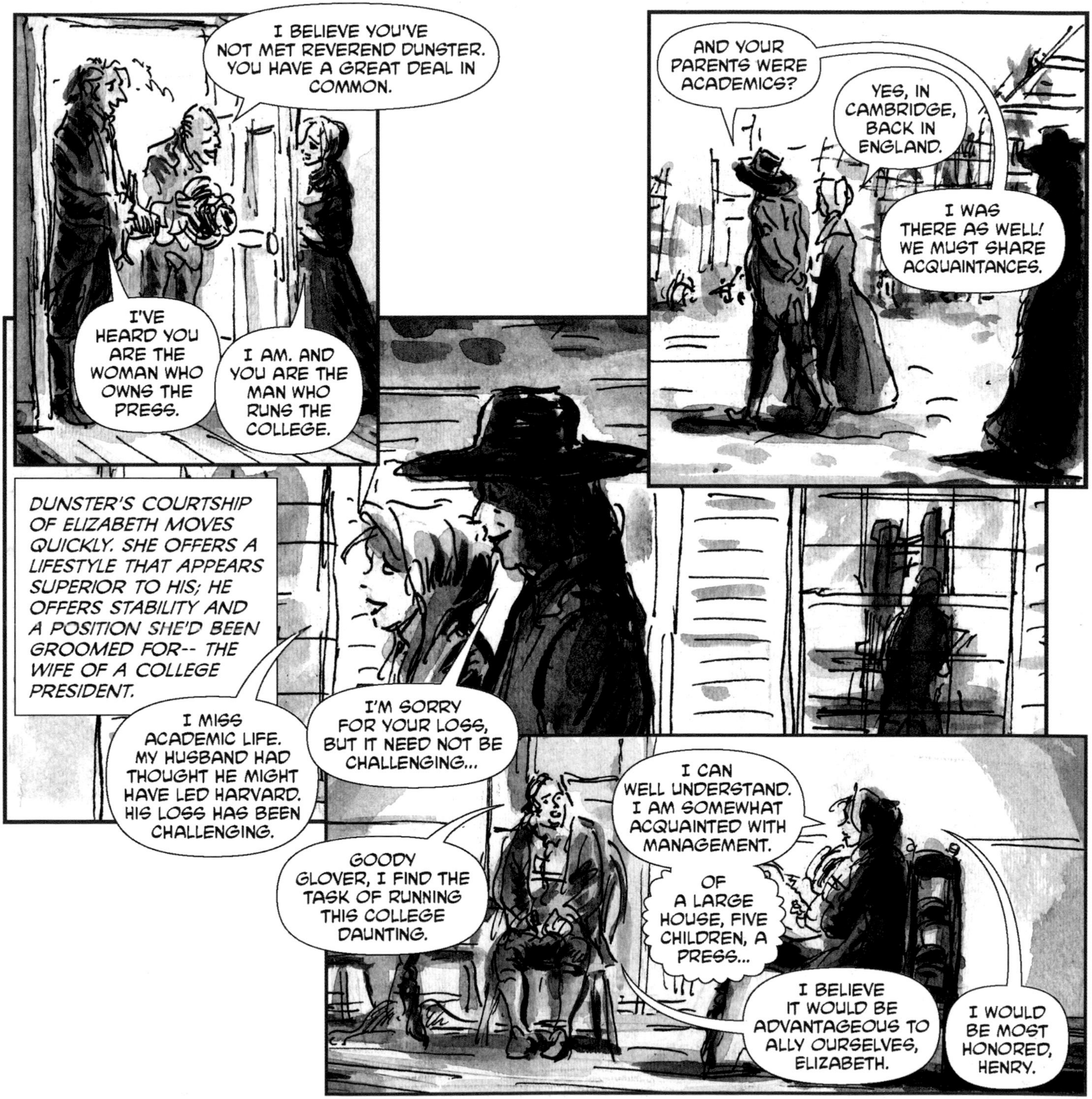

I BELIEVE YOU'VE NOT MET REVEREND DUNSTER. YOU HAVE A GREAT DEAL IN COMMON.
I'VE HEARD YOU ARE THE WOMAN WHO OWNS THE PRESS.
I AM. AND YOU ARE THE MAN WHO RUNS THE COLLEGE.
AND YOUR PARENTS WERE ACADEMICS?
YES, IN CAMBRIDGE, BACK IN ENGLAND.
I WAS THERE AS WELL! WE MUST SHARE ACQUAINTANCES.
DUNSTER'S COURTSHIP OF ELIZABETH MOVES QUICKLY. SHE OFFERS A LIFESTYLE THAT APPEARS SUPERIOR TO HIS; HE OFFERS STABILITY AND A POSITION SHE'D BEEN GROOMED FOR-- THE WIFE OF A COLLEGE PRESIDENT.
I MISS ACADEMIC LIFE. MY HUSBAND HAD THOUGHT HE MIGHT HAVE LED HARVARD. HIS LOSS HAS BEEN CHALLENGING.
I'M SORRY FOR YOUR LOSS, BUT IT NEED NOT BE CHALLENGING...
GOODY GLOVER, I FIND THE TASK OF RUNNING THIS COLLEGE DAUNTING.
I CAN WELL UNDERSTAND. I AM SOMEWHAT ACQUAINTED WITH MANAGEMENT.
OF A LARGE HOUSE, FIVE CHILDREN, A PRESS...
I BELIEVE IT WOULD BE ADVANTAGEOUS TO ALLY OURSELVES, ELIZABETH.
I WOULD BE MOST HONORED, HENRY.

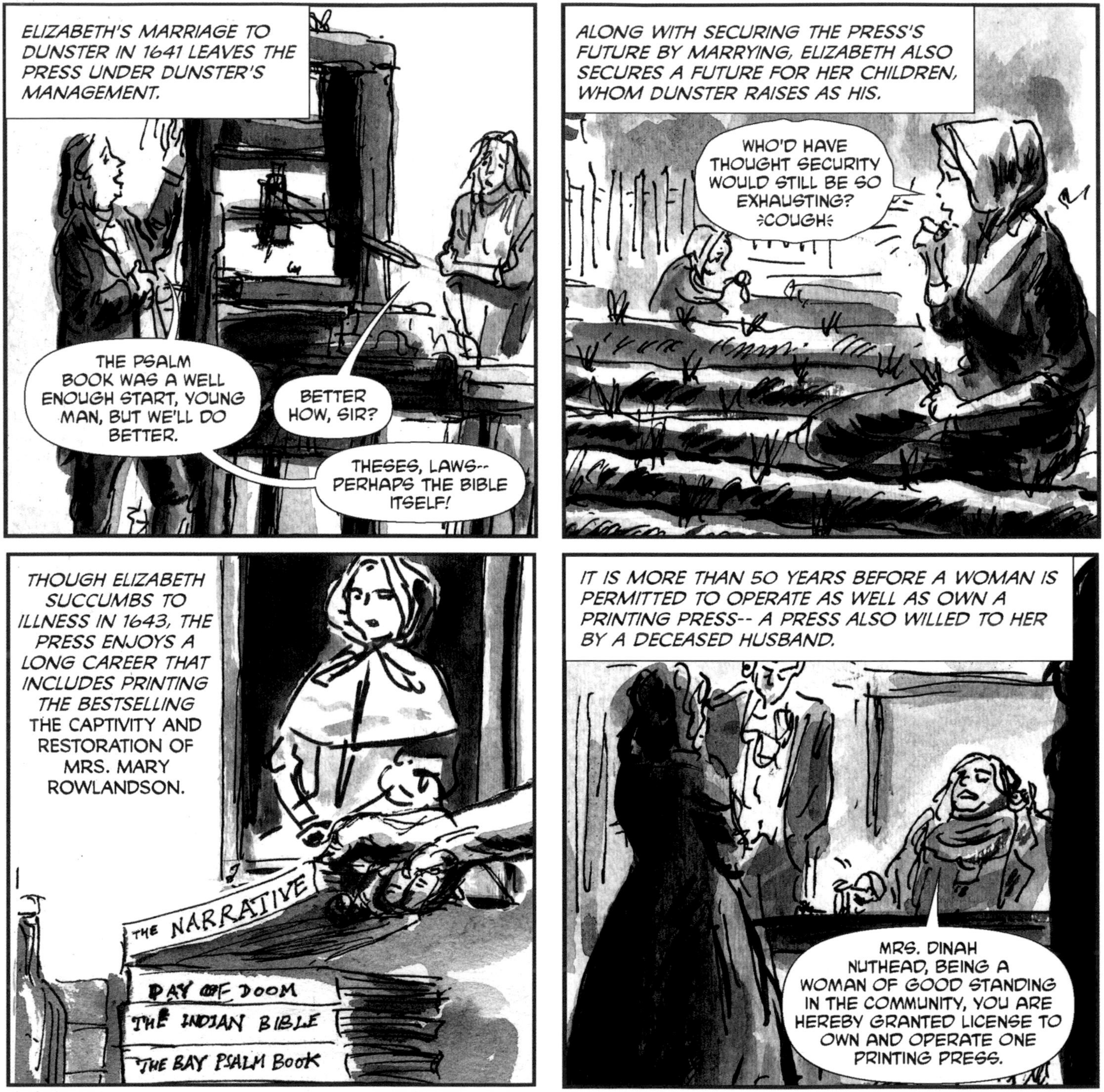
ELIZABETH'S MARRIAGE TO DUNSTER IN 1641 LEAVES THE PRESS UNDER DUNSTER'S MANAGEMENT.
THE PSALM BOOK WAS A WELL ENOUGH START, YOUNG MAN, BUT WE'LL DO BETTER.
BETTER HOW, SIR?
THESES, LAWS-- PERHAPS THE BIBLE ITSELF!
ALONG WITH SECURING THE PRESS'S FUTURE BY MARRYING, ELIZABETH ALSO SECURES A FUTURE FOR HER CHILDREN, WHOM DUNSTER RAISES AS HIS.
WHO'D HAVE THOUGHT SECURITY WOULD STILL BE SO EXHAUSTING? *COUGH*
THOUGH ELIZABETH SUCCUMBS TO ILLNESS IN 1643, THE PRESS ENJOYS A LONG CAREER THAT INCLUDES PRINTING THE BESTSELLING THE CAPTIVITY AND RESTORATION OF MRS. MARY ROWLANDSON.
THE NARRATIVE
DAY OF DOOM
THE INDIAN BIBLE
THE BAY PSALM BOOK
IT IS MORE THAN 50 YEARS BEFORE A WOMAN IS PERMITTED TO OPERATE AS WELL AS OWN A PRINTING PRESS-- A PRESS ALSO WILLED TO HER BY A DECEASED HUSBAND.
MRS. DINAH NUTHEAD, BEING A WOMAN OF GOOD STANDING IN THE COMMUNITY, YOU ARE HEREBY GRANTED LICENSE TO OWN AND OPERATE ONE PRINTING PRESS.

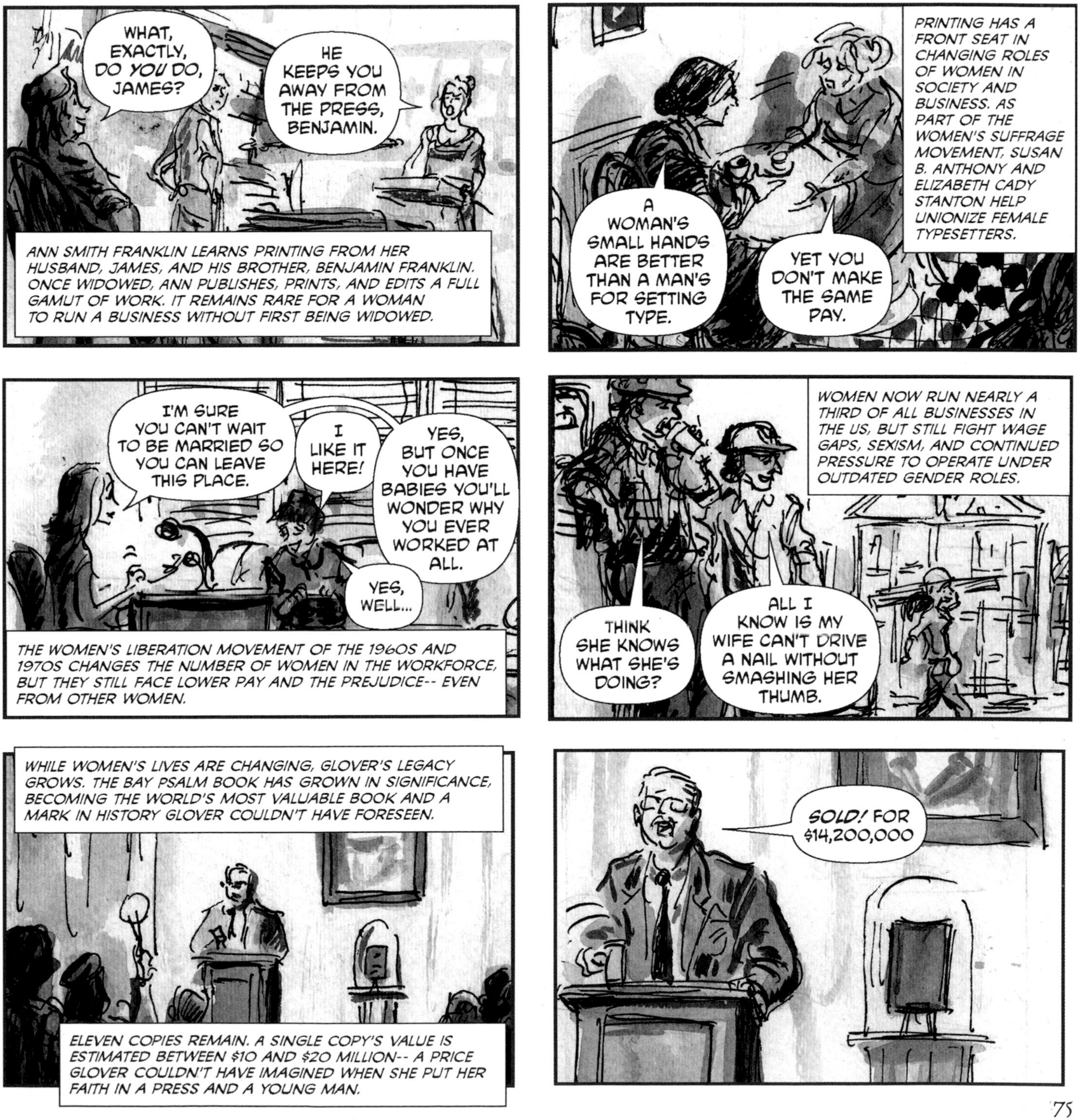
WHAT, EXACTLY, DO YOU DO, JAMES?
HE KEEPS YOU AWAY FROM THE PRESS, BENJAMIN.
ANN SMITH FRANKLIN LEARNS PRINTING FROM HER HUSBAND, JAMES, AND HIS BROTHER, BENJAMIN FRANKLIN. ONCE WIDOWED, ANN PUBLISHES, PRINTS, AND EDITS A FULL GAMUT OF WORK. IT REMAINS RARE FOR A WOMAN TO RUN A BUSINESS WITHOUT FIRST BEING WIDOWED.
PRINTING HAS A FRONT SEAT IN CHANGING ROLES OF WOMEN IN SOCIETY AND BUSINESS. AS PART OF THE WOMEN'S SUFFRAGE MOVEMENT, SUSAN B. ANTHONY AND ELIZABETH CADY STANTON HELP UNIONIZE FEMALE TYPESETTERS.
A WOMAN'S SMALL HANDS ARE BETTER THAN A MAN'S FOR SETTING TYPE.
YET YOU DON'T MAKE THE SAME PAY.
I'M SURE YOU CAN'T WAIT TO BE MARRIED SO YOU CAN LEAVE THIS PLACE.
I LIKE IT HERE!
YES, BUT ONCE YOU HAVE BABIES YOU'LL WONDER WHY YOU EVER WORKED AT ALL.
YES, WELL...
THE WOMEN'S LIBERATION MOVEMENT OF THE 1960S AND 1970S CHANGES THE NUMBER OF WOMEN IN THE WORKFORCE, BUT THEY STILL FACE LOWER PAY AND THE PREJUDICE-- EVEN FROM OTHER WOMEN.
WOMEN NOW RUN NEARLY A THIRD OF ALL BUSINESSES IN THE US, BUT STILL FIGHT WAGE GAPS, SEXISM, AND CONTINUED PRESSURE TO OPERATE UNDER OUTDATED GENDER ROLES.
THINK SHE KNOWS WHAT SHE'S DOING?
ALL I KNOW IS MY WIFE CAN'T DRIVE A NAIL WITHOUT SMASHING HER THUMB.
WHILE WOMEN'S LIVES ARE CHANGING, GLOVER'S LEGACY GROWS. THE BAY PSALM BOOK HAS GROWN IN SIGNIFICANCE, BECOMING THE WORLD'S MOST VALUABLE BOOK AND A MARK IN HISTORY GLOVER COULDN'T HAVE FORESEEN.
ELEVEN COPIES REMAIN. A SINGLE COPY'S VALUE IS ESTIMATED BETWEEN $10 AND $20 MILLION-- A PRICE GLOVER COULDN'T HAVE IMAGINED WHEN SHE PUT HER FAITH IN A PRESS AND A YOUNG MAN.
SOLD! FOR $14,200,000

HOLY LIBS

The *Bay Psalm Book* was the first book printed in colonial-era New England. There were approximately 1,700 copies of the first edition printed, of which only eleven copies are still known to exist. It goes without saying that a first edition of *The Bay Psalm Book* sells for a lot money, with a copy recently selling for over $14 million.

The translations were pretty poor, and the book was published along with a long list of corrections. Feel free to create your own translation of the title page on the right, filling in the nouns and verbs as prompted to create your own take on *The Bay Psalm Book*. Be careful, however! Blasphemy WILL get you banished from the colony!

THE
WHOLE
_____ OF PSALMES
(Noun)

Faithfully
_____ into ENGLISH
(Verb, Past Tense)

Whereunto is prefixed a discourse declaring not only

the lawfullness, but also the necessity of the

heavenly _____ of singing Scripture Psalmes in
(Noun)

the _____ of _____ .
(Plural Noun)   (Proper Noun)

Coll. III.

Let the _____ of _____ dwell plenteously
(Noun)   (Proper Noun)

in you, in all wisdome, teaching and exhorting one

another in _____ , _____ , and
(Plural Noun)   (Plural Noun)

Spirituall _____ , Singing to the _____
(Plural Noun)   (Proper Noun)

with _____ in your _____ .
(Noun)   (Plural Noun)

HOLY TEXT

THE
WHOLE
BOOK OF PSALMES

Faithfully
Translated into ENGLISH

Whereunto is prefixed a discourse declaring not only

the lawfullness, but also the necessity of the

heavenly Ordinance of singing Scripture Psalmes in

the Churches of God.

Coll. III.
Let the word of God dwell plenteously

in you, in all wisdome, teaching and exhorting one

another in Psalmes, Himnes, and

Spirituall Songs, Singing to the Lord

with grace in your hearts.

So, how did your *Bay Psalm Book* compare with the original?

I'm sure your spelling is more modern. Old texts would occasionally have some interesting spelling choices back then, especially the original *Bay Psalm Book* which was full of "Himnes" and "Psalmes."

One thing is for sure, however. Your *Bay Psalm Book* was scribbled in pen or pencil, whereas the original was printed on a movable type press, with each letter being positioned perfectly before stamping the sheet with the content. It took a lot of time to prepare a page for printing, and that has to be worth something.

Nothing against the pen or pencil you used, of course...

MAVERICK ISLAND

STORY BY J.L. Bell and Art by Joel Christian Gill

Slavery began in New England in the early 1600s, as in Britain's other New World colonies. The practice grew out of established customs of indentured servitude, and long or lifetime servitude for prisoners of war and Native people. Meanwhile, ships began to bring Africans to New England ports. In time, local legislatures passed laws enslaving certain people—in practice, people of color—for life, extending the same legal condition to their children.

Even before those laws were passed, however, there is evidence of race-based slavery. The following story is based on an anecdote from John Josselyn's "An Account of Two Voyages to New-England." Josselyn, a young upper-class Englishman, first visited the Massachusetts Bay Colony in 1638–39, although he didn't publish his description of that voyage until 1674. Josselyn's host on an island in Boston Harbor, Samuel Maverick, left no records about his decision to keep slaves.

In the twentieth century, Samuel Maverick's island was connected to the mainland with landfills. It is now the site of Logan Airport, and the city subway system has a station named Maverick.

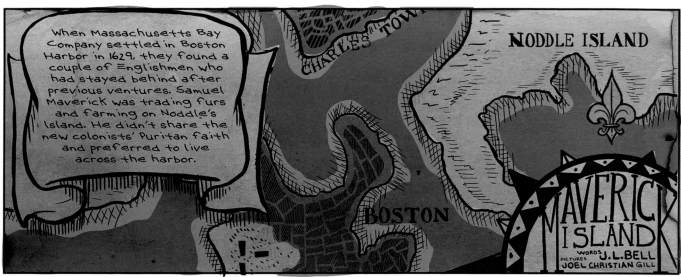

When Massachusetts Bay Company settled in Boston Harbor in 1629, they found a couple of Englishmen who had stayed behind after previous ventures. Samuel Maverick was trading furs and farming on Noddle's Island. He didn't share the new colonists' Puritan faith and preferred to live across the harbor.

NODDLE ISLAND

CHARLES TOWN

BOSTON

MAVERICK ISLAND

WORDS J. L. BELL
PICTURES JOEL CHRISTIAN GILL

In 1638, a young English gentleman named John Josselyn visited the colony.

He found Maverick a congenial host.

But one morning Josselyn was startled to hear a cry.

79

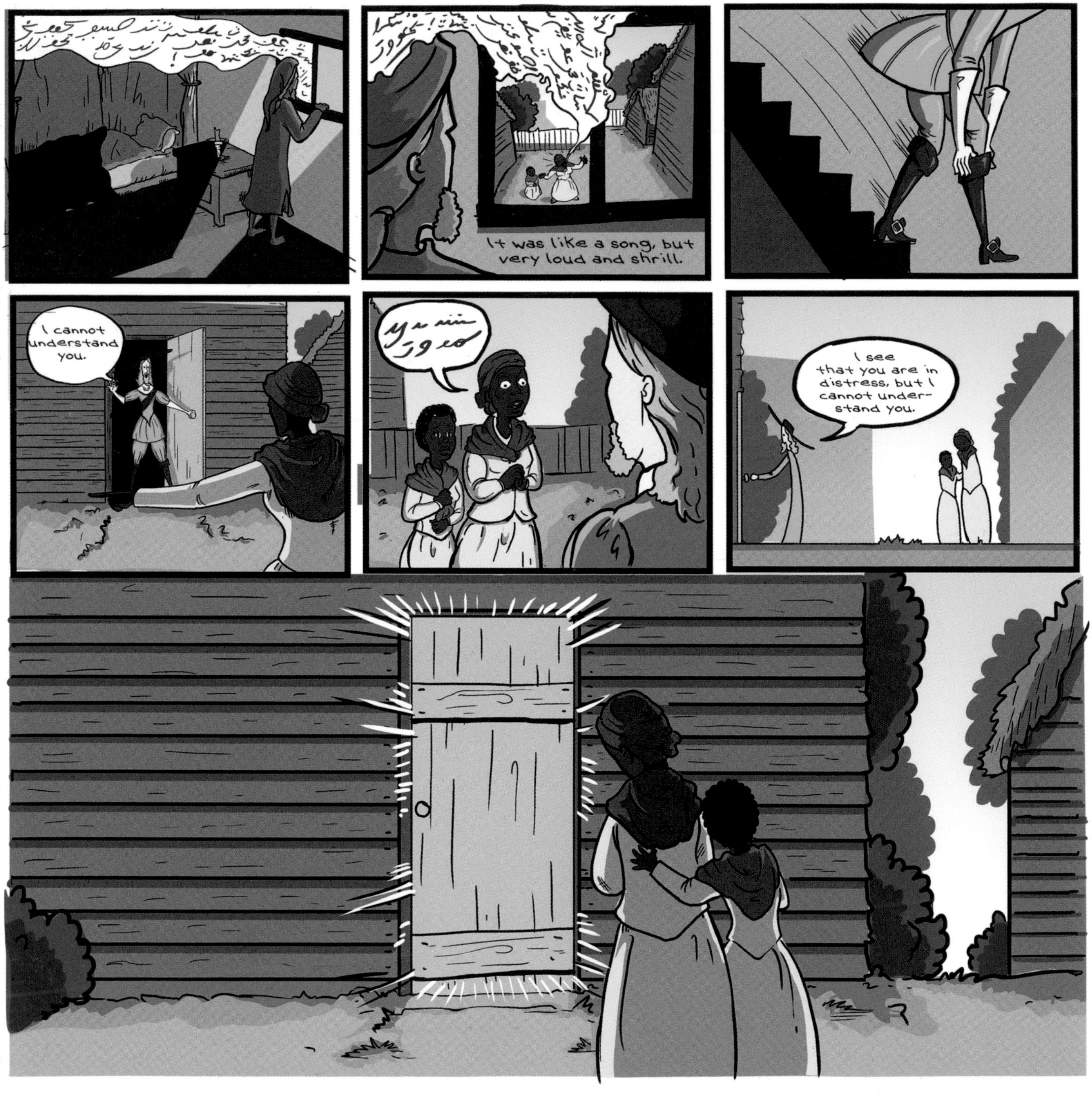
It was like a song, but very loud and shrill.
I cannot understand you.
I see that you are in distress, but I cannot understand you.

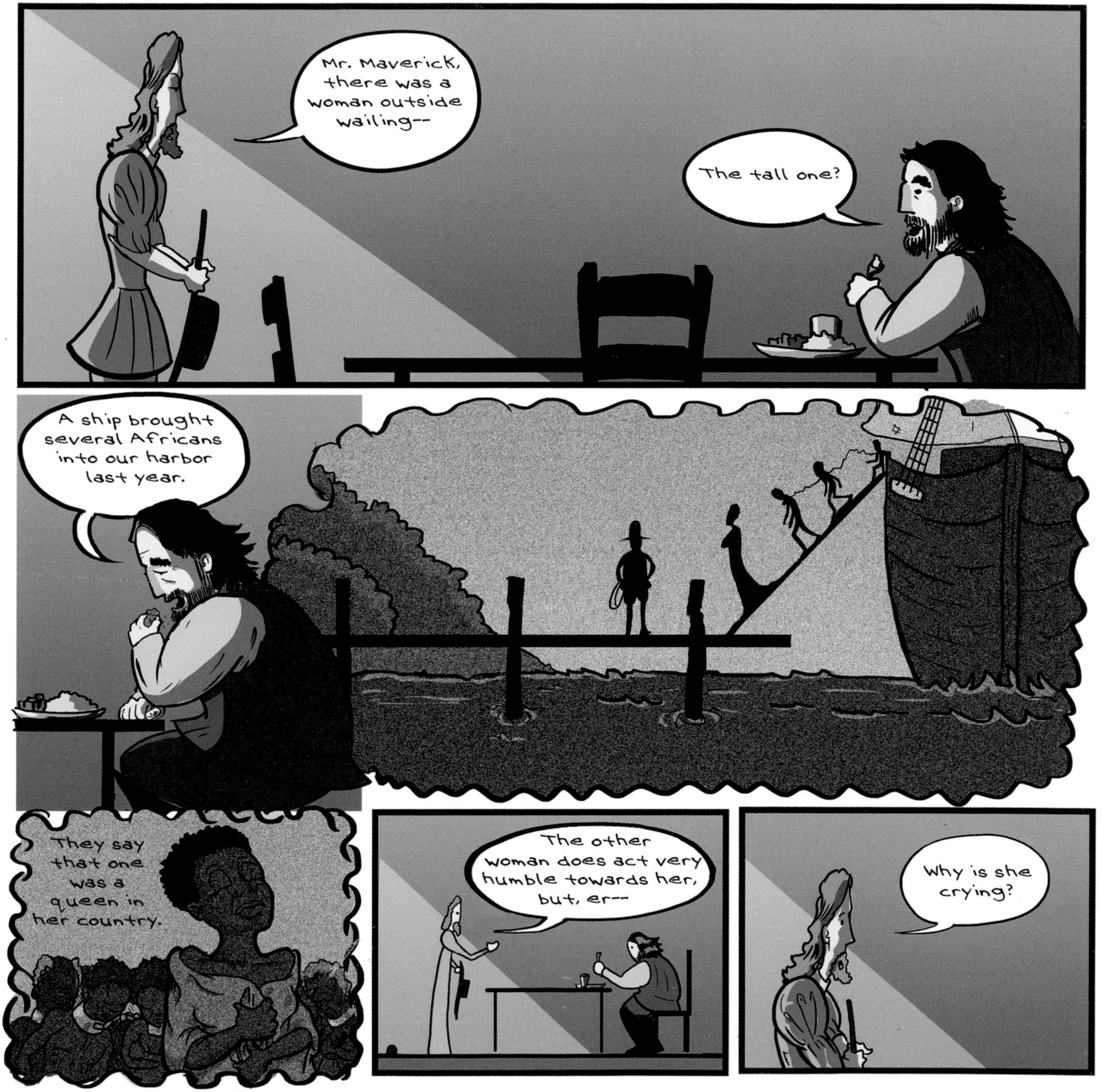
Mr. Maverick, there was a woman outside wailing--
The tall one?
A ship brought several Africans into our harbor last year.
They say that one was a queen in her country.
The other woman does act very humble towards her, but, er--
Why is she crying?

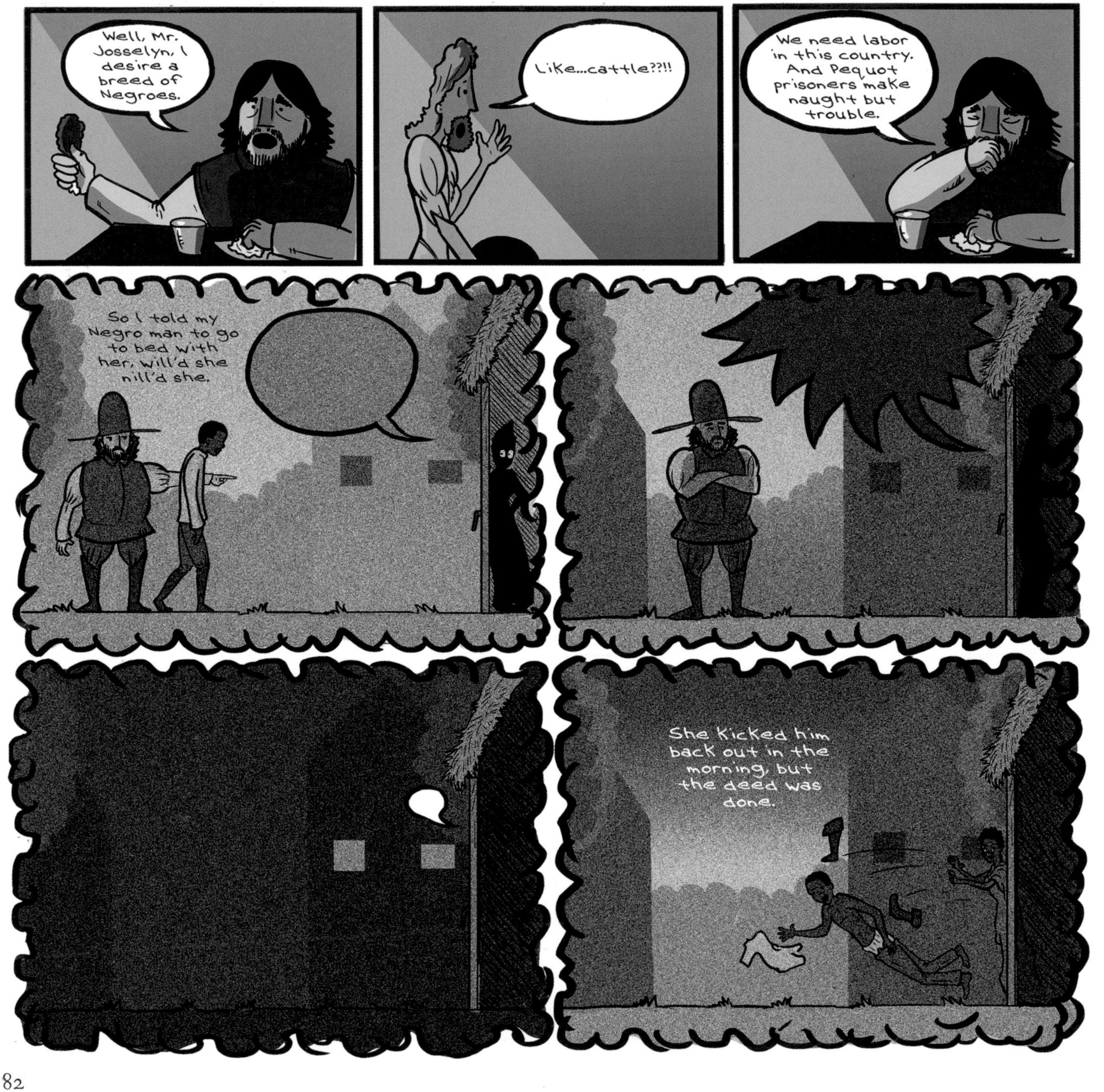
Well, Mr. Josselyn, I desire a breed of Negroes.
Like...cattle??!!
We need labor in this country. And Pequot prisoners make naught but trouble.
So I told my Negro man to go to bed with her, will'd she nill'd she.
She kicked him back out in the morning, but the deed was done.

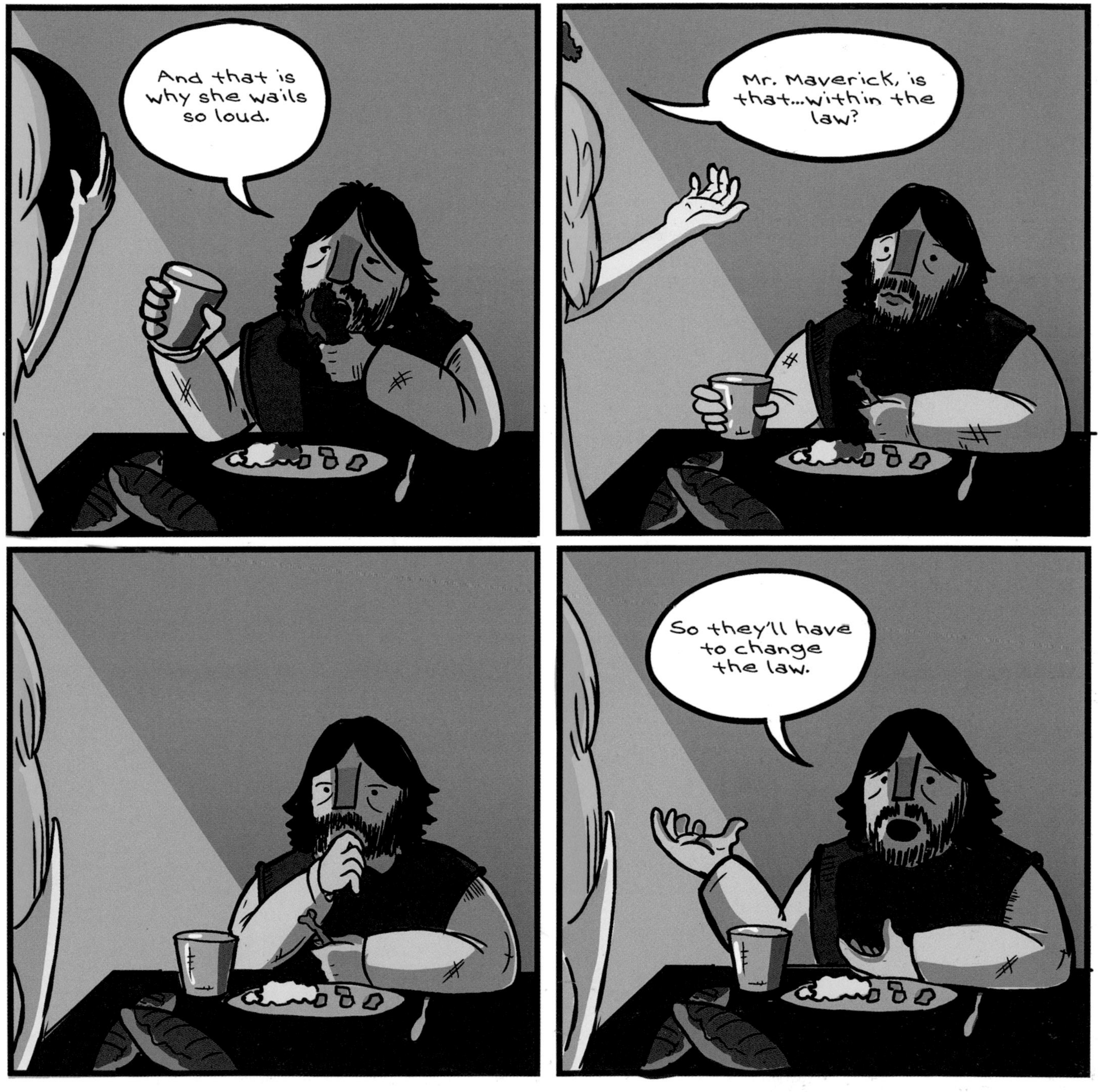

And that is why she wails so loud.
Mr. Maverick, is that...within the law?
So they'll have to change the law.

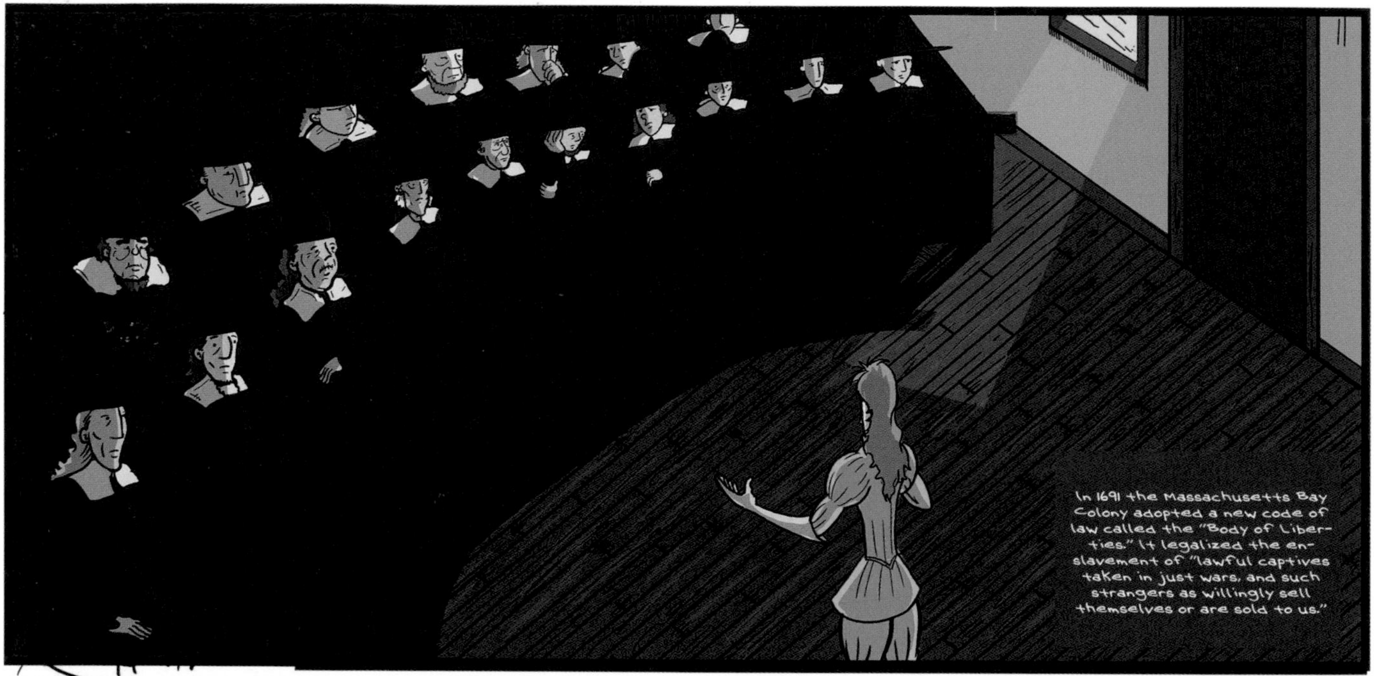
In 1691 the Massachusetts Bay Colony adopted a new code of law called the "Body of Liberties." It legalized the enslavement of "lawful captives taken in just wars, and such strangers as willingly sell themselves or are sold to us."

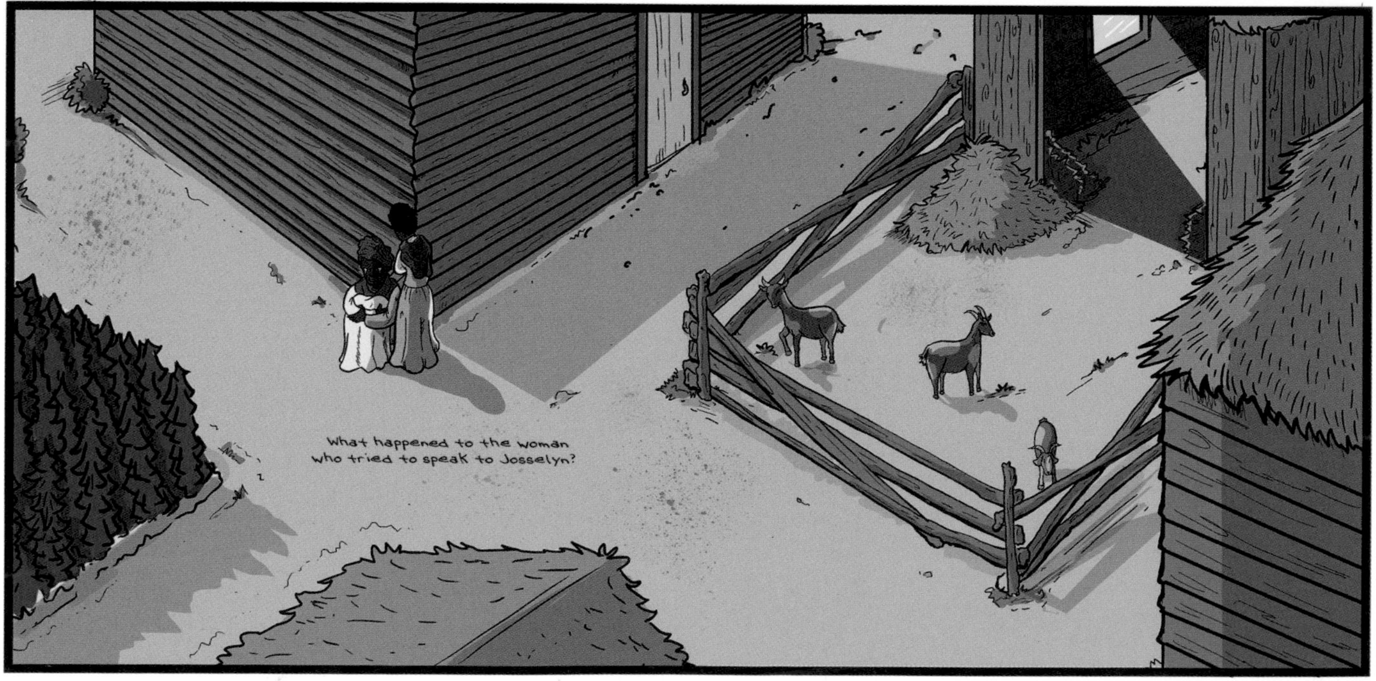
What happened to the woman who tried to speak to Josselyn?

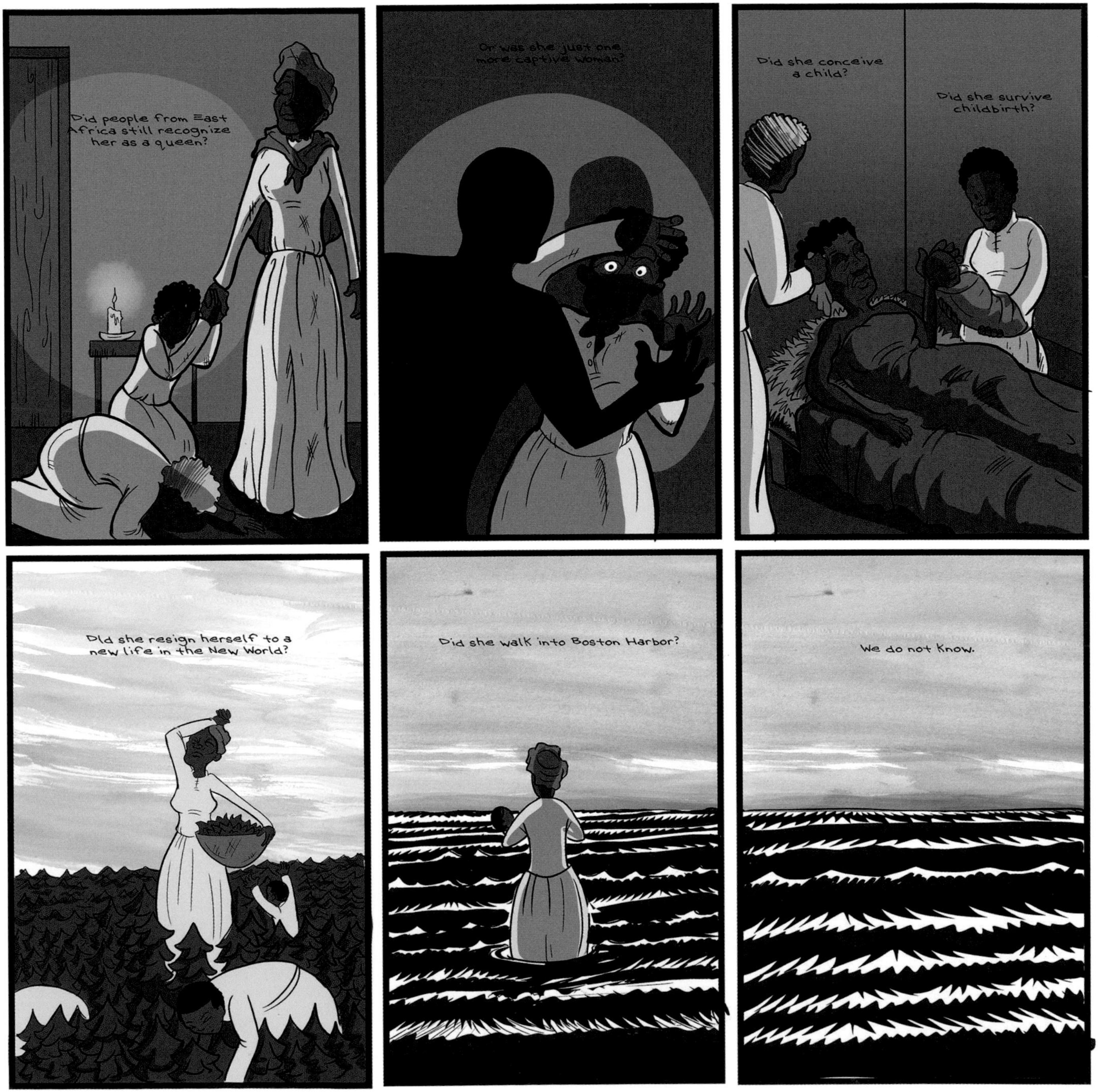
Did people from East Africa still recognize her as a queen?
Or was she just one more captive woman?
Did she conceive a child?
Did she survive childbirth?
Did she resign herself to a new life in the New World?
Did she walk into Boston Harbor?
We do not know.

New Medicine

Story by Walter W. Woodward, Art by Matt Dembicki,
Colors by Arsia Rozegar, and Letters by Jason Hanley

John Winthrop Jr., the son of Massachusetts's first governor, wore many hats. He came to the New World in 1631, where he spent a lot of his time studying the sciences and developing an interest in alchemy and medicine.

In 1657, he was elected governor of the Connecticut Colony, a seat he held—with the exception of one year—until his death in 1676. While governor, he also practiced medicine and alchemy, in accordance with the popular belief that alchemy, medicine, and prayer were all required for healing. Whether Winthrop was right wasn't the issue, however... what mattered was that his techniques worked better than other treatments that were available at the time.

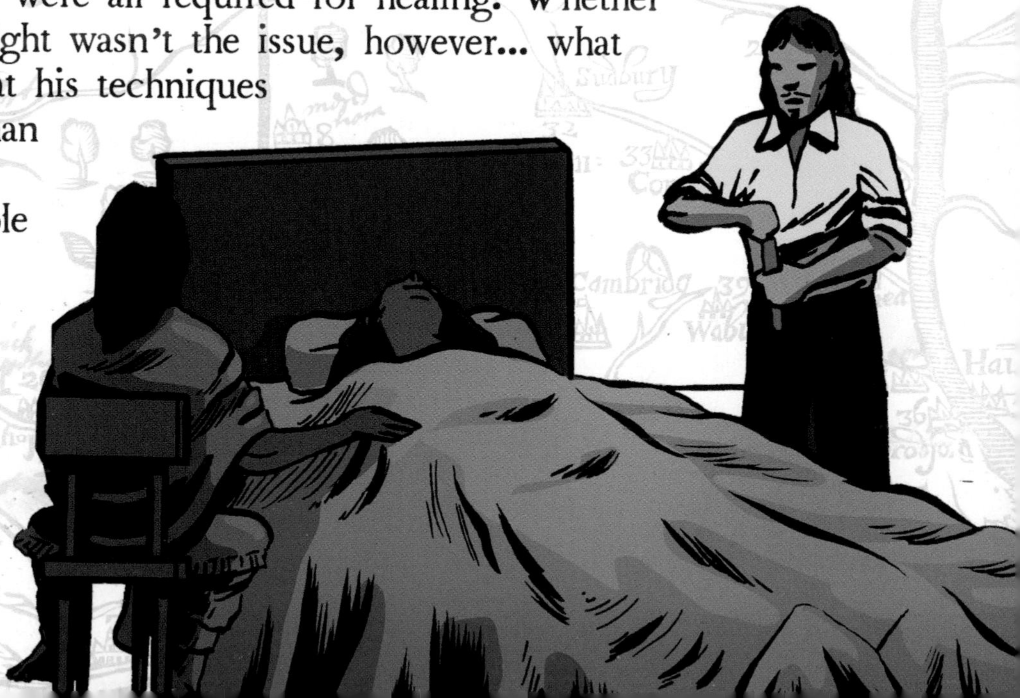

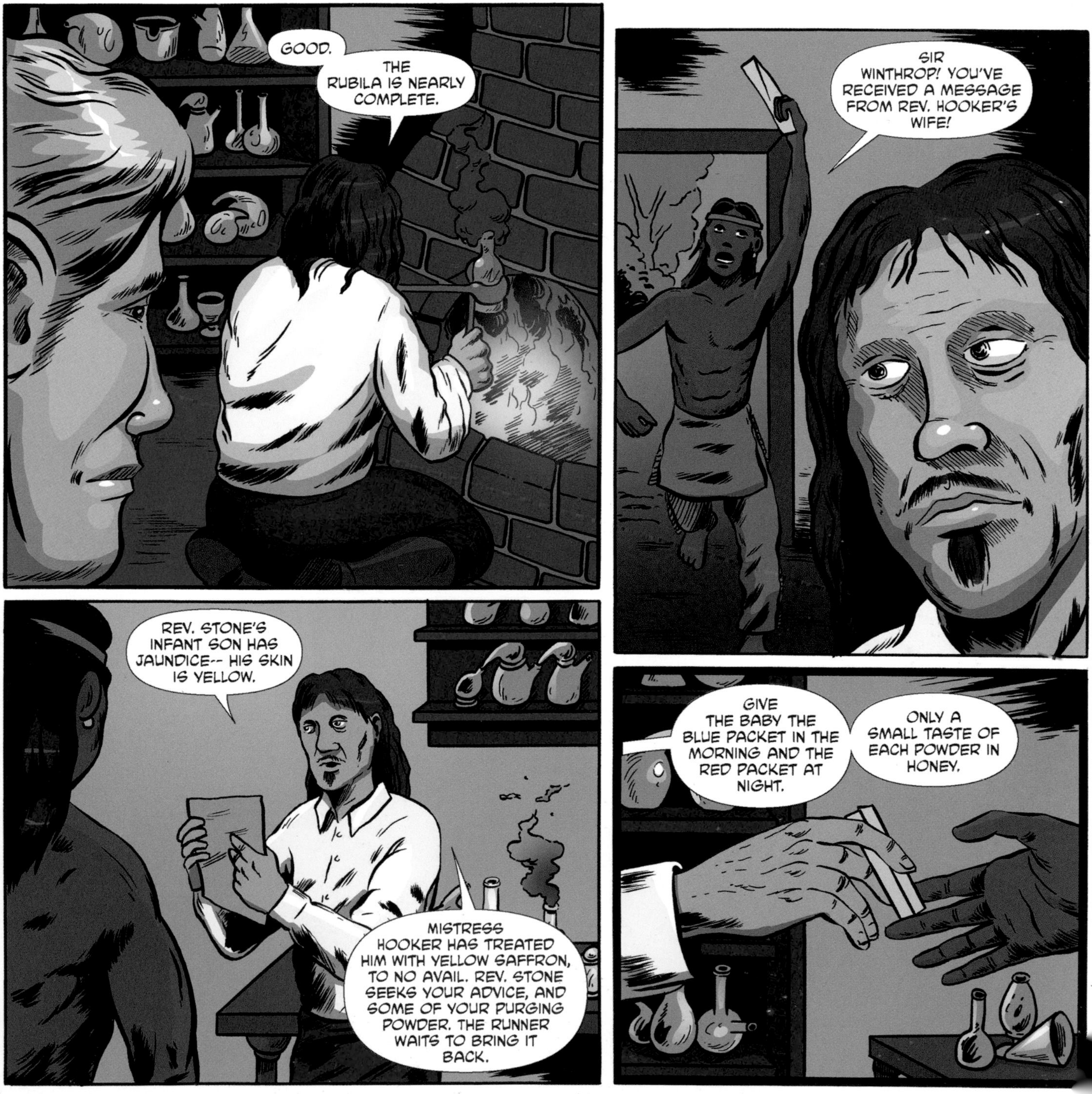
GOOD.
THE RUBILA IS NEARLY COMPLETE.
SIR WINTHROP! YOU'VE RECEIVED A MESSAGE FROM REV. HOOKER'S WIFE!
REV. STONE'S INFANT SON HAS JAUNDICE-- HIS SKIN IS YELLOW.
MISTRESS HOOKER HAS TREATED HIM WITH YELLOW SAFFRON, TO NO AVAIL. REV. STONE SEEKS YOUR ADVICE, AND SOME OF YOUR PURGING POWDER. THE RUNNER WAITS TO BRING IT BACK.
GIVE THE BABY THE BLUE PACKET IN THE MORNING AND THE RED PACKET AT NIGHT.
ONLY A SMALL TASTE OF EACH POWDER IN HONEY.

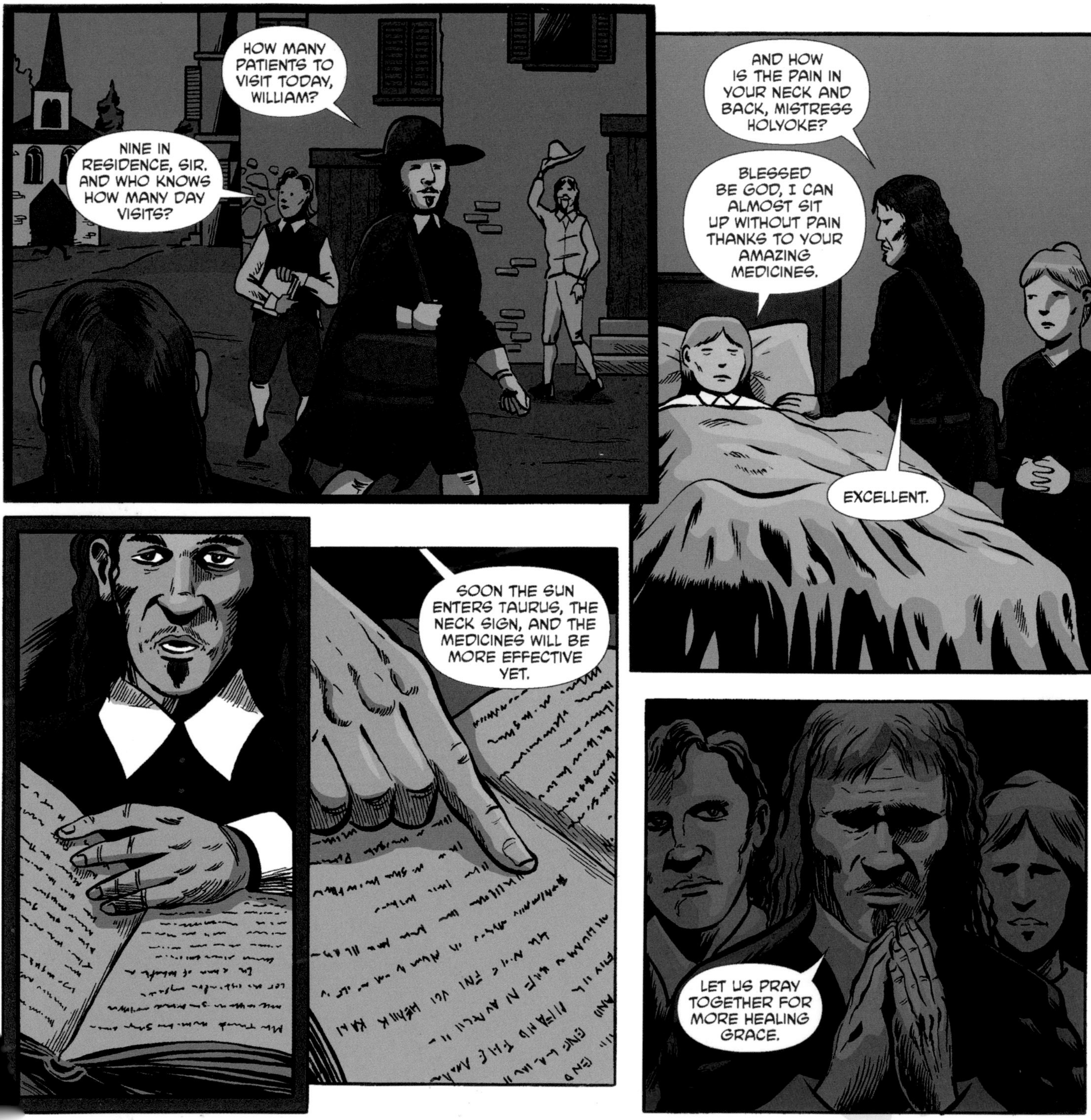
HOW MANY PATIENTS TO VISIT TODAY, WILLIAM?
NINE IN RESIDENCE, SIR. AND WHO KNOWS HOW MANY DAY VISITS?
AND HOW IS THE PAIN IN YOUR NECK AND BACK, MISTRESS HOLYOKE?
BLESSED BE GOD, I CAN ALMOST SIT UP WITHOUT PAIN THANKS TO YOUR AMAZING MEDICINES.
EXCELLENT.
SOON THE SUN ENTERS TAURUS, THE NECK SIGN, AND THE MEDICINES WILL BE MORE EFFECTIVE YET.
LET US PRAY TOGETHER FOR MORE HEALING GRACE.

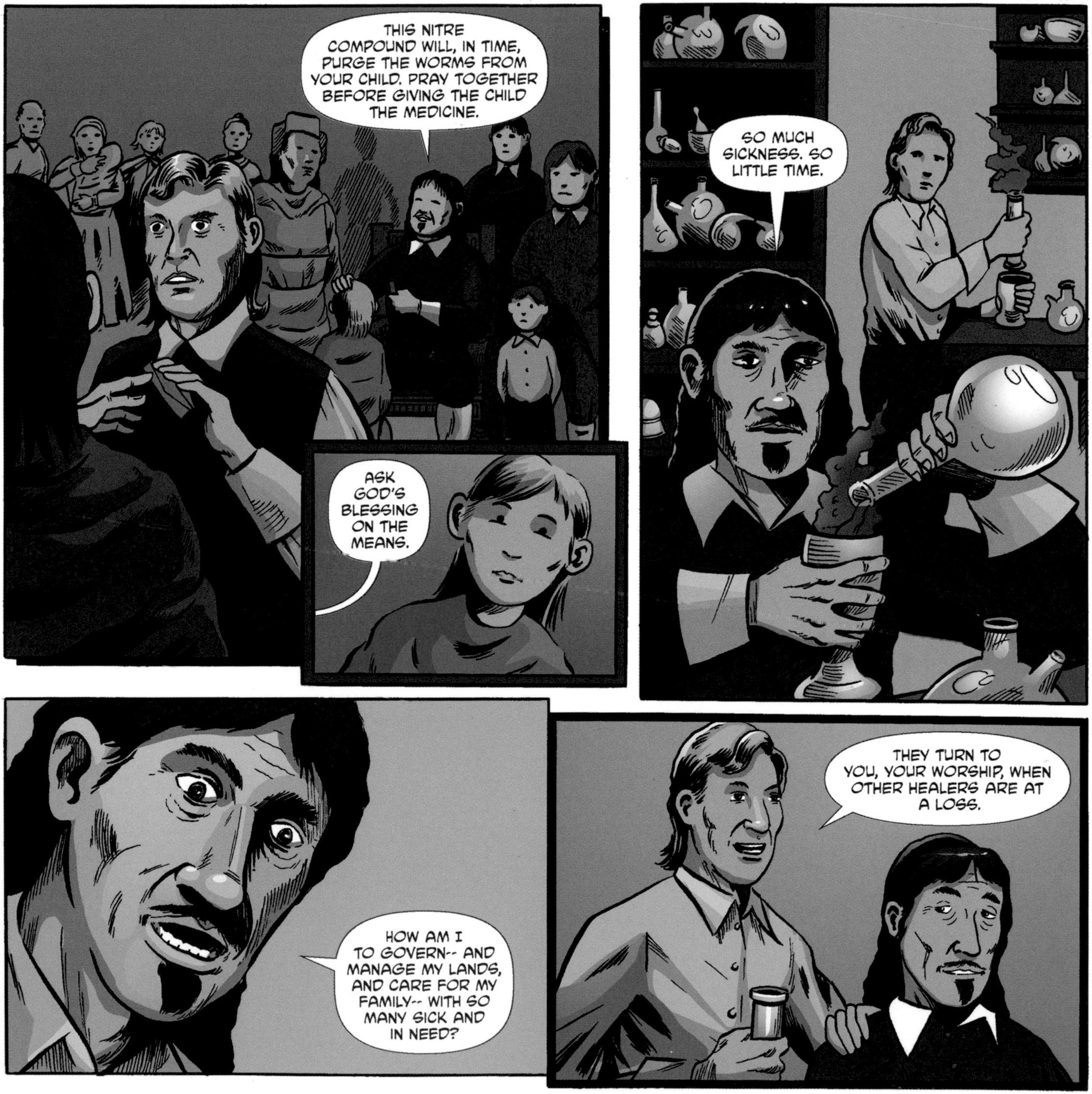
THIS NITRE COMPOUND WILL, IN TIME, PURGE THE WORMS FROM YOUR CHILD. PRAY TOGETHER BEFORE GIVING THE CHILD THE MEDICINE.
ASK GOD'S BLESSING ON THE MEANS.
SO MUCH SICKNESS. SO LITTLE TIME.
HOW AM I TO GOVERN-- AND MANAGE MY LANDS, AND CARE FOR MY FAMILY-- WITH SO MANY SICK AND IN NEED?
THEY TURN TO YOU, YOUR WORSHIP, WHEN OTHER HEALERS ARE AT A LOSS.

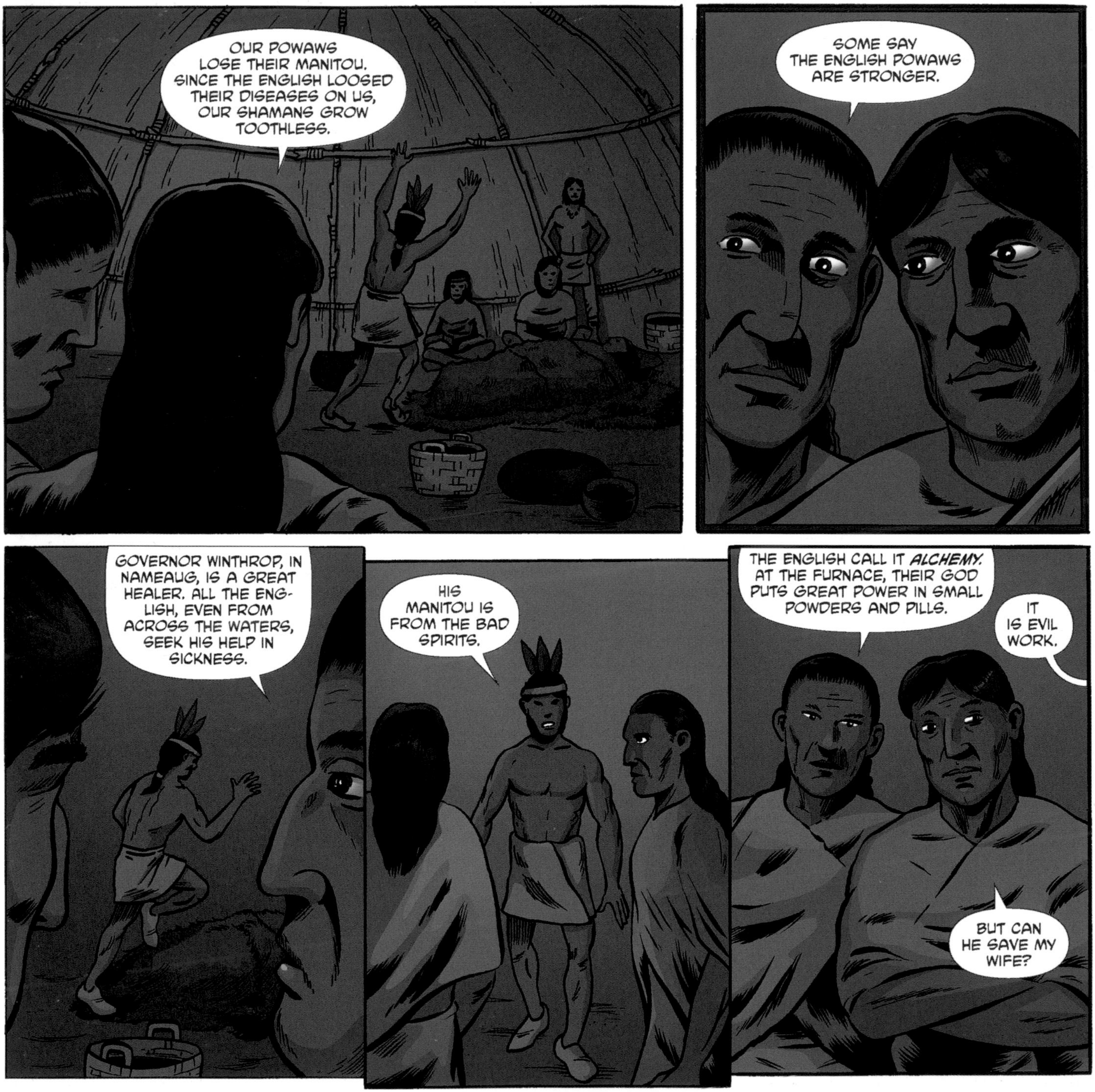

OUR POWAWS LOSE THEIR MANITOU. SINCE THE ENGLISH LOOSED THEIR DISEASES ON US, OUR SHAMANS GROW TOOTHLESS.
SOME SAY THE ENGLISH POWAWS ARE STRONGER.
GOVERNOR WINTHROP, IN NAMEAUG, IS A GREAT HEALER. ALL THE ENG-LISH, EVEN FROM ACROSS THE WATERS, SEEK HIS HELP IN SICKNESS.
HIS MANITOU IS FROM THE BAD SPIRITS.
THE ENGLISH CALL IT *ALCHEMY.* AT THE FURNACE, THEIR GOD PUTS GREAT POWER IN SMALL POWDERS AND PILLS.
IT IS EVIL WORK.
BUT CAN HE SAVE MY WIFE?

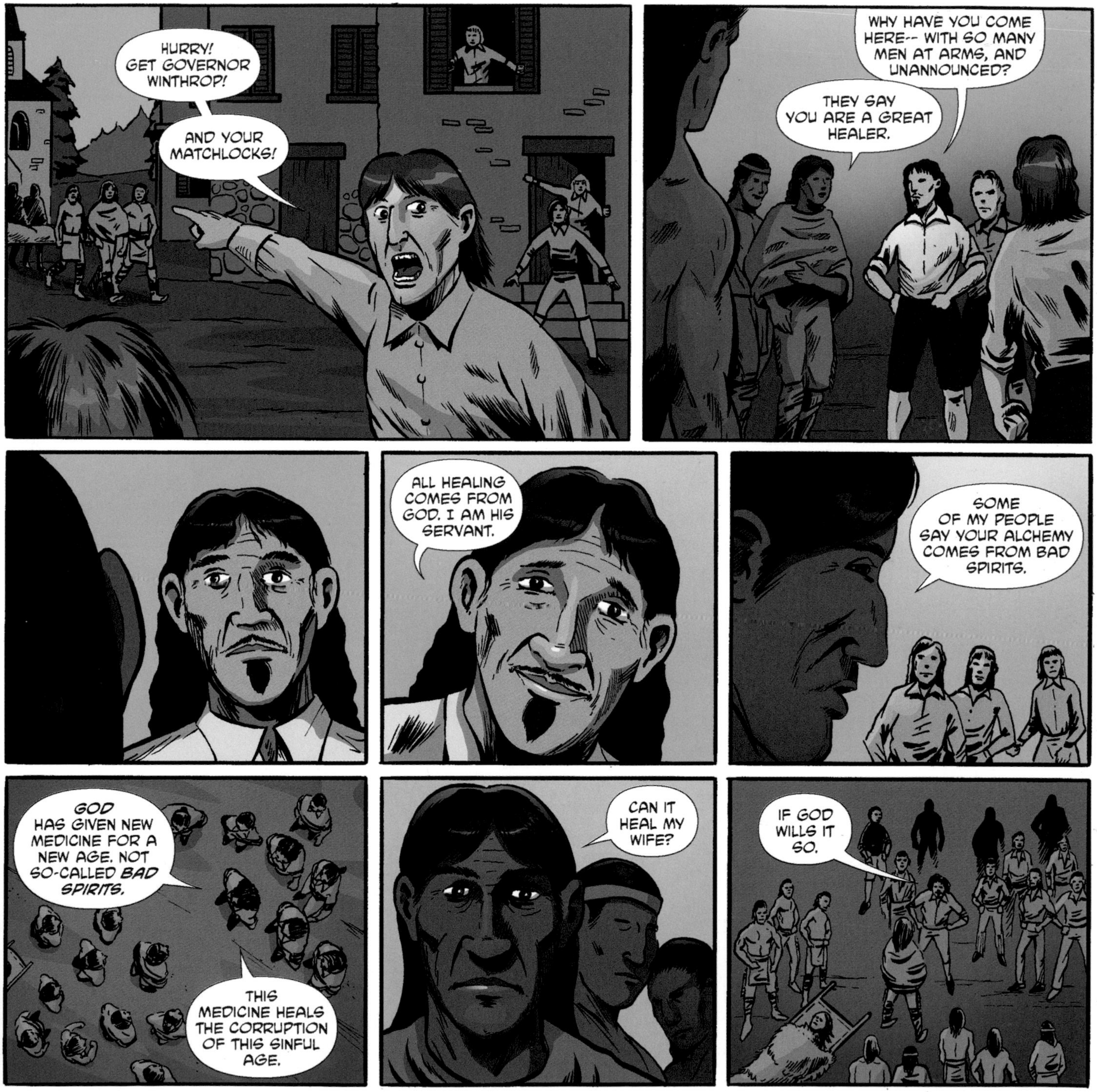
HURRY! GET GOVERNOR WINTHROP!
AND YOUR MATCHLOCKS!
WHY HAVE YOU COME HERE-- WITH SO MANY MEN AT ARMS, AND UNANNOUNCED?
THEY SAY YOU ARE A GREAT HEALER.
ALL HEALING COMES FROM GOD. I AM HIS SERVANT.
SOME OF MY PEOPLE SAY YOUR ALCHEMY COMES FROM BAD SPIRITS.
GOD HAS GIVEN NEW MEDICINE FOR A NEW AGE. NOT SO-CALLED *BAD SPIRITS.*
THIS MEDICINE HEALS THE CORRUPTION OF THIS SINFUL AGE.
CAN IT HEAL MY WIFE?
IF GOD WILLS IT SO.

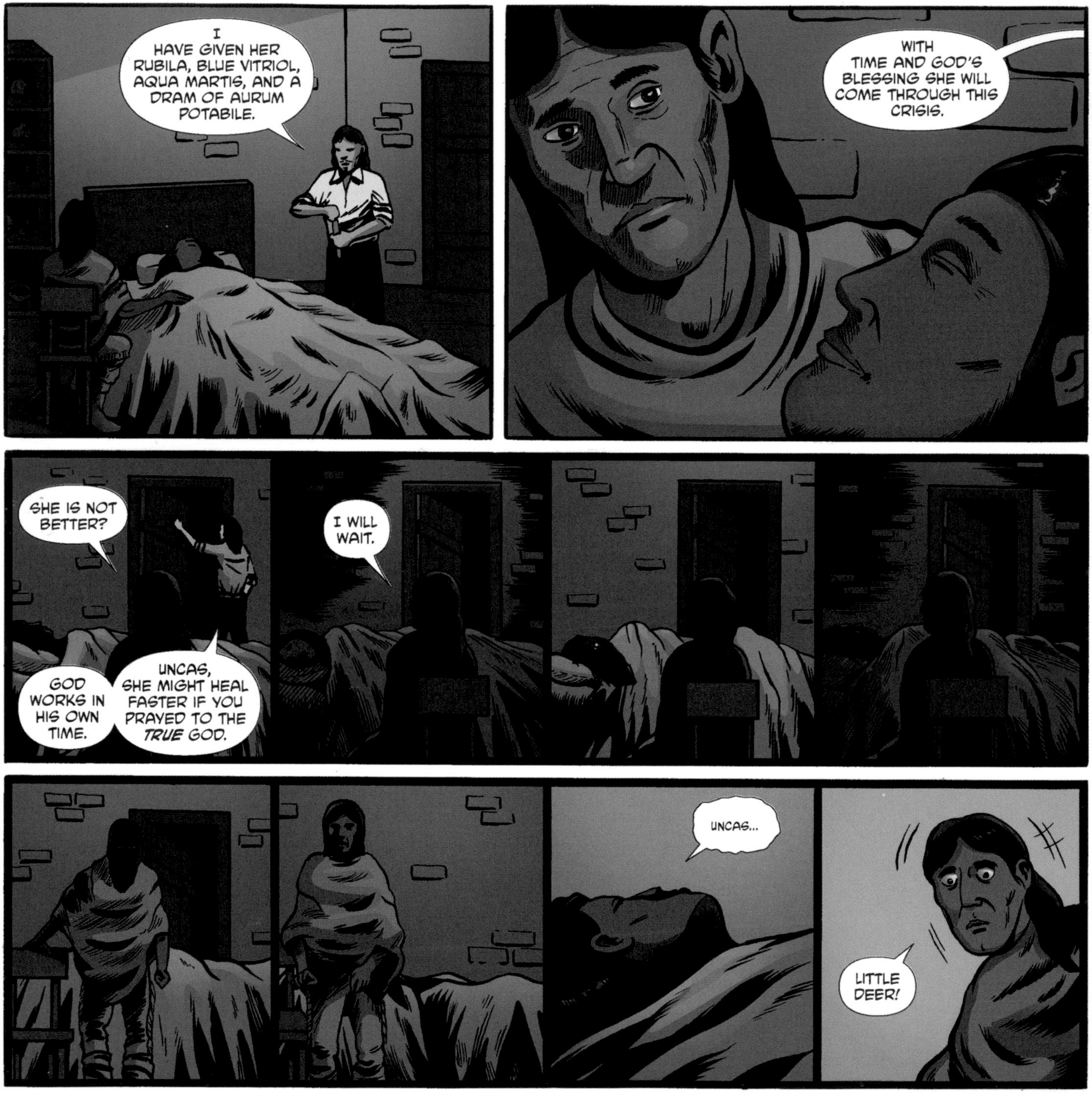
I HAVE GIVEN HER RUBILA, BLUE VITRIOL, AQUA MARTIS, AND A DRAM OF AURUM POTABILE.
WITH TIME AND GOD'S BLESSING SHE WILL COME THROUGH THIS CRISIS.
SHE IS NOT BETTER?
GOD WORKS IN HIS OWN TIME.
UNCAS, SHE MIGHT HEAL FASTER IF YOU PRAYED TO THE *TRUE* GOD.
I WILL WAIT.
UNCAS...
LITTLE DEER!

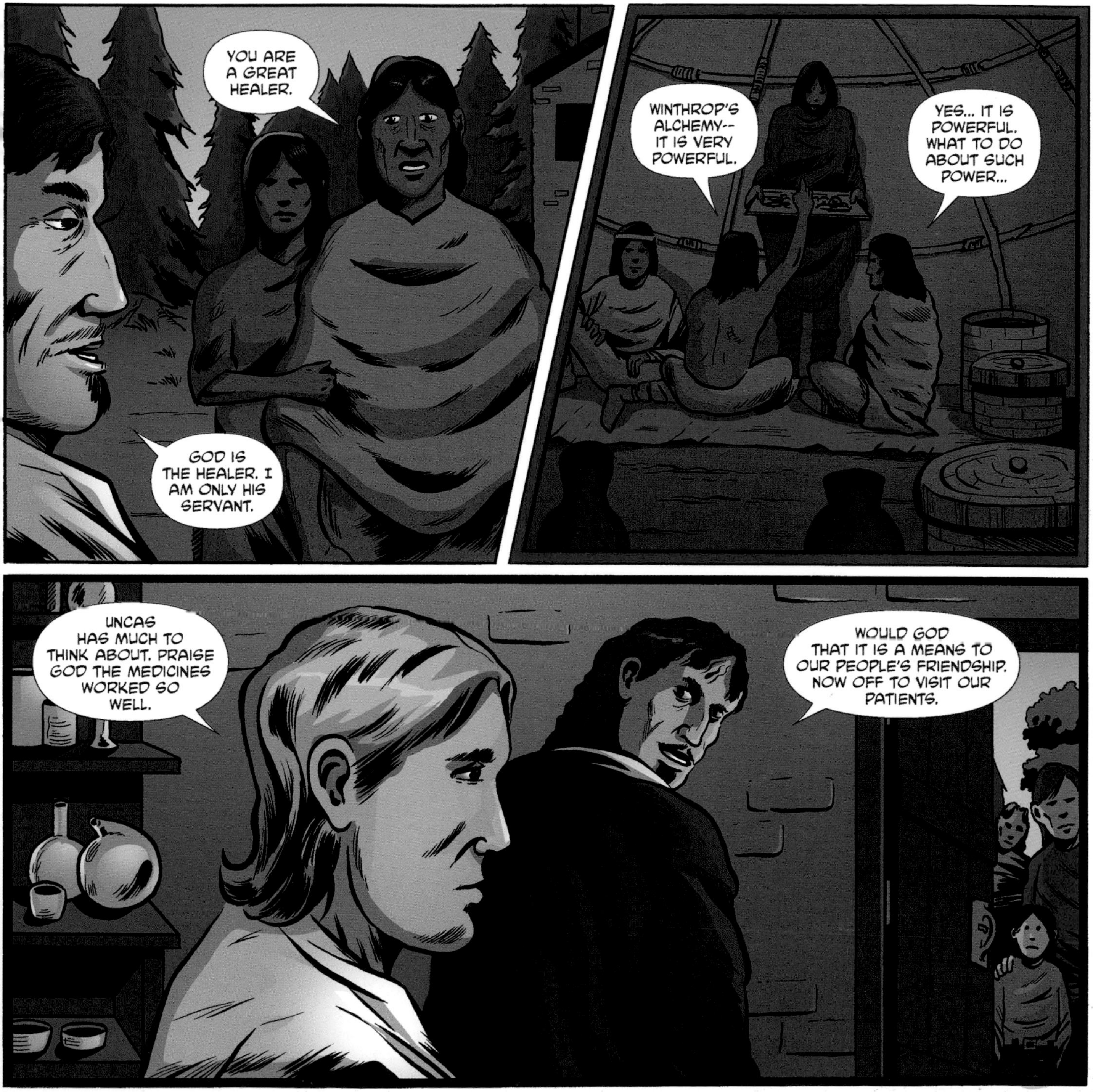
YOU ARE A GREAT HEALER.
GOD IS THE HEALER. I AM ONLY HIS SERVANT.
WINTHROP'S ALCHEMY-- IT IS VERY POWERFUL.
YES... IT IS POWERFUL. WHAT TO DO ABOUT SUCH POWER...
UNCAS HAS MUCH TO THINK ABOUT. PRAISE GOD THE MEDICINES WORKED SO WELL.
WOULD GOD THAT IT IS A MEANS TO OUR PEOPLE'S FRIENDSHIP. NOW OFF TO VISIT OUR PATIENTS.

LOST TRIBE
Story by A. David Lewis and Art by JT Waldman

NEWPORT, Rhode Island, is home to the first permanent and surviving Jewish settlement in the United States.

However, when Mordecai Campanal and his kinsmen arrived on its shores in the late 1650s, their future felt anything but certain.

Widespread anti-Semitism, legal opposition, and British occupation all threatened the existence of what would become the oldest synagogue in America—and one of the sites the first President of the United States visited in 1790.

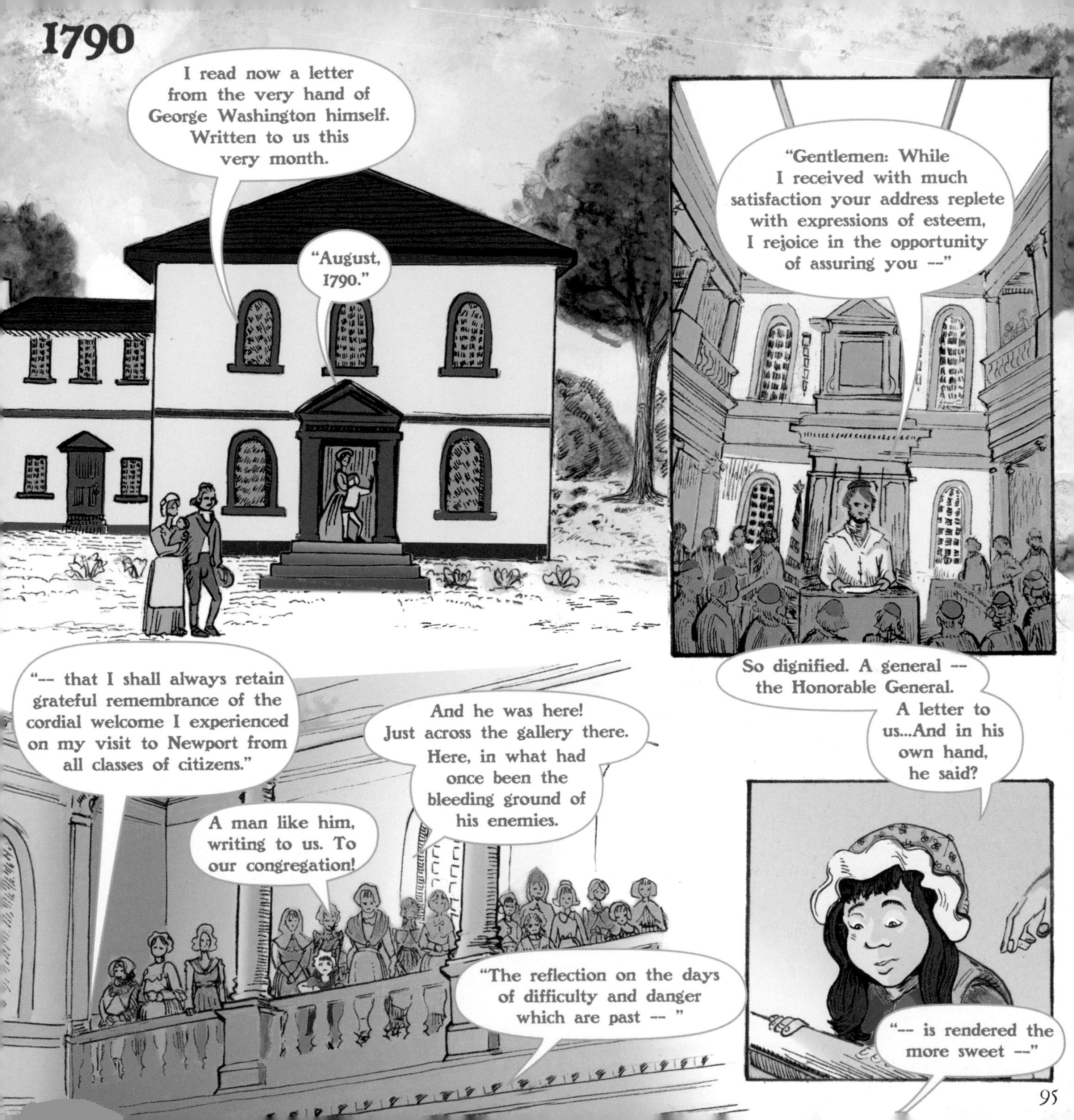
1790
I read now a letter from the very hand of George Washington himself. Written to us this very month.
"August, 1790."
"Gentlemen: While I received with much satisfaction your address replete with expressions of esteem, I rejoice in the opportunity of assuring you --"
"-- that I shall always retain grateful remembrance of the cordial welcome I experienced on my visit to Newport from all classes of citizens."
A man like him, writing to us. To our congregation!
And he was here! Just across the gallery there. Here, in what had once been the bleeding ground of his enemies.
So dignified. A general -- the Honorable General.
A letter to us...And in his own hand, he said?
"The reflection on the days of difficulty and danger which are past -- "
"-- is rendered the more sweet --"

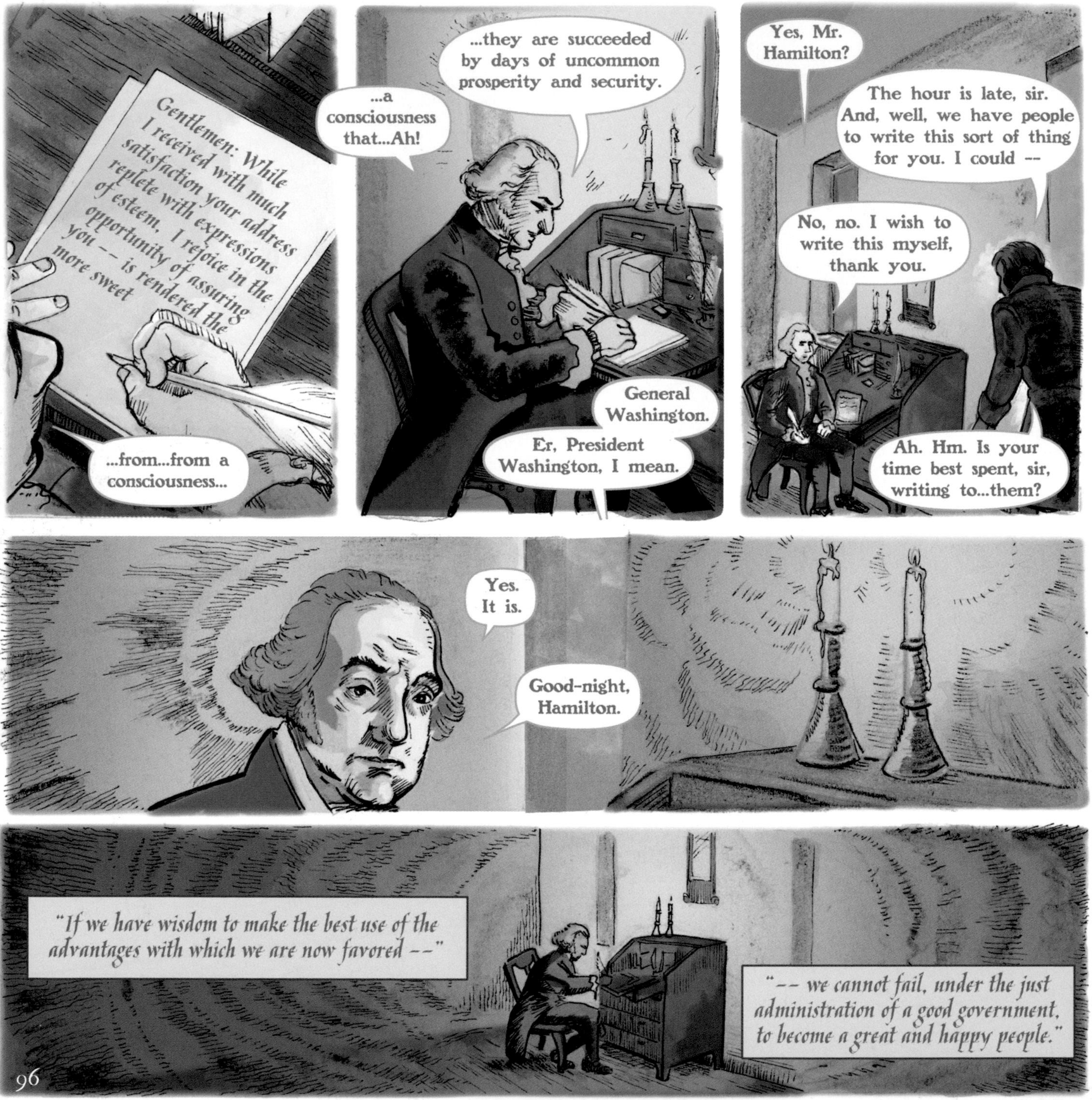
Gentlemen: While I received with much satisfaction your address replete with expressions of esteem, I rejoice in the opportunity of assuring you -- is rendered the more sweet
...from...from a consciousness...
...a consciousness that...Ah!
...they are succeeded by days of uncommon prosperity and security.
General Washington.
Er, President Washington, I mean.
Yes, Mr. Hamilton?
The hour is late, sir. And, well, we have people to write this sort of thing for you. I could --
No, no. I wish to write this myself, thank you.
Ah. Hm. Is your time best spent, sir, writing to...them?
Yes. It is.
Good-night, Hamilton.
"If we have wisdom to make the best use of the advantages with which we are now favored --"
"-- we cannot fail, under the just administration of a good government, to become a great and happy people."

1778

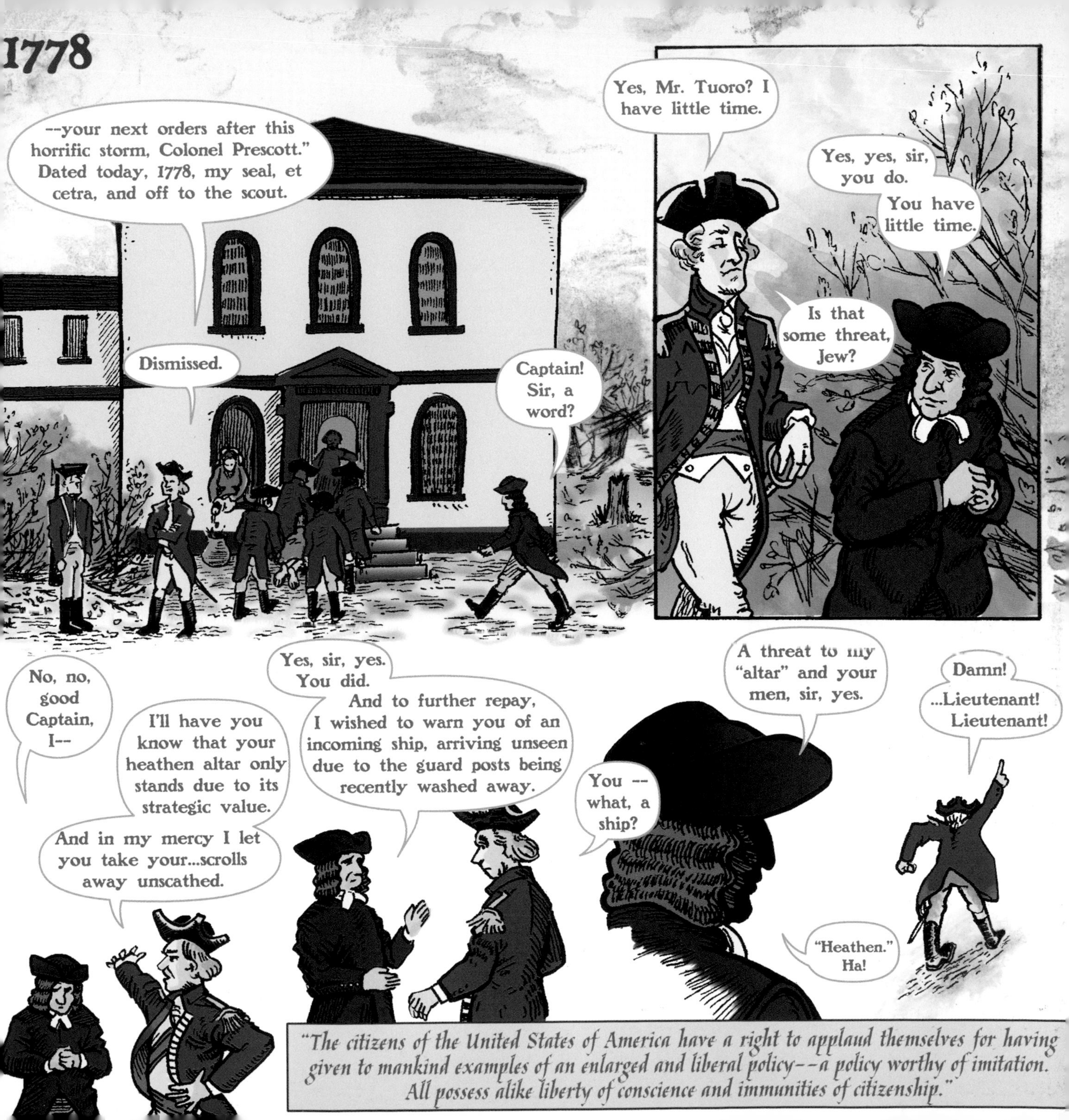
--your next orders after this horrific storm, Colonel Prescott." Dated today, 1778, my seal, et cetra, and off to the scout.
Dismissed.
Captain! Sir, a word?
Yes, Mr. Tuoro? I have little time.
Yes, yes, sir, you do.
You have little time.
Is that some threat, Jew?
No, no, good Captain, I--
I'll have you know that your heathen altar only stands due to its strategic value.
And in my mercy I let you take your...scrolls away unscathed.
Yes, sir, yes. You did.
And to further repay, I wished to warn you of an incoming ship, arriving unseen due to the guard posts being recently washed away.
You -- what, a ship?
A threat to my "altar" and your men, sir, yes.
Damn! ...Lieutenant! Lieutenant!
"Heathen." Ha!
"The citizens of the United States of America have a right to applaud themselves for having given to mankind examples of an enlarged and liberal policy--a policy worthy of imitation. All possess alike liberty of conscience and immunities of citizenship."

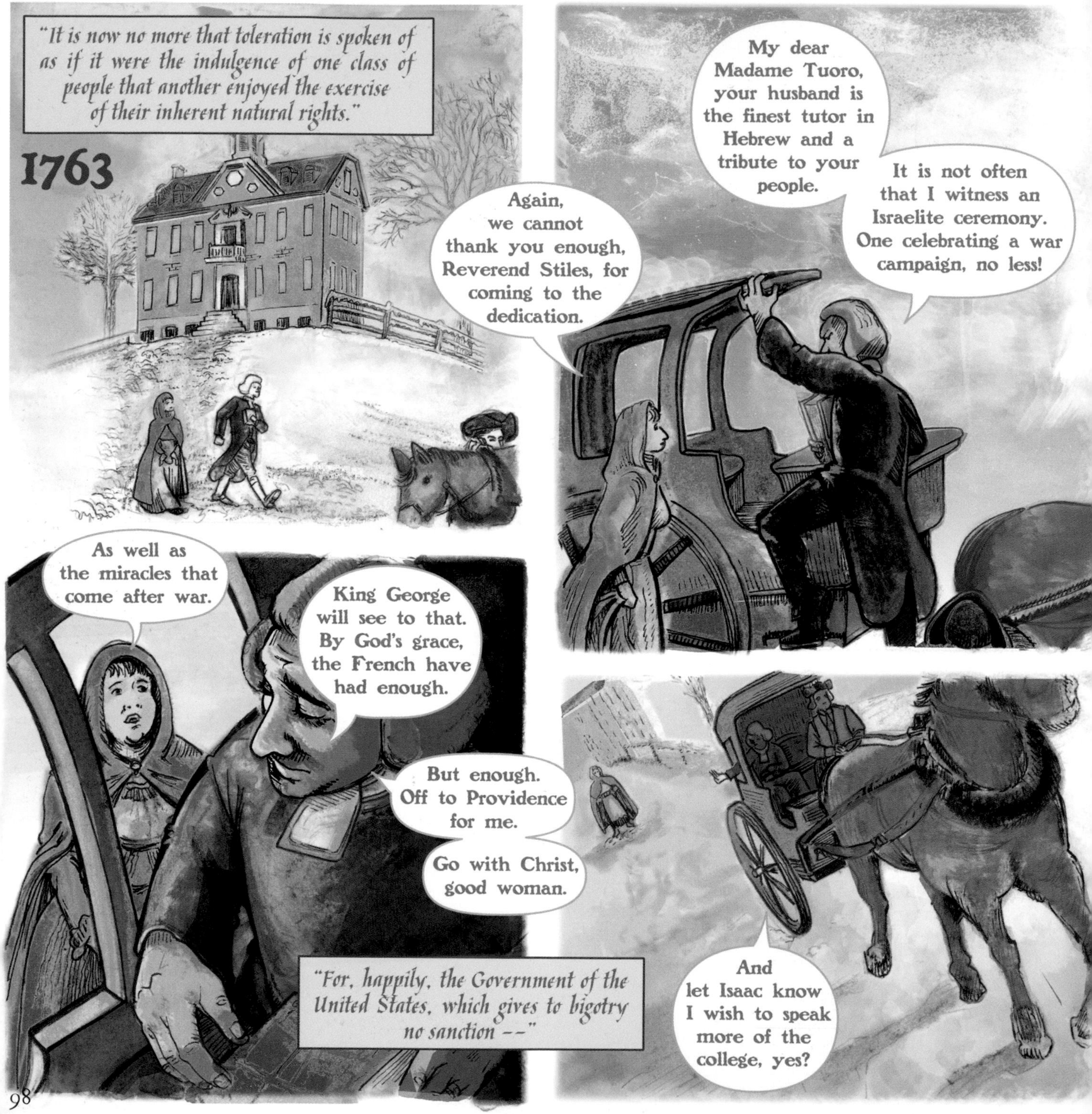
"It is now no more that toleration is spoken of as if it were the indulgence of one class of people that another enjoyed the exercise of their inherent natural rights."
1763
Again, we cannot thank you enough, Reverend Stiles, for coming to the dedication.
My dear Madame Tuoro, your husband is the finest tutor in Hebrew and a tribute to your people.
It is not often that I witness an Israelite ceremony. One celebrating a war campaign, no less!
As well as the miracles that come after war.
King George will see to that. By God's grace, the French have had enough.
But enough. Off to Providence for me.
Go with Christ, good woman.
"For, happily, the Government of the United States, which gives to bigotry no sanction --"
And let Isaac know I wish to speak more of the college, yes?

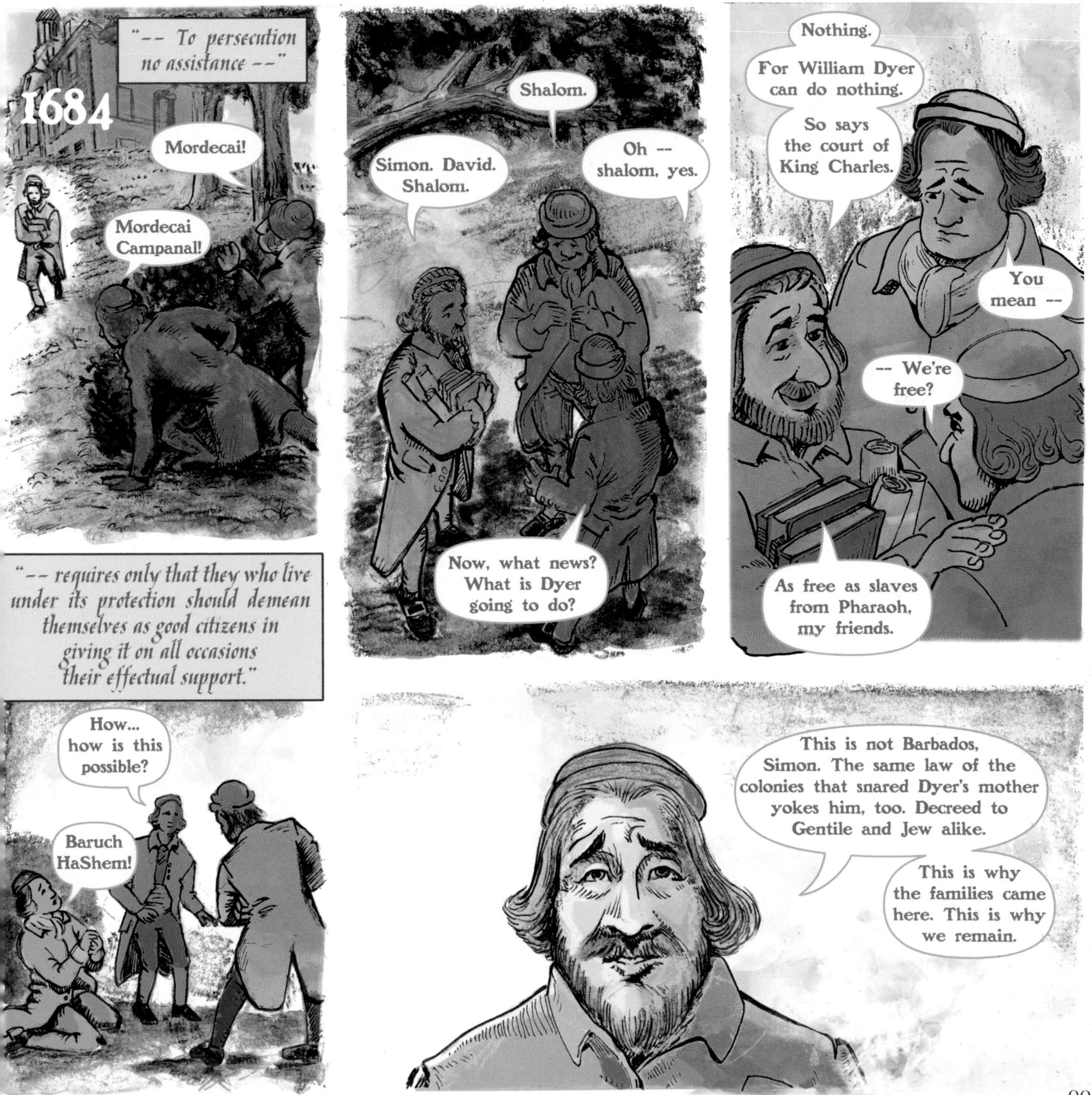
"-- To persecution no assistance --"
1684
Mordecai!
Mordecai Campanal!
Shalom.
Simon. David. Shalom.
Oh -- shalom, yes.
Now, what news? What is Dyer going to do?
Nothing.
For William Dyer can do nothing.
So says the court of King Charles.
You mean --
-- We're free?
As free as slaves from Pharaoh, my friends.
"-- requires only that they who live under its protection should demean themselves as good citizens in giving it on all occasions their effectual support."
How... how is this possible?
Baruch HaShem!
This is not Barbados, Simon. The same law of the colonies that snared Dyer's mother yokes him, too. Decreed to Gentile and Jew alike.
This is why the families came here. This is why we remain.

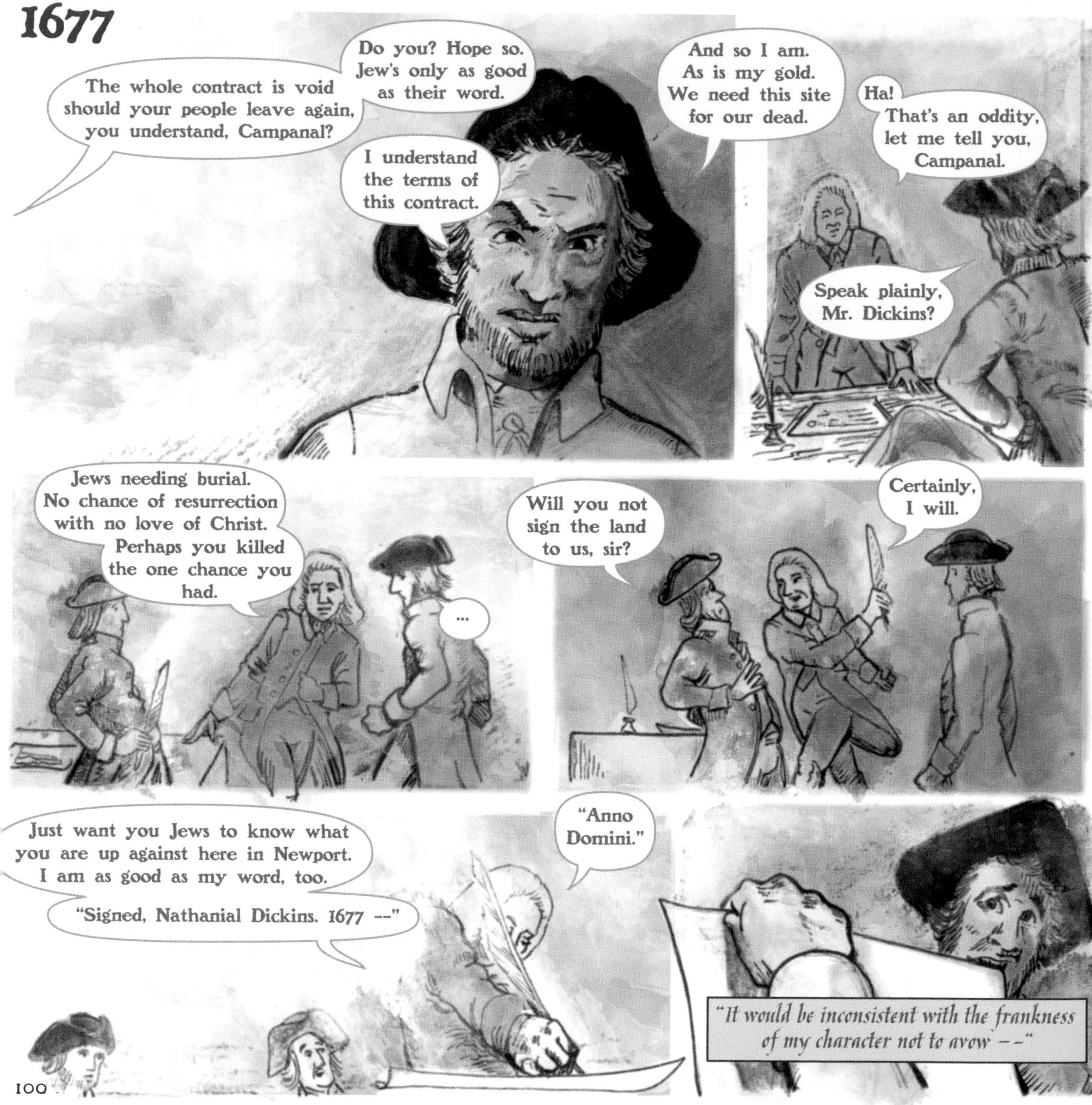
1677
The whole contract is void should your people leave again, you understand, Campanal?
Do you? Hope so. Jew's only as good as their word.
I understand the terms of this contract.
And so I am. As is my gold. We need this site for our dead.
Ha! That's an oddity, let me tell you, Campanal.
Speak plainly, Mr. Dickins?
Jews needing burial. No chance of resurrection with no love of Christ.
Perhaps you killed the one chance you had.
...
Will you not sign the land to us, sir?
Certainly, I will.
Just want you Jews to know what you are up against here in Newport. I am as good as my word, too.
"Signed, Nathanial Dickins. 1677 --"
"Anno Domini."
"It would be inconsistent with the frankness of my character not to avow --"

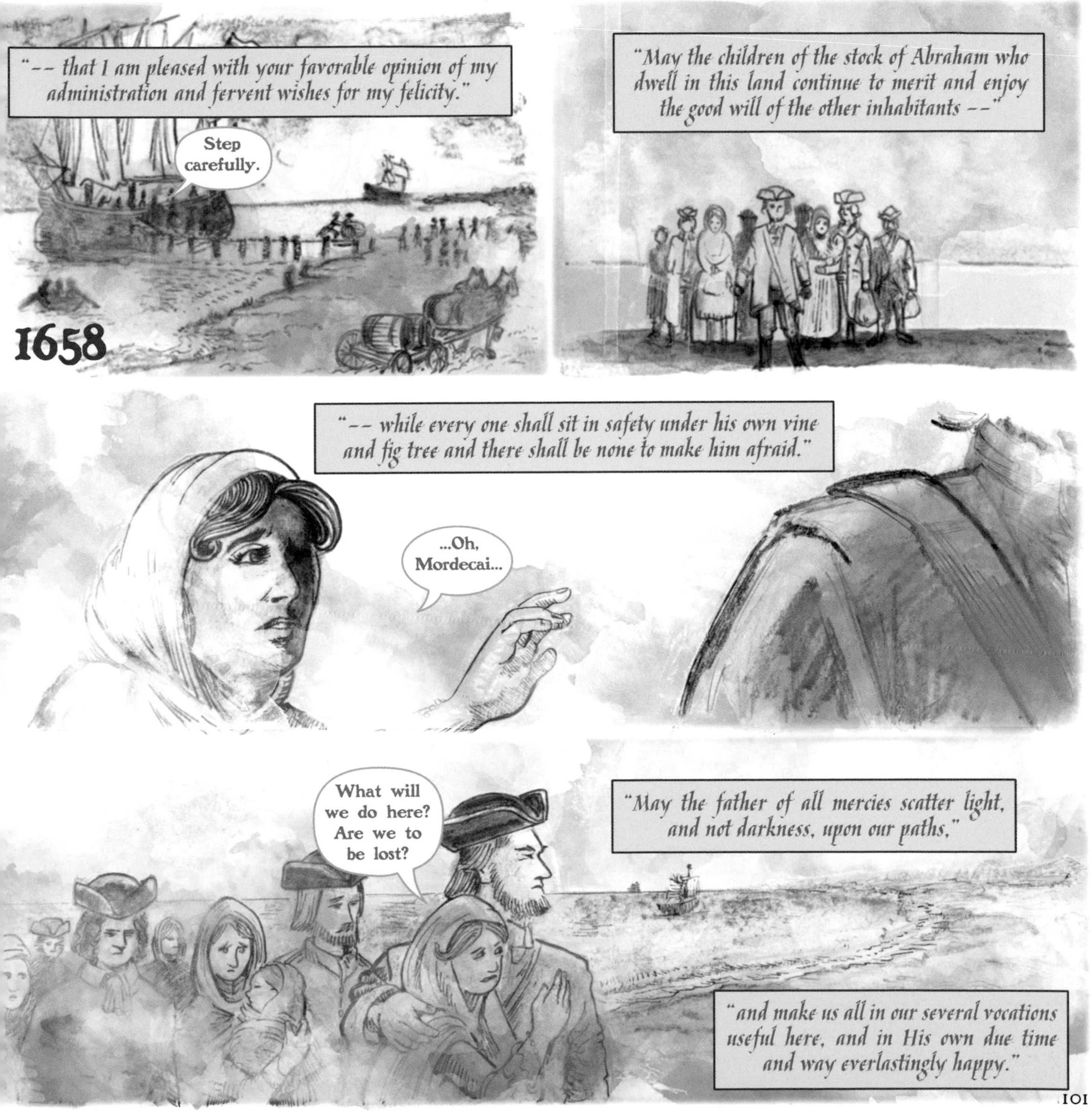
"-- that I am pleased with your favorable opinion of my administration and fervent wishes for my felicity."
Step carefully.
1658
"May the children of the stock of Abraham who dwell in this land continue to merit and enjoy the good will of the other inhabitants --"
"-- while every one shall sit in safety under his own vine and fig tree and there shall be none to make him afraid."
...Oh, Mordecai...
What will we do here? Are we to be lost?
"May the father of all mercies scatter light, and not darkness, upon our paths,"
"and make us all in our several vocations useful here, and in His own due time and way everlastingly happy."

John Eliot authored the first translation of the Bible to a Native language: Massachusett, to be exact. This was the first Bible printed in North America, and it was printed on Elizabeth Glover's printing press. John Eliot carried this Bible with him as part of his role as the "apostle to the Indians." Below is a reproduction of the first page.

Kesteonn muttaok Chap. i. *nequtta tashikquinnu.*

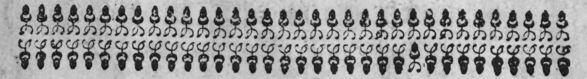

NEGONNE OOSUKKUHWHONK *MOSES*,

Ne asoweetamuk

GENESIS.

CHAP. I.

Eske kutchissik *a* ayum God a Psal.
Kesuk kah Ohke. 33.6.
2 Kah Ohke mô matta & 136.
kuhkenauunneunkquttinnoo 5.
kah monteagunninno, kah Act.14.
pohkenum woskeche moo- 15.
nôi, kah Nashauanit popom- & 17.
shau woskeche nippekontu. 24.
3 Onk noowau God *b* wequaiaj, kah mô Hebr.
wequai. 11.3.
4 Kah wunnaumun God wequai ne en b 2Cor.
wunnegen: Kah wutchadchaûbe-ponumun 4.6.
God noeu wequai kah noeu pohkenum.
5 Kah wuttissowêtamun God wequai Kesukod, kah pohkenum wuttissoweetamun
Nukon: kah mô wunnonkooook kah mo
mohtompog negonne kesuk.
6 Kah noowau God *c* sepakehtamoudj c Psal.
nôeu nippekontu, kah chadchapemoudj na- 136.5.
shauweit nippe wutch nippekontu. Jer.10.
7 Kah ayimup God sepakehtamóonk, kah 12. &
wutchadchabeponumunnap nashaueu nippe 51.15.
agwu, uttiyeu agwu sepakehtamóonk, kah
nashaueu nippekontu ...

13 Kah mo wunnonkooook, kah mo mohtompog shwekesukod.
14 Kah noowau God, *f* Wequanantéga- f Deut.
nohettich ut wussepakehtamoowonganit ke- 4.19.
sukquash, & pohshehettich ut nashauwe ke- Psal.
sukod, kah ut nashauwe nukkonut, kah kuk- 136. 7.
kineasuonganuhhettich, kah uttoocheyeu-
hettich, kah kesukodtauowuhhettich, kah
kodtummooowuhhettich.
15 Kah n nag wequanantéganuóhettich
ut sepakehtamoowonganit wequasunnóhet-
tich ohke, onk mô n nih.
16 Kah ayum God neesunash missiyeuash
wequanantéganash, wequananteg mohtag na-
nânumoomoo kesukod, wequananteg peasik
nananu noomoo nukon, kah anogqsog.
17 Kah uponuh God wussepakehtamoo-
onganit kesukquash, woh wequohsumwog
ohke.
18 Onk woh *g* wunnananumunneau kesukod kah nukon, kah pohshémoo nashaueu g Jer.
wequai, kah nashaueu pohkénum, kah wun- 31.35.
naumun God ne en wunnegen.

This Indian Work

Story by Tara Alexander and Art by Dale Rawlings

John Eliot can be credited with many "firsts." He was one of the editors of *The Bay Psalm Book*, the first book printed in America. He was the first to translate the Bible to a Native American language. The *Mamusse Wunneetupanatamwe Up-Biblum God,* published in the Massachusett language, was also the first Christian Bible printed in America. Eliot also authored the first political book printed in North America—a book that also had the distinction of being the first banned book in North America.

Despite all of these achievements, Eliot is mostly remembered for his missionary work. He attempted to establish Native American towns where he could preach the Bible and create Christian communities. The people in these towns were known as "Praying Indians." The title of this story comes from the opening line of a letter Eliot wrote to Robert Boyle, which read, "Your constant care of, and steadfast affection unto this Indian work... do greatly oblige my heart to honor you..."

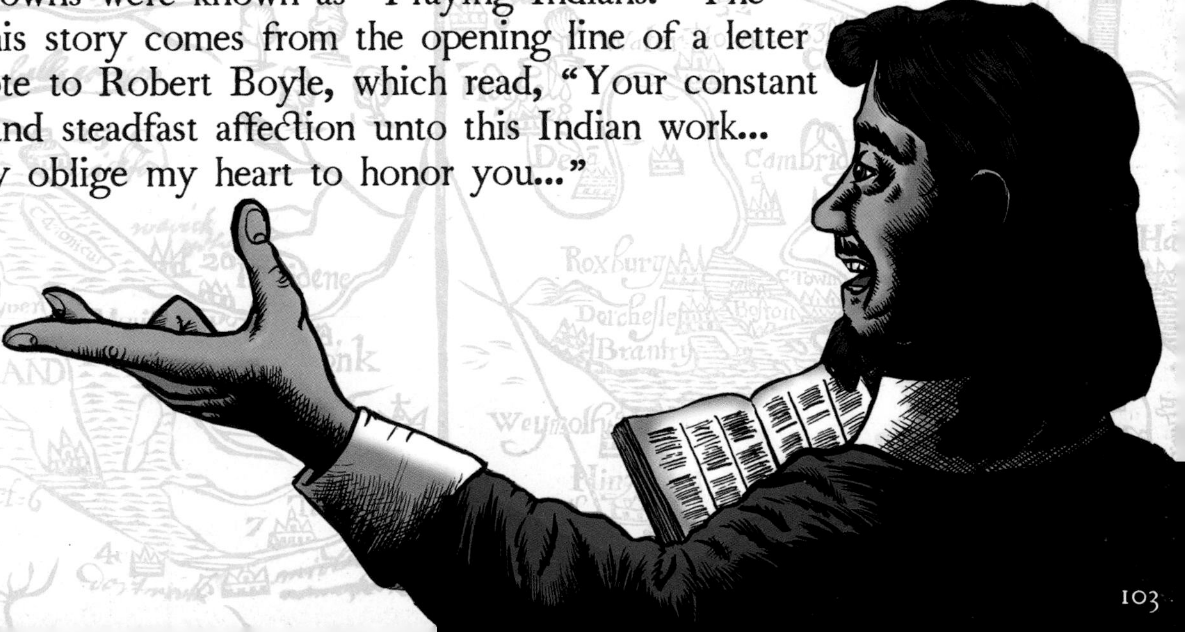

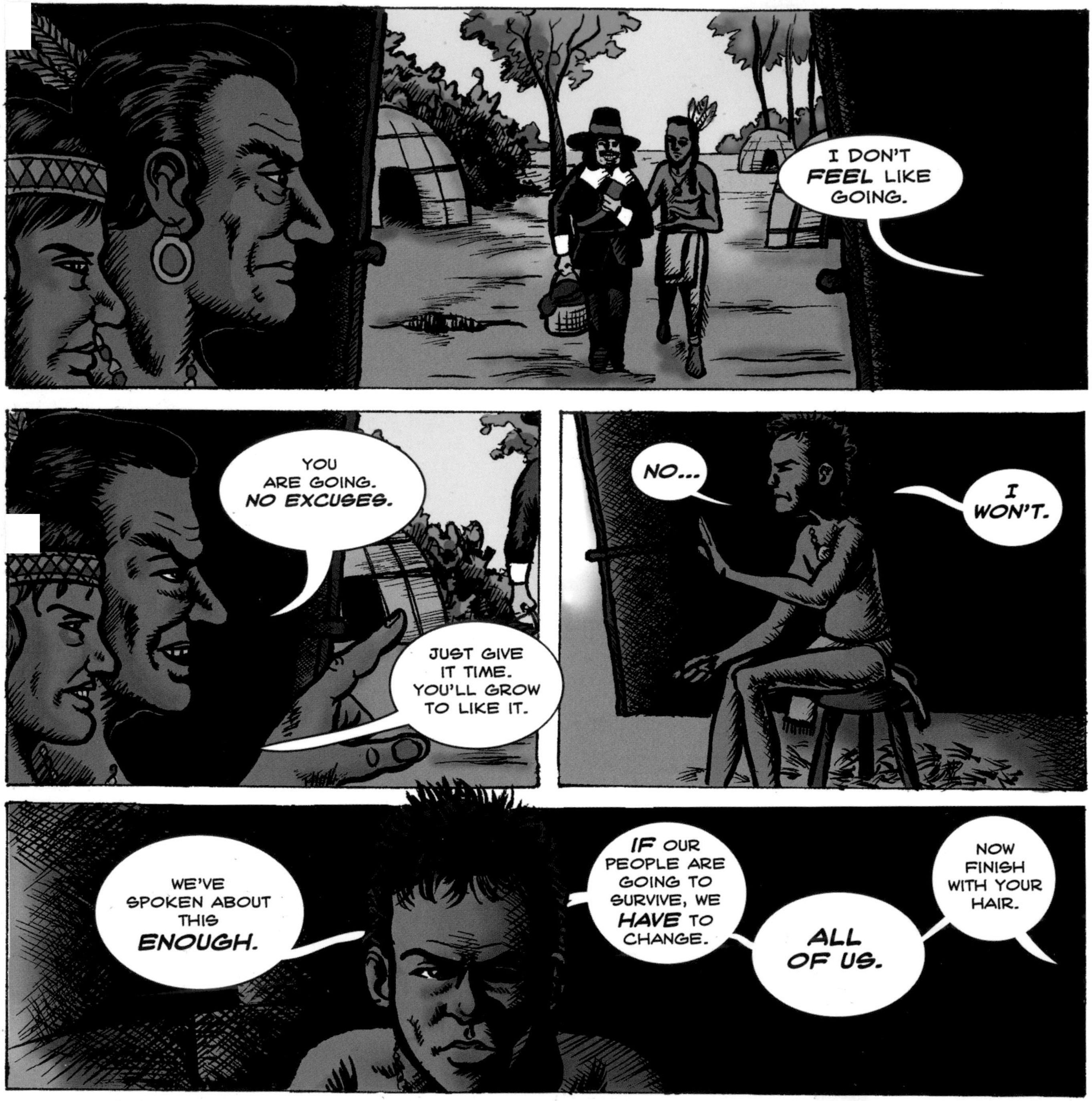
I DON'T FEEL LIKE GOING.
YOU ARE GOING. NO EXCUSES.
JUST GIVE IT TIME. YOU'LL GROW TO LIKE IT.
NO...
I WON'T.
WE'VE SPOKEN ABOUT THIS ENOUGH.
IF OUR PEOPLE ARE GOING TO SURVIVE, WE HAVE TO CHANGE.
ALL OF US.
NOW FINISH WITH YOUR HAIR.

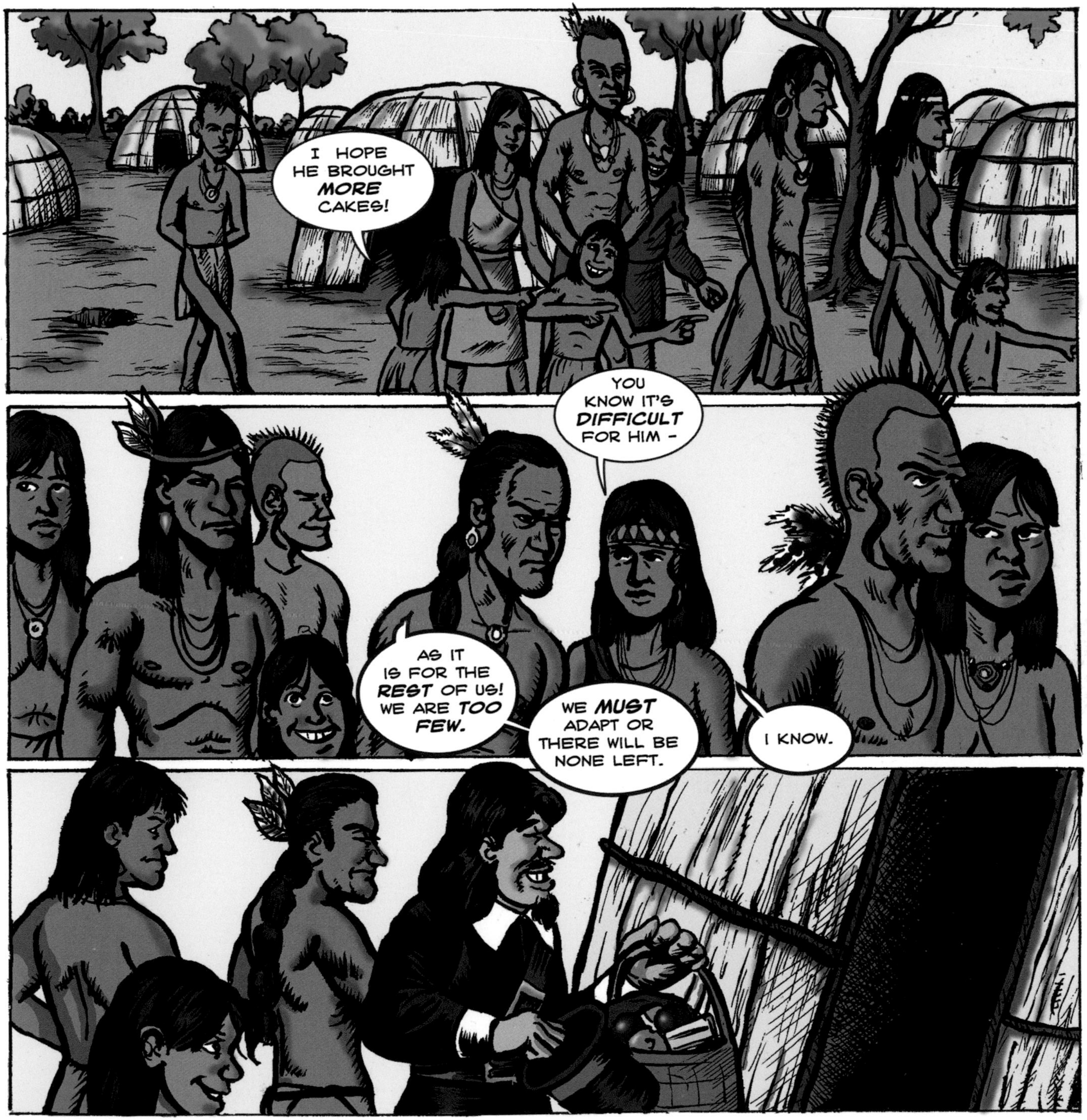
I HOPE HE BROUGHT MORE CAKES!
YOU KNOW IT'S DIFFICULT FOR HIM -
AS IT IS FOR THE REST OF US! WE ARE TOO FEW.
WE MUST ADAPT OR THERE WILL BE NONE LEFT.
I KNOW.

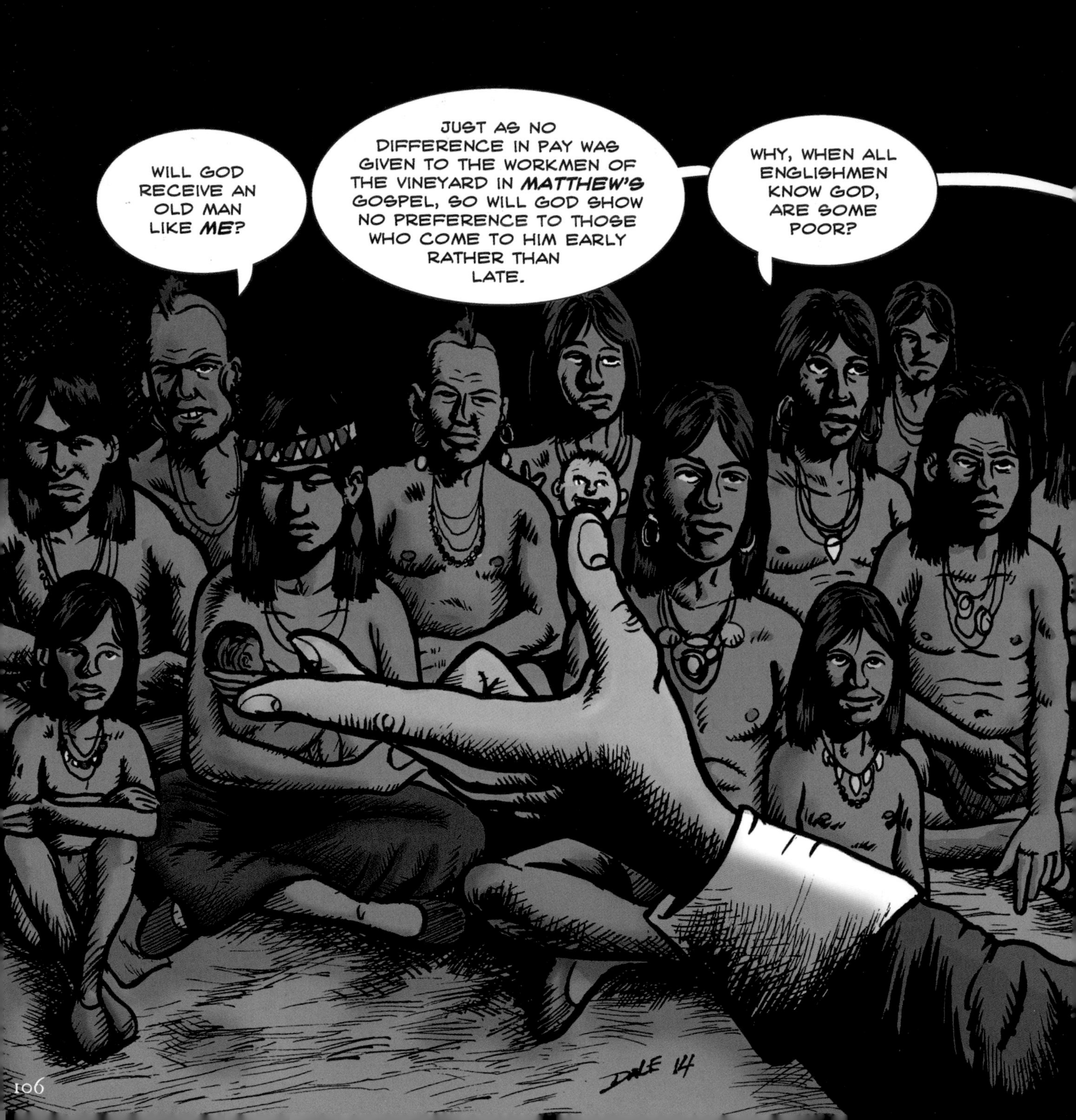
WILL GOD RECEIVE AN OLD MAN LIKE *ME*?
JUST AS NO DIFFERENCE IN PAY WAS GIVEN TO THE WORKMEN OF THE VINEYARD IN *MATTHEW'S* GOSPEL, SO WILL GOD SHOW NO PREFERENCE TO THOSE WHO COME TO HIM EARLY RATHER THAN LATE.
WHY, WHEN ALL ENGLISHMEN KNOW GOD, ARE SOME POOR?
DALE 14

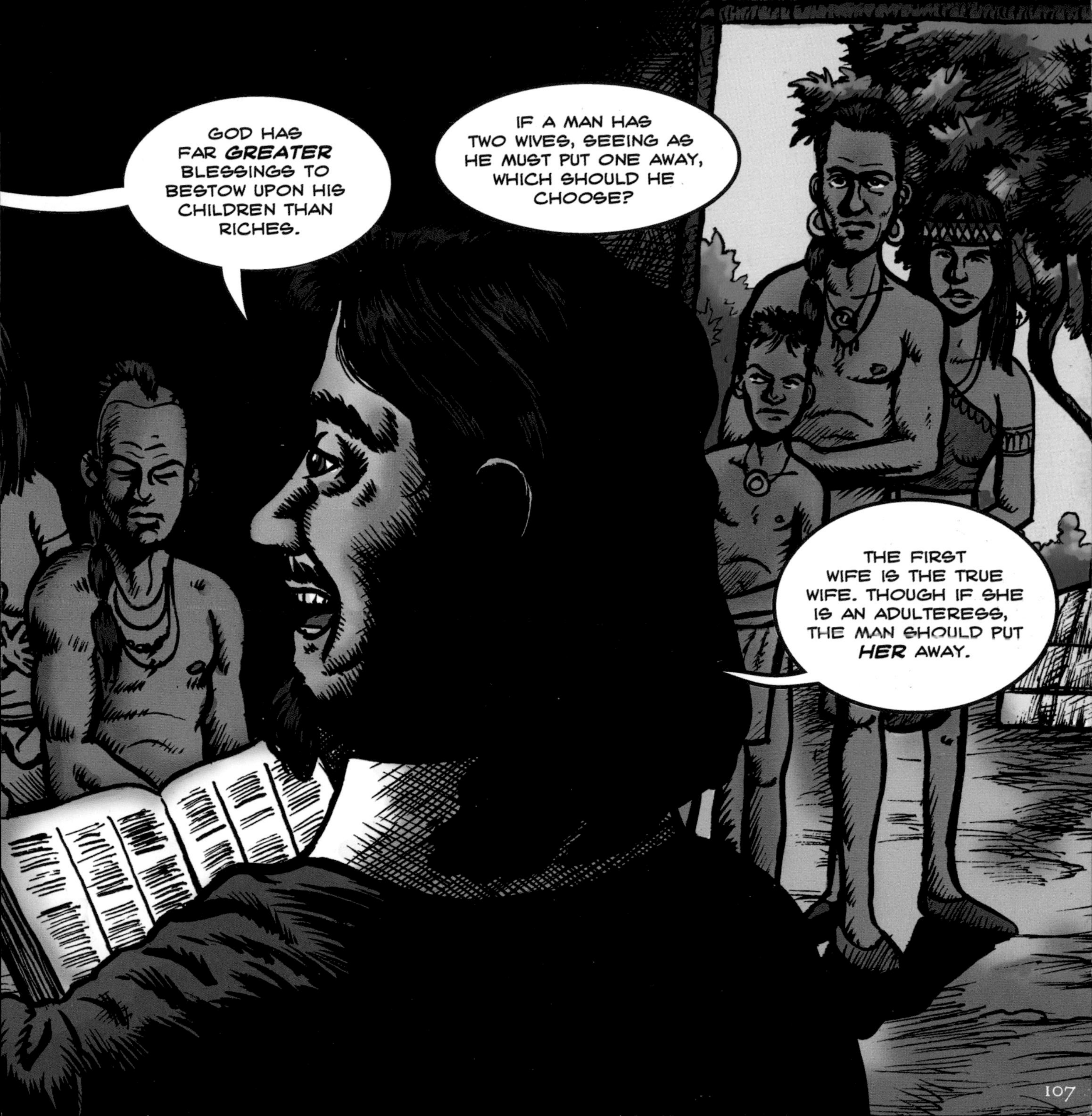
GOD HAS FAR GREATER BLESSINGS TO BESTOW UPON HIS CHILDREN THAN RICHES.
IF A MAN HAS TWO WIVES, SEEING AS HE MUST PUT ONE AWAY, WHICH SHOULD HE CHOOSE?
THE FIRST WIFE IS THE TRUE WIFE. THOUGH IF SHE IS AN ADULTERESS, THE MAN SHOULD PUT HER AWAY.

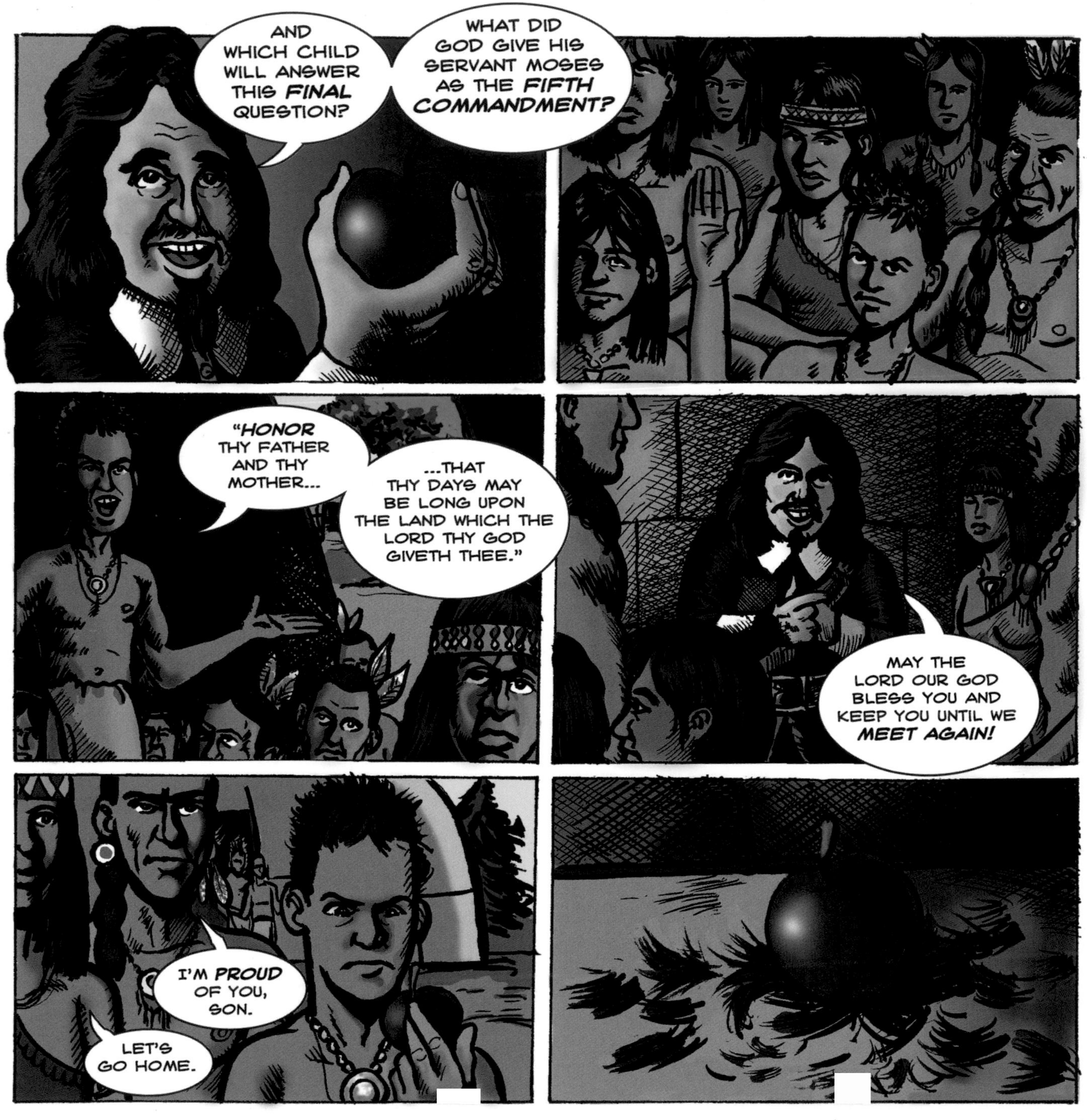
AND WHICH CHILD WILL ANSWER THIS FINAL QUESTION?
WHAT DID GOD GIVE HIS SERVANT MOSES AS THE FIFTH COMMANDMENT?
"HONOR THY FATHER AND THY MOTHER...
...THAT THY DAYS MAY BE LONG UPON THE LAND WHICH THE LORD THY GOD GIVETH THEE."
MAY THE LORD OUR GOD BLESS YOU AND KEEP YOU UNTIL WE MEET AGAIN!
I'M PROUD OF YOU, SON.
LET'S GO HOME.

Sui Generis, a Short Introduction to Ezekiel Cheever

Story by Christina Rice, Art by Steve Harrison,
and Letters by Jason Hanley

The Boston Latin School, which was established in 1635, was the first public school in America and set a standard for public education that has persisted to this day.

One of the school's earliest headmasters was a man named Ezekiel Cheever, who had a long history of teaching in America before taking the job at the Boston Latin School.

Cheever worked for more than seventy years as a teacher, but his longest, last, and most memorable tenure was his time spent in the Latin School. His publication *Accidence: A Short Introduction to the Latin Tongue* appeared in twenty editions by 1785 and was again published in 1838. It came to be regarded as the standard Latin textbook throughout colonial New England.

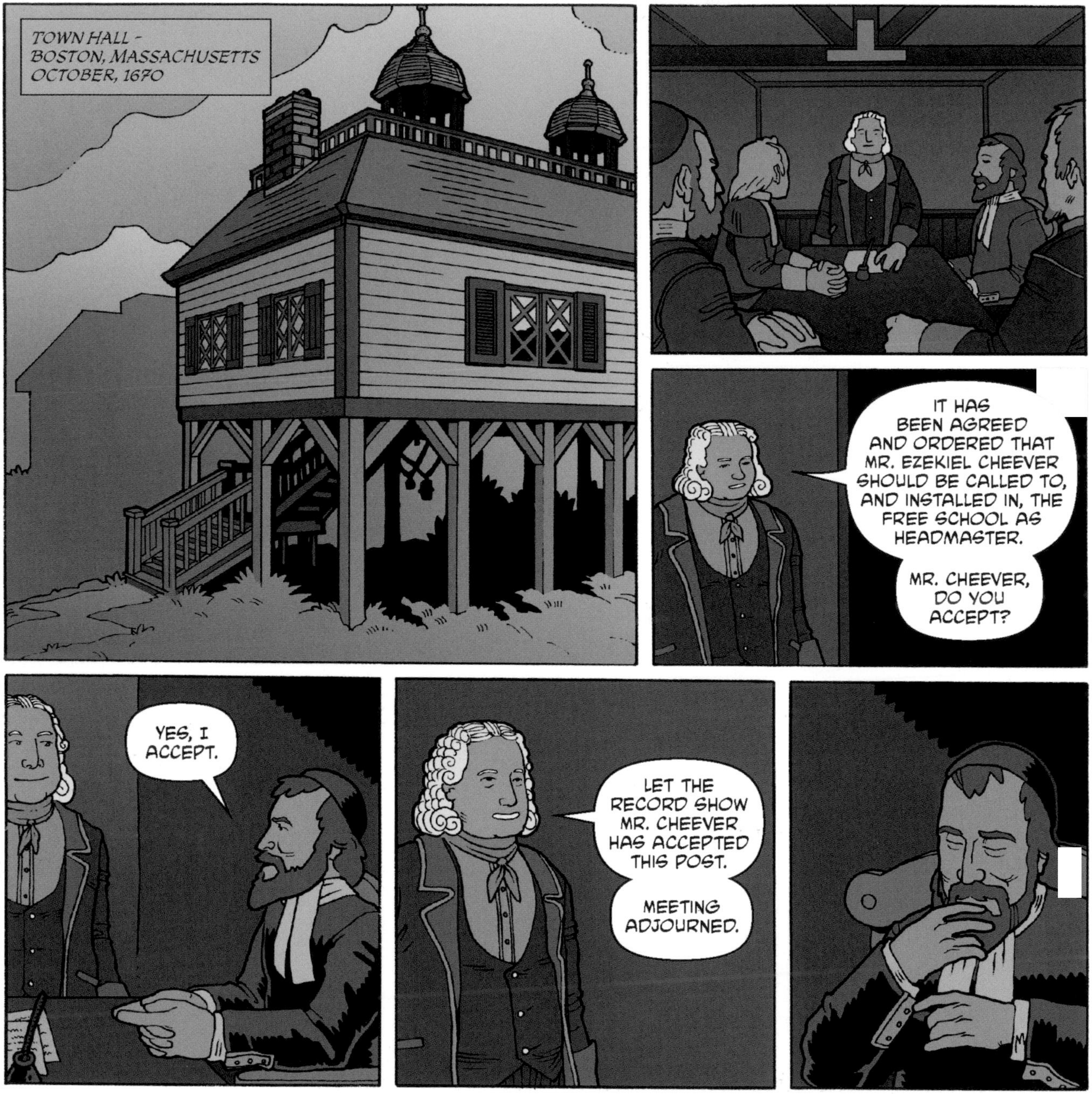
TOWN HALL - BOSTON, MASSACHUSETTS OCTOBER, 1670
IT HAS BEEN AGREED AND ORDERED THAT MR. EZEKIEL CHEEVER SHOULD BE CALLED TO, AND INSTALLED IN, THE FREE SCHOOL AS HEADMASTER.
MR. CHEEVER, DO YOU ACCEPT?
YES, I ACCEPT.
LET THE RECORD SHOW MR. CHEEVER HAS ACCEPTED THIS POST.
MEETING ADJOURNED.

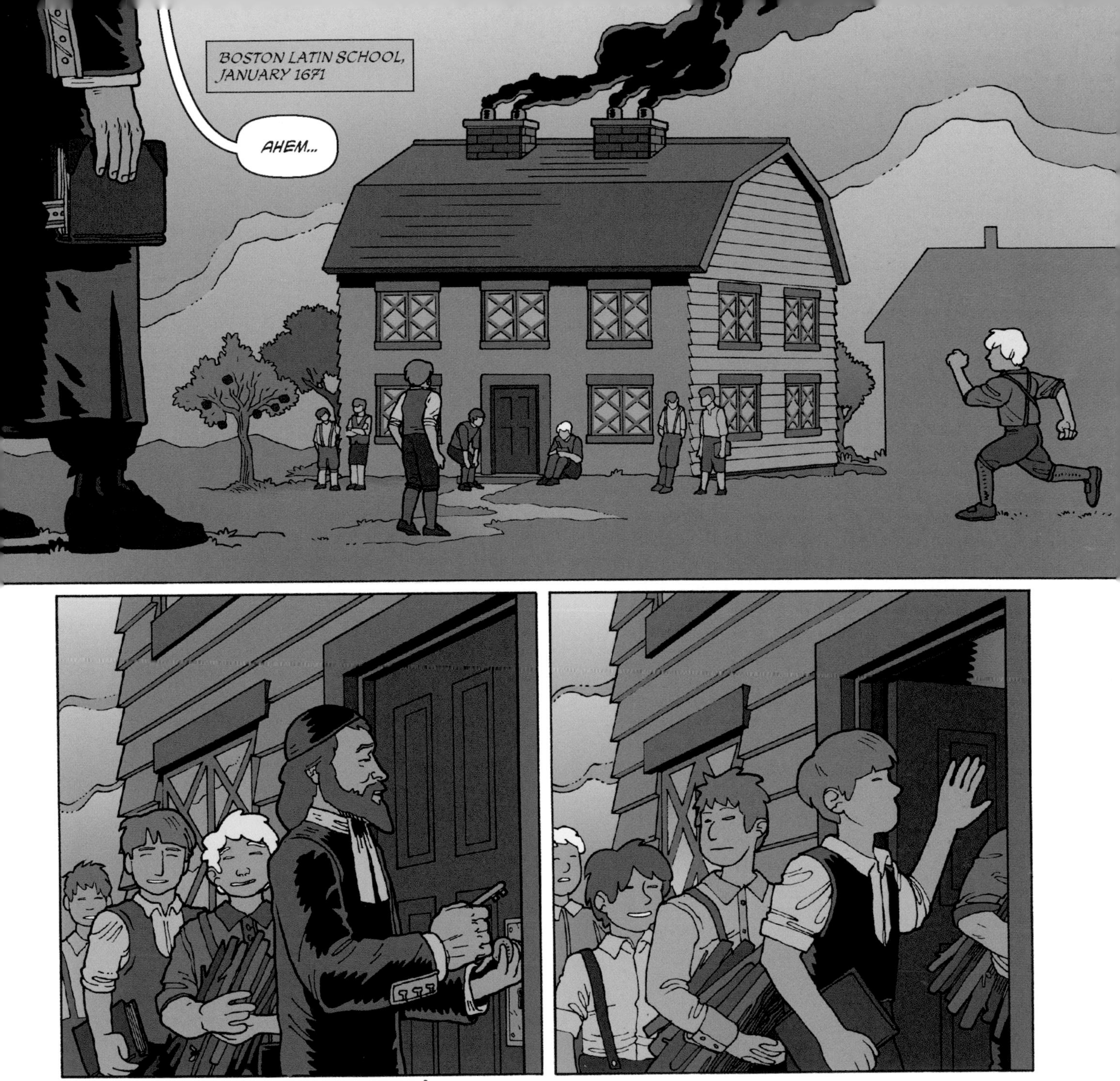
BOSTON LATIN SCHOOL,
JANUARY 1671
AHEM...

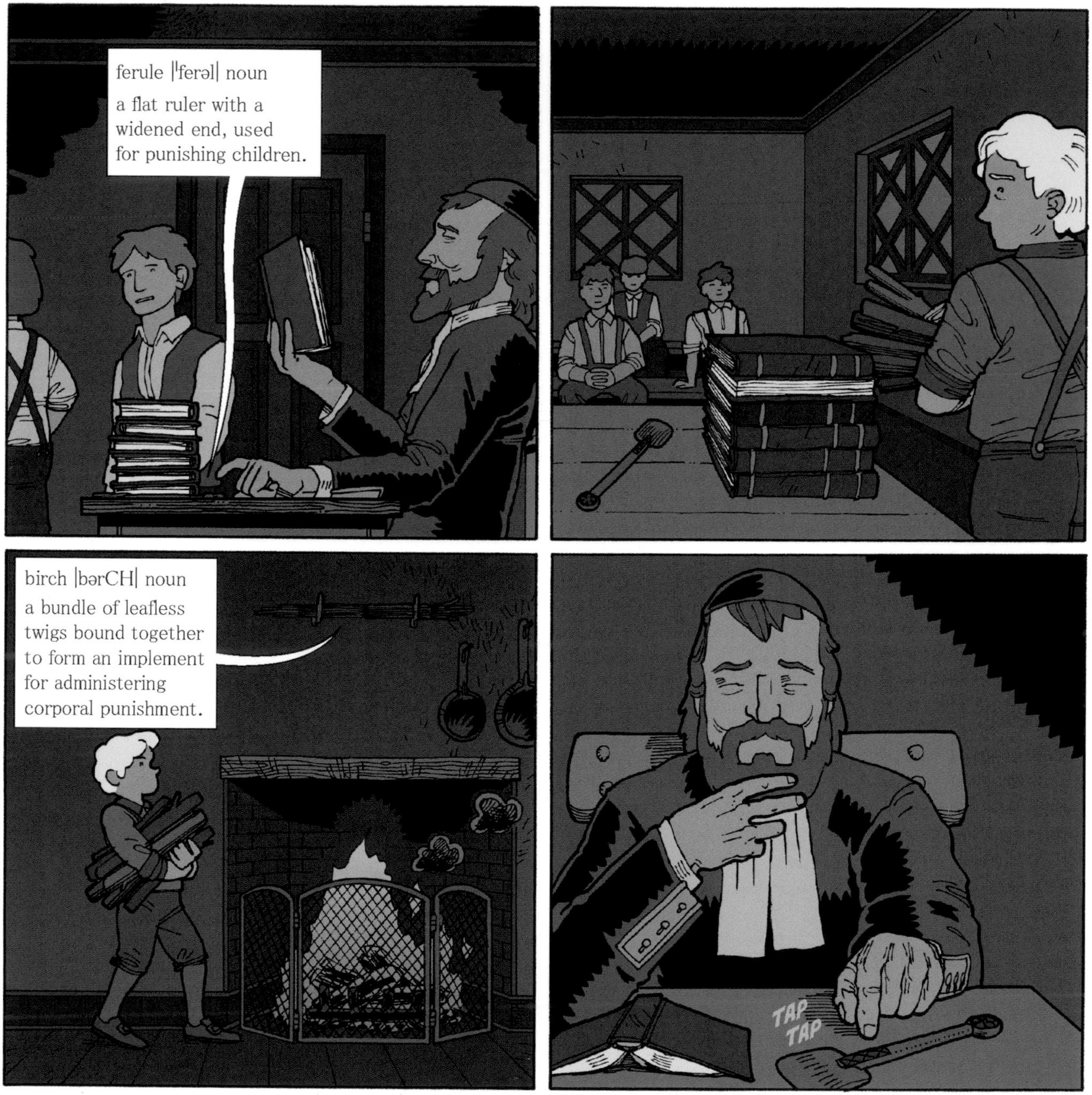
ferule |ˈferəl| noun
a flat ruler with a widened end, used for punishing children.
birch |bərCH| noun
a bundle of leafless twigs bound together to form an implement for administering corporal punishment.
TAP TAP

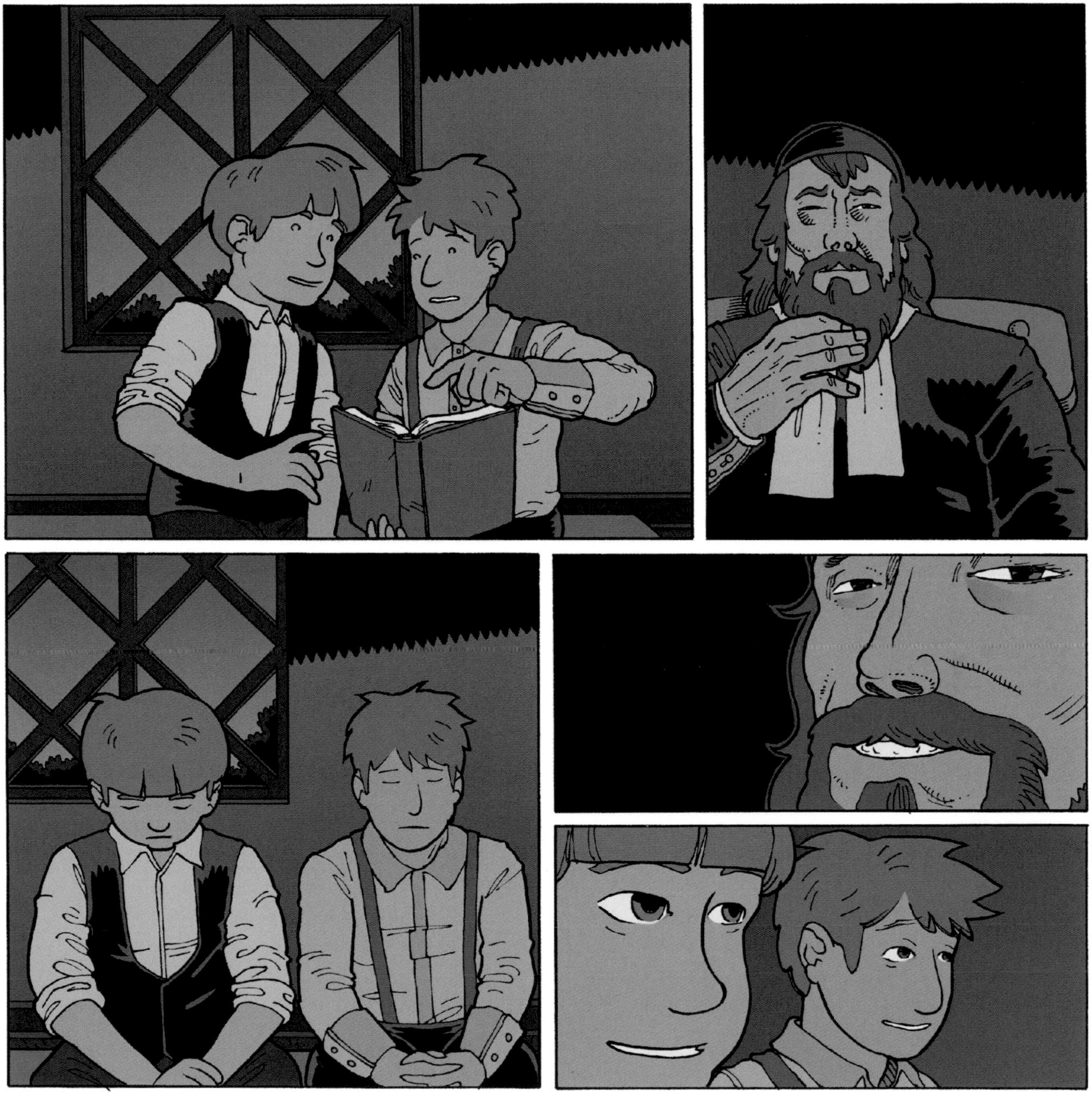

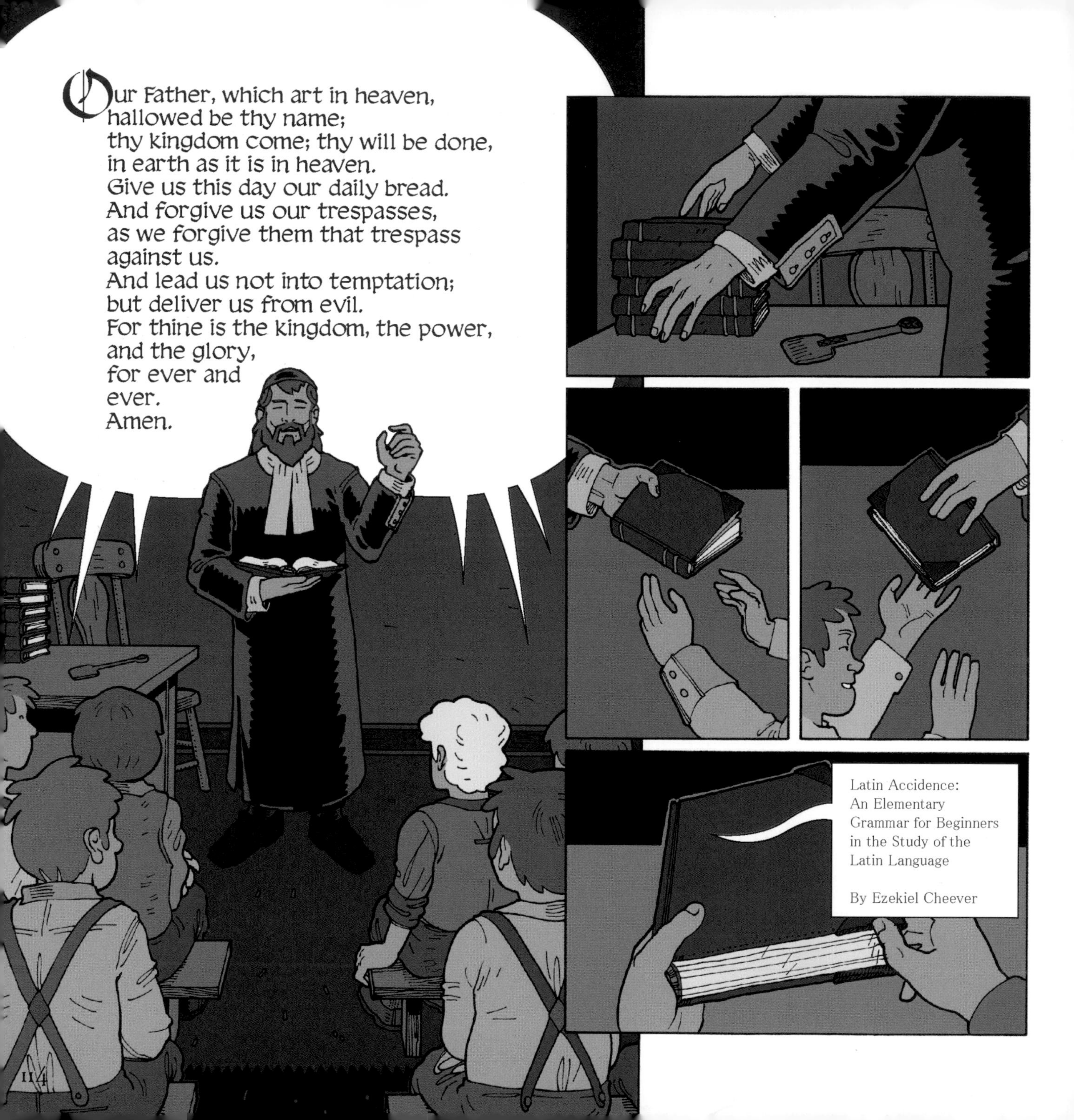
Our Father, which art in heaven,
hallowed be thy name;
thy kingdom come; thy will be done,
in earth as it is in heaven.
Give us this day our daily bread.
And forgive us our trespasses,
as we forgive them that trespass
against us.
And lead us not into temptation;
but deliver us from evil.
For thine is the kingdom, the power,
and the glory,
for ever and
ever.
Amen.
Latin Accidence:
An Elementary
Grammar for Beginners
in the Study of the
Latin Language
By Ezekiel Cheever

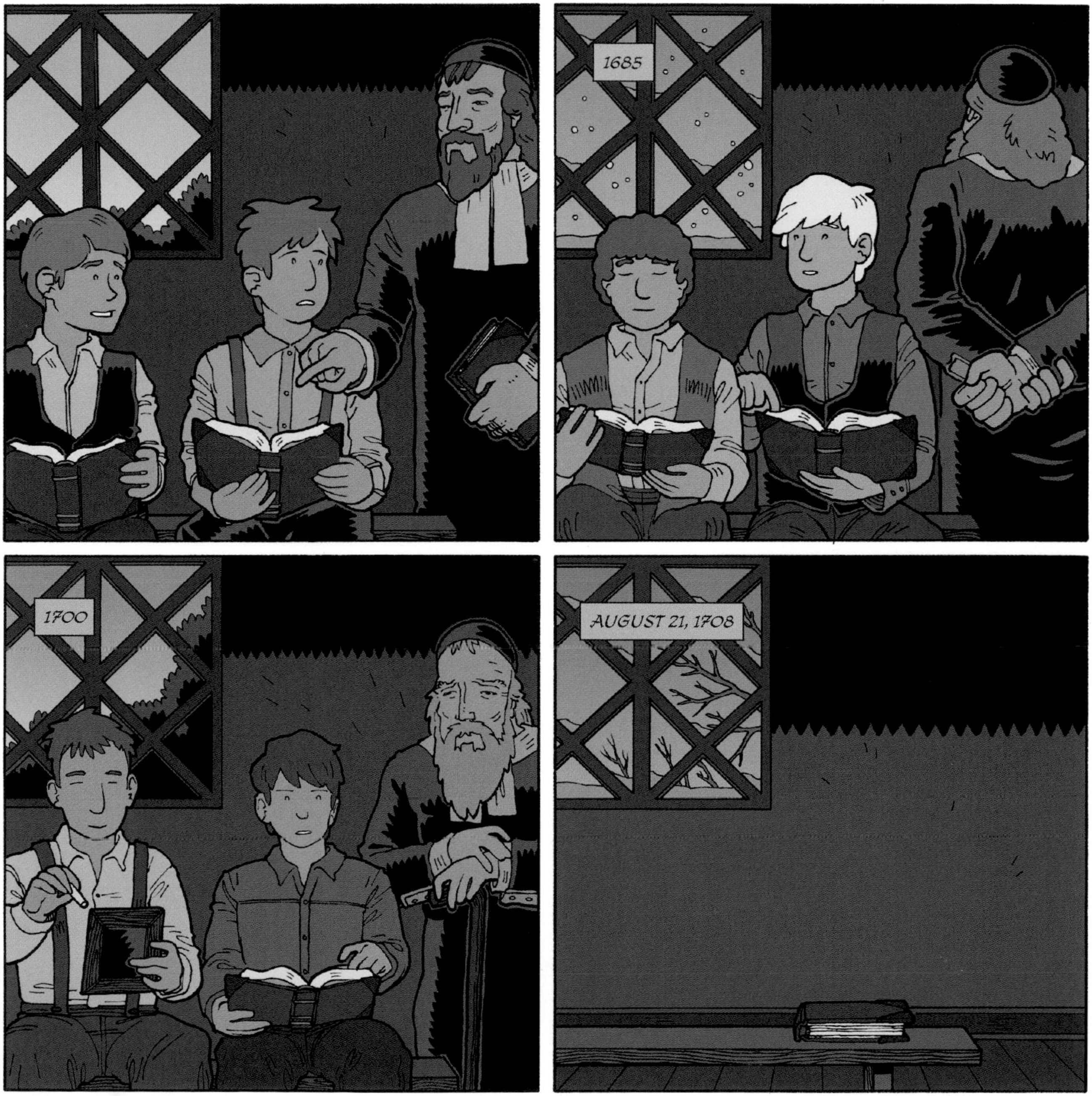
1685
1700
AUGUST 21, 1708

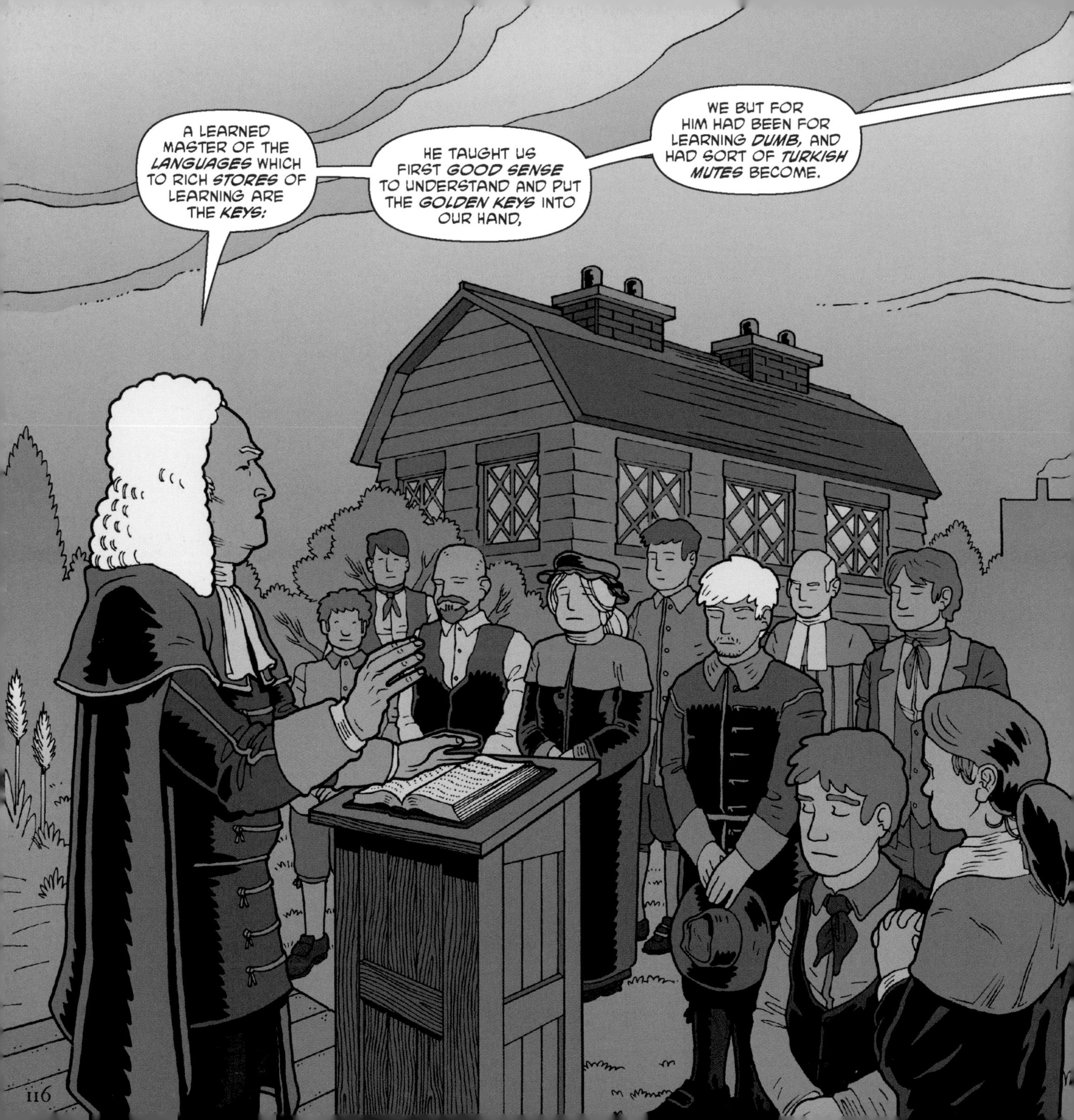
A LEARNED MASTER OF THE LANGUAGES WHICH TO RICH STORES OF LEARNING ARE THE KEYS:
HE TAUGHT US FIRST GOOD SENSE TO UNDERSTAND AND PUT THE GOLDEN KEYS INTO OUR HAND,
WE BUT FOR HIM HAD BEEN FOR LEARNING DUMB, AND HAD SORT OF TURKISH MUTES BECOME.

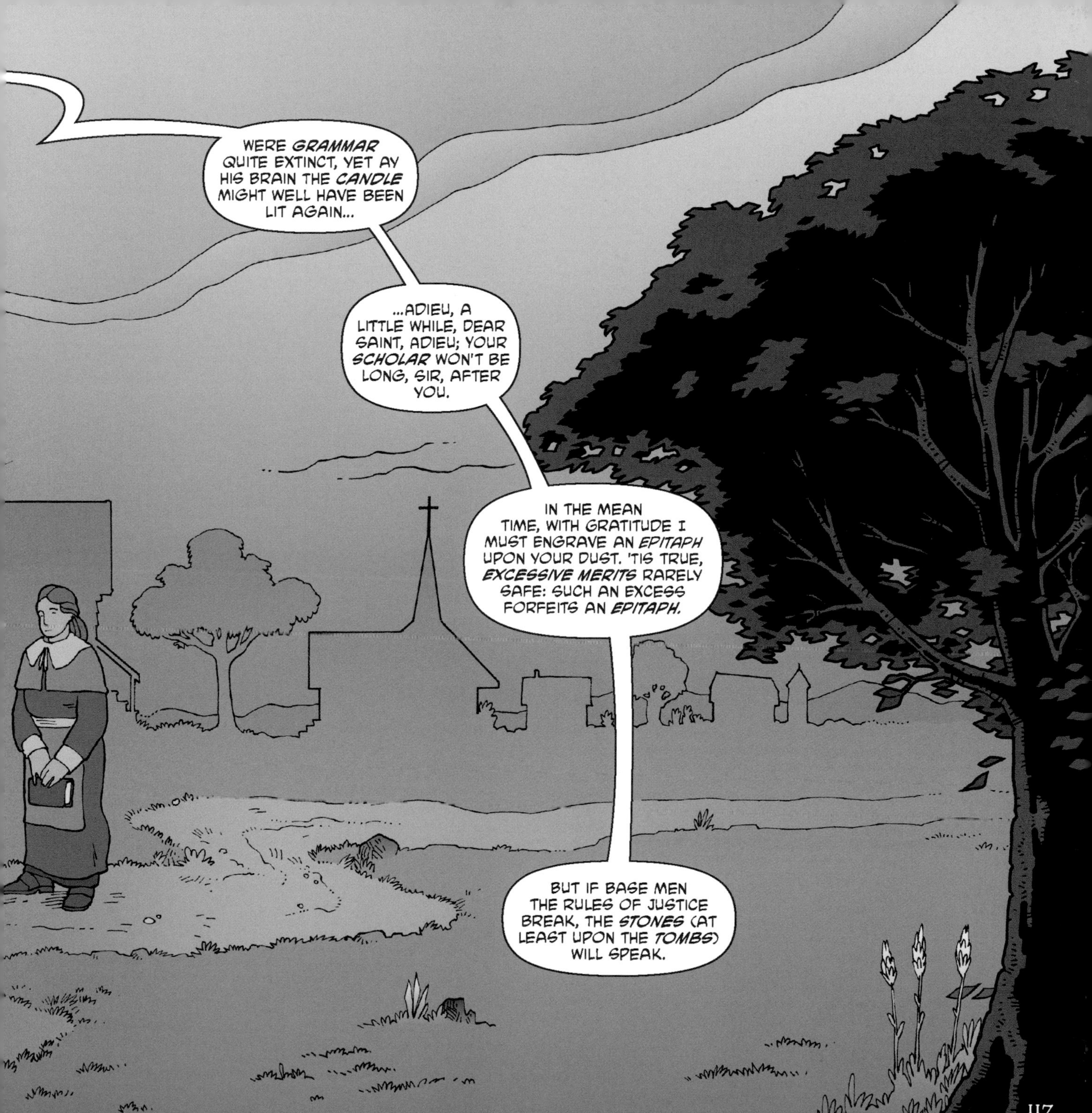
WERE *GRAMMAR* QUITE EXTINCT, YET AY HIS BRAIN THE *CANDLE* MIGHT WELL HAVE BEEN LIT AGAIN...
...ADIEU, A LITTLE WHILE, DEAR SAINT, ADIEU; YOUR *SCHOLAR* WON'T BE LONG, SIR, AFTER YOU.
IN THE MEAN TIME, WITH GRATITUDE I MUST ENGRAVE AN *EPITAPH* UPON YOUR DUST. 'TIS TRUE, *EXCESSIVE MERITS* RARELY SAFE: SUCH AN EXCESS FORFEITS AN *EPITAPH.*
BUT IF BASE MEN THE RULES OF JUSTICE BREAK, THE *STONES* (AT LEAST UPON THE *TOMBS*) WILL SPEAK.

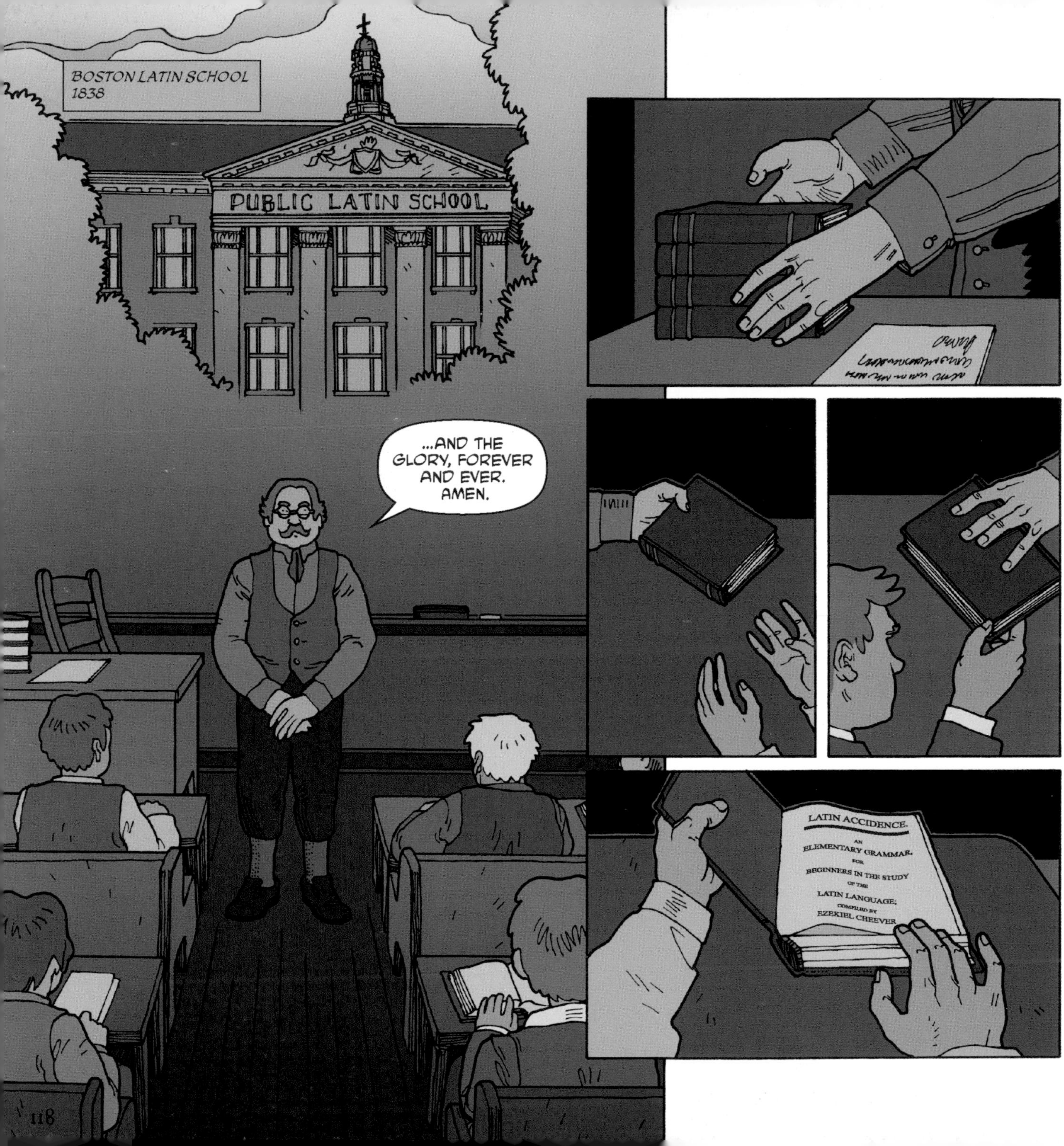

BOSTON LATIN SCHOOL
1838
PUBLIC LATIN SCHOOL
...AND THE GLORY, FOREVER AND EVER. AMEN.
LATIN ACCIDENCE.
AN
ELEMENTARY GRAMMAR,
FOR
BEGINNERS IN THE STUDY
OF THE
LATIN LANGUAGE;
COMPILED BY
EZEKIEL CHEEVER

Interested in learning Latin? Below is the first page of Cheever's *Latin Accidence*. The book was used long after Ezekiel Cheever's death in 1708. In fact, there were twenty editions released by 1785! This page is taken from the 1838 version.

OF THE LATIN LETTERS AND POINTS, &c.

THE Latin letters are commonly formed like the English. K, W, Y, and Z, are not properly Latin letters, though sometimes used in Latin words derived from other languages; the rest of the Latin letters are the same as those of the English.

Capital letters are used in the beginning of sentences, verses, and proper names.

Letters are either vowels or consonants.

A vowel may be fully and perfectly sounded of itself; and there are five Latin vowels, *a, e, i, o, u;* to which is added the Greek vowel *y.*

A consonant cannot be sounded without a vowel; all the letters, except the vowels, are called consonants; *j* and *v* are always consonants.

A diphthong is two vowels joined together in one syllable; and the Latin diphthongs are chiefly six — *æ, œ, ai, au, ei, eu.*

Instead of *æ* and *œ*, we commonly pronounce (*e*); *c*, before *e, i, y, æ, œ*, is sounded like *s.*

Ti, before a vowel, is sounded like *si*, unless *s* goes before the *t.*

Beside the letters, there are other characters, viz.

A period, marked thus (.) which is put at the end of a sentence.

A colon, thus (:) a semicolon, thus (;) a comma, thus (,) are shorter stops or pauses, the sense being still continued;

King Philip

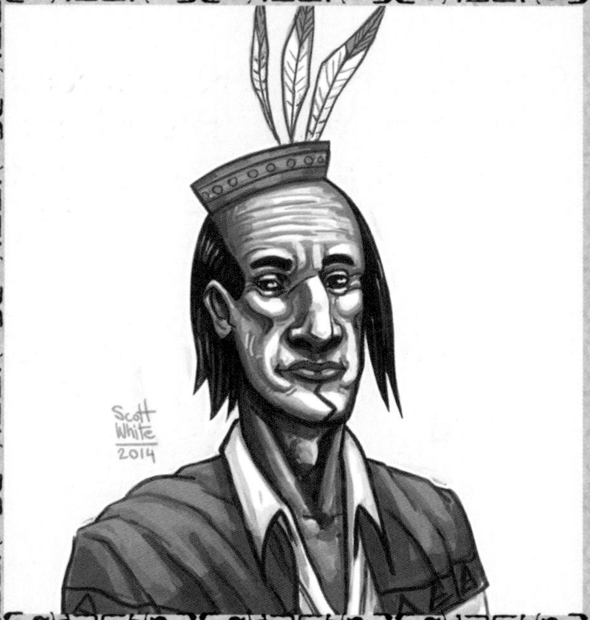
Scott
White
2014

Real Name: Metacomet
Occupation: Wampanoag Sachem
Legal Status: Member of the Wampanoag tribe
Place of Birth: Patuxet (Plymouth)
Bio: Metacomet was the second son of the Wampanoag Sachem Massasoit (who played a significant role in helping the Plymouth Colony survive) and became Sachem upon the early death of his older brother, Wamsutta. Metacomet tried to cœxist with the colonists, learning English, aiding in trade, and legally taking the English name Philip. However, tensions began to rise as the English continued to claim Native land, and the once autonomous Wampanoag people were largely disarmed and forced to comply with British law.

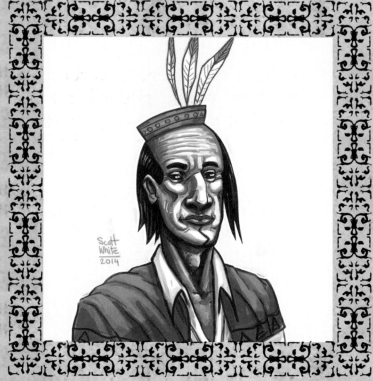

As a result of the rising tensions, Native American tribes began to raid colonial towns. First they attacked isolated homes, then smaller towns and supply lines, and finally the town of Springfield, which was almost entirely burned to the ground. The colonies eventually joined together and declared war on the Native Americans in 1675. The war was long fought, and while casualties on both sides were heavy, the long-term effects on Native American tribes were completely devastating.

Jason Rodriguez and Scott White

Church and Anawan
Story by Nate DiMeo and Art by Mal Jones

The Great Migration, in which tens of thousands of English colonists came to the New World, resulted in a large portion of Native American land being taken over by the colonists. The Wampanoag Sachem, Metacomet (known to the English as King Philip), believed that his treaty with the settlers of Plymouth protected Wampanoag land... but he was wrong.

John Sassoman, a Harvard-educated Wampanoag and Christian convert who was also an advisor to Metacomet, told the Governor of Plymouth that Metacomet was planning to gather allies and attack English settlements. Shortly after that, Sassoman was found dead.

Metacomet was cleared of the murder, but three Wampanoag were convicted and hung. The verdict created friction between the Wampanoag and the Plymouth settlers, and this tension eventually led to war.

In August 1676, Metacomet was hunted down and killed by forces led by Major Benjamin Church. The Wampanoag continued to fight, however, under the leadership of a man named Anawan...

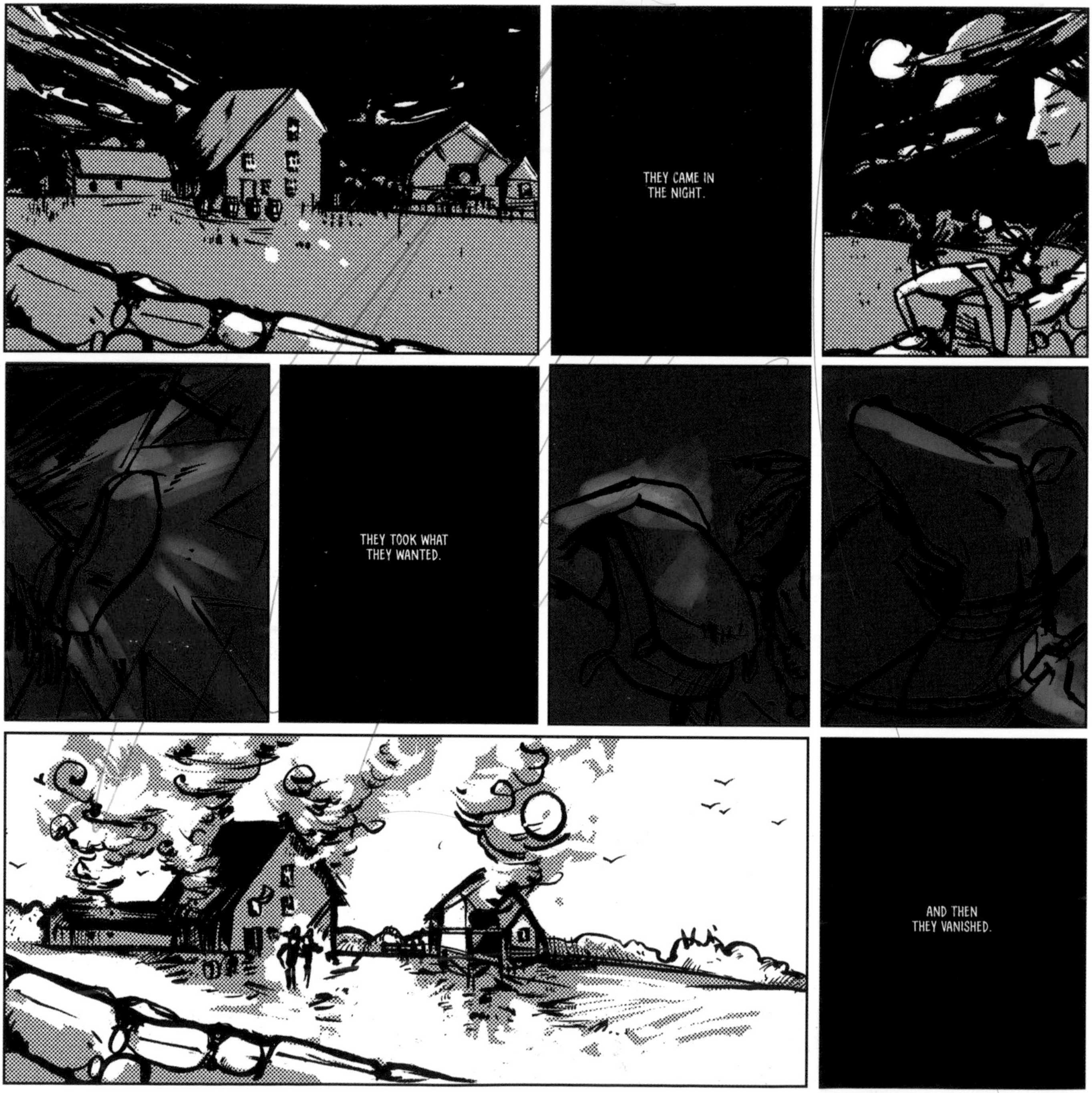
THEY CAME IN THE NIGHT.
THEY TOOK WHAT THEY WANTED.
AND THEN THEY VANISHED.

IN THE SUMMER OF MY THIRTY-SEVENTH YEAR, I RETURNED HOME AFTER A YEAR AT WAR TO TEND TO MY FIELDS AND TO MY FAMILY.

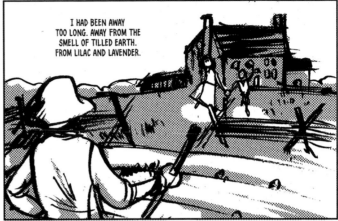

I HAD BEEN AWAY TOO LONG. AWAY FROM THE SMELL OF TILLED EARTH. FROM LILAC AND LAVENDER.

FROM THE BREEZE THAT CARRIED SALT AIR UP FROM RHODE ISLAND SOUND TO OUR HOME AT LITTLE COMPTON.

OR "SOGKONATE," AS OUR INDIAN NEIGHBORS CALLED OUR MUTUAL HOME WHERE THE LAND MET THE SEA.

WHAT CHEER, CAPTAIN?

GOOD EVENING TO YOU, SIR!

IT IS *ANAWAN*, SIR.

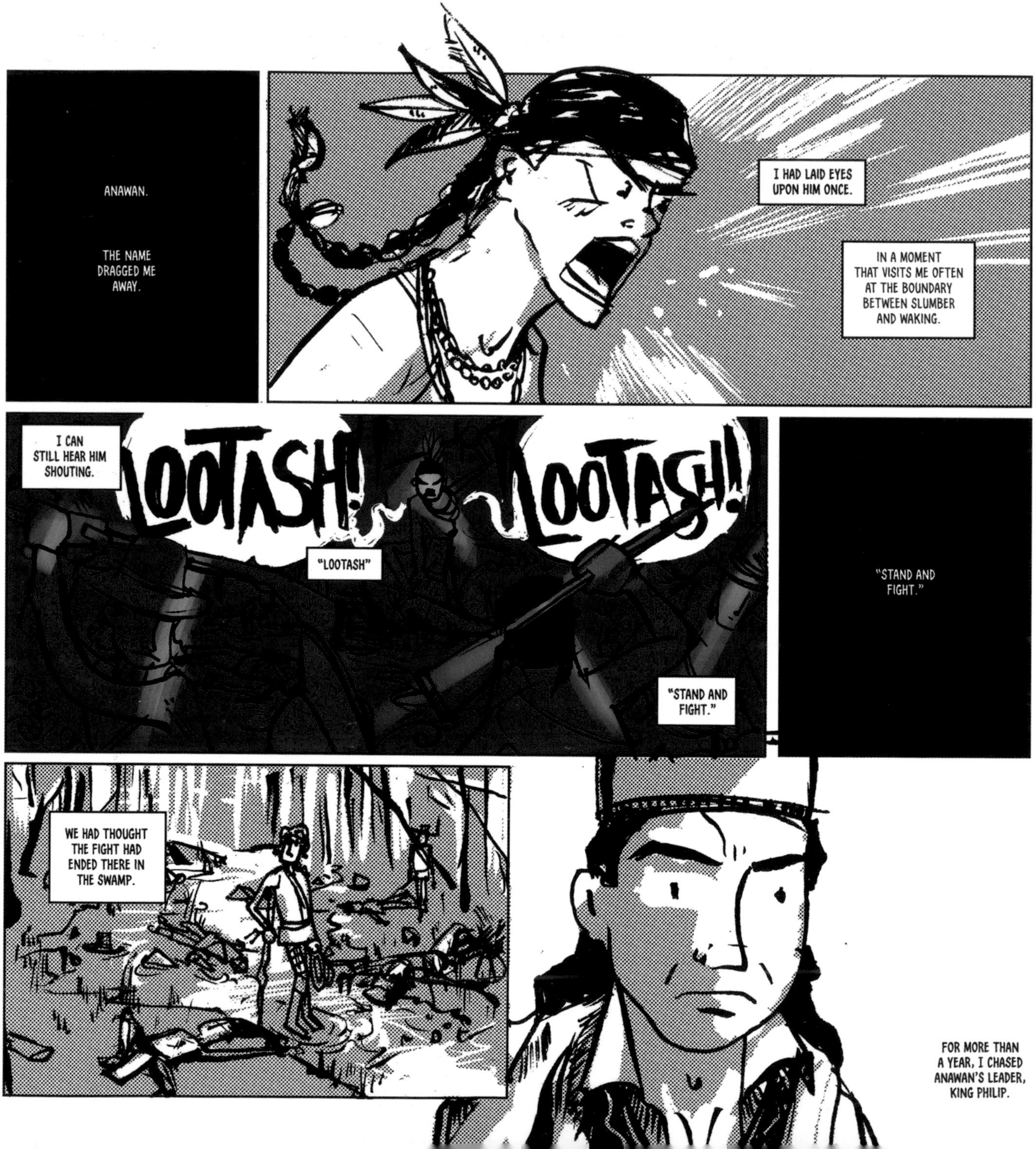
ANAWAN.
THE NAME DRAGGED ME AWAY.
I HAD LAID EYES UPON HIM ONCE.
IN A MOMENT THAT VISITS ME OFTEN AT THE BOUNDARY BETWEEN SLUMBER AND WAKING.
I CAN STILL HEAR HIM SHOUTING.
LOOTASH!
LOOTASH!!
"LOOTASH"
"STAND AND FIGHT."
"STAND AND FIGHT."
WE HAD THOUGHT THE FIGHT HAD ENDED THERE IN THE SWAMP.
FOR MORE THAN A YEAR, I CHASED ANAWAN'S LEADER, KING PHILIP.

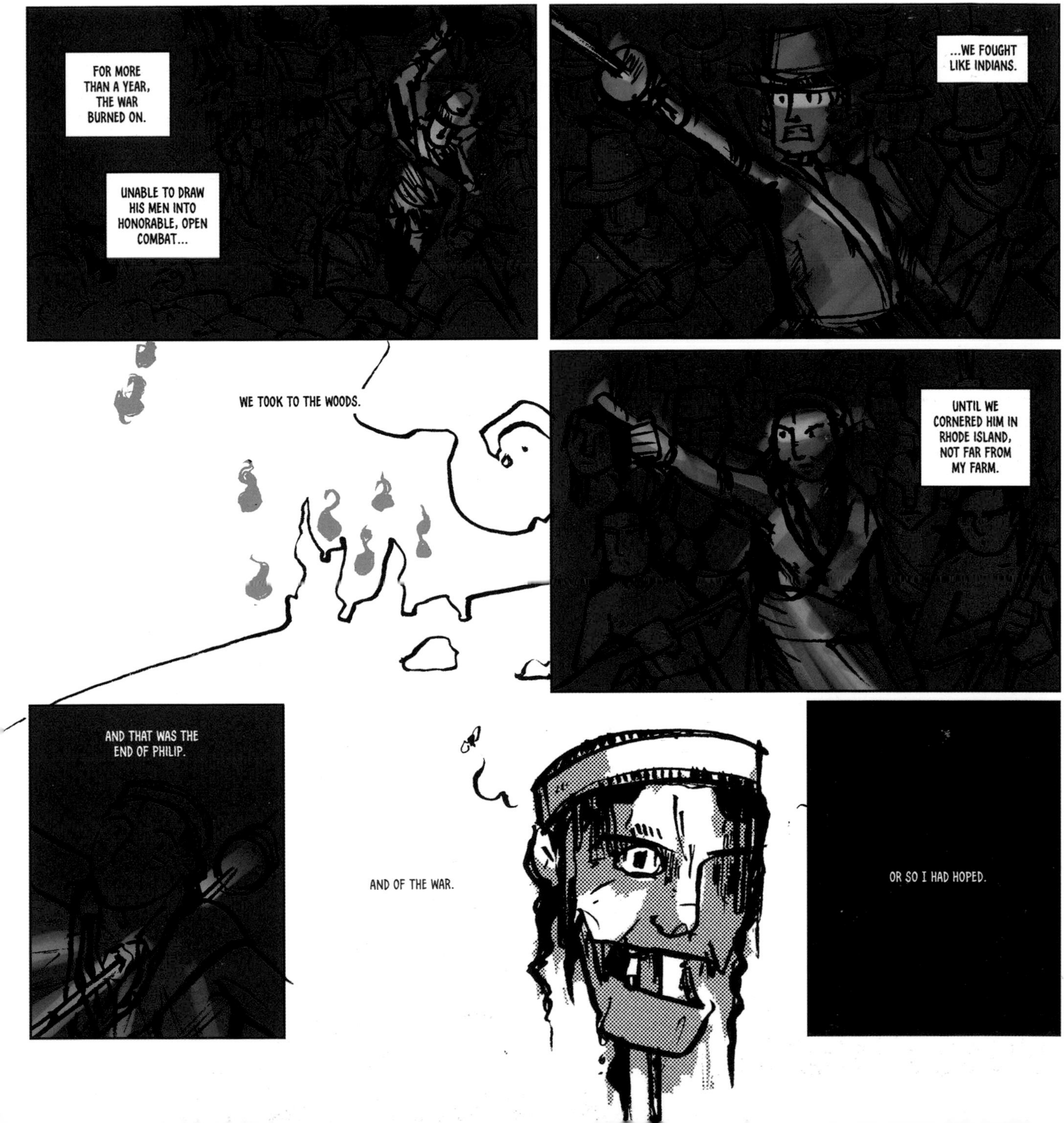
FOR MORE THAN A YEAR, THE WAR BURNED ON.
UNABLE TO DRAW HIS MEN INTO HONORABLE, OPEN COMBAT...
...WE FOUGHT LIKE INDIANS.
WE TOOK TO THE WOODS.
UNTIL WE CORNERED HIM IN RHODE ISLAND, NOT FAR FROM MY FARM.
AND THAT WAS THE END OF PHILIP.
AND OF THE WAR.
OR SO I HAD HOPED.

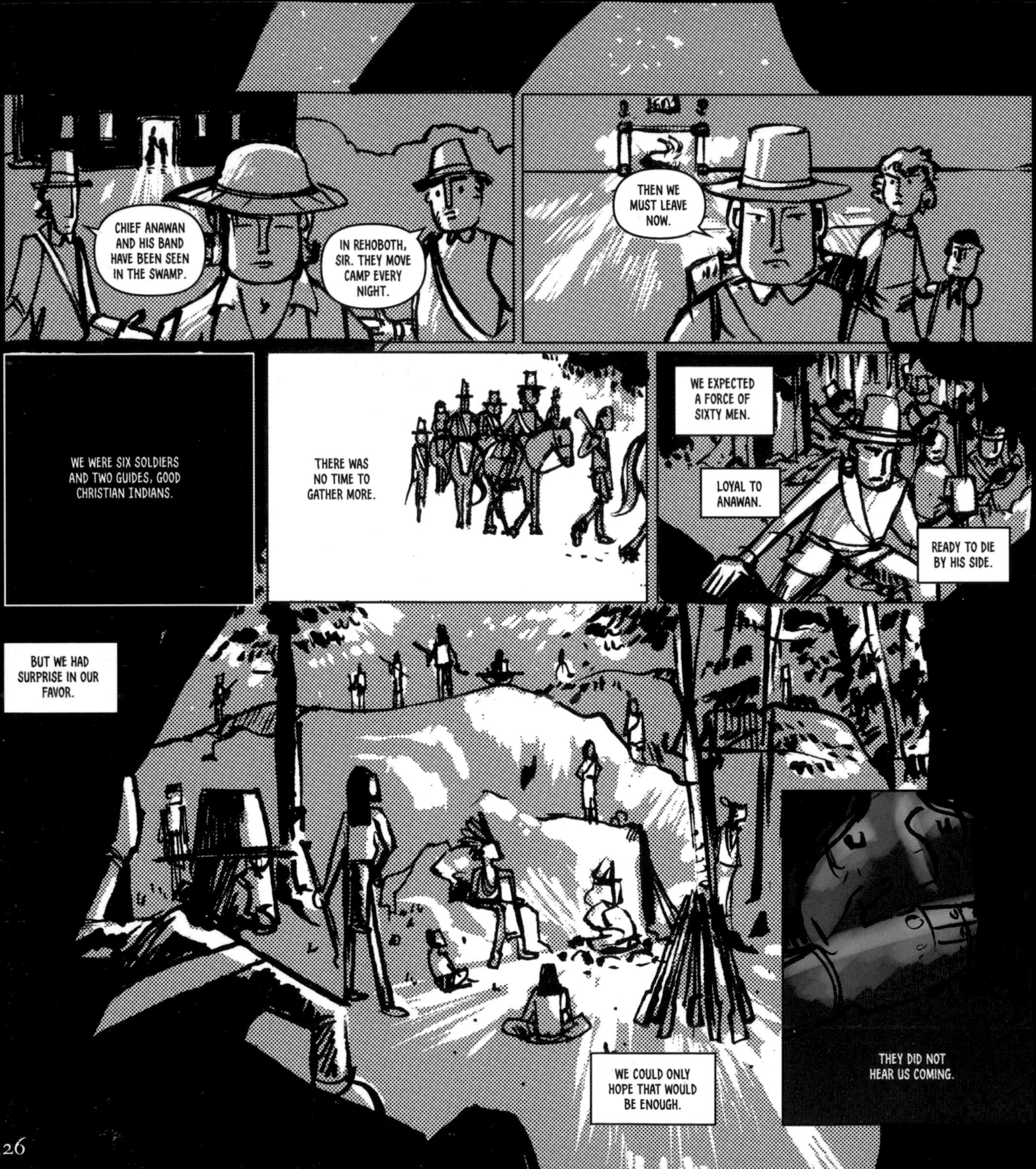
CHIEF ANAWAN AND HIS BAND HAVE BEEN SEEN IN THE SWAMP.
IN REHOBOTH, SIR. THEY MOVE CAMP EVERY NIGHT.
THEN WE MUST LEAVE NOW.
WE WERE SIX SOLDIERS AND TWO GUIDES, GOOD CHRISTIAN INDIANS.
THERE WAS NO TIME TO GATHER MORE.
WE EXPECTED A FORCE OF SIXTY MEN.
LOYAL TO ANAWAN.
READY TO DIE BY HIS SIDE.
BUT WE HAD SURPRISE IN OUR FAVOR.
WE COULD ONLY HOPE THAT WOULD BE ENOUGH.
THEY DID NOT HEAR US COMING.

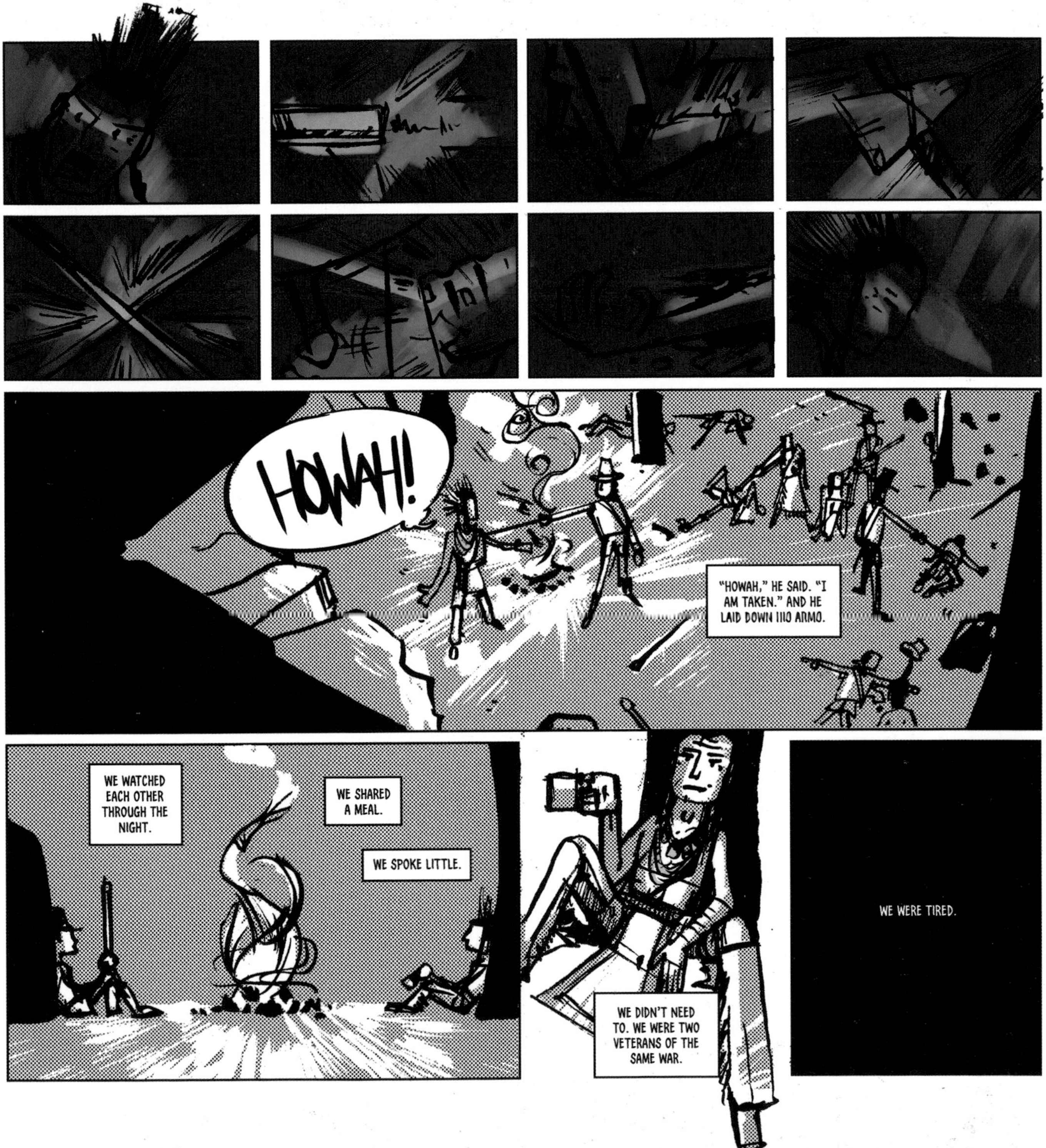
HOWAH!
"HOWAH," HE SAID. "I AM TAKEN." AND HE LAID DOWN HIS ARMS.
WE WATCHED EACH OTHER THROUGH THE NIGHT.
WE SHARED A MEAL.
WE SPOKE LITTLE.
WE DIDN'T NEED TO. WE WERE TWO VETERANS OF THE SAME WAR.
WE WERE TIRED.

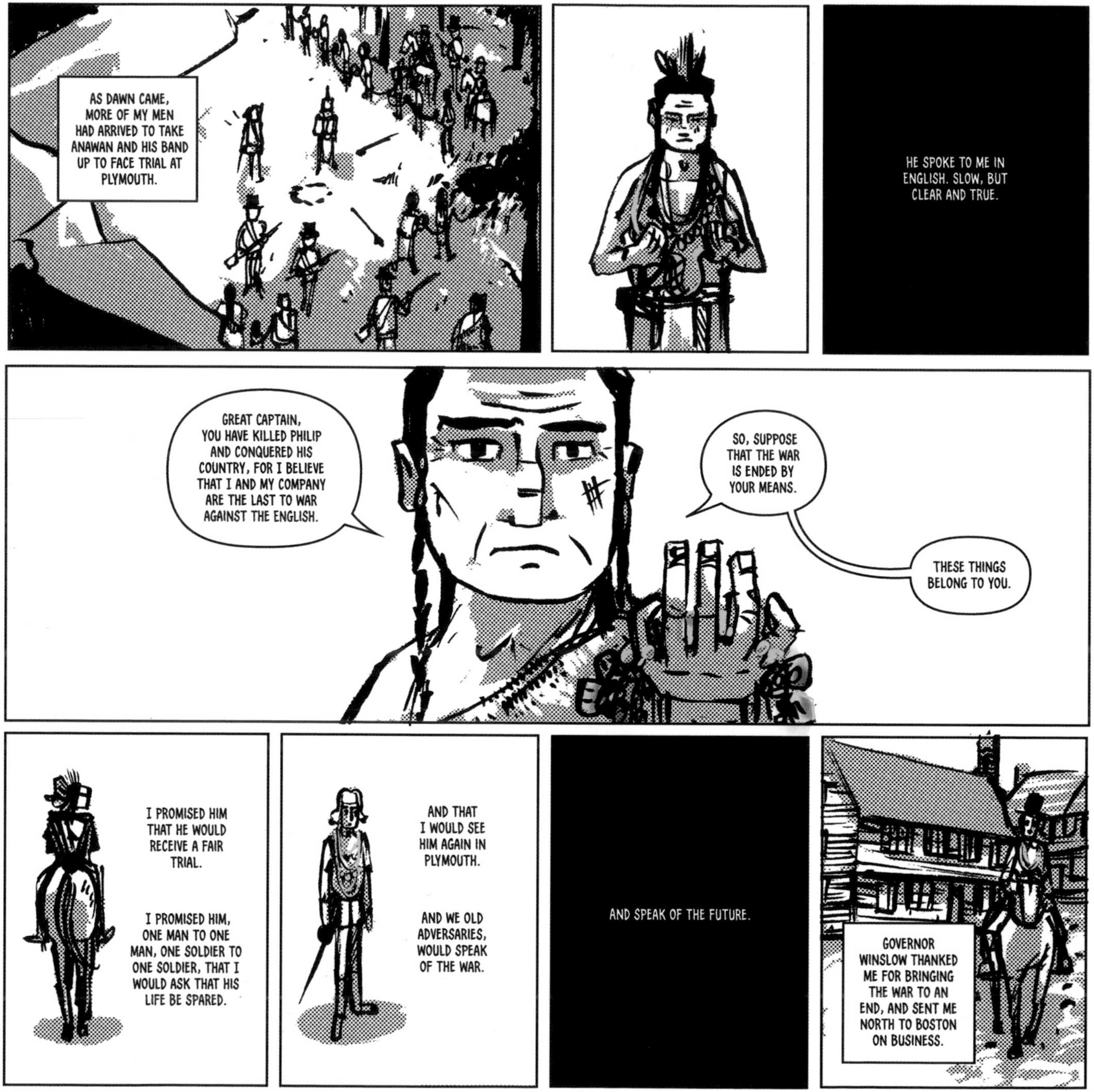

AS DAWN CAME, MORE OF MY MEN HAD ARRIVED TO TAKE ANAWAN AND HIS BAND UP TO FACE TRIAL AT PLYMOUTH.
HE SPOKE TO ME IN ENGLISH. SLOW, BUT CLEAR AND TRUE.
GREAT CAPTAIN, YOU HAVE KILLED PHILIP AND CONQUERED HIS COUNTRY, FOR I BELIEVE THAT I AND MY COMPANY ARE THE LAST TO WAR AGAINST THE ENGLISH.
SO, SUPPOSE THAT THE WAR IS ENDED BY YOUR MEANS.
THESE THINGS BELONG TO YOU.
I PROMISED HIM THAT HE WOULD RECEIVE A FAIR TRIAL.
I PROMISED HIM, ONE MAN TO ONE MAN, ONE SOLDIER TO ONE SOLDIER, THAT I WOULD ASK THAT HIS LIFE BE SPARED.
AND THAT I WOULD SEE HIM AGAIN IN PLYMOUTH.
AND WE OLD ADVERSARIES, WOULD SPEAK OF THE WAR.
AND SPEAK OF THE FUTURE.
GOVERNOR WINSLOW THANKED ME FOR BRINGING THE WAR TO AN END, AND SENT ME NORTH TO BOSTON ON BUSINESS.

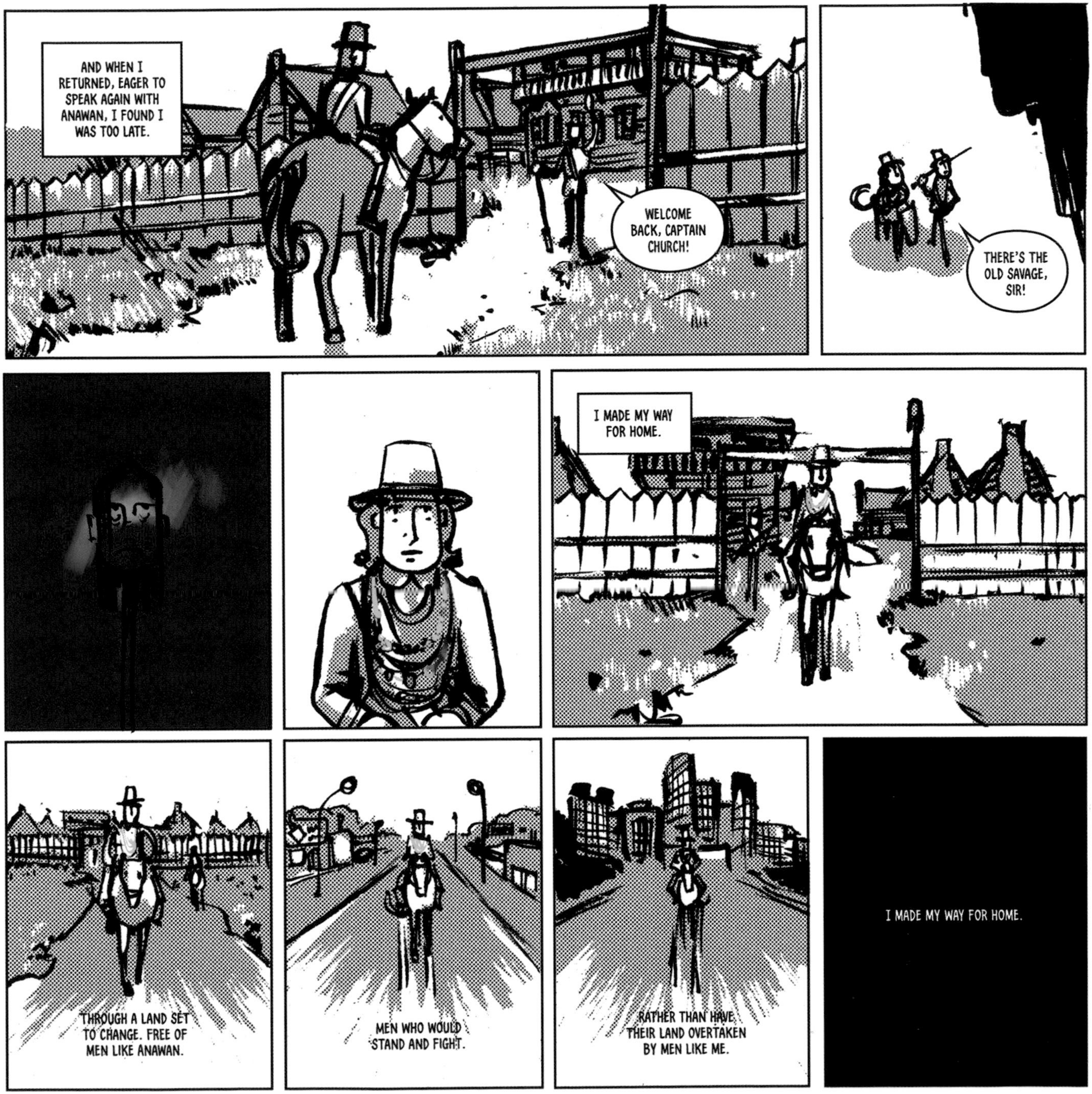
AND WHEN I RETURNED, EAGER TO SPEAK AGAIN WITH ANAWAN, I FOUND I WAS TOO LATE.
WELCOME BACK, CAPTAIN CHURCH!
THERE'S THE OLD SAVAGE, SIR!
I MADE MY WAY FOR HOME.
THROUGH A LAND SET TO CHANGE. FREE OF MEN LIKE ANAWAN.
MEN WHO WOULD STAND AND FIGHT.
RATHER THAN HAVE THEIR LAND OVERTAKEN BY MEN LIKE ME.
I MADE MY WAY FOR HOME.

WRITTEN BY NATE DIMEO / ILLUSTRATED BY MAL JONES

THE HANGING OF GEORGE BURROUGHS
Story and Art by Rafer Roberts

If you ever sat down to watch a production of *The Crucible*, you'd have seen a play in which witchcraft accusations were primarily the result of affairs and longstanding grudges. Although the latter cause was true to an extent, at the core of these grudges is a much richer history than what is presented in Arthur Miller's play.

The truth is, many of Salem's residents had memories of King Philip's War and the subsequent skirmishes in Maine that forced colonists out of the frontier and back into towns like Salem. The grudges that these colonists held were from a time long before the trials began—a time when many people lost their entire families, while others seemed to come out of the conflicts unscathed.

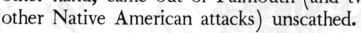

Mercy Lewis, for example, lost her entire family to Native American attacks on Falmouth, Maine. George Burroughs, on the other hand, came out of Falmouth (and two other Native American attacks) unscathed.

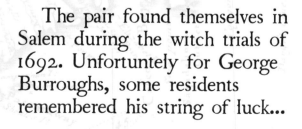

The pair found themselves in Salem during the witch trials of 1692. Unfortuntely for George Burroughs, some residents remembered his string of luck...

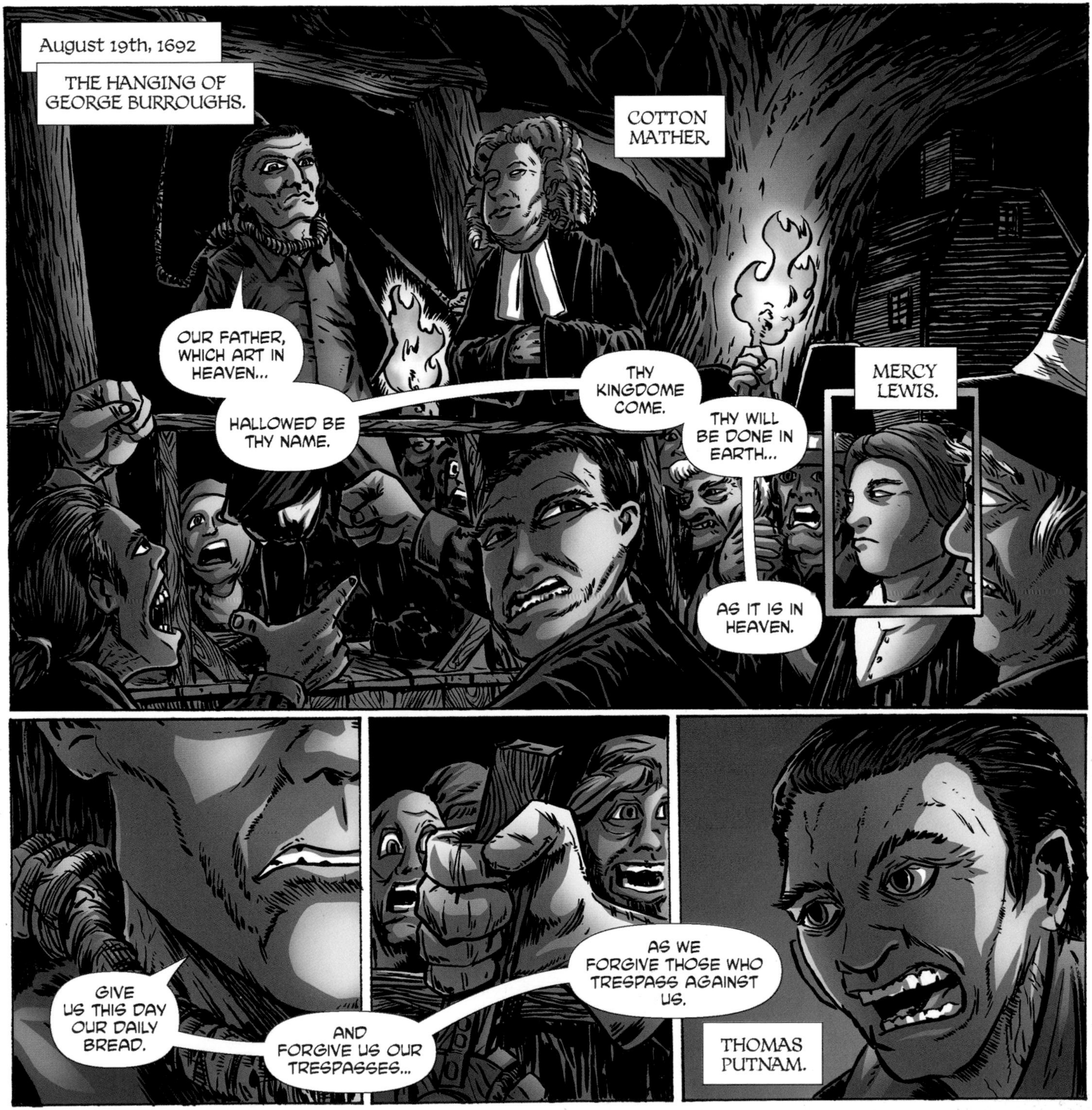

August 19th, 1692
THE HANGING OF GEORGE BURROUGHS.
COTTON MATHER
OUR FATHER, WHICH ART IN HEAVEN...
HALLOWED BE THY NAME.
THY KINGDOME COME.
THY WILL BE DONE IN EARTH...
AS IT IS IN HEAVEN.
MERCY LEWIS.
GIVE US THIS DAY OUR DAILY BREAD.
AND FORGIVE US OUR TRESPASSES...
AS WE FORGIVE THOSE WHO TRESPASS AGAINST US.
THOMAS PUTNAM.

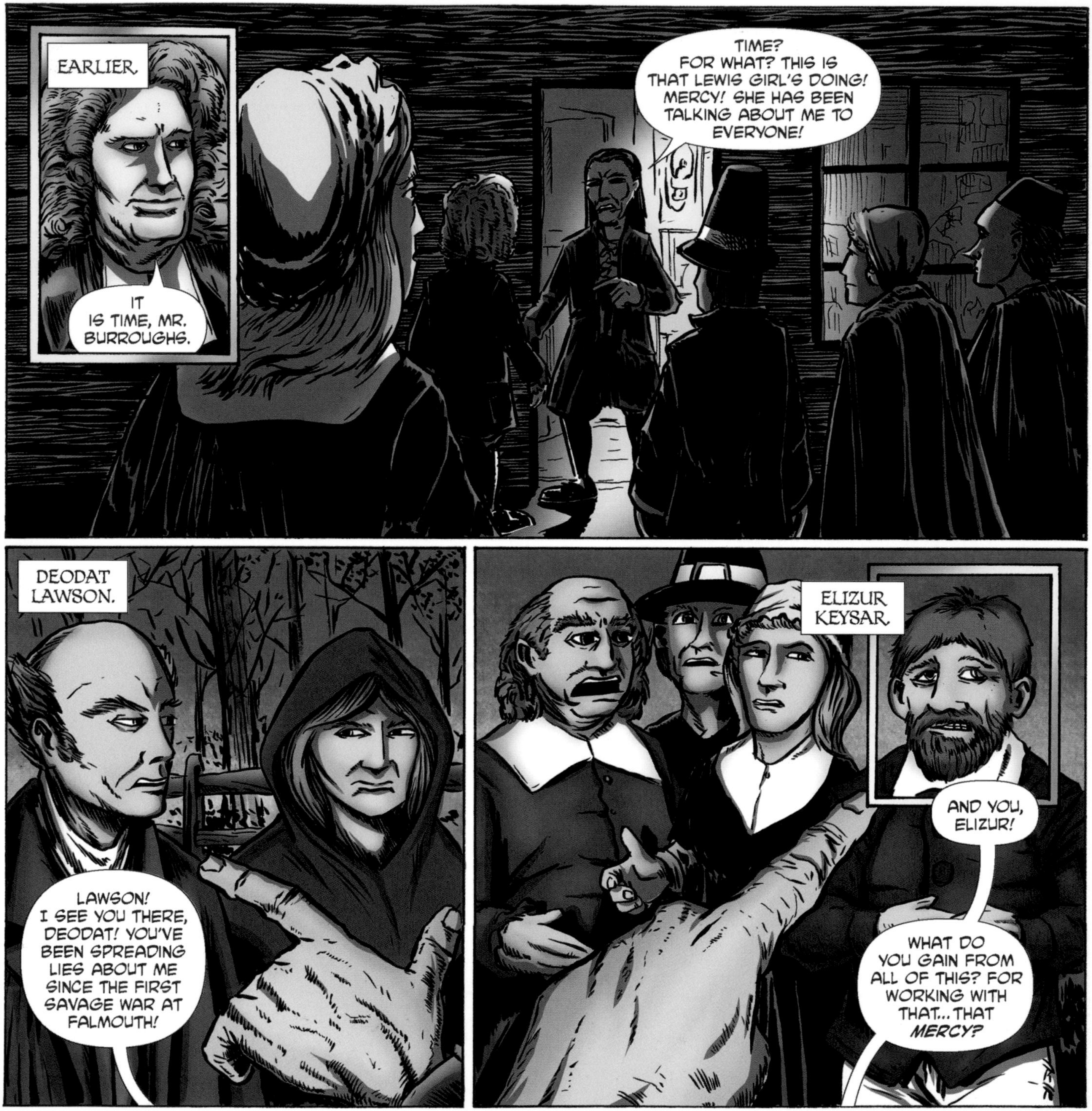
EARLIER.
IT IS TIME, MR. BURROUGHS.
TIME? FOR WHAT? THIS IS THAT LEWIS GIRL'S DOING! MERCY! SHE HAS BEEN TALKING ABOUT ME TO EVERYONE!
DEODAT LAWSON.
LAWSON! I SEE YOU THERE, DEODAT! YOU'VE BEEN SPREADING LIES ABOUT ME SINCE THE FIRST SAVAGE WAR AT FALMOUTH!
ELIZUR KEYSAR.
AND YOU, ELIZUR!
WHAT DO YOU GAIN FROM ALL OF THIS? FOR WORKING WITH THAT...THAT *MERCY?*

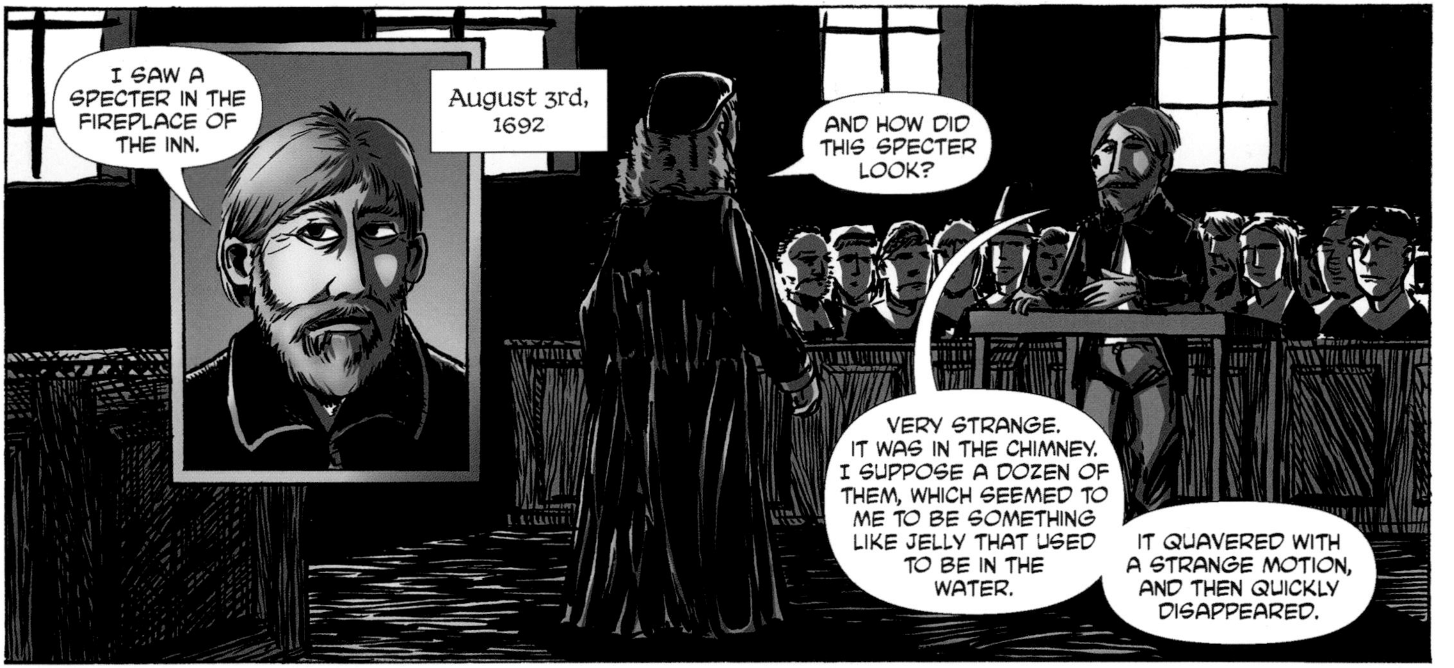
August 3rd, 1692
I SAW A SPECTER IN THE FIREPLACE OF THE INN.
AND HOW DID THIS SPECTER LOOK?
VERY STRANGE. IT WAS IN THE CHIMNEY. I SUPPOSE A DOZEN OF THEM, WHICH SEEMED TO ME TO BE SOMETHING LIKE JELLY THAT USED TO BE IN THE WATER.
IT QUAVERED WITH A STRANGE MOTION, AND THEN QUICKLY DISAPPEARED.

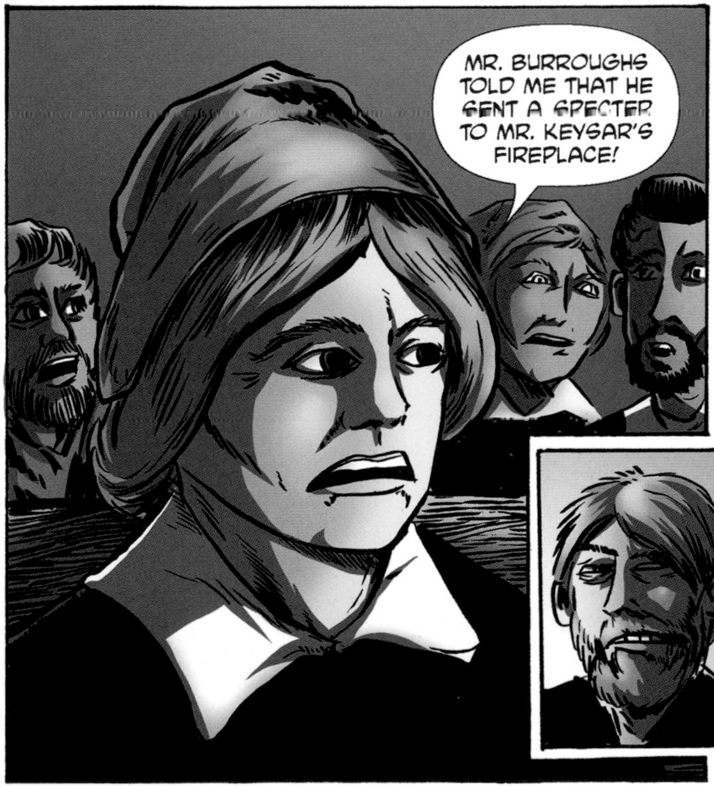
MR. BURROUGHS TOLD ME THAT HE SENT A SPECTER TO MR. KEYSAR'S FIREPLACE!

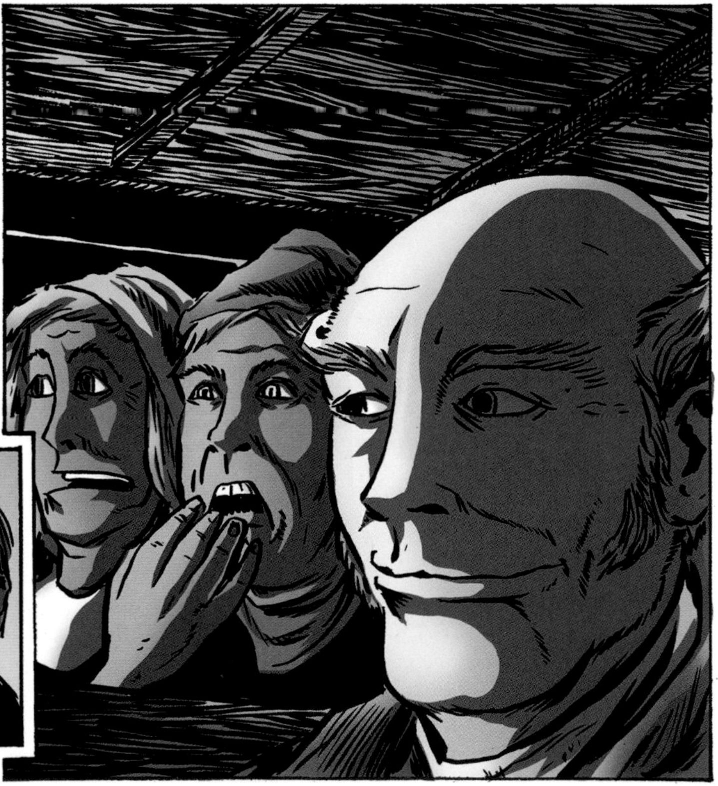

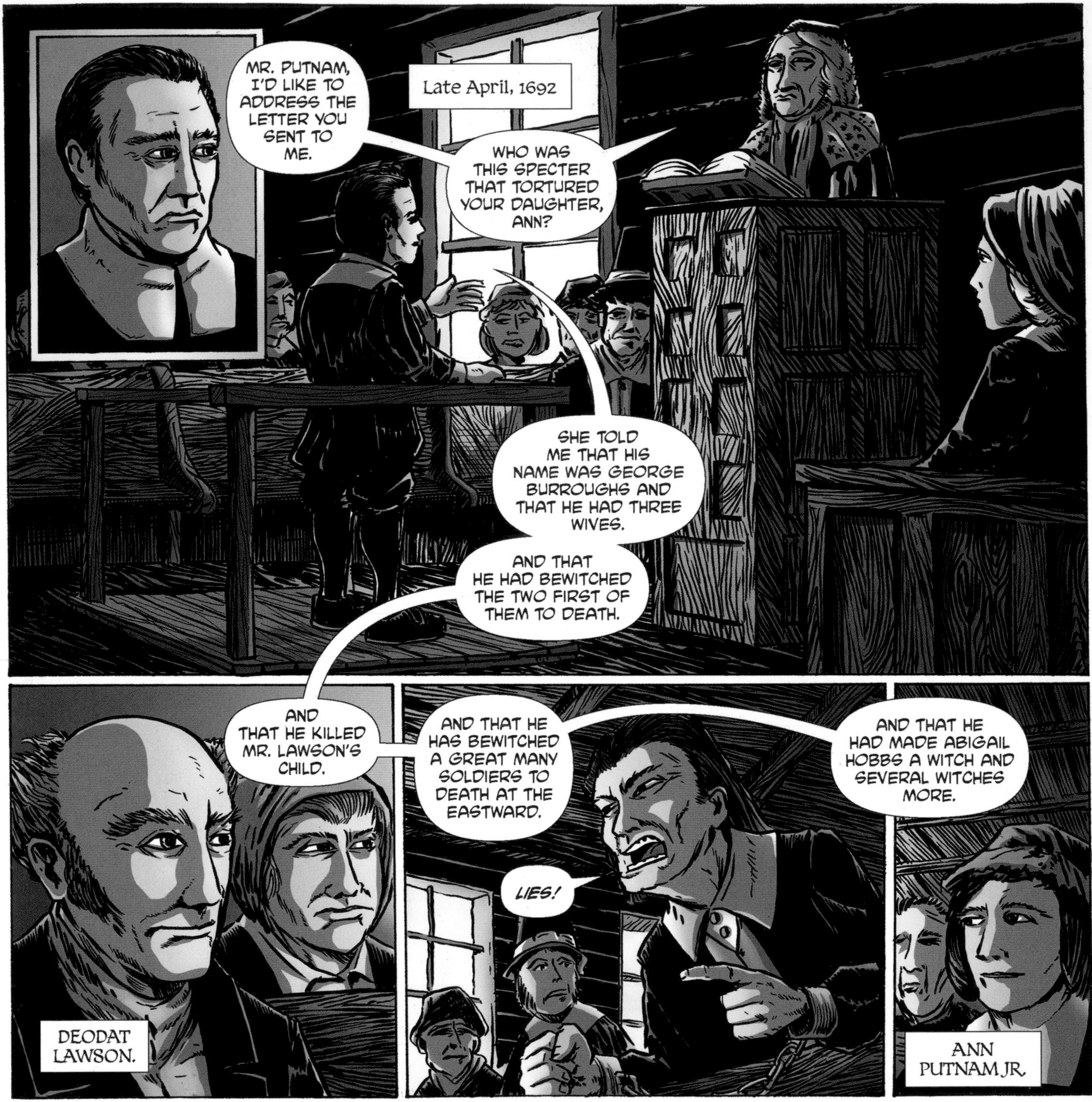
Late April, 1692
MR. PUTNAM, I'D LIKE TO ADDRESS THE LETTER YOU SENT TO ME.
WHO WAS THIS SPECTER THAT TORTURED YOUR DAUGHTER, ANN?
SHE TOLD ME THAT HIS NAME WAS GEORGE BURROUGHS AND THAT HE HAD THREE WIVES.
AND THAT HE HAD BEWITCHED THE TWO FIRST OF THEM TO DEATH.
AND THAT HE KILLED MR. LAWSON'S CHILD.
DEODAT LAWSON.
AND THAT HE HAS BEWITCHED A GREAT MANY SOLDIERS TO DEATH AT THE EASTWARD.
LIES!
AND THAT HE HAD MADE ABIGAIL HOBBS A WITCH AND SEVERAL WITCHES MORE.
ANN PUTNAM JR.

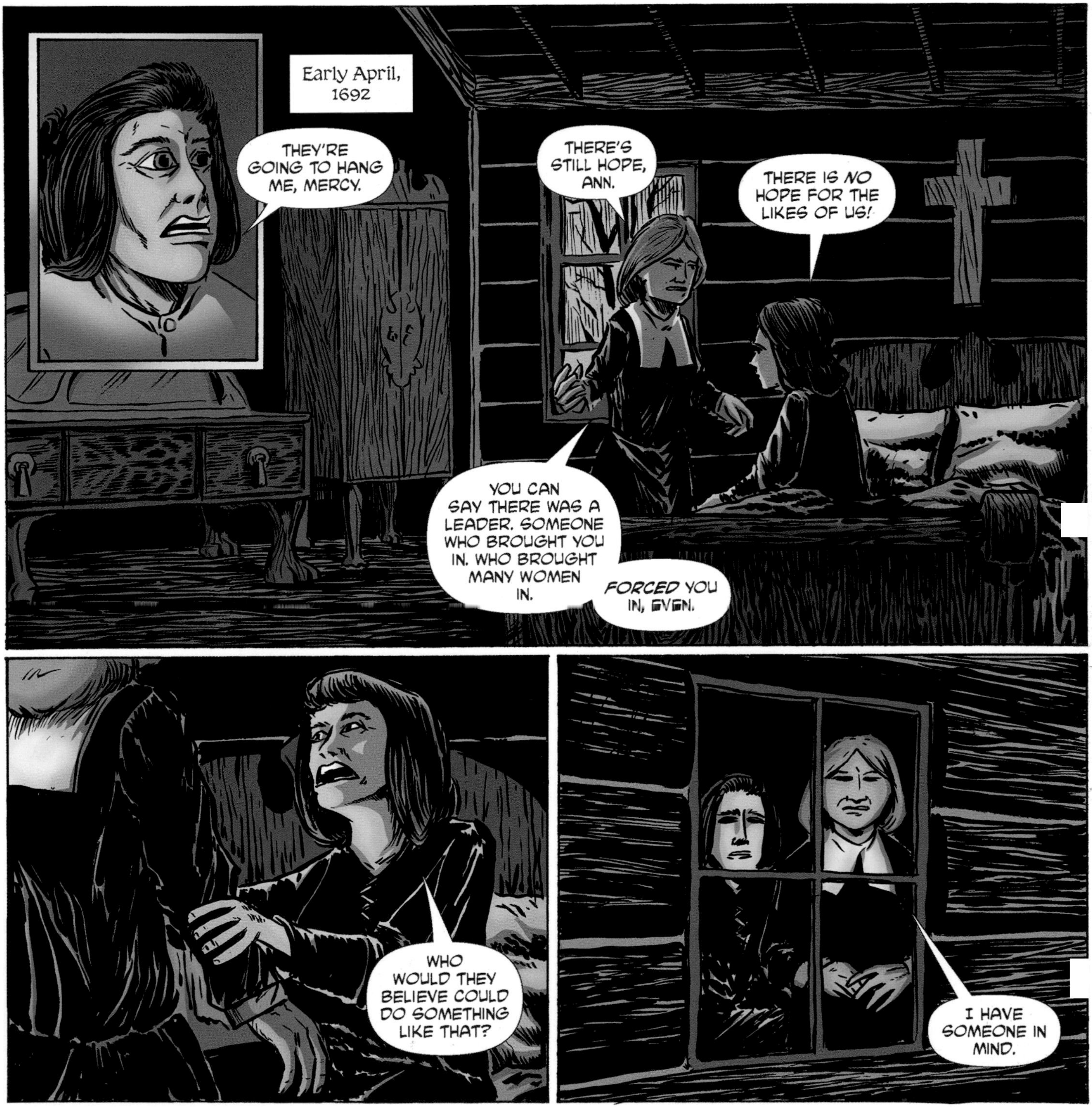

Early April, 1692
THEY'RE GOING TO HANG ME, MERCY.
THERE'S STILL HOPE, ANN.
THERE IS NO HOPE FOR THE LIKES OF US!
YOU CAN SAY THERE WAS A LEADER. SOMEONE WHO BROUGHT YOU IN. WHO BROUGHT MANY WOMEN IN.
FORCED YOU IN, EVEN.
WHO WOULD THEY BELIEVE COULD DO SOMETHING LIKE THAT?
I HAVE SOMEONE IN MIND.

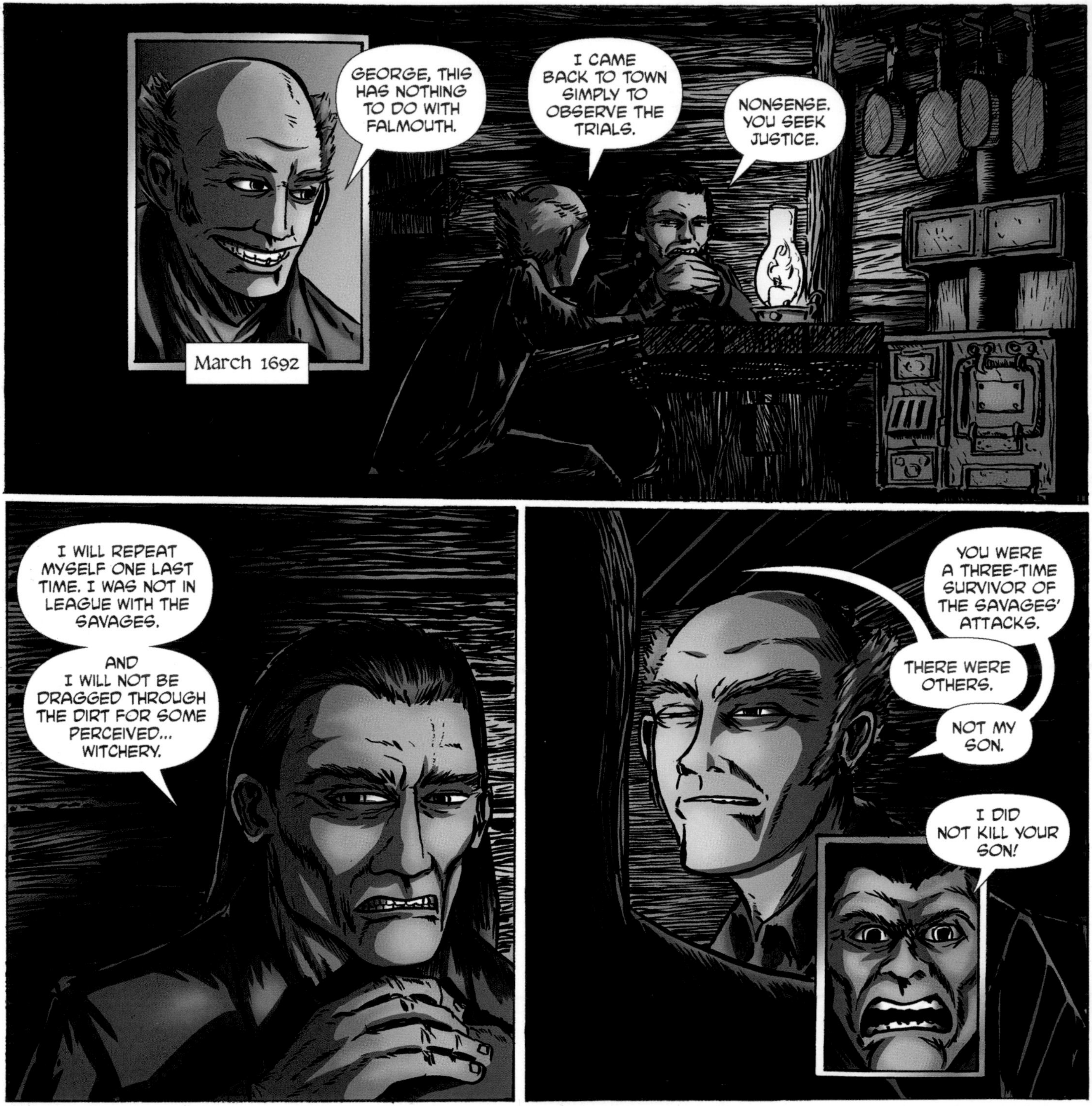
March 1692
GEORGE, THIS HAS NOTHING TO DO WITH FALMOUTH.
I CAME BACK TO TOWN SIMPLY TO OBSERVE THE TRIALS.
NONSENSE. YOU SEEK JUSTICE.
I WILL REPEAT MYSELF ONE LAST TIME. I WAS NOT IN LEAGUE WITH THE SAVAGES.
AND I WILL NOT BE DRAGGED THROUGH THE DIRT FOR SOME PERCEIVED... WITCHERY.
YOU WERE A THREE-TIME SURVIVOR OF THE SAVAGES' ATTACKS.
THERE WERE OTHERS.
NOT MY SON.
I DID NOT KILL YOUR SON!

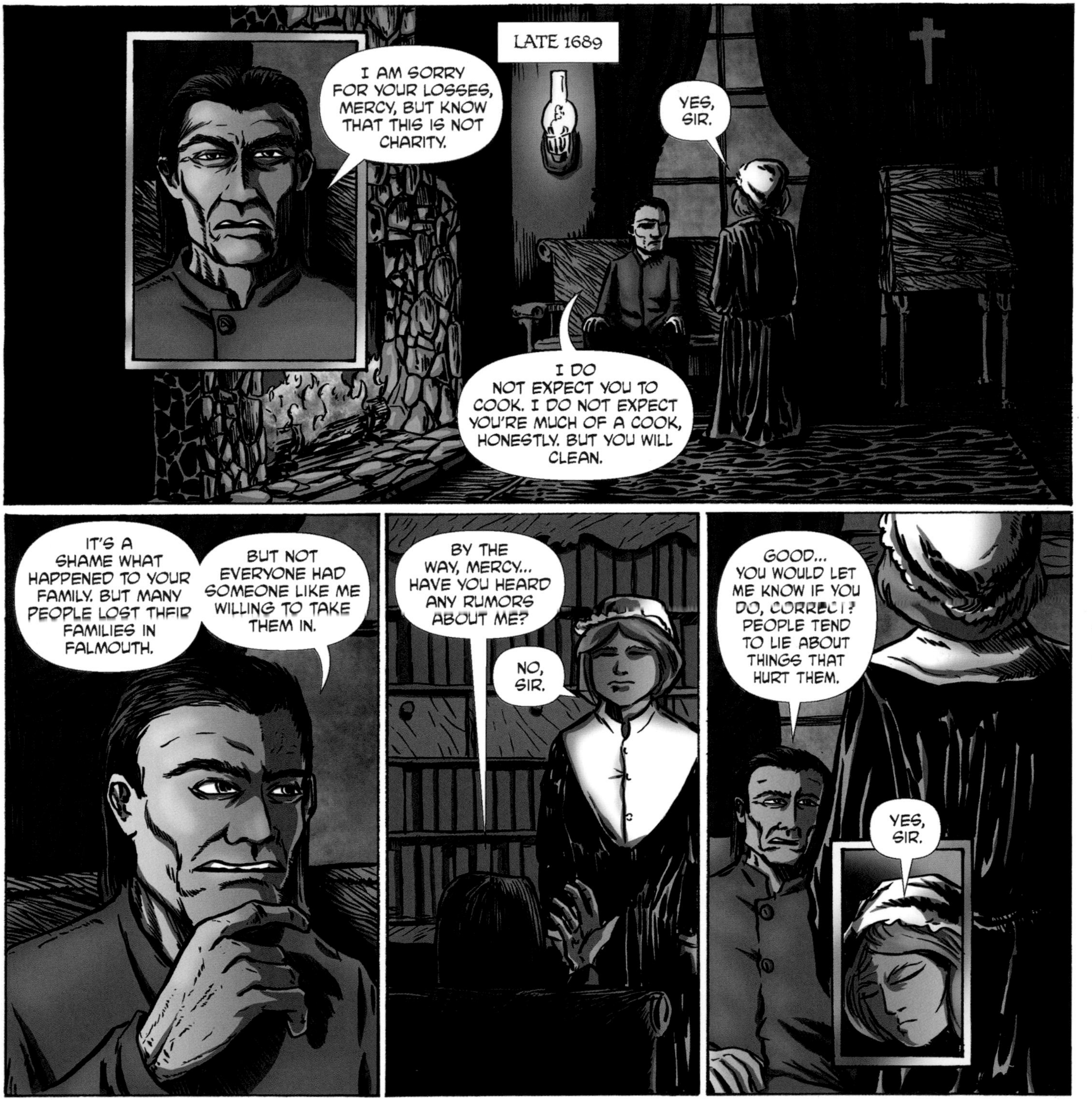
LATE 1689
I AM SORRY FOR YOUR LOSSES, MERCY, BUT KNOW THAT THIS IS NOT CHARITY.
YES, SIR.
I DO NOT EXPECT YOU TO COOK. I DO NOT EXPECT YOU'RE MUCH OF A COOK, HONESTLY. BUT YOU WILL CLEAN.
IT'S A SHAME WHAT HAPPENED TO YOUR FAMILY. BUT MANY PEOPLE LOST THEIR FAMILIES IN FALMOUTH.
BUT NOT EVERYONE HAD SOMEONE LIKE ME WILLING TO TAKE THEM IN.
BY THE WAY, MERCY... HAVE YOU HEARD ANY RUMORS ABOUT ME?
NO, SIR.
GOOD... YOU WOULD LET ME KNOW IF YOU DO, CORRECT? PEOPLE TEND TO LIE ABOUT THINGS THAT HURT THEM.
YES, SIR.

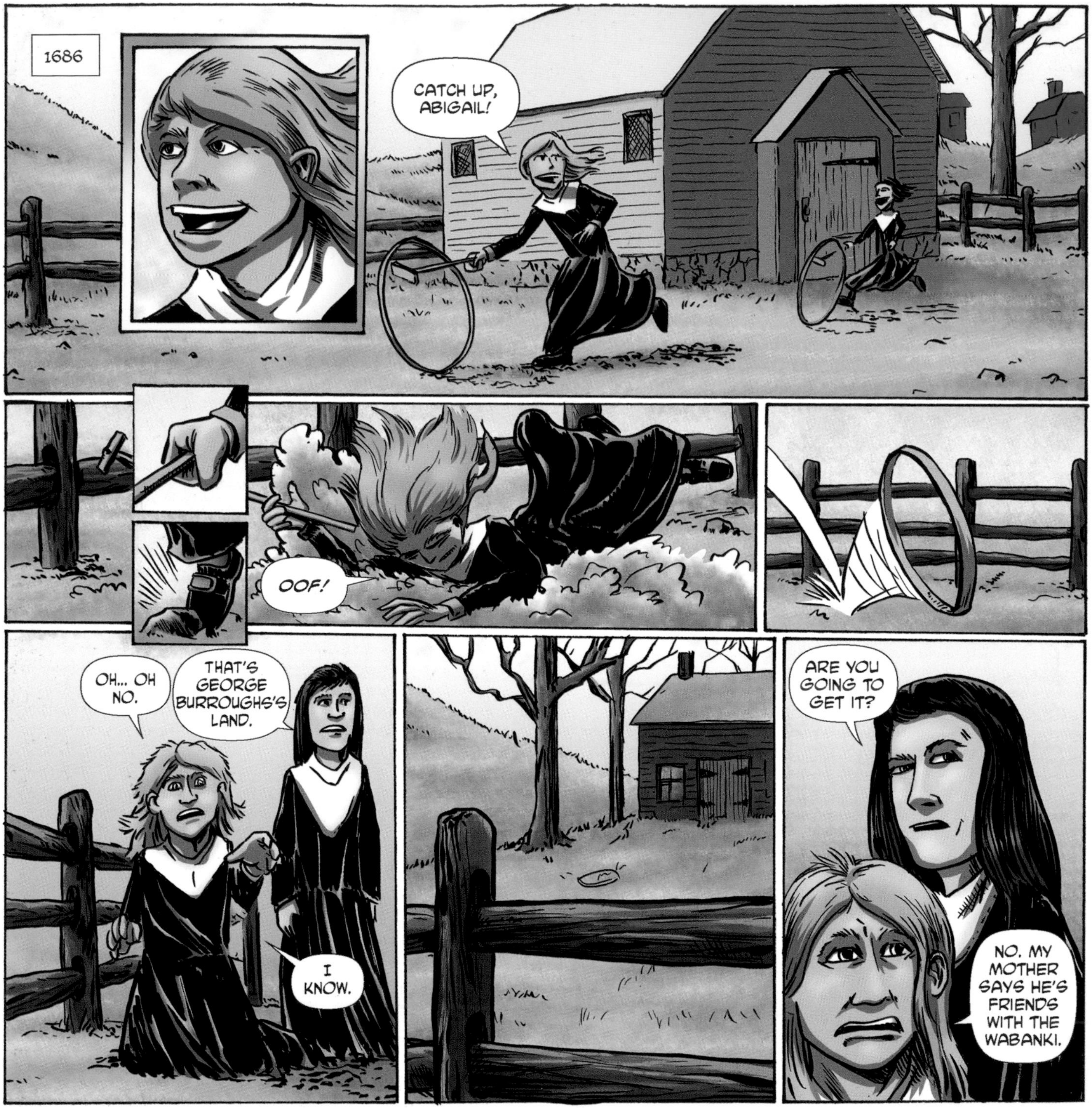
1686
CATCH UP, ABIGAIL!
OOF!
OH... OH NO.
THAT'S GEORGE BURROUGHS'S LAND.
I KNOW.
ARE YOU GOING TO GET IT?
NO. MY MOTHER SAYS HE'S FRIENDS WITH THE WABANKI.

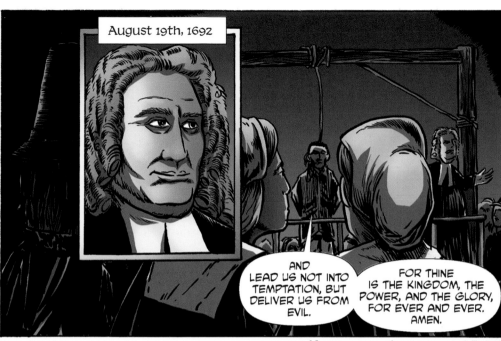

August 19th, 1692

AND LEAD US NOT INTO TEMPTATION, BUT DELIVER US FROM EVIL.

FOR THINE IS THE KINGDOM, THE POWER, AND THE GLORY, FOR EVER AND EVER. AMEN.

OF COURSE HE CAN RECITE THE LORD'S PRAYER. HE'S BEEN FOOLING US AS A MINISTER HIS WHOLE LIFE.

THAT'S WHAT HE DOES. FOOLS PEOPLE.

THEN YOUR DAUGHTER TURNS TO THE DEVIL, THOMAS.

THEN YOUR NIECE TURNS, SAMUEL.

WHOSE DAUGHTER IS NEXT?

DO WE SPARE THIS WITCH'S LIFE JUST BECAUSE HE CAN RECITE THE LORD'S PRAYER?

I THOUGHT NOT.

139

The Missing Cheese
Story and Art by Sarah Winifred Searle

Puritan America was, for women, a time of tremendous restriction. For those with an "entrepreneurial spirit," their best bet was to marry a supportive man who would allow them a certain amount of autonomy, giving them the status to make such endeavors socially acceptable.

One of these women was Mary Huntris. A series of court records chronicles her struggle for independence and the archnemesis she gained along the way.

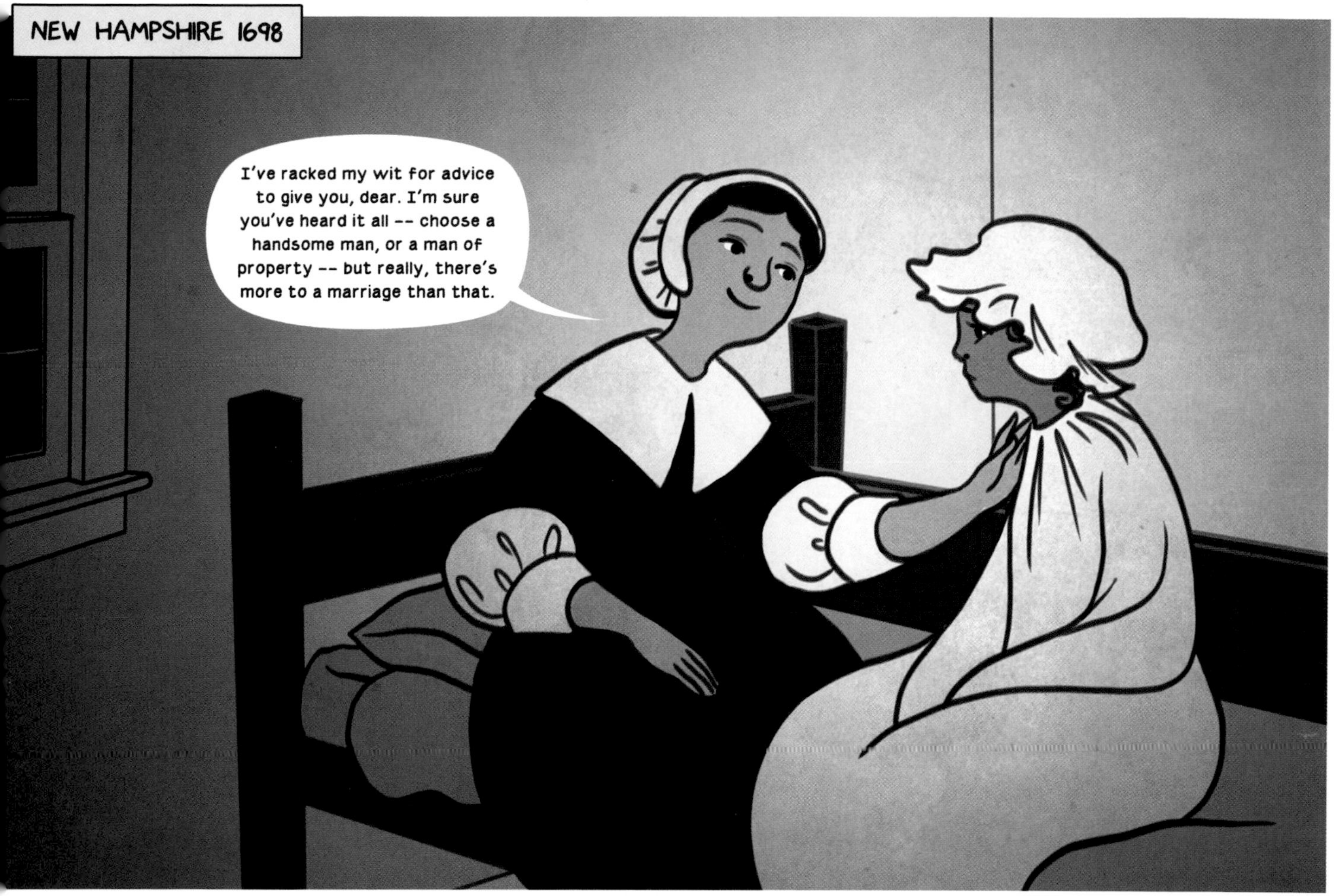
NEW HAMPSHIRE 1698
I've racked my wit for advice to give you, dear. I'm sure you've heard it all -- choose a handsome man, or a man of property -- but really, there's more to a marriage than that.

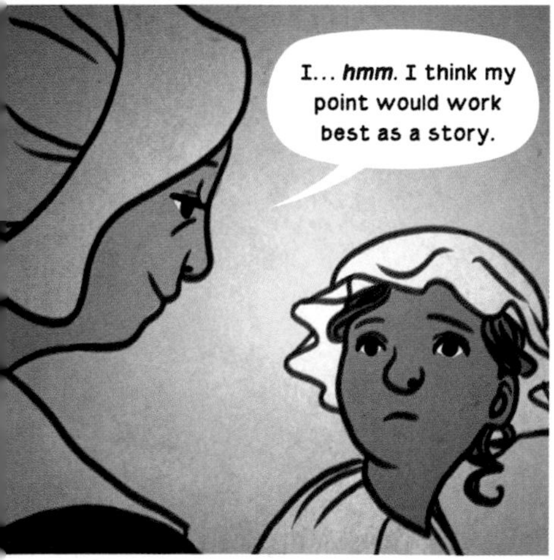
I... *hmm*. I think my point would work best as a story.

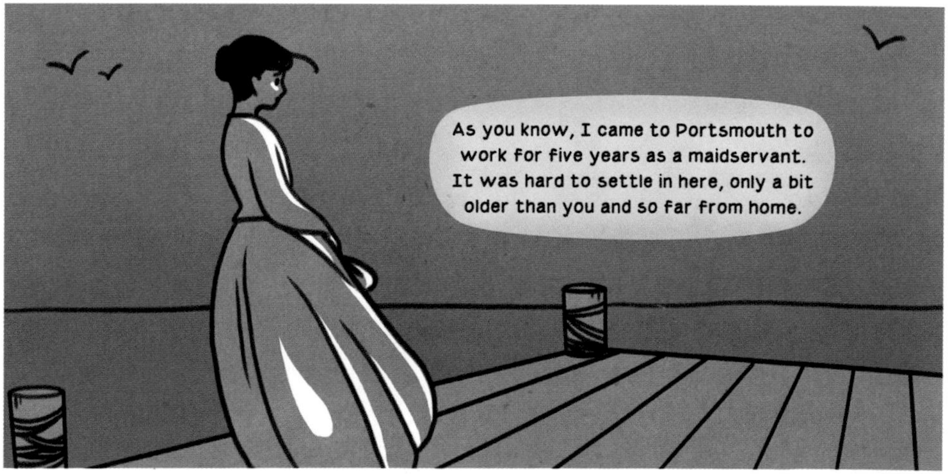
As you know, I came to Portsmouth to work for five years as a maidservant. It was hard to settle in here, only a bit older than you and so far from home.

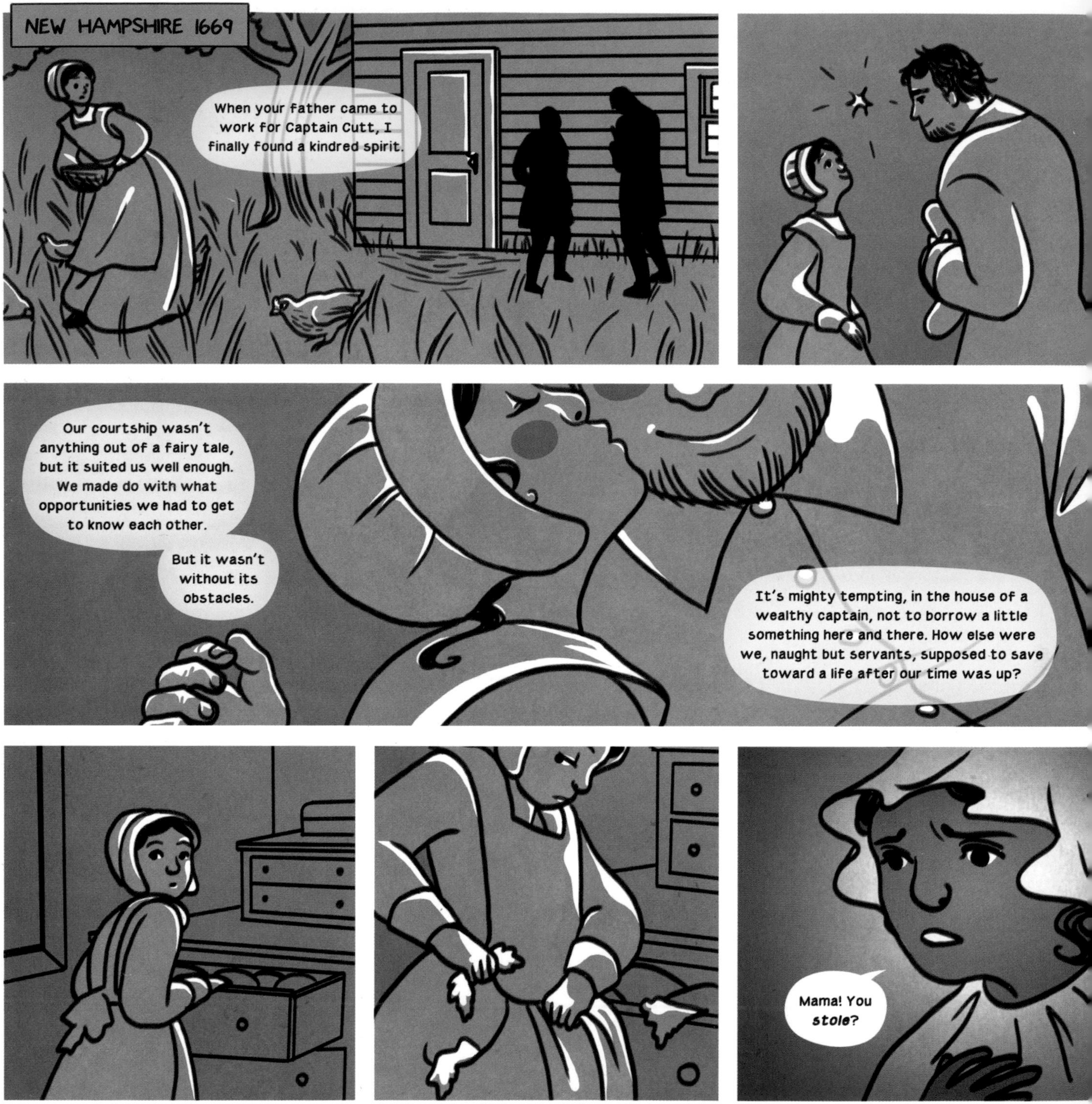
NEW HAMPSHIRE 1669
When your father came to work for Captain Cutt, I finally found a kindred spirit.
Our courtship wasn't anything out of a fairy tale, but it suited us well enough. We made do with what opportunities we had to get to know each other.
But it wasn't without its obstacles.
It's mighty tempting, in the house of a wealthy captain, not to borrow a little something here and there. How else were we, naught but servants, supposed to save toward a life after our time was up?
Mama! You *stole*?

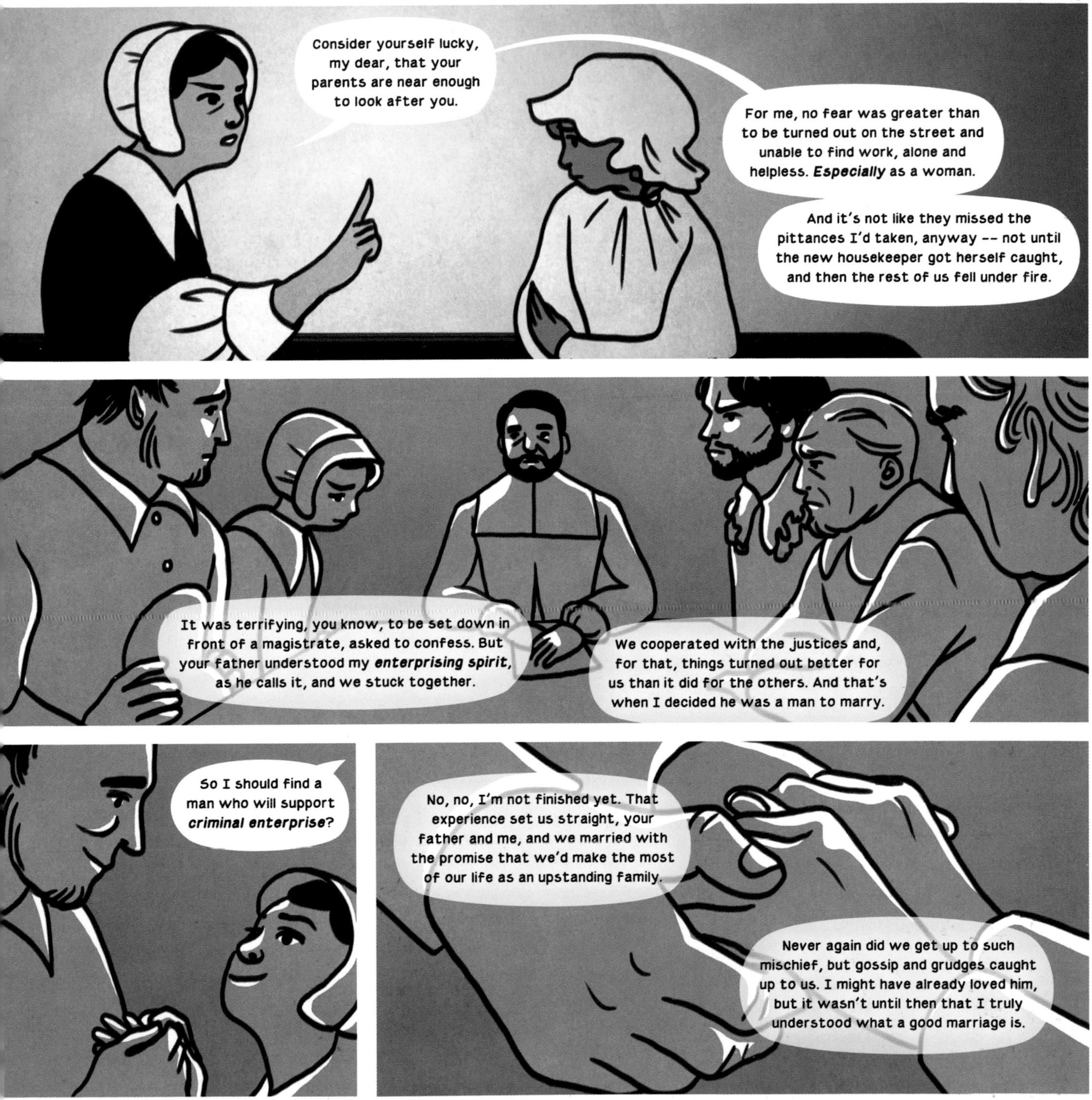
Consider yourself lucky, my dear, that your parents are near enough to look after you.
For me, no fear was greater than to be turned out on the street and unable to find work, alone and helpless. *Especially* as a woman.
And it's not like they missed the pittances I'd taken, anyway -- not until the new housekeeper got herself caught, and then the rest of us fell under fire.
It was terrifying, you know, to be set down in front of a magistrate, asked to confess. But your father understood my *enterprising spirit*, as he calls it, and we stuck together.
We cooperated with the justices and, for that, things turned out better for us than it did for the others. And that's when I decided he was a man to marry.
So I should find a man who will support *criminal enterprise*?
No, no, I'm not finished yet. That experience set us straight, your father and me, and we married with the promise that we'd make the most of our life as an upstanding family.
Never again did we get up to such mischief, but gossip and grudges caught up to us. I might have already loved him, but it wasn't until then that I truly understood what a good marriage is.

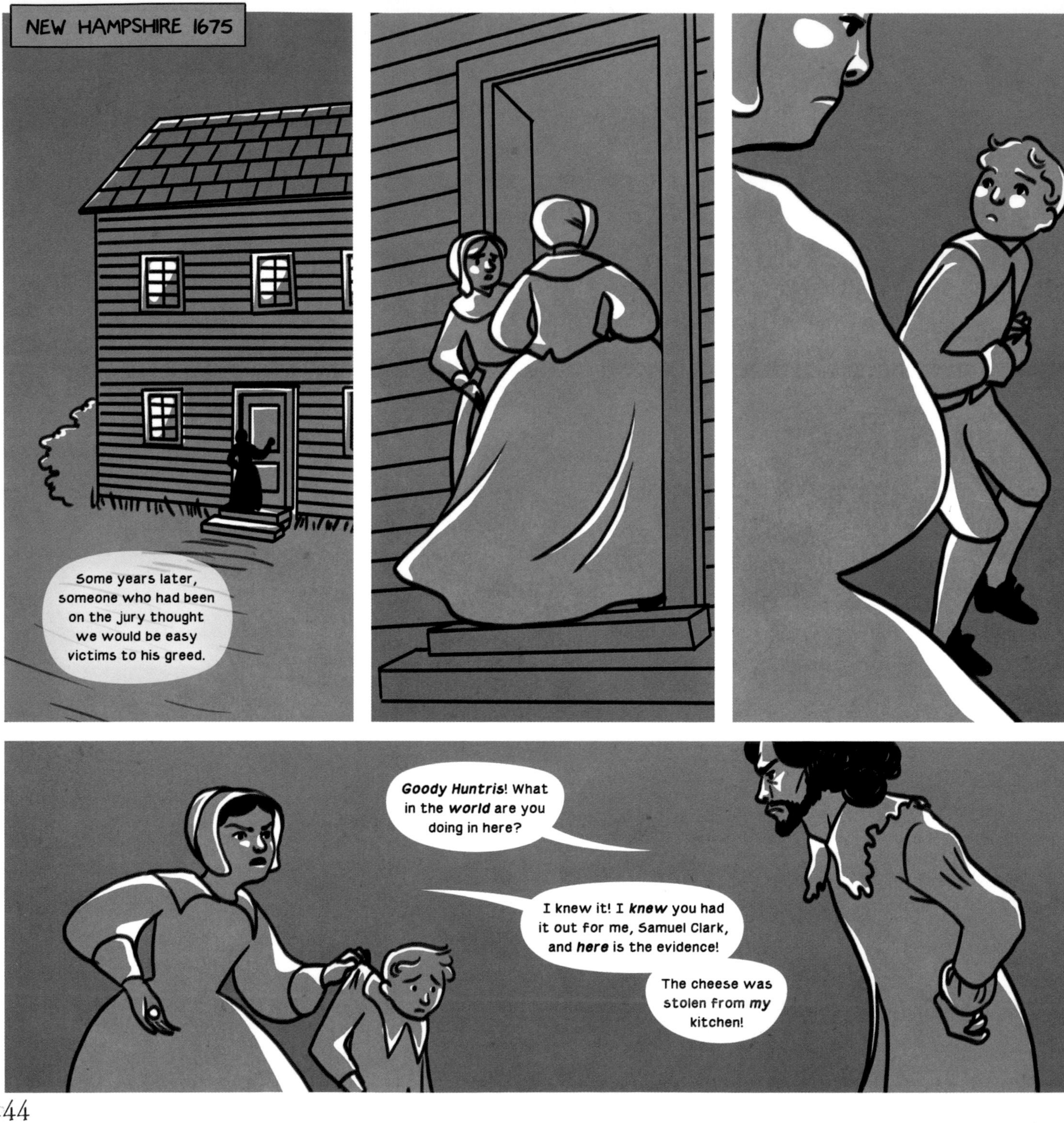
NEW HAMPSHIRE 1675
Some years later, someone who had been on the jury thought we would be easy victims to his greed.
Goody Huntris! What in the *world* are you doing in here?
I knew it! I *knew* you had it out for me, Samuel Clark, and *here* is the evidence!
The cheese was stolen from *my* kitchen!

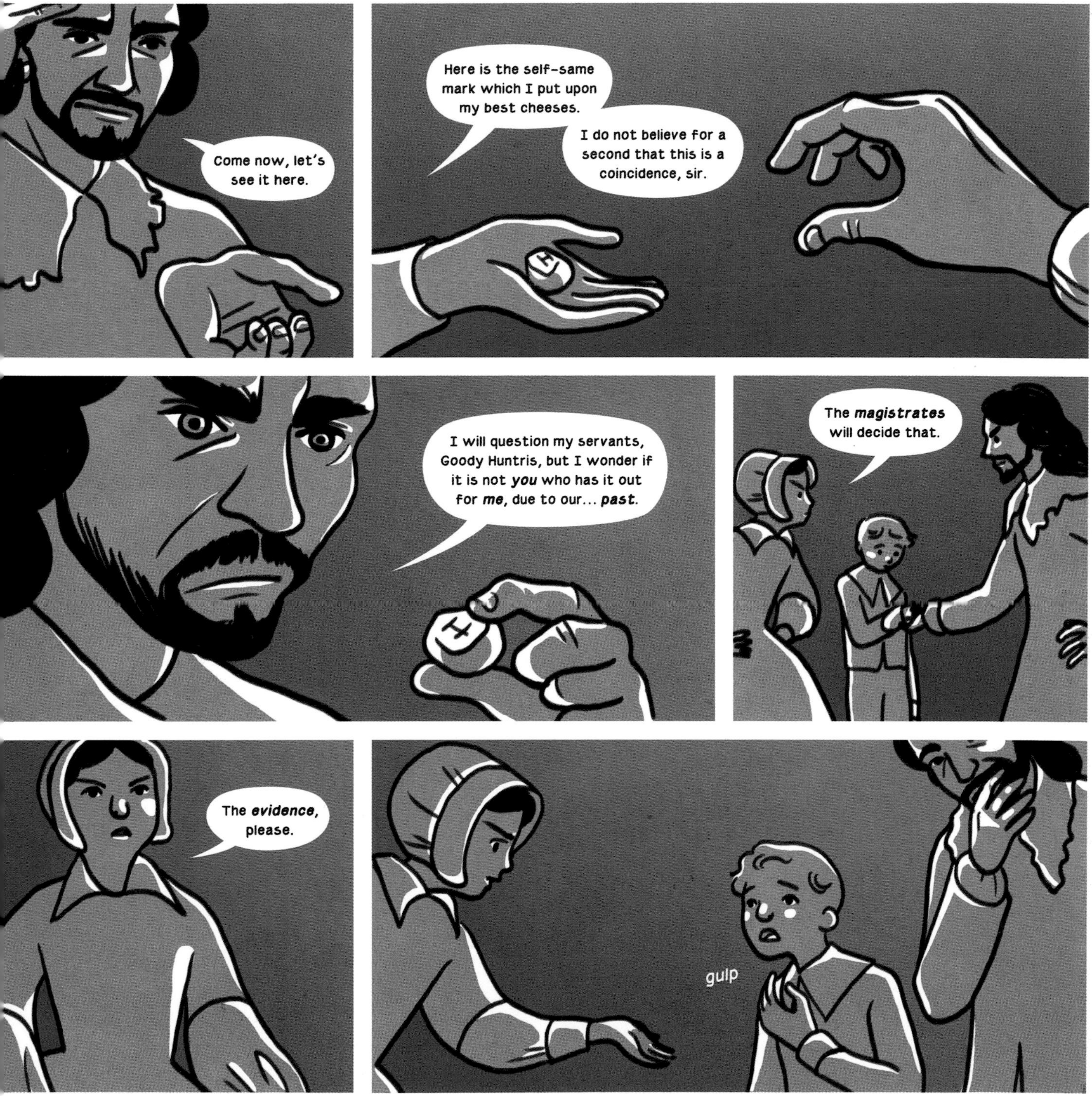
Come now, let's see it here.
Here is the self-same mark which I put upon my best cheeses.
I do not believe for a second that this is a coincidence, sir.
I will question my servants, Goody Huntris, but I wonder if it is not *you* who has it out for *me*, due to our... *past*.
The *magistrates* will decide that.
The *evidence*, please.
gulp

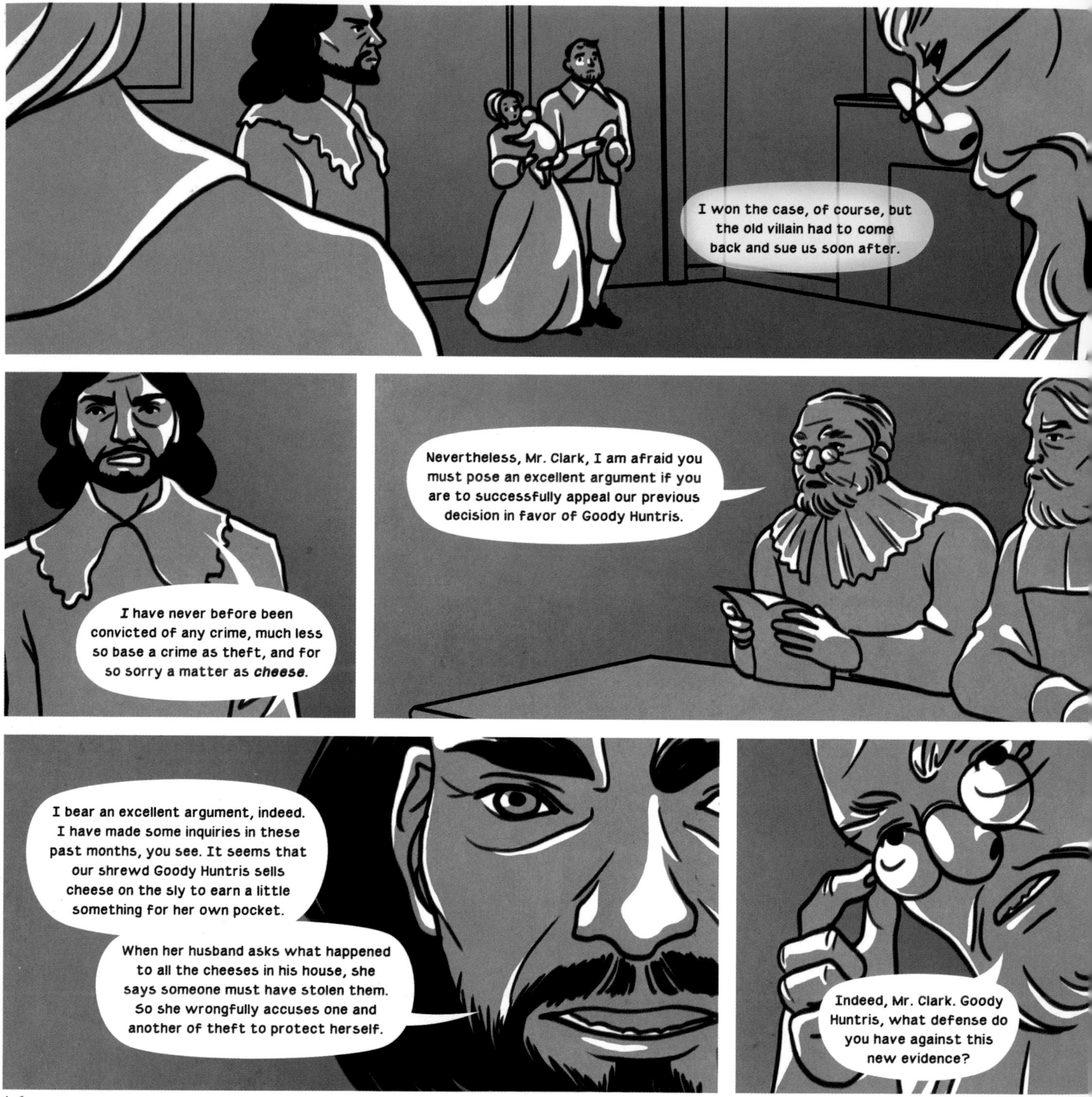
I won the case, of course, but the old villain had to come back and sue us soon after.
I have never before been convicted of any crime, much less so base a crime as theft, and for so sorry a matter as *cheese*.
Nevertheless, Mr. Clark, I am afraid you must pose an excellent argument if you are to successfully appeal our previous decision in favor of Goody Huntris.
I bear an excellent argument, indeed. I have made some inquiries in these past months, you see. It seems that our shrewd Goody Huntris sells cheese on the sly to earn a little something for her own pocket.
When her husband asks what happened to all the cheeses in his house, she says someone must have stolen them. So she wrongfully accuses one and another of theft to protect herself.
Indeed, Mr. Clark. Goody Huntris, what defense do you have against this new evidence?

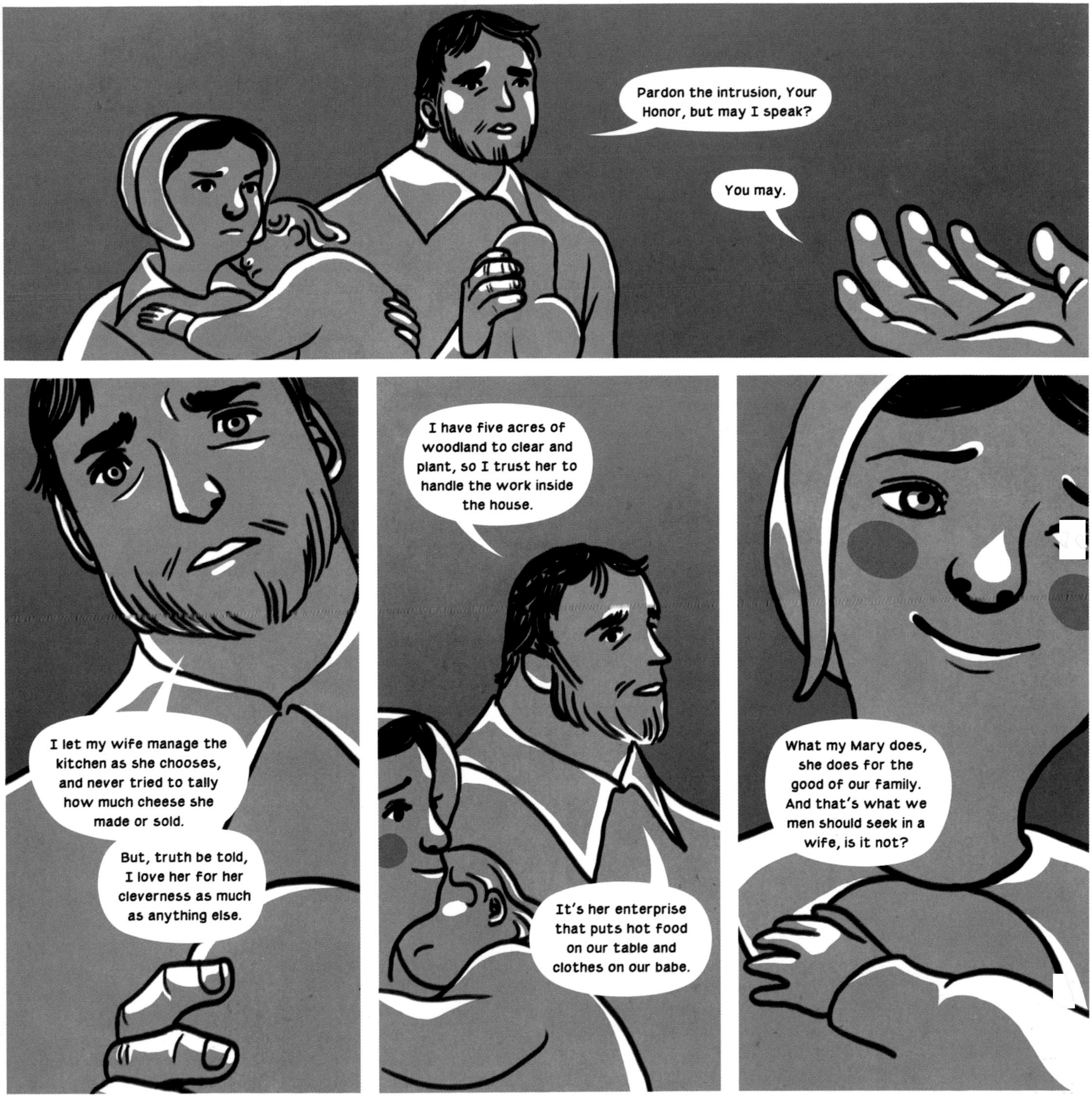
Pardon the intrusion, Your Honor, but may I speak?
You may.
I let my wife manage the kitchen as she chooses, and never tried to tally how much cheese she made or sold.
But, truth be told, I love her for her cleverness as much as anything else.
I have five acres of woodland to clear and plant, so I trust her to handle the work inside the house.
It's her enterprise that puts hot food on our table and clothes on our babe.
What my Mary does, she does for the good of our family. And that's what we men should seek in a wife, is it not?

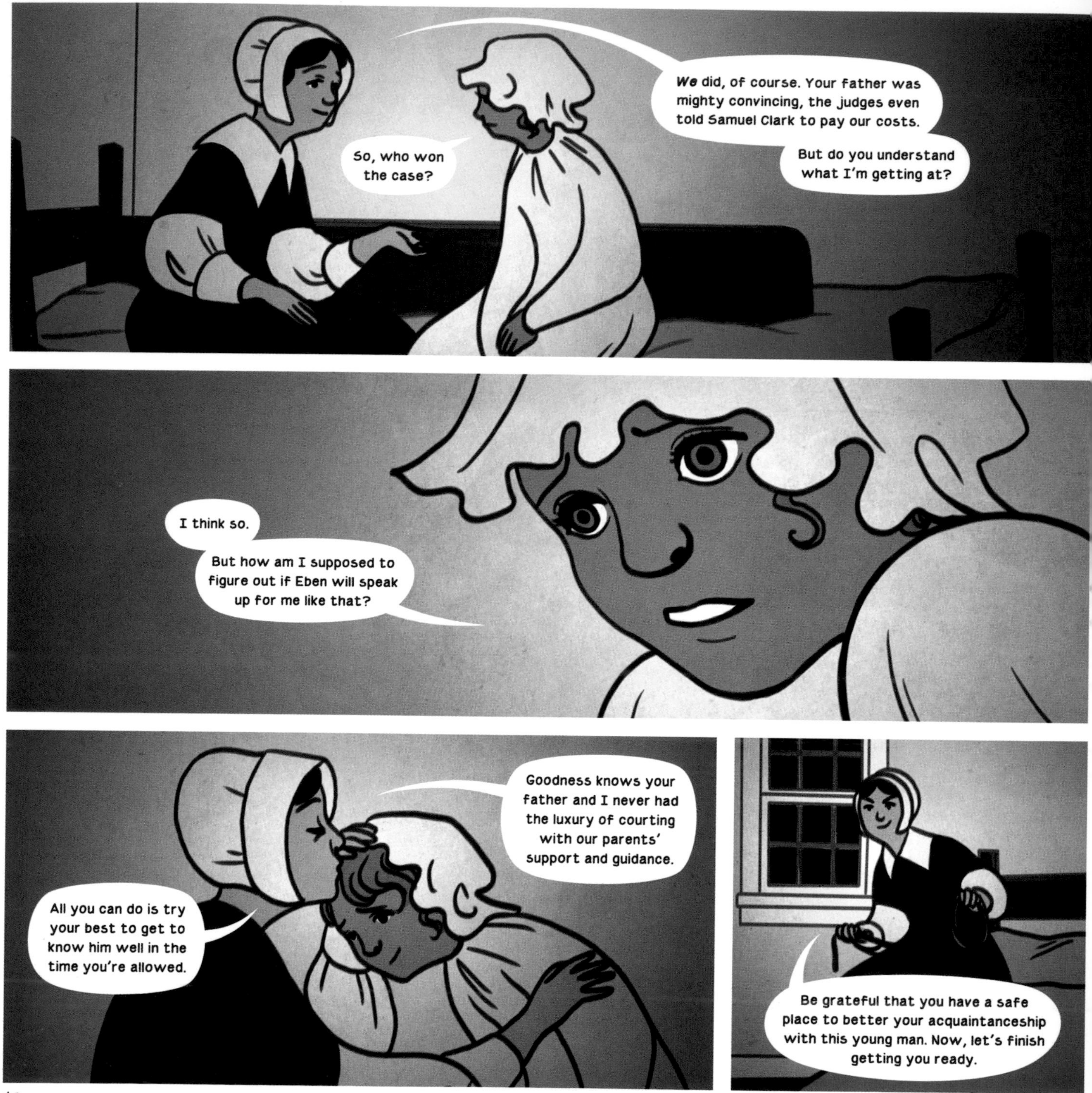
So, who won the case?
We did, of course. Your father was mighty convincing, the judges even told Samuel Clark to pay our costs.
But do you understand what I'm getting at?
I think so.
But how am I supposed to figure out if Eben will speak up for me like that?
Goodness knows your father and I never had the luxury of courting with our parents' support and guidance.
All you can do is try your best to get to know him well in the time you're allowed.
Be grateful that you have a safe place to better your acquaintanceship with this young man. Now, let's finish getting you ready.

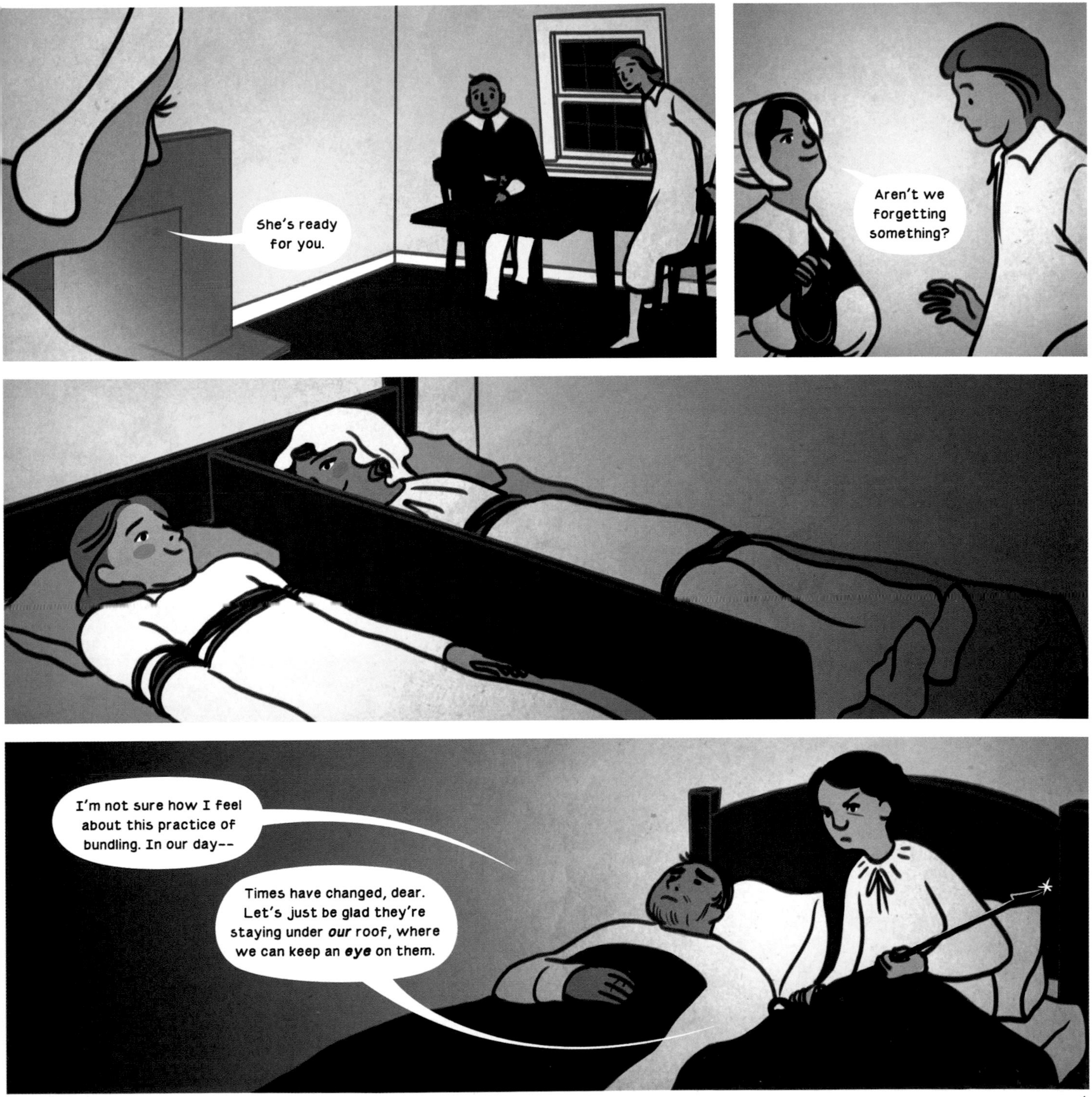
She's ready for you.
Aren't we forgetting something?
I'm not sure how I feel about this practice of bundling. In our day--
Times have changed, dear. Let's just be glad they're staying under *our* roof, where we can keep an *eye* on them.

Captives: The Stories of Eunice and John Williams

Story and Art by Dan Mazur

1702 saw the start of Queen Anne's War, the second of four French and Indian Wards. Colonies in New England fought against French and Indian forces based in Quebec.

In 1704, Queen Anne's War came to the town of Deerfield, Massachusetts. A group of French fighters who were allied with men of the Abenaki and Mohawk tribes descended upon the town, killing many of the residents. Deerfield's minster, John Williams was taken captive along with his wife and four of their children, including seven year old Eunice. The two youngest Williams children, including an infant, were killed in the raid, and the surviving family members were brought to Canada. Eunice's mother, weak from recent childbirth, was unable to keep up on the journey north and was killed along the way.

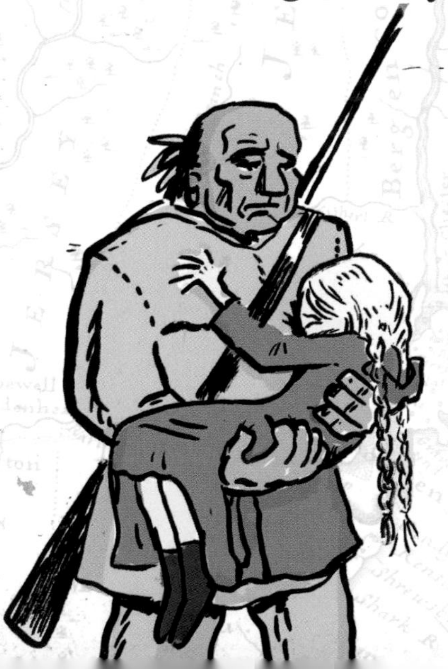

Eunice was separated from her family and taken in by a group of Catholic Mohawks near Montreal. Over the next three years her father and brothers and sisters were released, but John's attempts to ransom Eunice were unsuccessful.

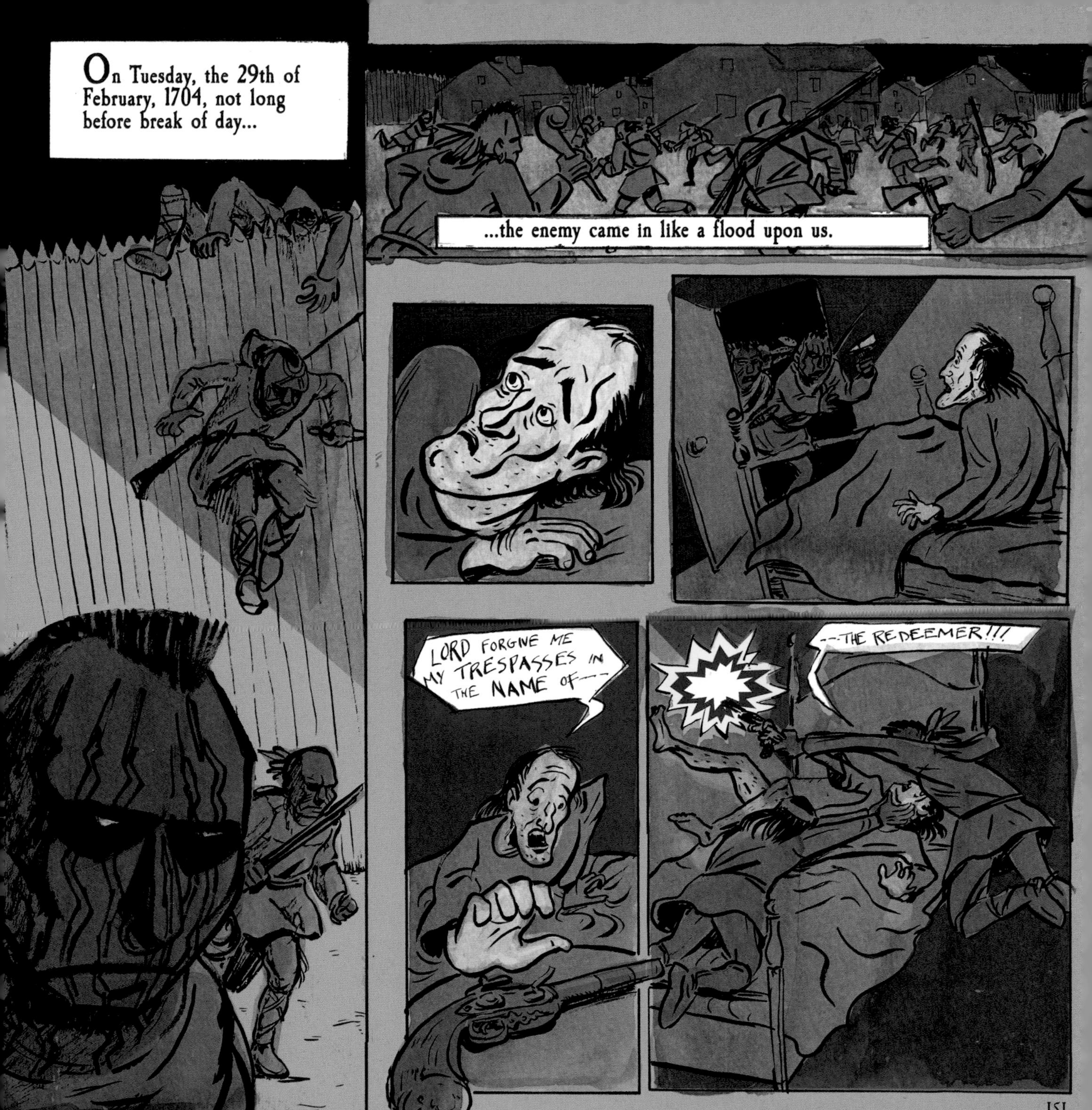
On Tuesday, the 29th of February, 1704, not long before break of day...
...the enemy came in like a flood upon us.
LORD FORGIVE ME MY TRESPASSES IN THE NAME OF---
--THE REDEEMER!!!

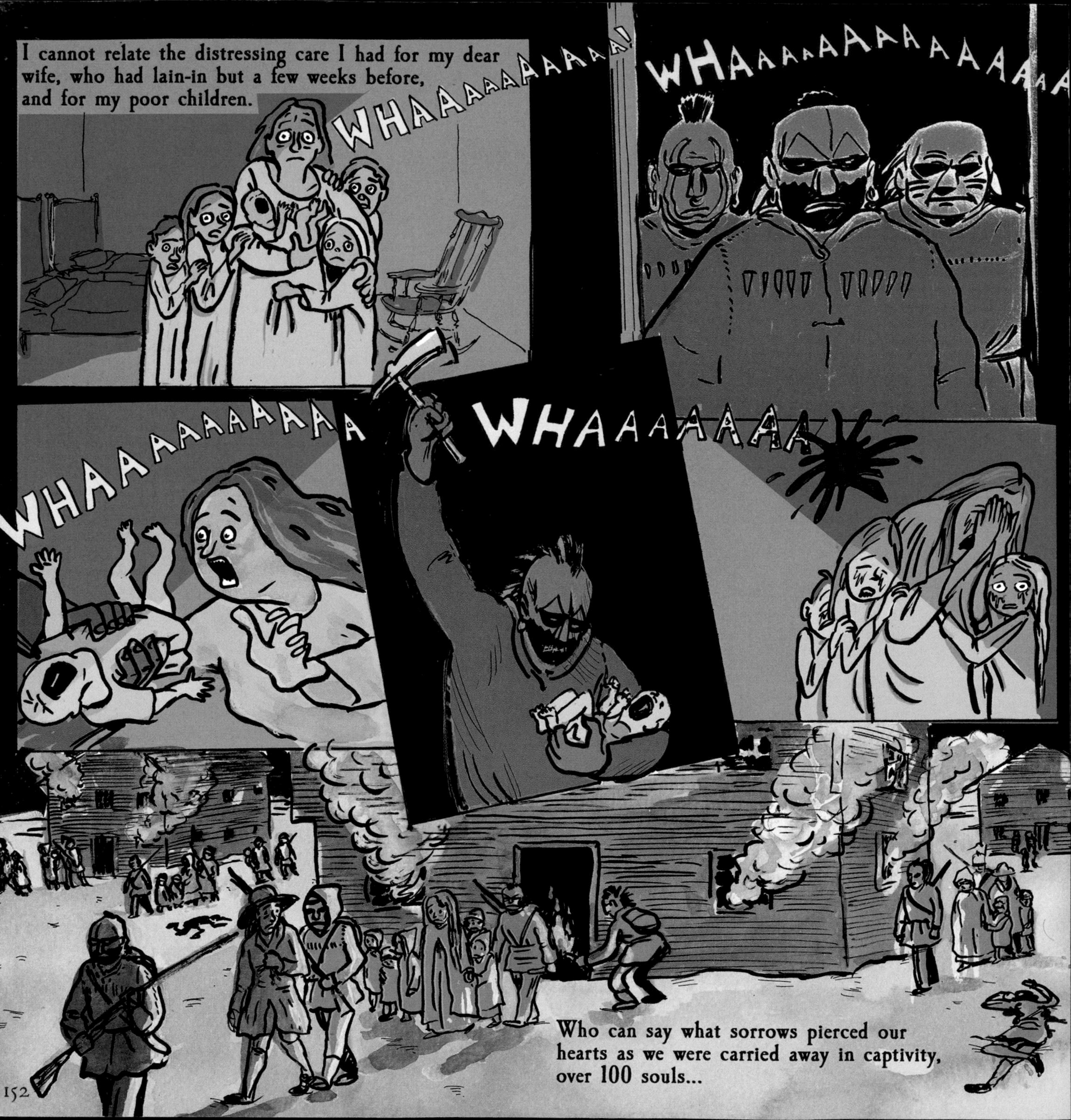
I cannot relate the distressing care I had for my dear wife, who had lain-in but a few weeks before, and for my poor children.
WHAAAAAAAAAAAA!
WHAAAAAAAAAAAAA
WHAAAAAAAAAAAA
WHAAAAAAAAA
Who can say what sorrows pierced our hearts as we were carried away in captivity, over 100 souls...

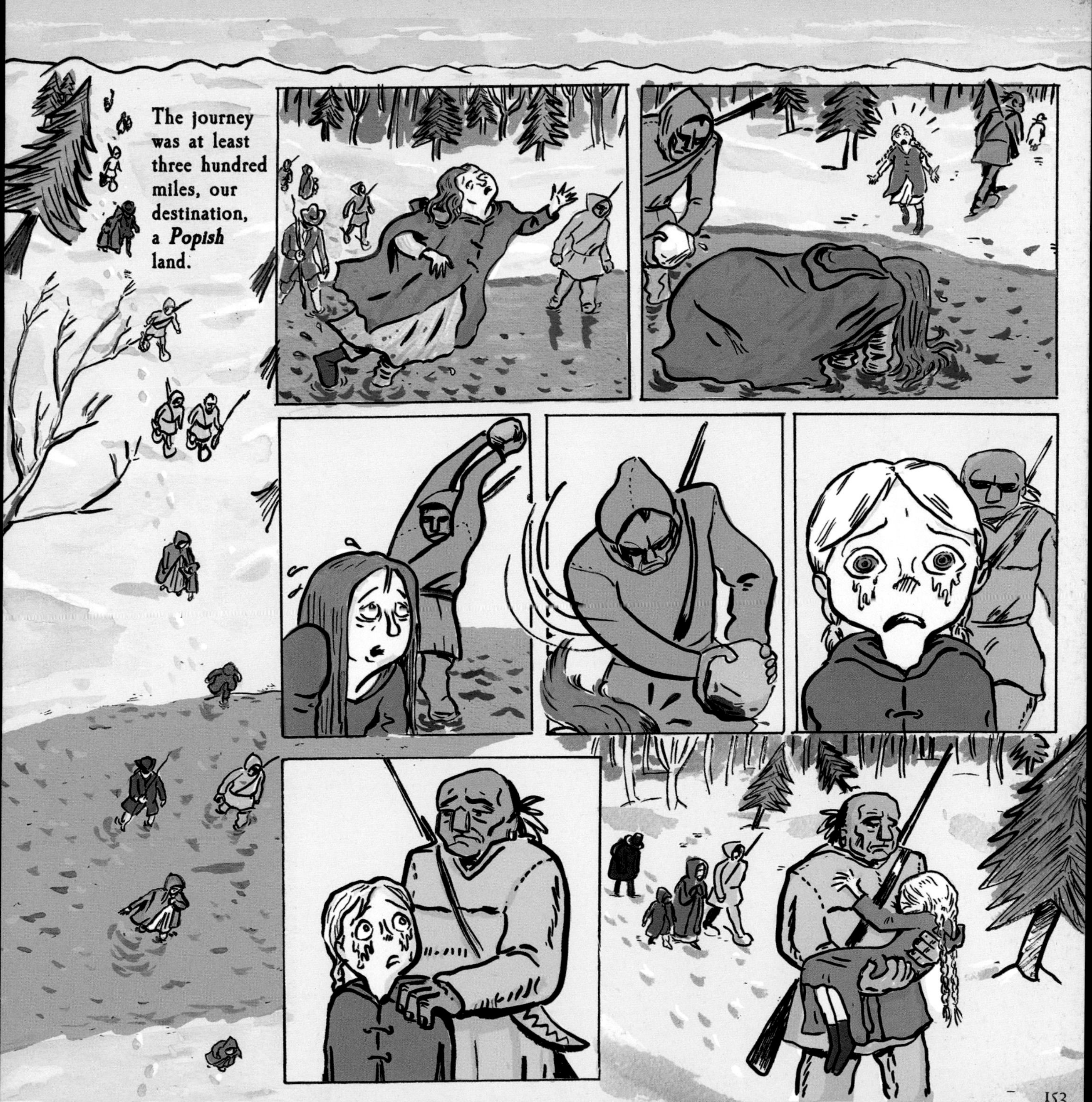
The journey was at least three hundred miles, our destination, a *Popish* land.

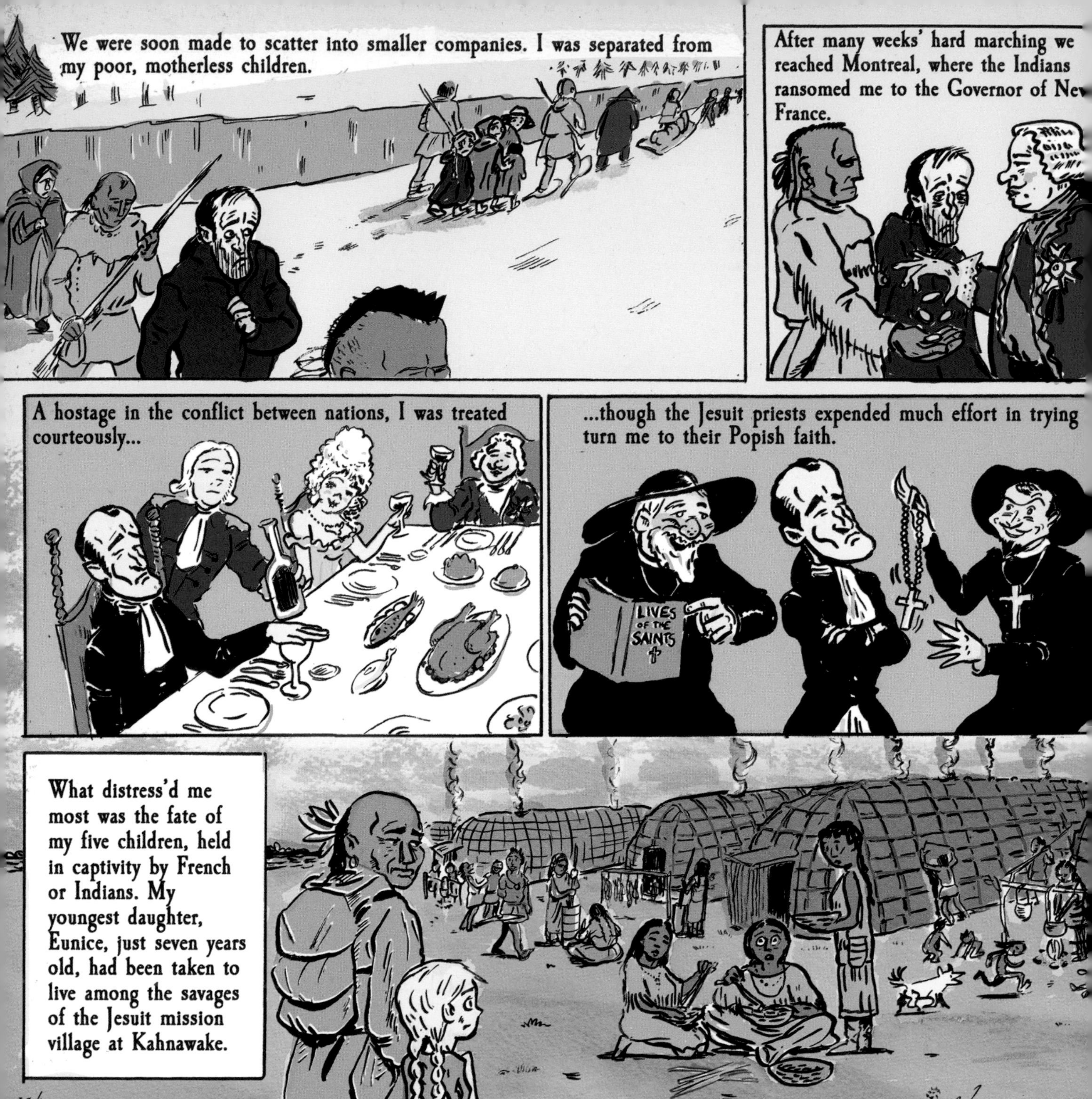

We were soon made to scatter into smaller companies. I was separated from my poor, motherless children.
After many weeks' hard marching we reached Montreal, where the Indians ransomed me to the Governor of Ne
France.
A hostage in the conflict between nations, I was treated courteously...
...though the Jesuit priests expended much effort in trying turn me to their Popish faith.
LIVES OF THE SAINTS
What distress'd me most was the fate of my five children, held in captivity by French or Indians. My youngest daughter, Eunice, just seven years old, had been taken to live among the savages of the Jesuit mission village at Kahnawake.

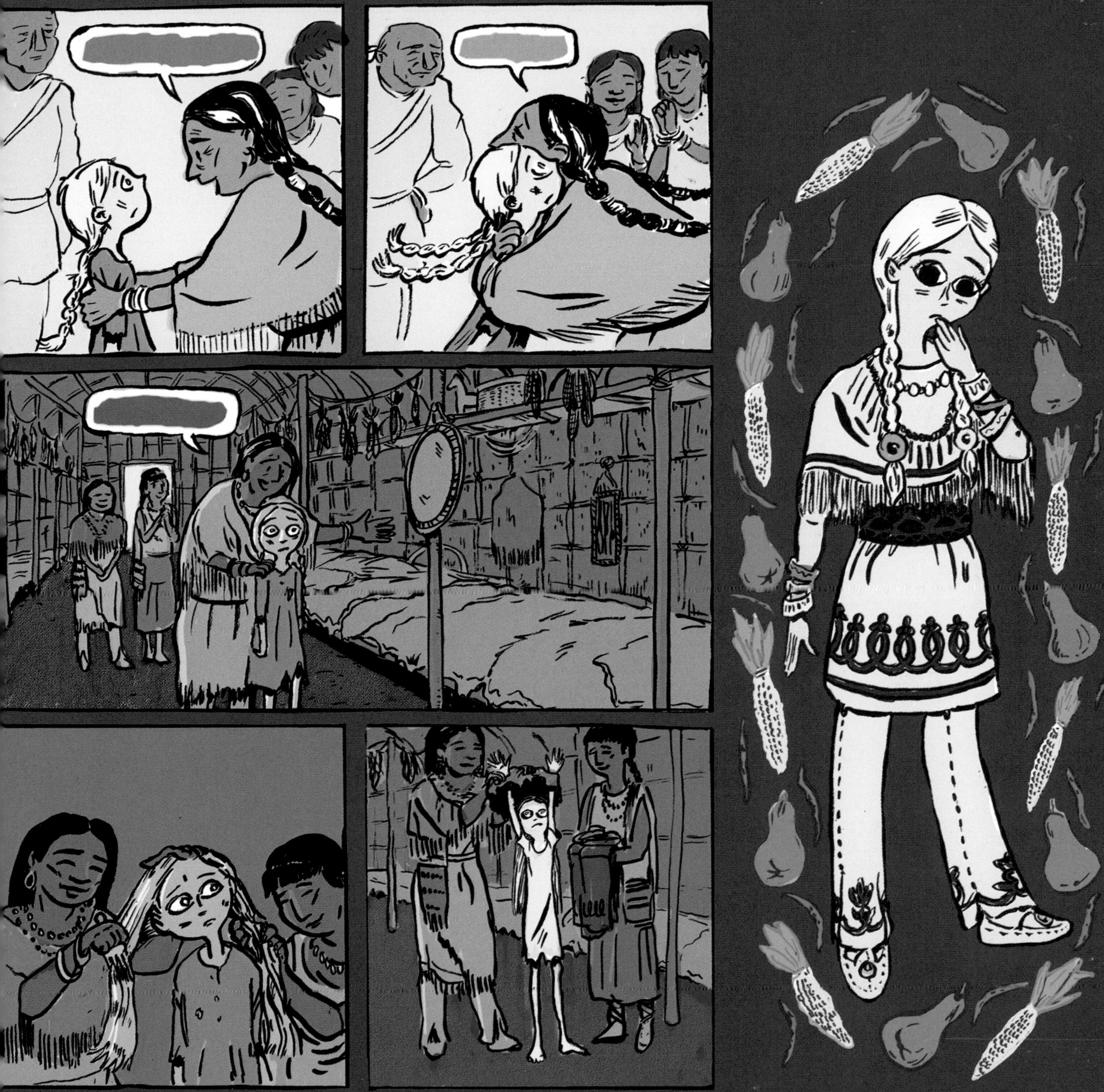

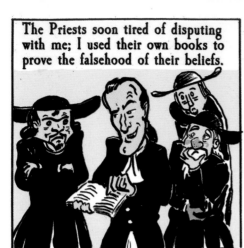

The Priests soon tired of disputing with me; I used their own books to prove the falsehood of their beliefs.

It was proffered that if I would stay and adopt their religion, I would have a fine house and an honorable position.

YOU HAVE MANIFESTED MUCH SORROW FOR YOUR SEPARATION FROM YOUR CHILDREN. ACCEPT, AND YOU SHALL HAVE THEM ALL WITH YOU!

MY CHILDREN...

...ARE DEARER TO ME THAN ALL THE WORLD!" BUT I WOULD NOT DENY CHRIST AND HIS TRUTHS FOR THE HAVING OF THEM!!!

..."FOR WHAT IS A MAN PROFITED IF HE GAIN THE WHOLE WORLD, AND LOSE HIS OWN SOUL?

Finally, the Governor arranged for me a brief visit with my youngest daughter.

WHAT DID SHE SAY?

SHE SAID THAT THEY WOULD SOONER PART WITH THEIR OWN HEARTS THAN WITH YOUR CHILD!

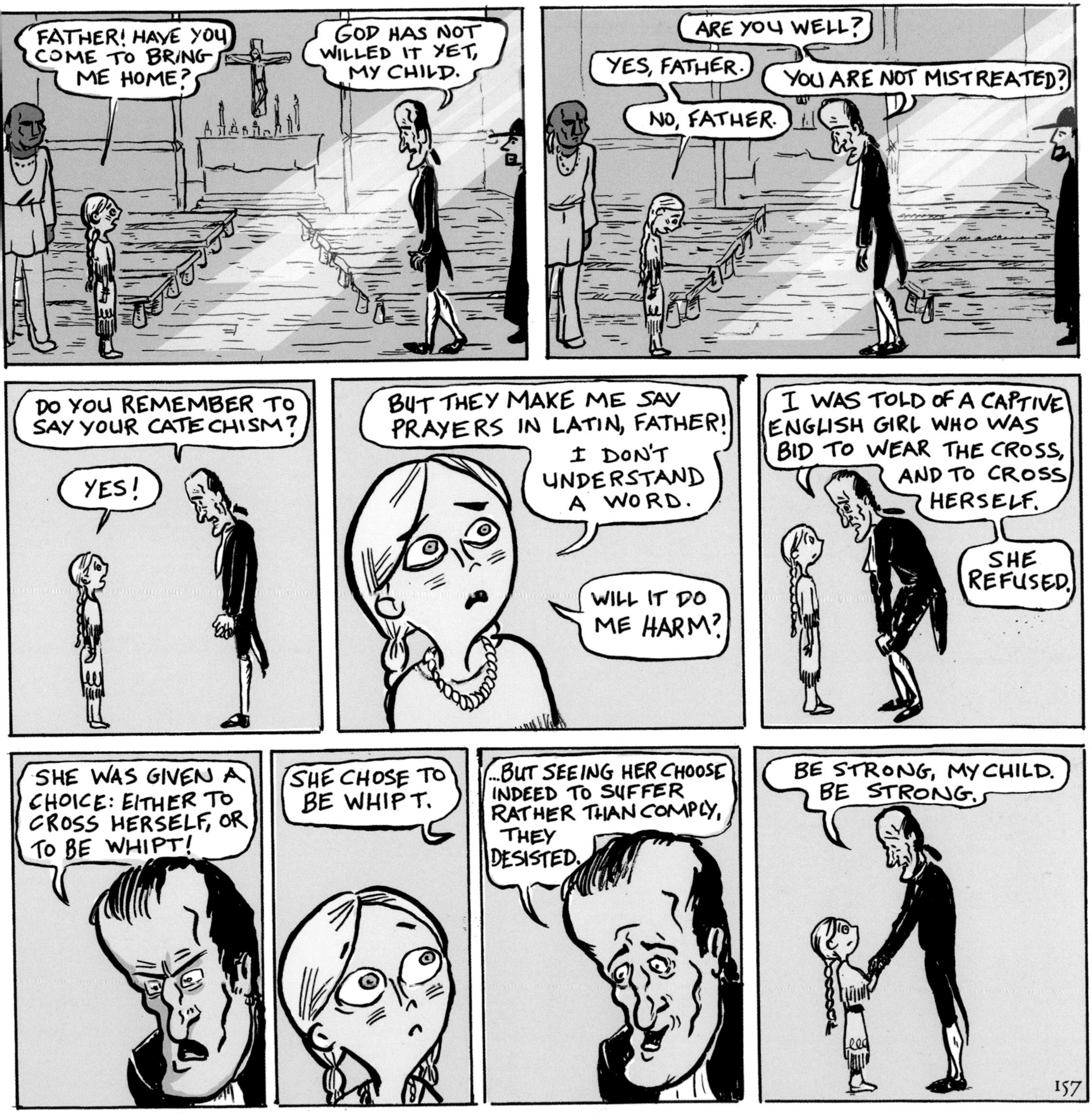
FATHER! HAVE YOU COME TO BRING ME HOME?
GOD HAS NOT WILLED IT YET, MY CHILD.
ARE YOU WELL?
YES, FATHER.
YOU ARE NOT MISTREATED?
NO, FATHER.
DO YOU REMEMBER TO SAY YOUR CATECHISM?
YES!
BUT THEY MAKE ME SAY PRAYERS IN LATIN, FATHER!
I DON'T UNDERSTAND A WORD.
WILL IT DO ME HARM?
I WAS TOLD OF A CAPTIVE ENGLISH GIRL WHO WAS BID TO WEAR THE CROSS, AND TO CROSS HERSELF.
SHE REFUSED.
SHE WAS GIVEN A CHOICE: EITHER TO CROSS HERSELF, OR TO BE WHIPT!
SHE CHOSE TO BE WHIPT.
...BUT SEEING HER CHOOSE INDEED TO SUFFER RATHER THAN COMPLY, THEY DESISTED.
BE STRONG, MY CHILD. BE STRONG.

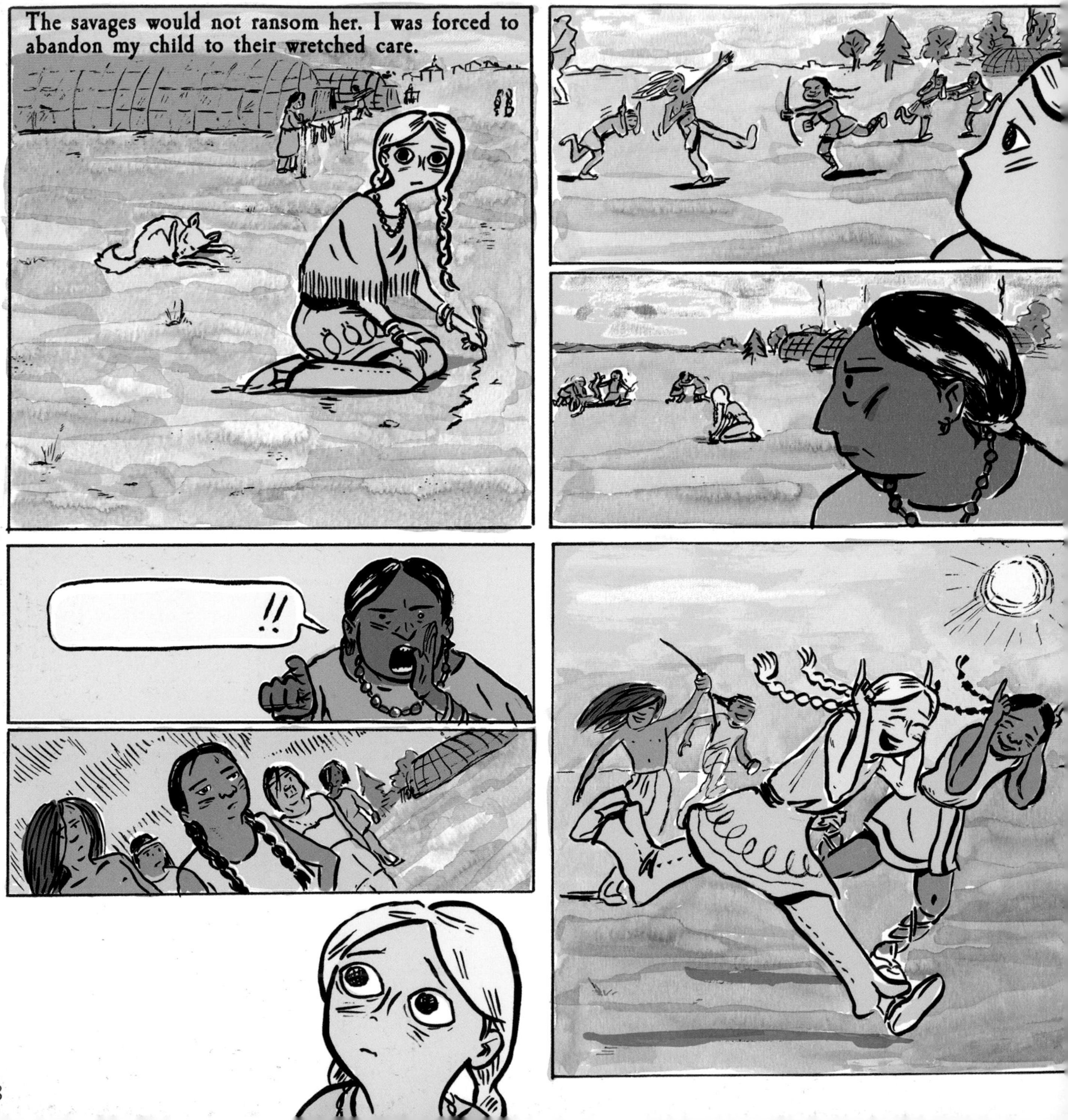

The savages would not ransom her. I was forced to abandon my child to their wretched care.
!!

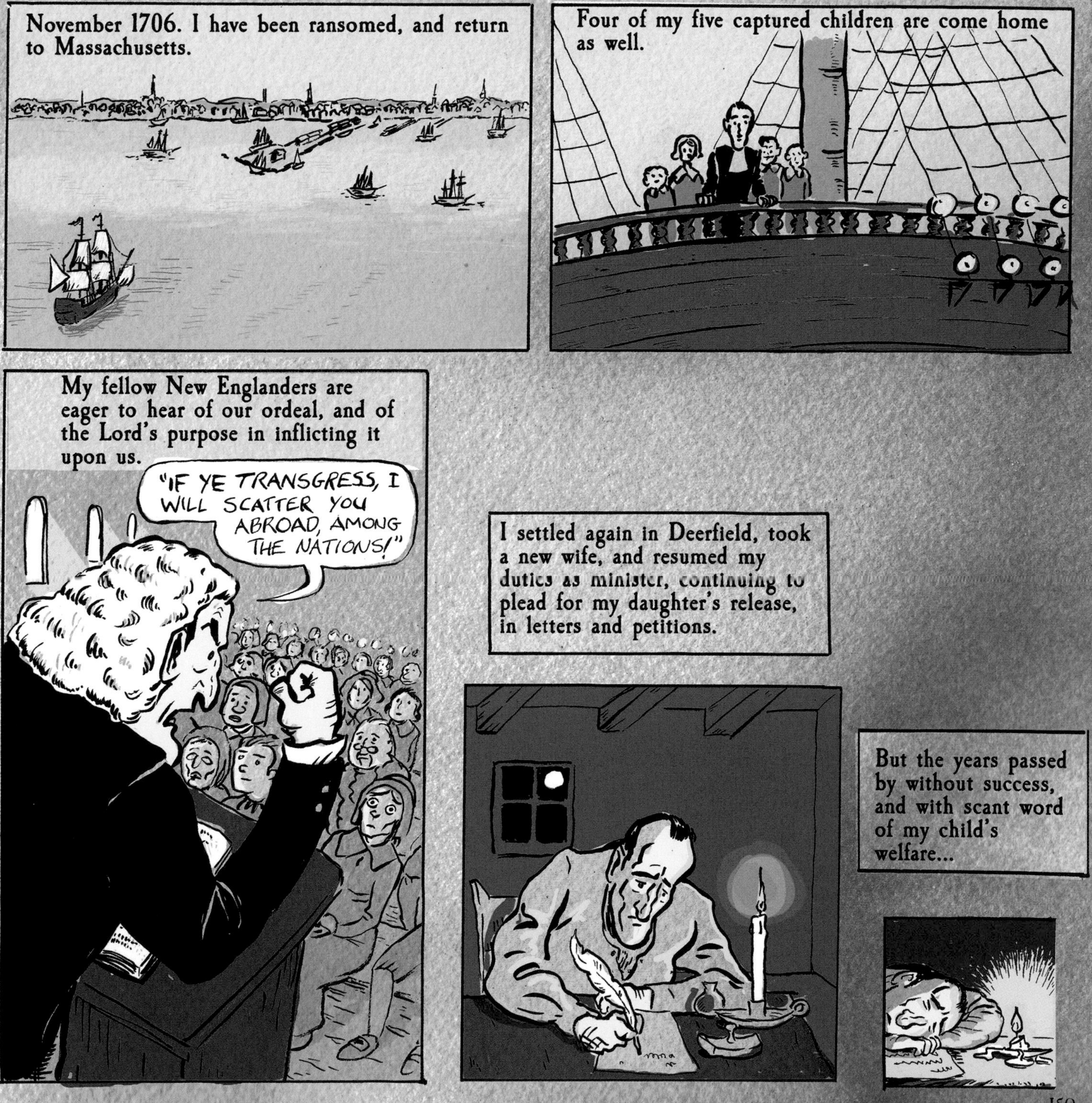
November 1706. I have been ransomed, and return to Massachusetts.
Four of my five captured children are come home as well.
My fellow New Englanders are eager to hear of our ordeal, and of the Lord's purpose in inflicting it upon us.
"IF YE TRANSGRESS, I WILL SCATTER YOU ABROAD, AMONG THE NATIONS!"
I settled again in Deerfield, took a new wife, and resumed my duties as minister, continuing to plead for my daughter's release, in letters and petitions.
But the years passed by without success, and with scant word of my child's welfare...

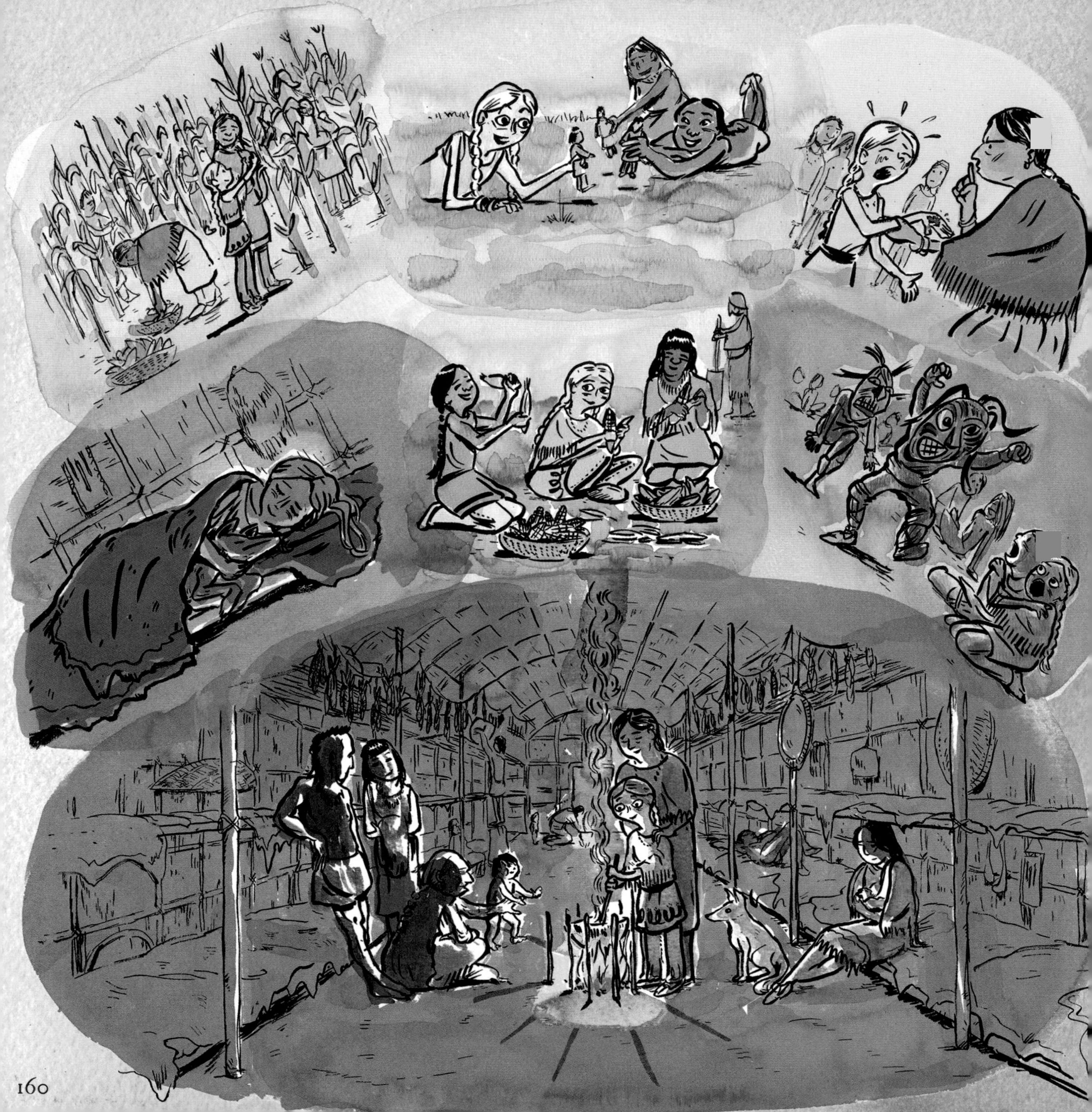

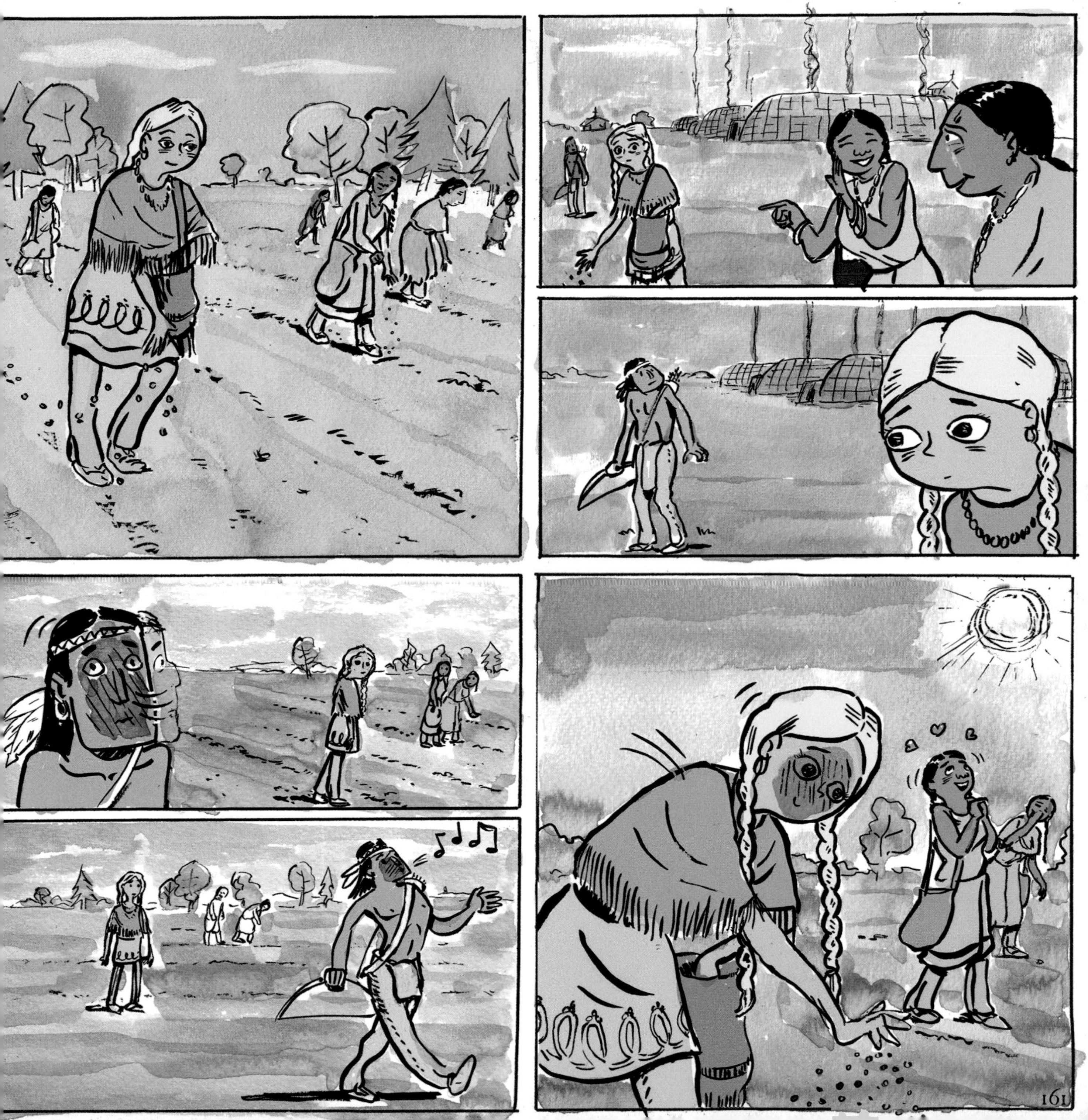

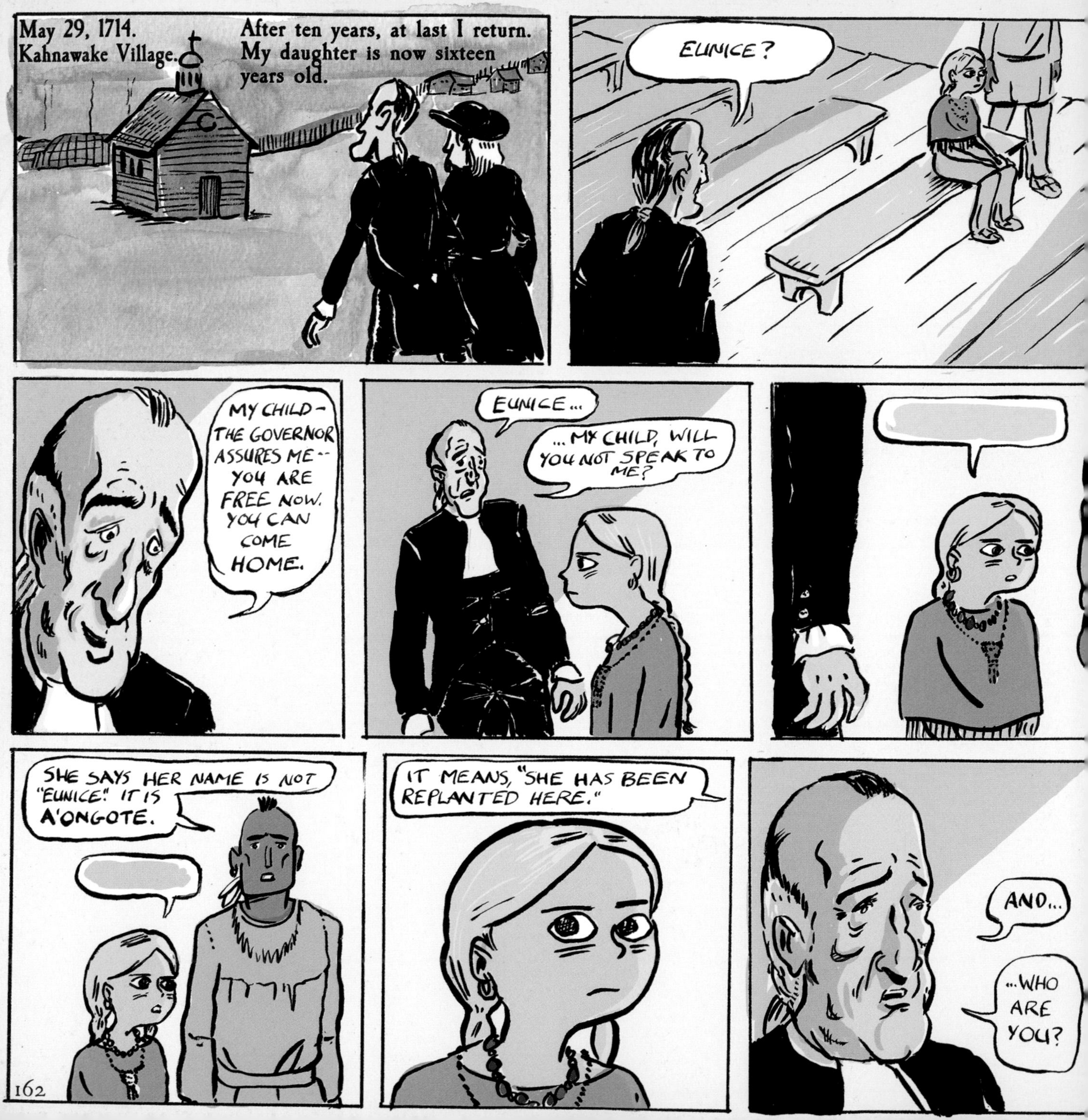
May 29, 1714.
Kahnawake Village.
After ten years, at last I return. My daughter is now sixteen years old.
EUNICE?
MY CHILD - THE GOVERNOR ASSURES ME -- YOU ARE FREE NOW. YOU CAN COME HOME.
EUNICE...
...MY CHILD, WILL YOU NOT SPEAK TO ME?
SHE SAYS HER NAME IS NOT "EUNICE." IT IS A'ONGOTE.
IT MEANS, "SHE HAS BEEN REPLANTED HERE."
AND...
...WHO ARE YOU?

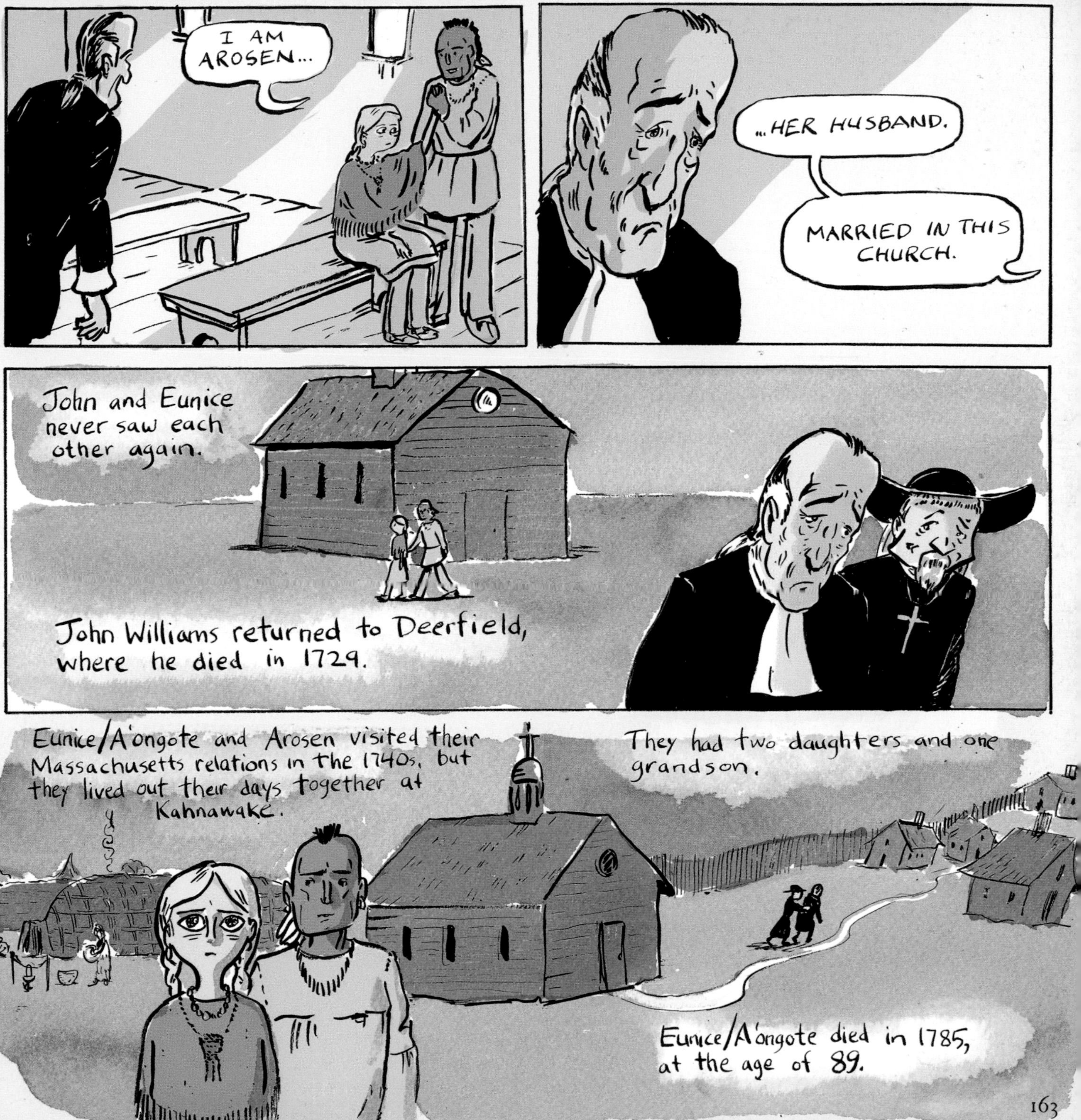
I AM AROSEN...
...HER HUSBAND.
MARRIED IN THIS CHURCH.
John and Eunice never saw each other again.
John Williams returned to Deerfield, where he died in 1729.
Eunice/A'ongote and Arosen visited their Massachusetts relations in the 1740s, but they lived out their days together at Kahnawake.
They had two daughters and one grandson.
Eunice/A'ongote died in 1785, at the age of 89.

Glooscap and the New Men

Story by Josh O'Neil and Art by James Comey

Glooscap was an important figure in Wabanaki folklore, playing the role of the creator of the first humans in Mi'kmaq and Penobscot tales. In the Abeneki myth, Glooscap did not create the first humans (they believed it was Tabaldak, who created people out of stones) but he did try to stop humans from hunting, believing that their hunting would eventually kill all of the animals and upset the delicate balance of nature.

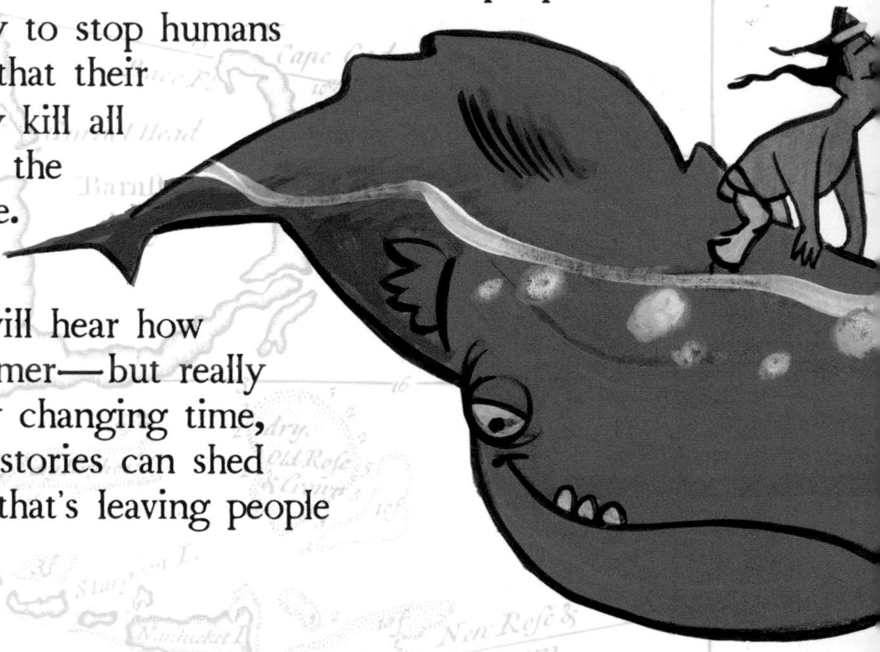

In this vignette, we will hear how Glooscap found the summer—but really this is a tale of a rapidly changing time, and how our best-loved stories can shed light even on the world that's leaving people behind.

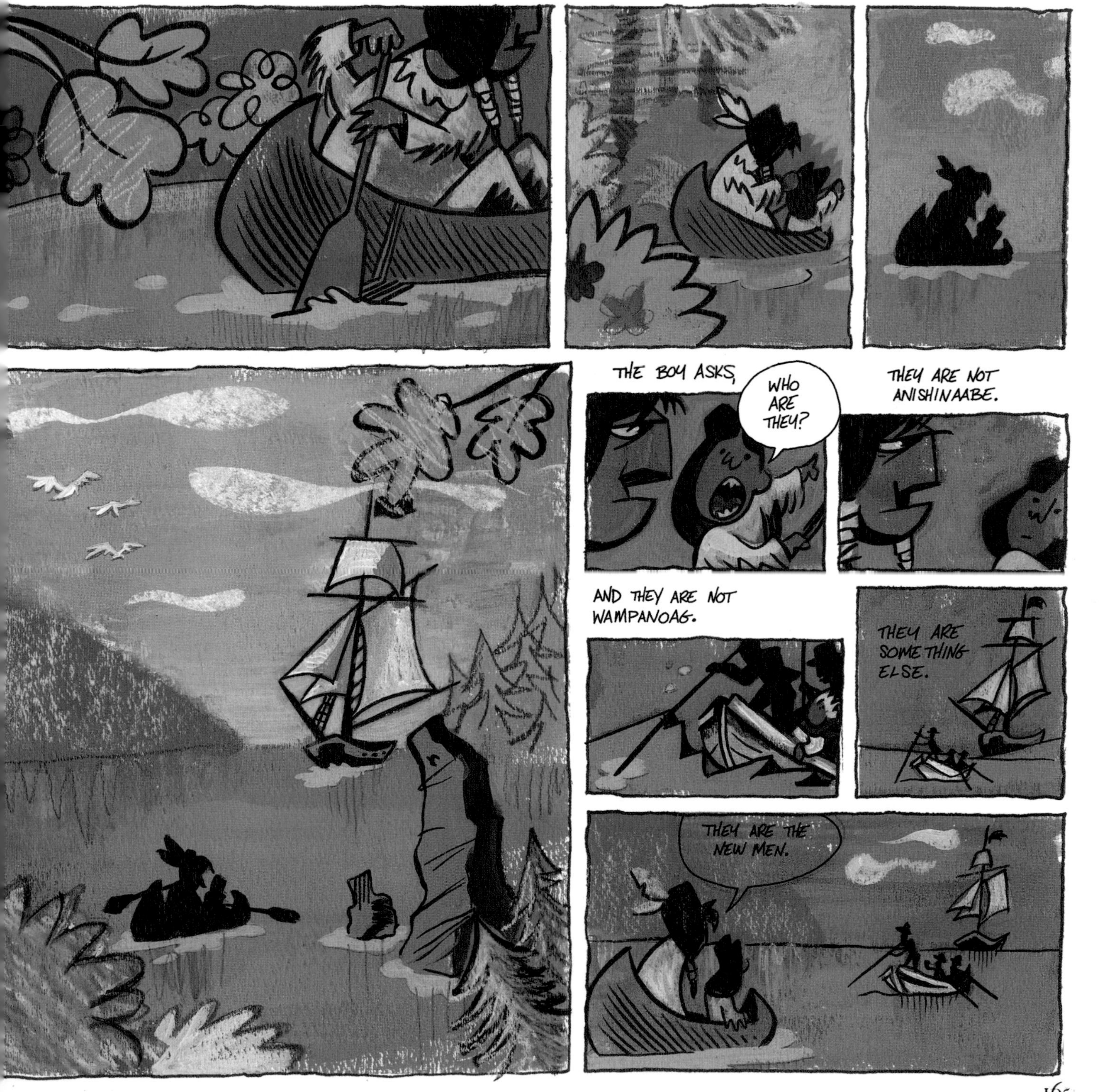
THE BOY ASKS,
WHO ARE THEY?
THEY ARE NOT ANISHINAABE.
AND THEY ARE NOT WAMPANOAG.
THEY ARE SOMETHING ELSE.
THEY ARE THE NEW MEN.

WHERE DO THE NEW MEN COME FROM?

DO YOU REMEMBER THE STORY OF HOW GLOOSCAP FOUND THE SUMMER?

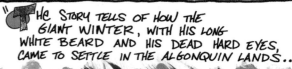

"THE STORY TELLS OF HOW THE GIANT WINTER, WITH HIS LONG WHITE BEARD AND HIS DEAD HARD EYES, CAME TO SETTLE IN THE ALGONQUIN LANDS..."

I DO!

AND HOW DOES IT GO?

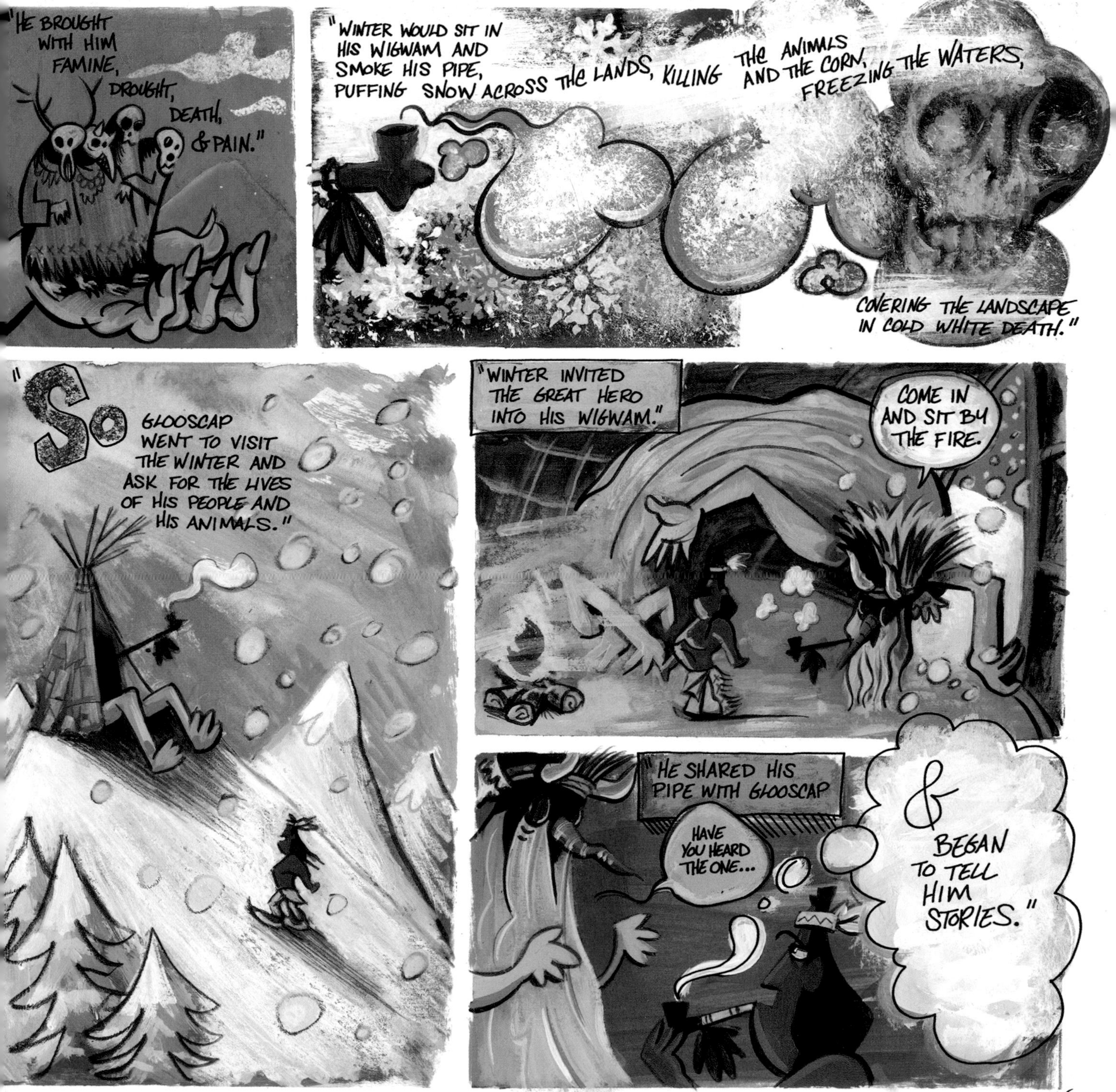

"HE BROUGHT WITH HIM FAMINE, DROUGHT, DEATH, & PAIN."
"WINTER WOULD SIT IN HIS WIGWAM AND SMOKE HIS PIPE, PUFFING SNOW ACROSS THE LANDS, KILLING THE ANIMALS AND THE CORN, FREEZING THE WATERS,
COVERING THE LANDSCAPE IN COLD WHITE DEATH."
"SO GLOOSCAP WENT TO VISIT THE WINTER AND ASK FOR THE LIVES OF HIS PEOPLE AND HIS ANIMALS."
"WINTER INVITED THE GREAT HERO INTO HIS WIGWAM."
COME IN AND SIT BY THE FIRE.
"HE SHARED HIS PIPE WITH GLOOSCAP
HAVE YOU HEARD THE ONE...
& BEGAN TO TELL HIM STORIES."

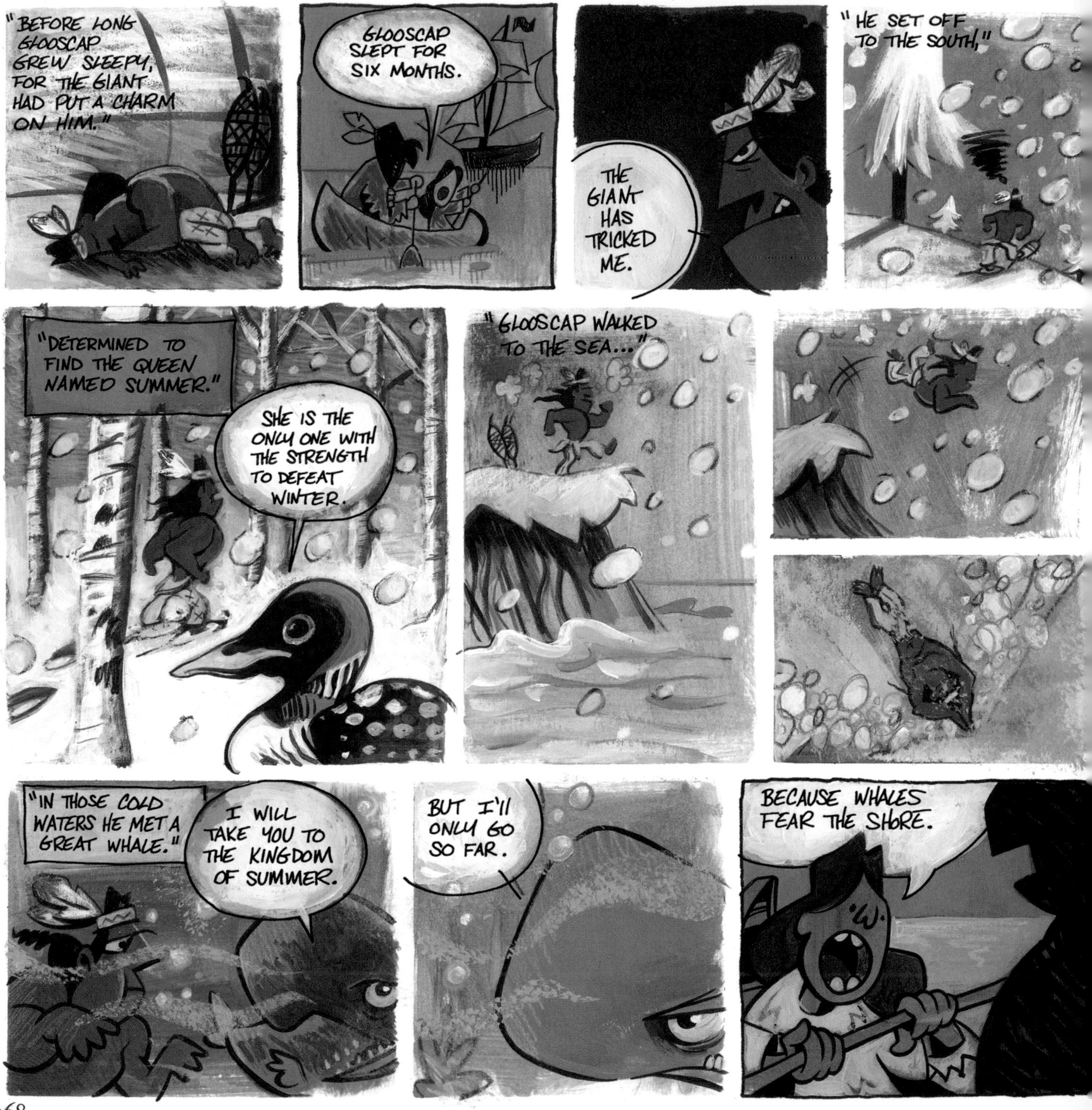
"BEFORE LONG GLOOSCAP GREW SLEEPY, FOR THE GIANT HAD PUT A CHARM ON HIM."
GLOOSCAP SLEPT FOR SIX MONTHS.
THE GIANT HAS TRICKED ME.
"HE SET OFF TO THE SOUTH,"
"DETERMINED TO FIND THE QUEEN NAMED SUMMER."
SHE IS THE ONLY ONE WITH THE STRENGTH TO DEFEAT WINTER.
"GLOOSCAP WALKED TO THE SEA..."
"IN THOSE COLD WATERS HE MET A GREAT WHALE."
I WILL TAKE YOU TO THE KINGDOM OF SUMMER.
BUT I'LL ONLY GO SO FAR.
BECAUSE WHALES FEAR THE SHORE.

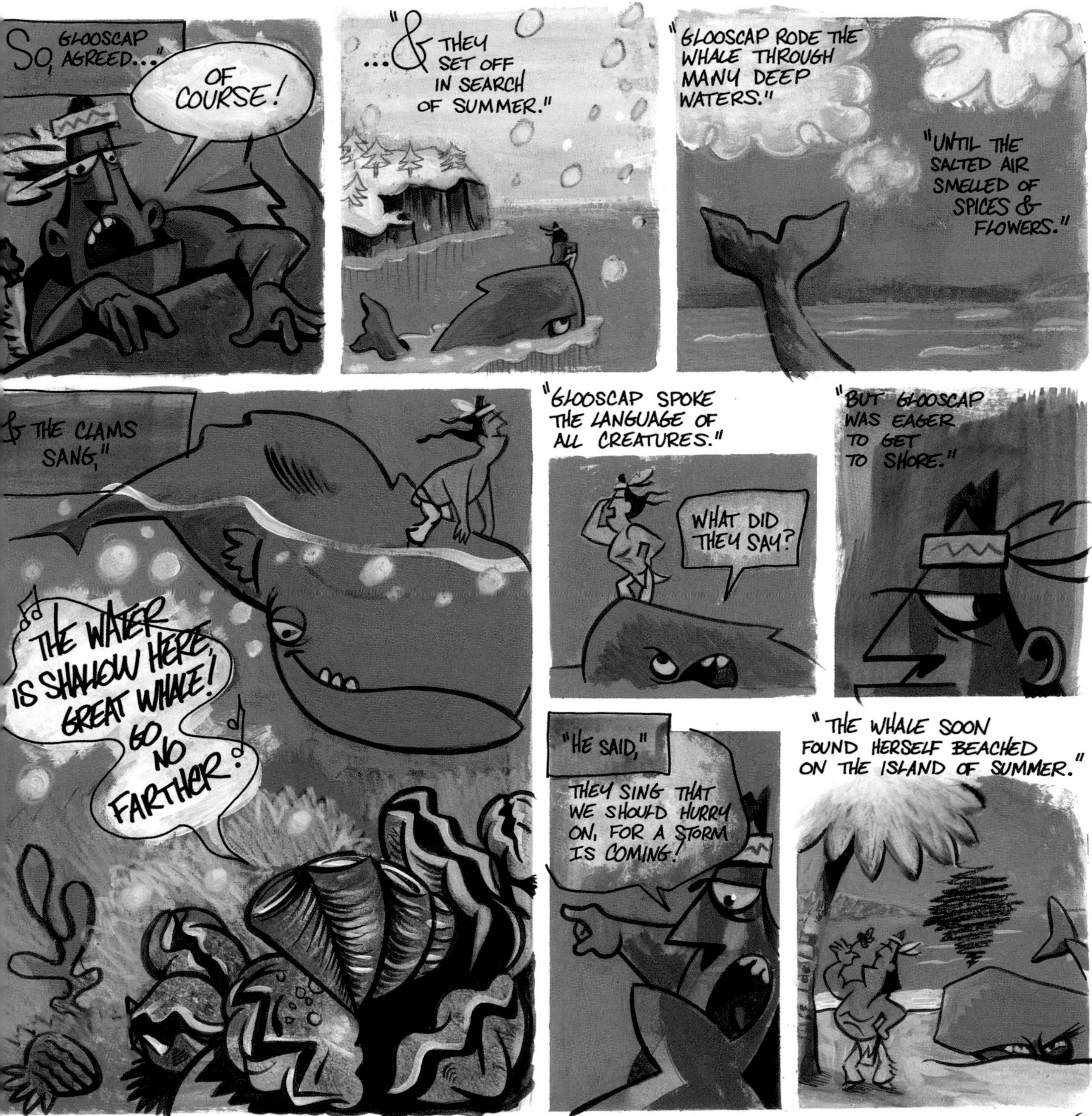
"So, Glooscap agreed..."
Of course!
"...& they set off in search of summer."
"Glooscap rode the whale through many deep waters."
"Until the salted air smelled of spices & flowers."
"& the clams sang,"
The water is shallow here, great whale! Go no farther!
"Glooscap spoke the language of all creatures."
What did they say?
"But Glooscap was eager to get to shore."
"He said,"
They sing that we should hurry on, for a storm is coming!
"The whale soon found herself beached on the island of summer."

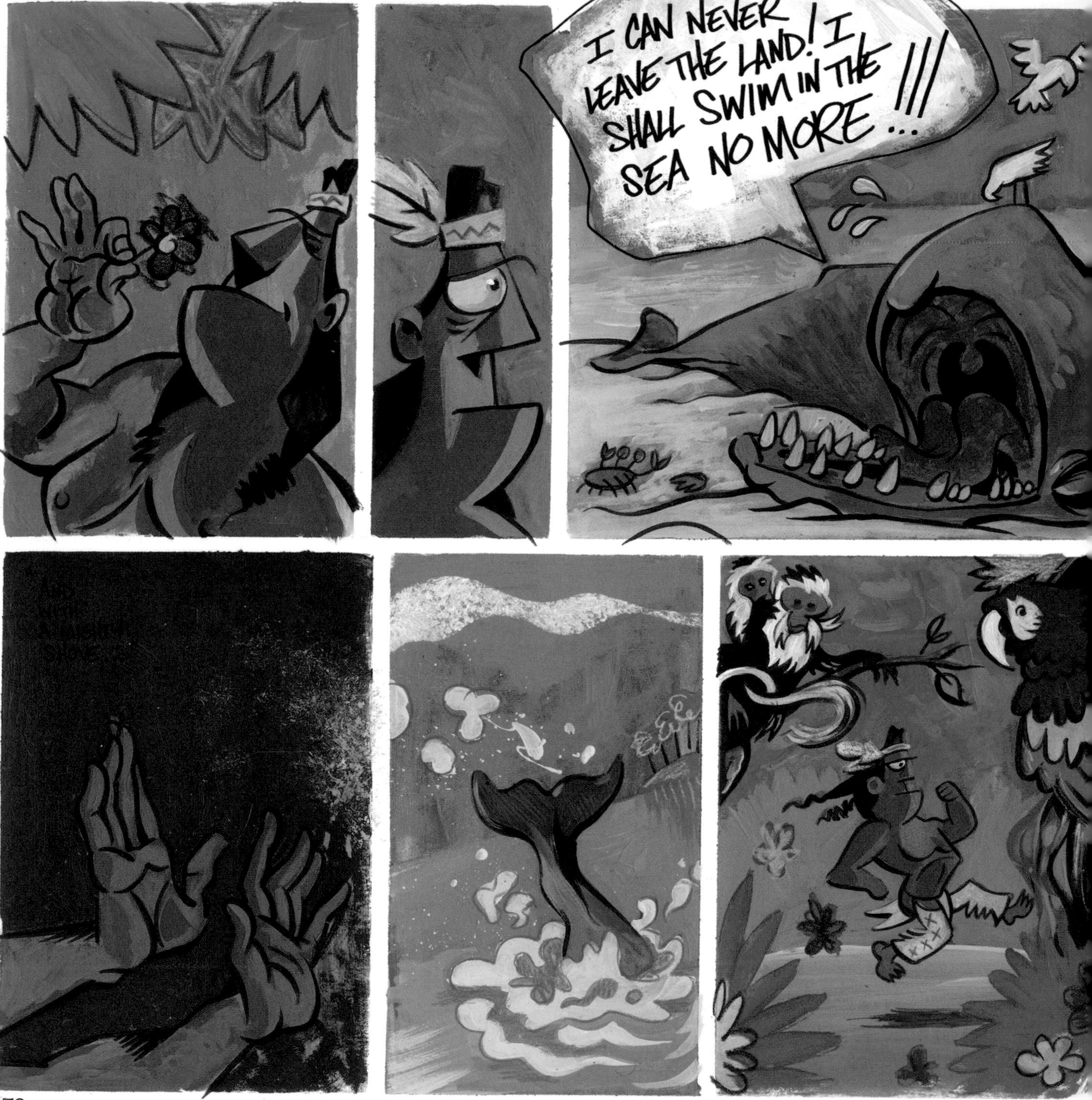
I CAN NEVER LEAVE THE LAND! I SHALL SWIM IN THE SEA NO MORE...!!!

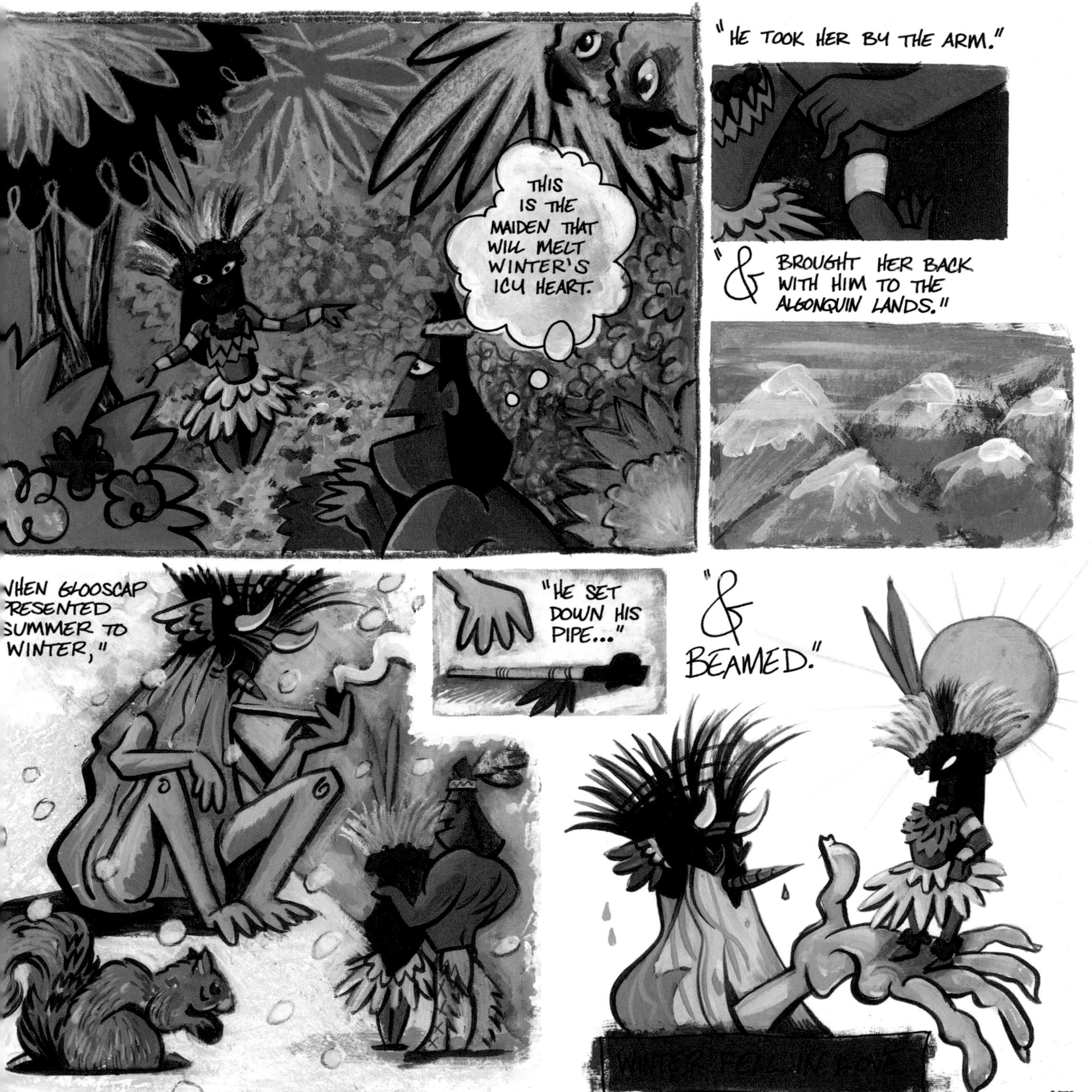
THIS IS THE MAIDEN THAT WILL MELT WINTER'S ICY HEART.
"HE TOOK HER BY THE ARM."
"& BROUGHT HER BACK WITH HIM TO THE ALGONQUIN LANDS."
WHEN GLOOSCAP PRESENTED SUMMER TO WINTER,"
"HE SET DOWN HIS PIPE..."
"& BEAMED."
WINTER FELL IN LOVE

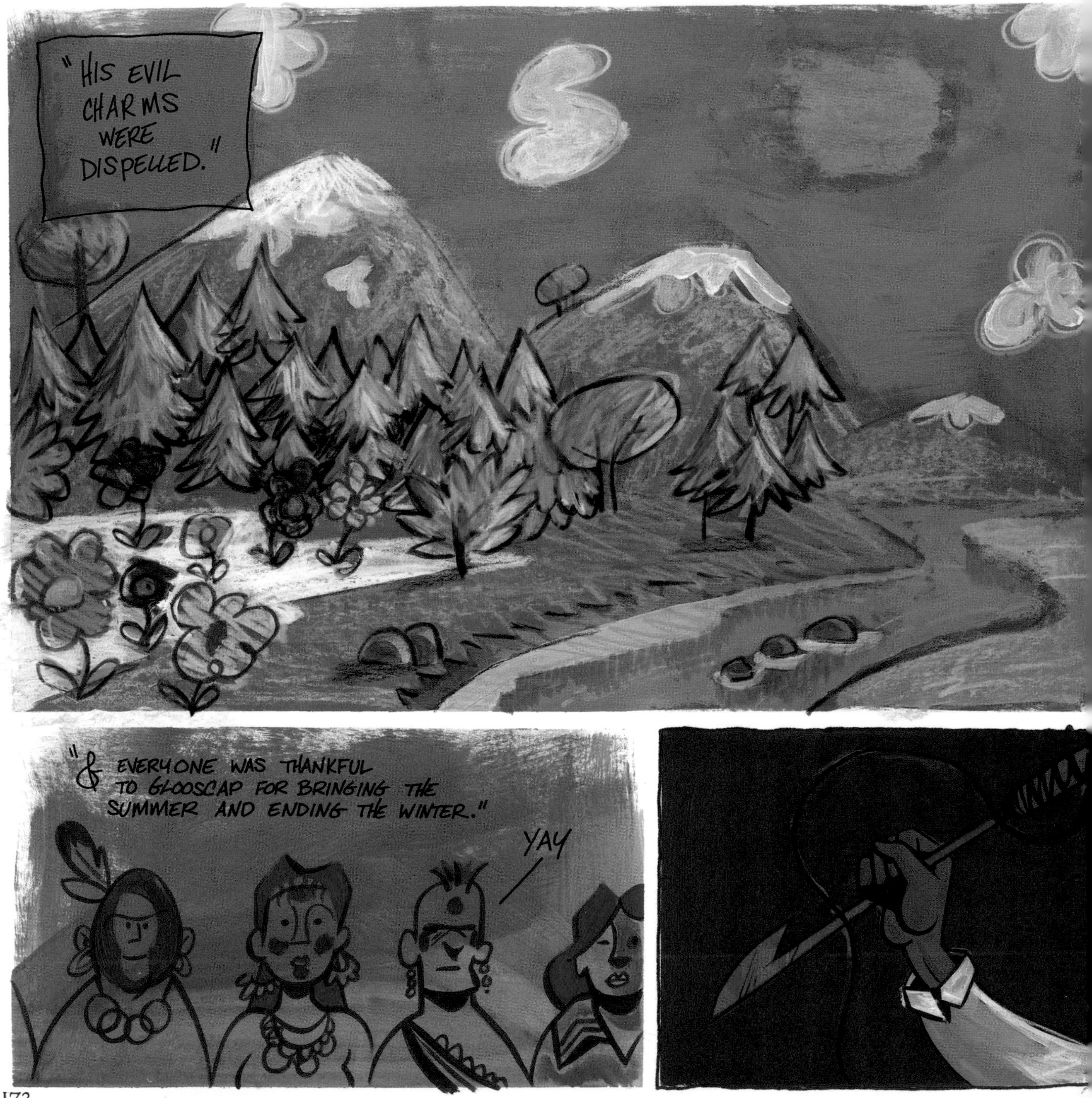
"HIS EVIL CHARMS WERE DISPELLED."
"& EVERYONE WAS THANKFUL TO GLOOSCAP FOR BRINGING THE SUMMER AND ENDING THE WINTER."
YAY

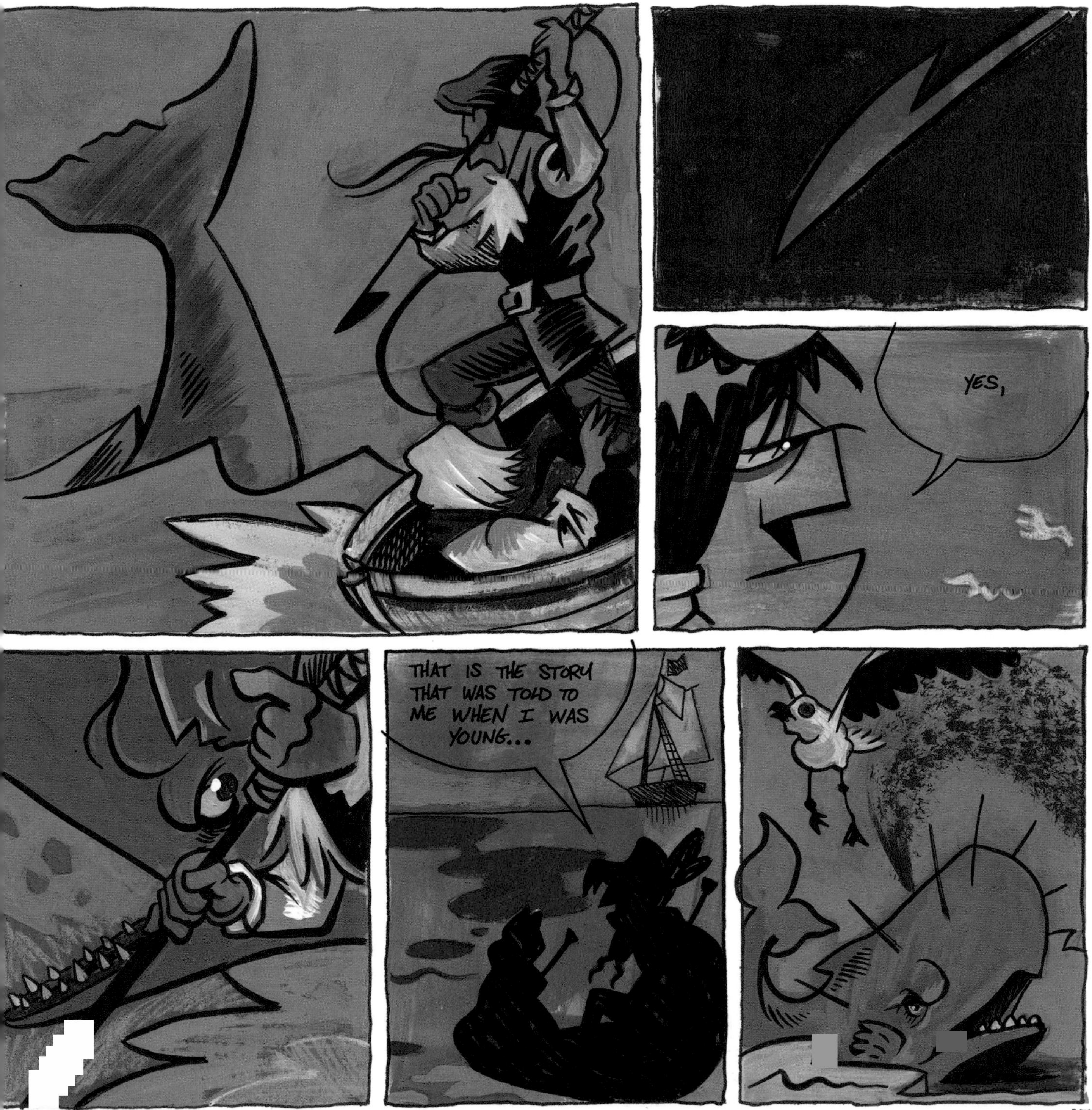
YES,
THAT IS THE STORY THAT WAS TOLD TO ME WHEN I WAS YOUNG...

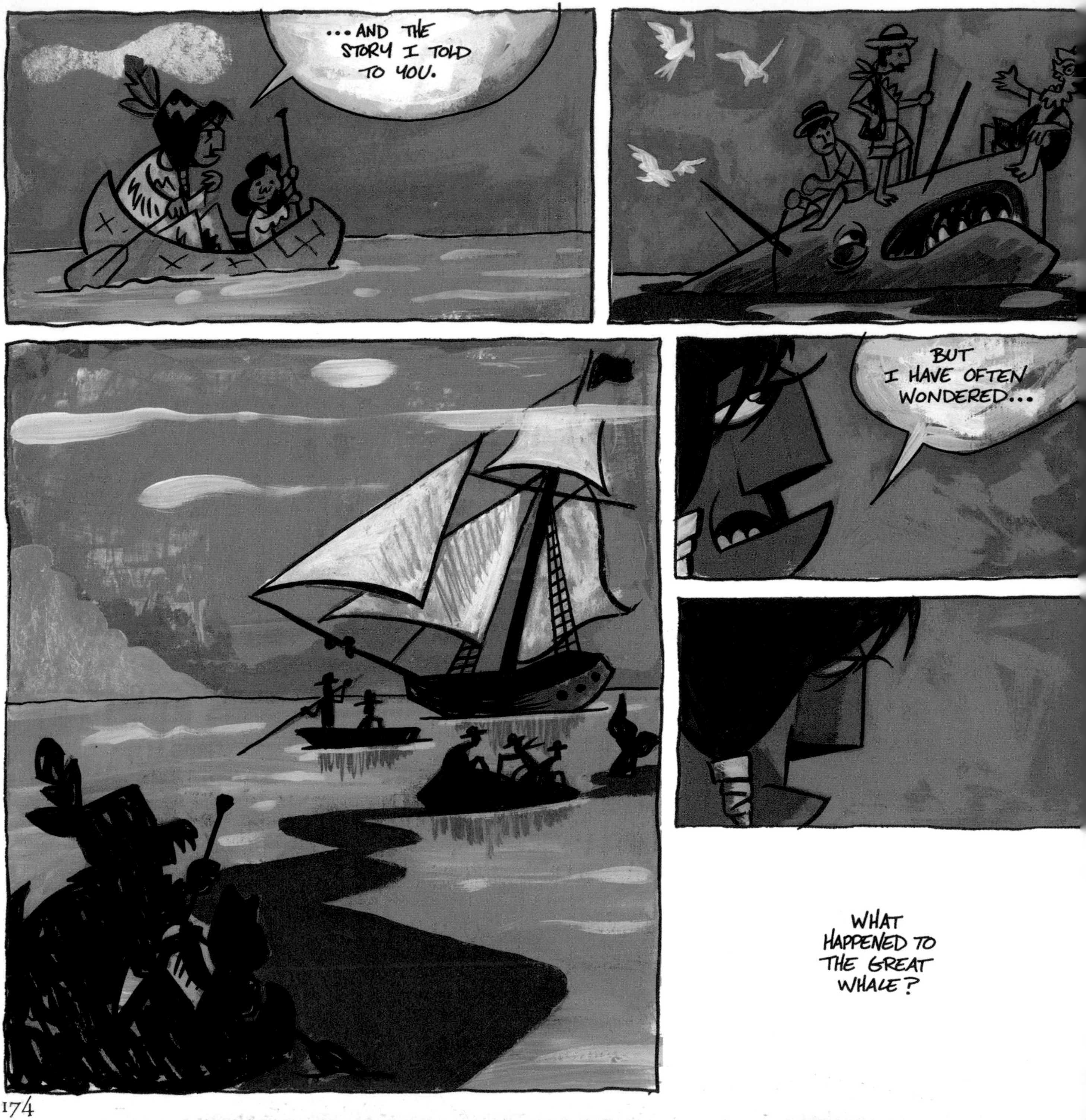
...AND THE STORY I TOLD TO YOU.
BUT I HAVE OFTEN WONDERED...
WHAT HAPPENED TO THE GREAT WHALE?

Chasing Monsters

Story and Art by Charles Fetherolf

Whaling in America was nothing new, as Native Americans employed a technique called drift whaling in which they would harvest whales that had washed up on shore. Early on, colonists started shore whaling—hunting whales that were close to shore. However, once people realized how valuable sperm oil was (which was harvested by boiling the blubber of sperm whales), colonial whalers began to hunt farther from shore, and Nantucket and New Bedford became important whaling ports.

For the most part, the whaling industry operated independently from the societies in Boston, Plymouth, and beyond. Many Native Americans and African Americans crewed the whaling ships, which offered a lucrative but dangerous job to any who were willing to take the chance.

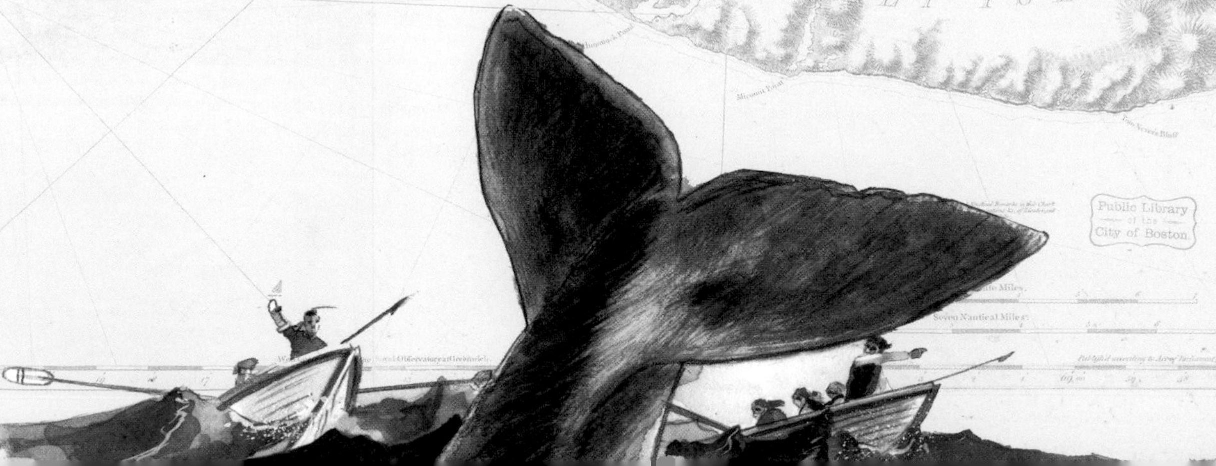
Public Library of the City of Boston
Seven Nautical Miles.

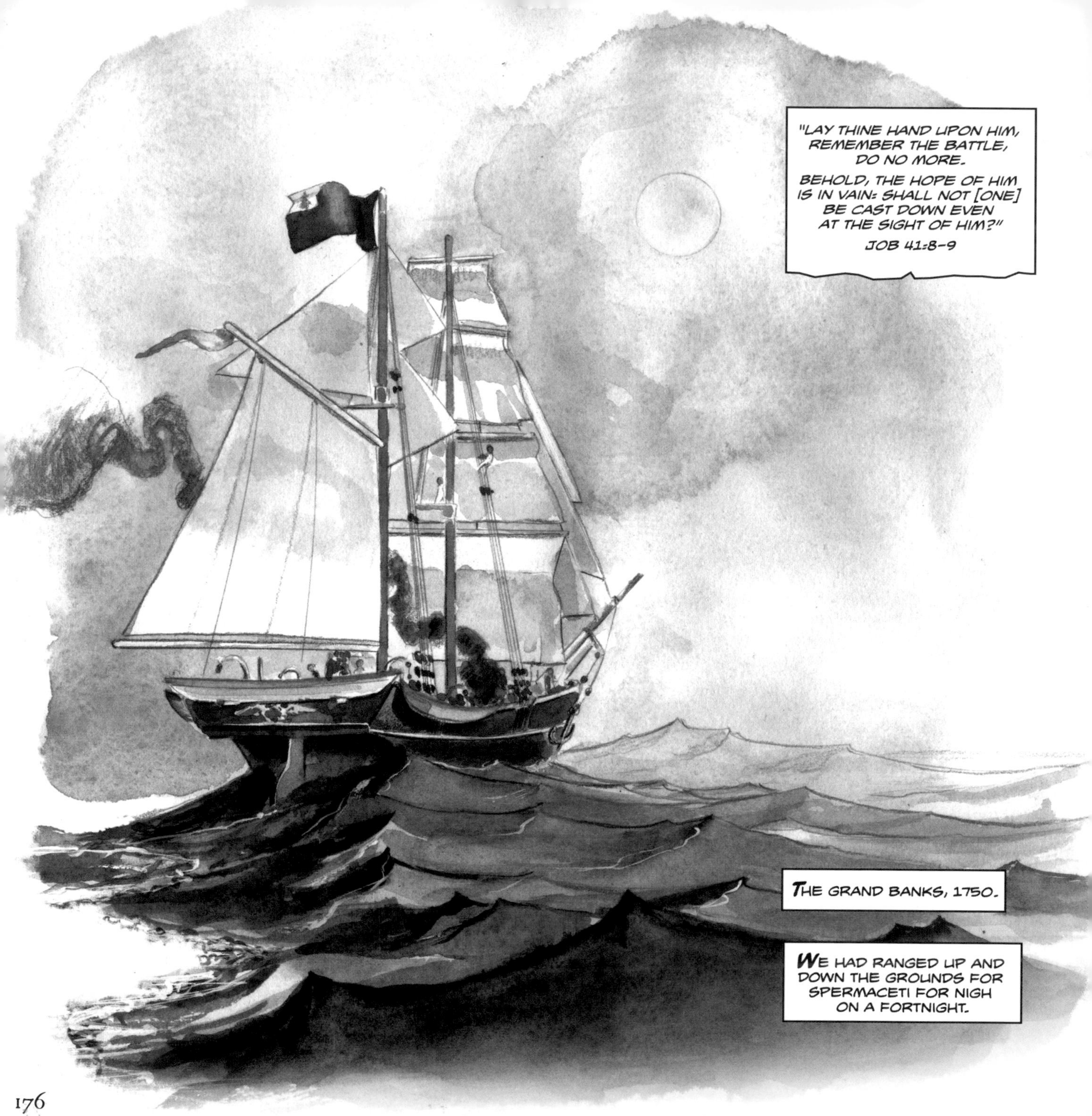
"LAY THINE HAND UPON HIM, REMEMBER THE BATTLE, DO NO MORE.
BEHOLD, THE HOPE OF HIM IS IN VAIN: SHALL NOT [ONE] BE CAST DOWN EVEN AT THE SIGHT OF HIM?"
JOB 41:8-9
THE GRAND BANKS, 1750.
WE HAD RANGED UP AND DOWN THE GROUNDS FOR SPERMACETI FOR NIGH ON A FORTNIGHT.

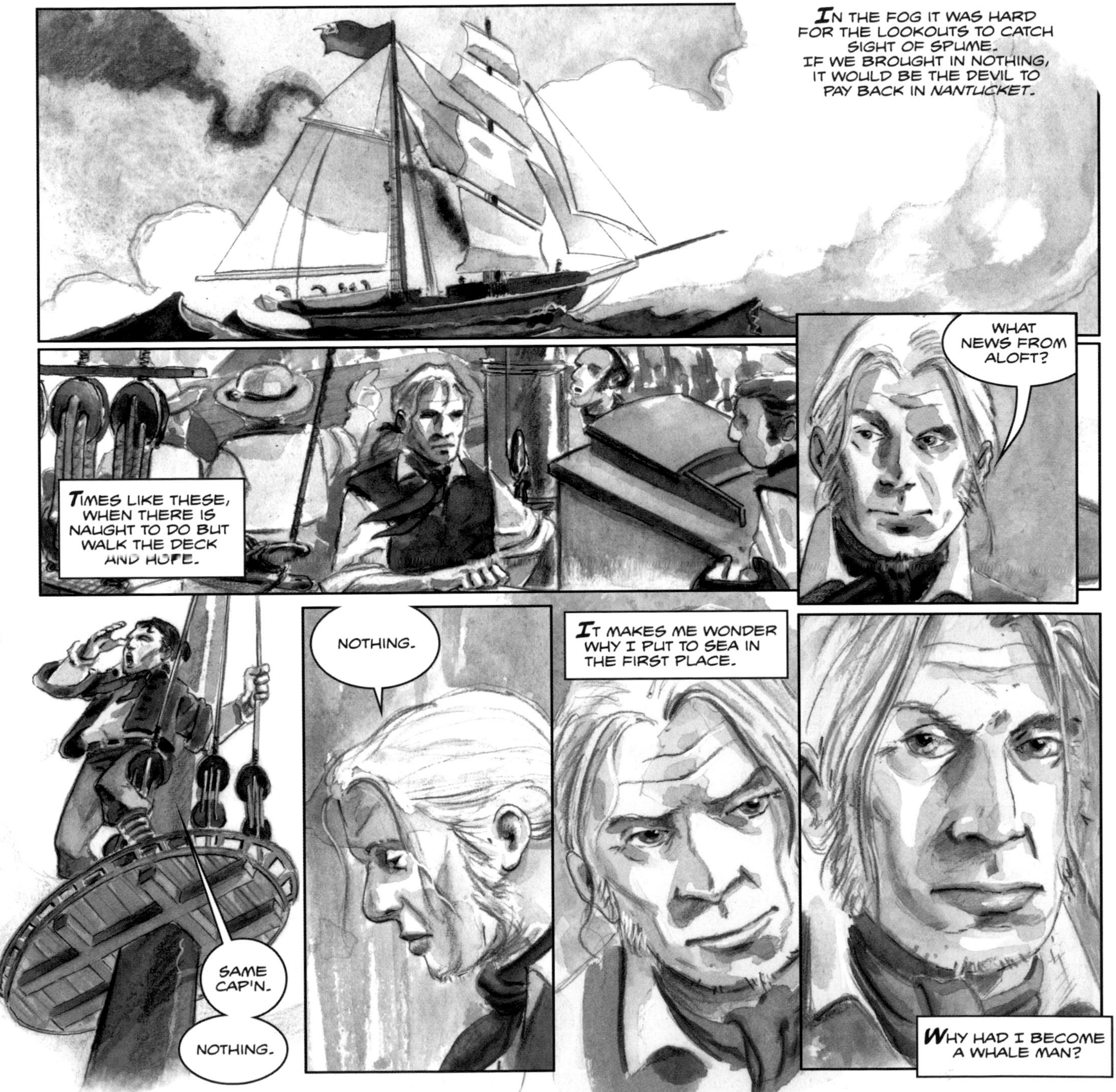
IN THE FOG IT WAS HARD FOR THE LOOKOUTS TO CATCH SIGHT OF SPUME. IF WE BROUGHT IN NOTHING, IT WOULD BE THE DEVIL TO PAY BACK IN *NANTUCKET*.
TIMES LIKE THESE, WHEN THERE IS NAUGHT TO DO BUT WALK THE DECK AND HOPE.
WHAT NEWS FROM ALOFT?
SAME CAP'N.
NOTHING.
NOTHING.
IT MAKES ME WONDER WHY I PUT TO SEA IN THE FIRST PLACE.
WHY HAD I BECOME A WHALE MAN?

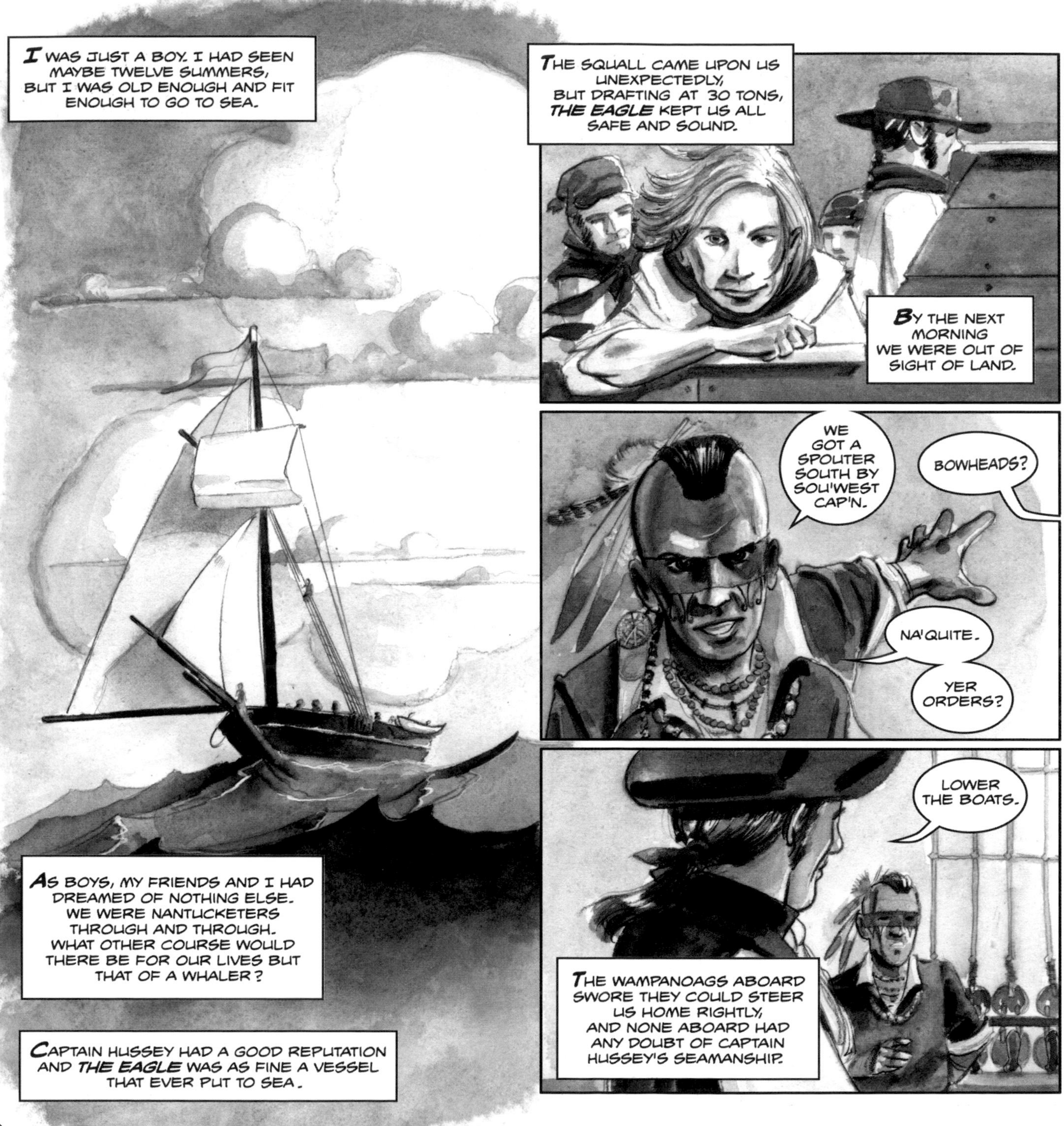
I WAS JUST A BOY. I HAD SEEN MAYBE TWELVE SUMMERS, BUT I WAS OLD ENOUGH AND FIT ENOUGH TO GO TO SEA.
AS BOYS, MY FRIENDS AND I HAD DREAMED OF NOTHING ELSE. WE WERE NANTUCKETERS THROUGH AND THROUGH. WHAT OTHER COURSE WOULD THERE BE FOR OUR LIVES BUT THAT OF A WHALER?
CAPTAIN HUSSEY HAD A GOOD REPUTATION AND THE EAGLE WAS AS FINE A VESSEL THAT EVER PUT TO SEA.
THE SQUALL CAME UPON US UNEXPECTEDLY, BUT DRAFTING AT 30 TONS, THE EAGLE KEPT US ALL SAFE AND SOUND.
BY THE NEXT MORNING WE WERE OUT OF SIGHT OF LAND.
WE GOT A SPOUTER SOUTH BY SOU'WEST CAP'N.
BOWHEADS?
NA'QUITE.
YER ORDERS?
LOWER THE BOATS.
THE WAMPANOAGS ABOARD SWORE THEY COULD STEER US HOME RIGHTLY, AND NONE ABOARD HAD ANY DOUBT OF CAPTAIN HUSSEY'S SEAMANSHIP.

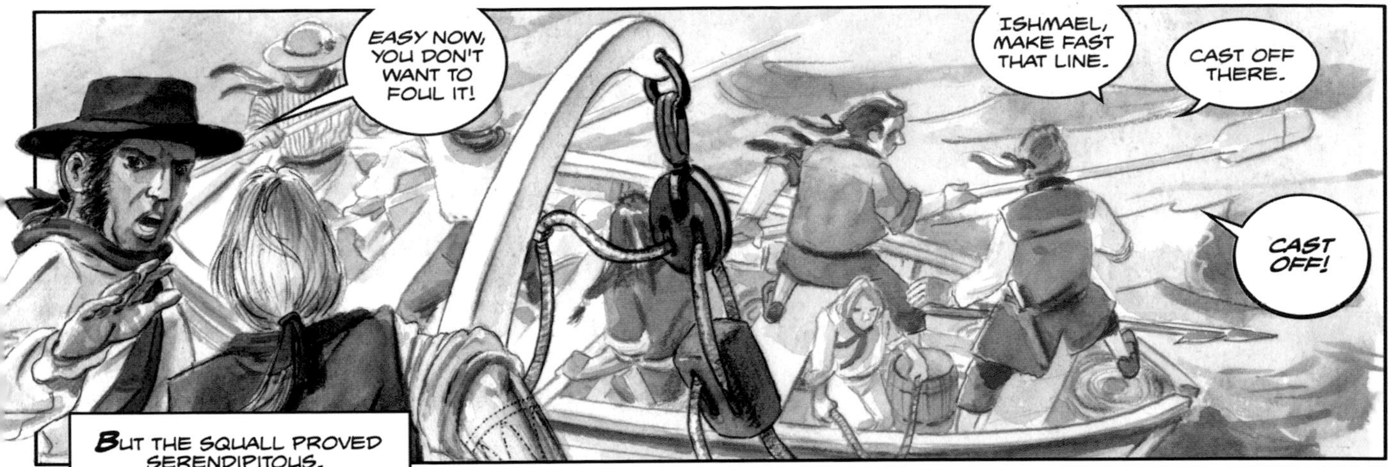
EASY NOW, YOU DON'T WANT TO FOUL IT!
ISHMAEL, MAKE FAST THAT LINE.
CAST OFF THERE.
CAST OFF!
BUT THE SQUALL PROVED SERENDIPITOUS. AFTER A WEEK OF CRUISING WITH NO WHALES SIGHTED, HERE WE SAW SPUMES APLENTY!

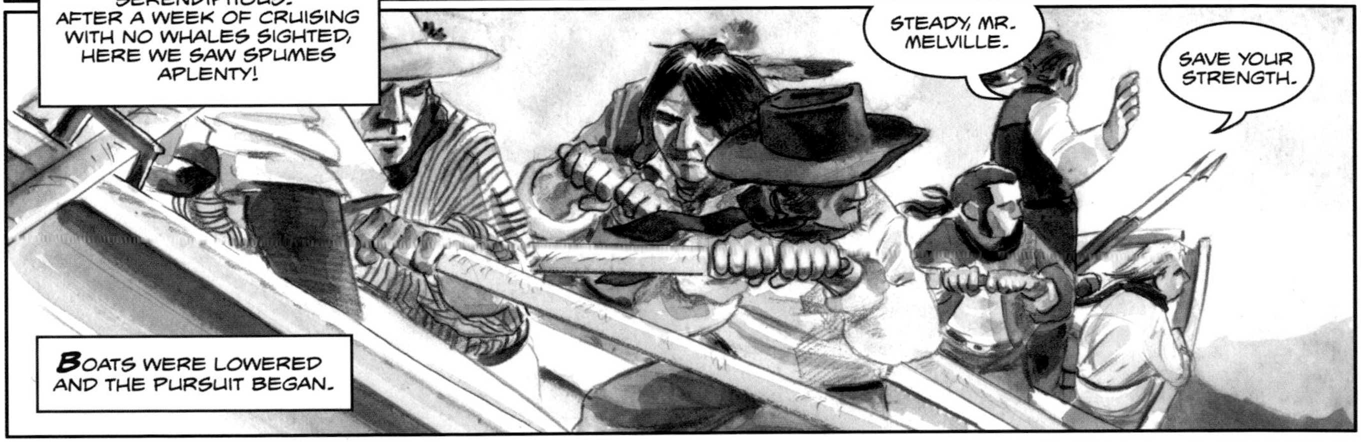
STEADY, MR. MELVILLE.
SAVE YOUR STRENGTH.
BOATS WERE LOWERED AND THE PURSUIT BEGAN.

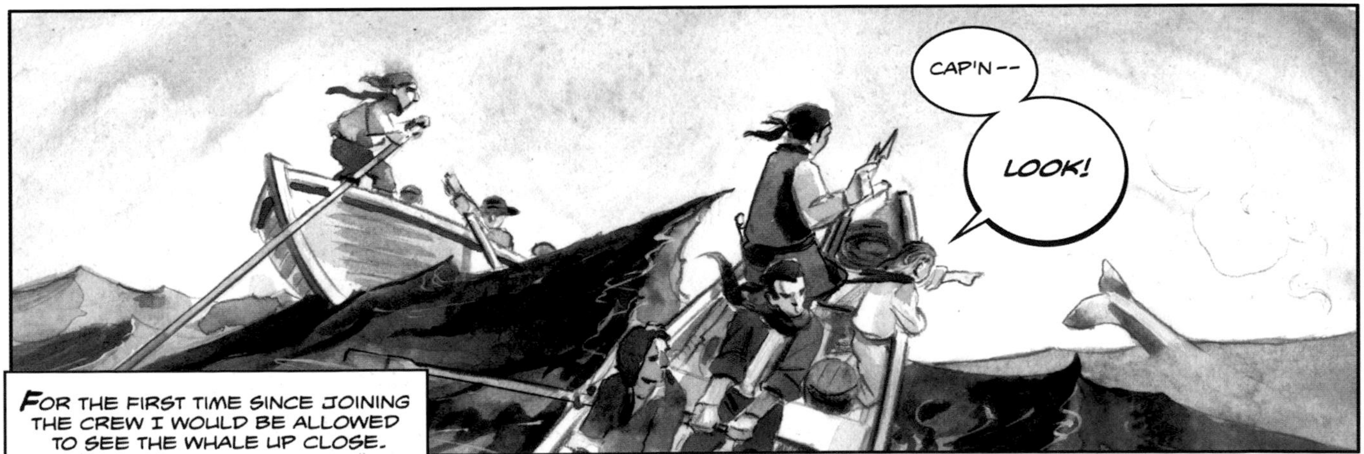
CAP'N --
LOOK!
FOR THE FIRST TIME SINCE JOINING THE CREW I WOULD BE ALLOWED TO SEE THE WHALE UP CLOSE.

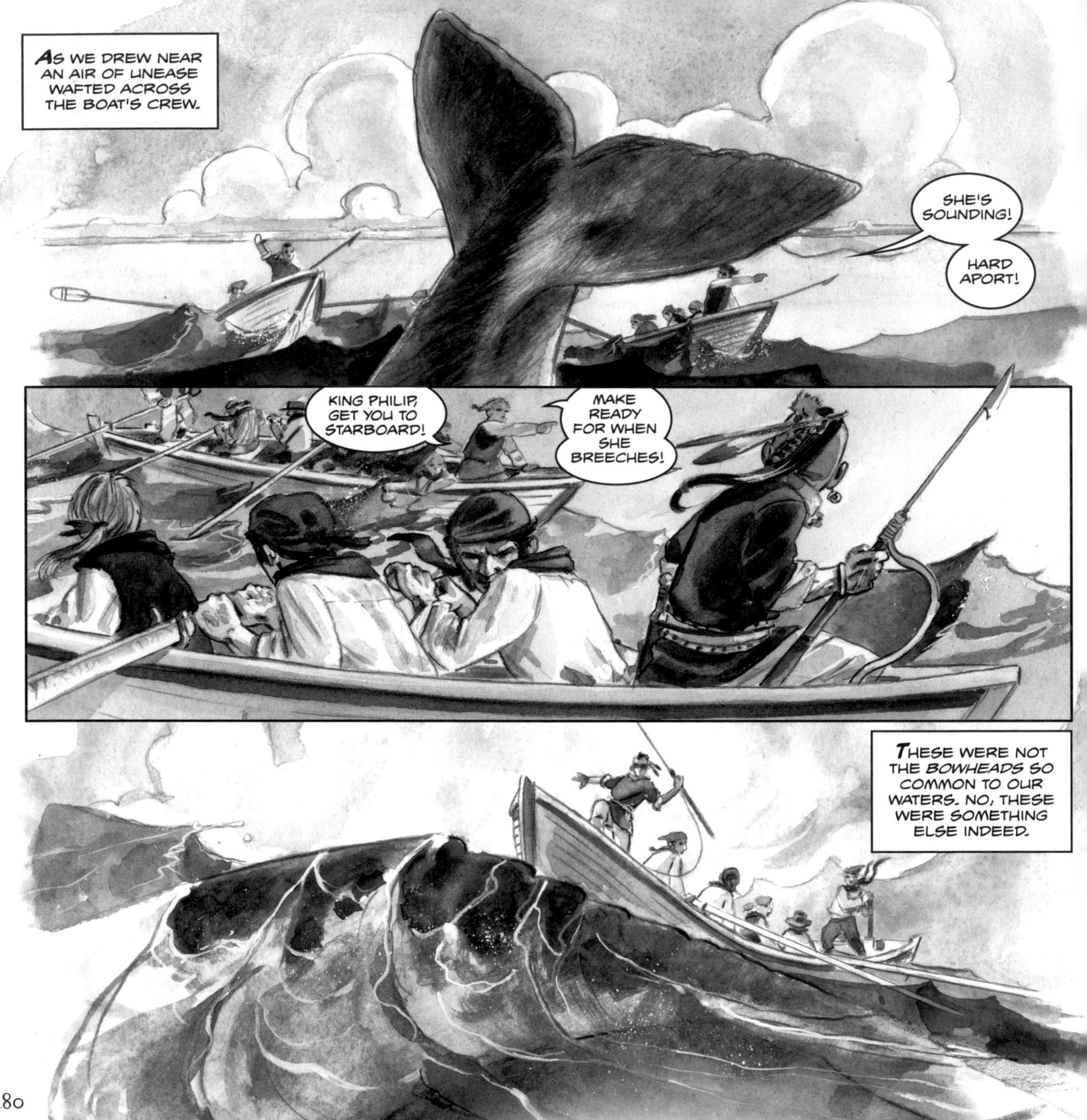
AS WE DREW NEAR AN AIR OF UNEASE WAFTED ACROSS THE BOAT'S CREW.
SHE'S SOUNDING!
HARD APORT!
KING PHILIP, GET YOU TO STARBOARD!
MAKE READY FOR WHEN SHE BREECHES!
THESE WERE NOT THE *BOWHEADS* SO COMMON TO OUR WATERS. NO, THESE WERE SOMETHING ELSE INDEED.

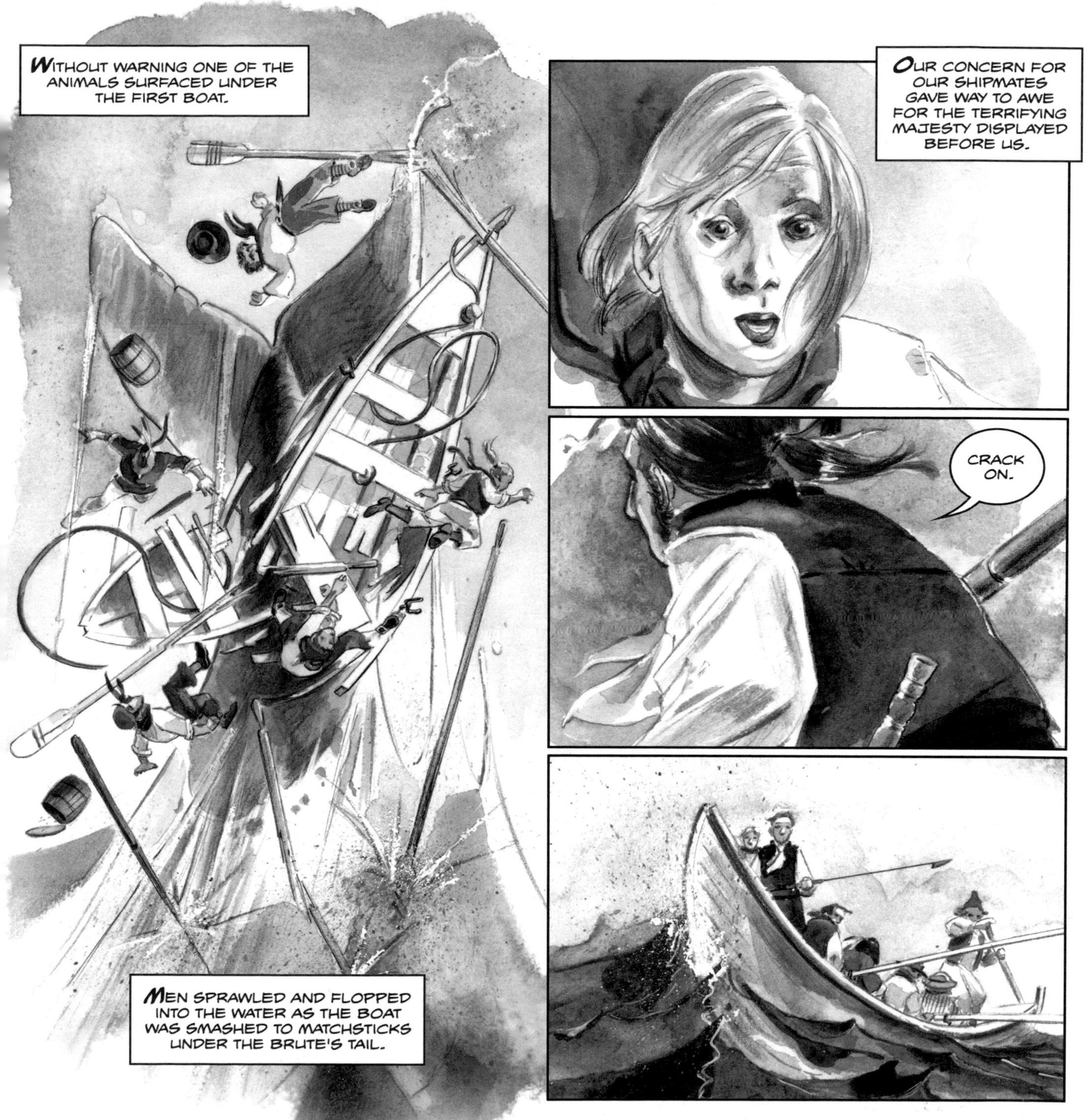
WITHOUT WARNING ONE OF THE ANIMALS SURFACED UNDER THE FIRST BOAT.
MEN SPRAWLED AND FLOPPED INTO THE WATER AS THE BOAT WAS SMASHED TO MATCHSTICKS UNDER THE BRUTE'S TAIL.
OUR CONCERN FOR OUR SHIPMATES GAVE WAY TO AWE FOR THE TERRIFYING MAJESTY DISPLAYED BEFORE US.
CRACK ON.

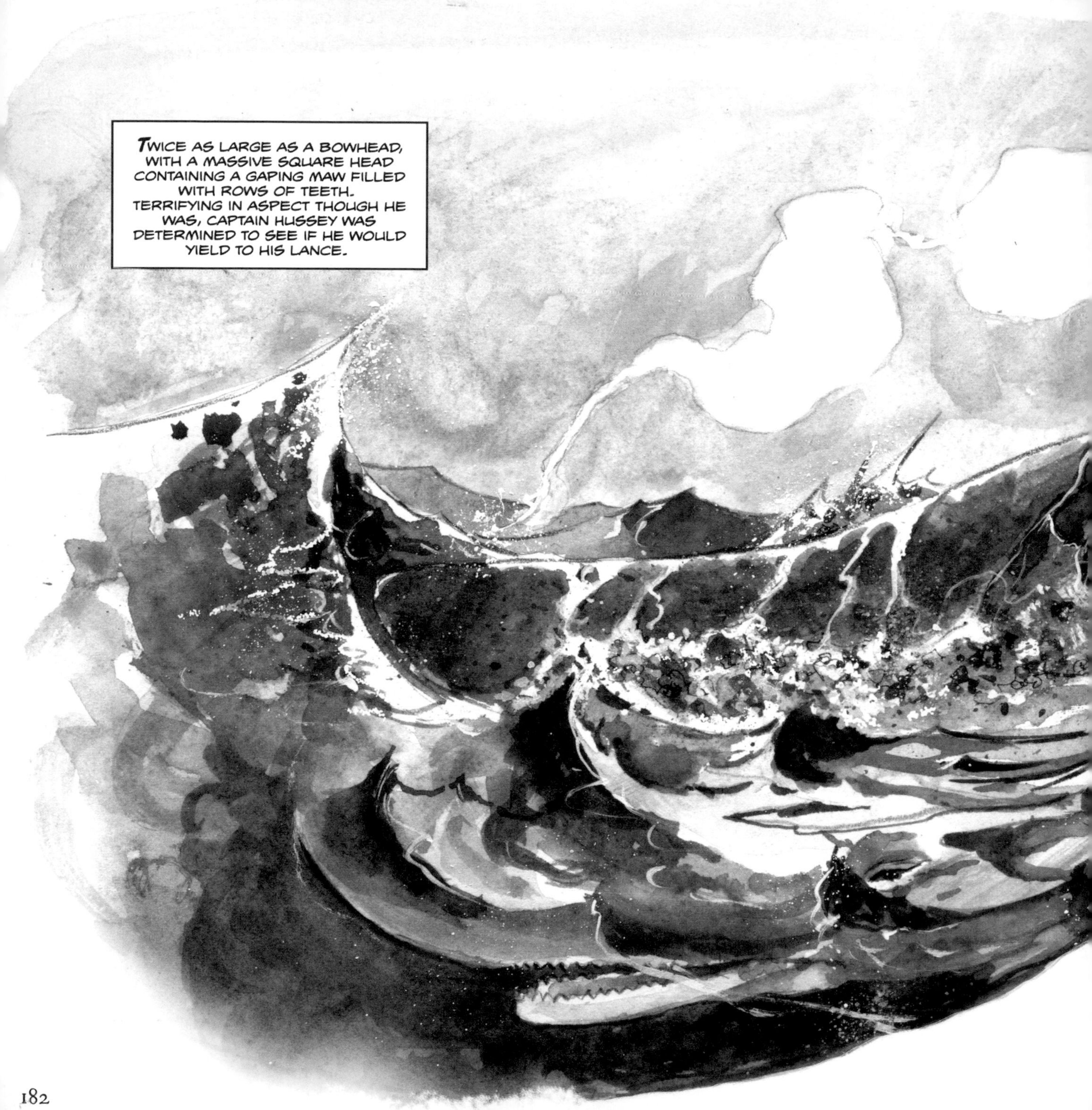
TWICE AS LARGE AS A BOWHEAD, WITH A MASSIVE SQUARE HEAD CONTAINING A GAPING MAW FILLED WITH ROWS OF TEETH. TERRIFYING IN ASPECT THOUGH HE WAS, CAPTAIN HUSSEY WAS DETERMINED TO SEE IF HE WOULD YIELD TO HIS LANCE.

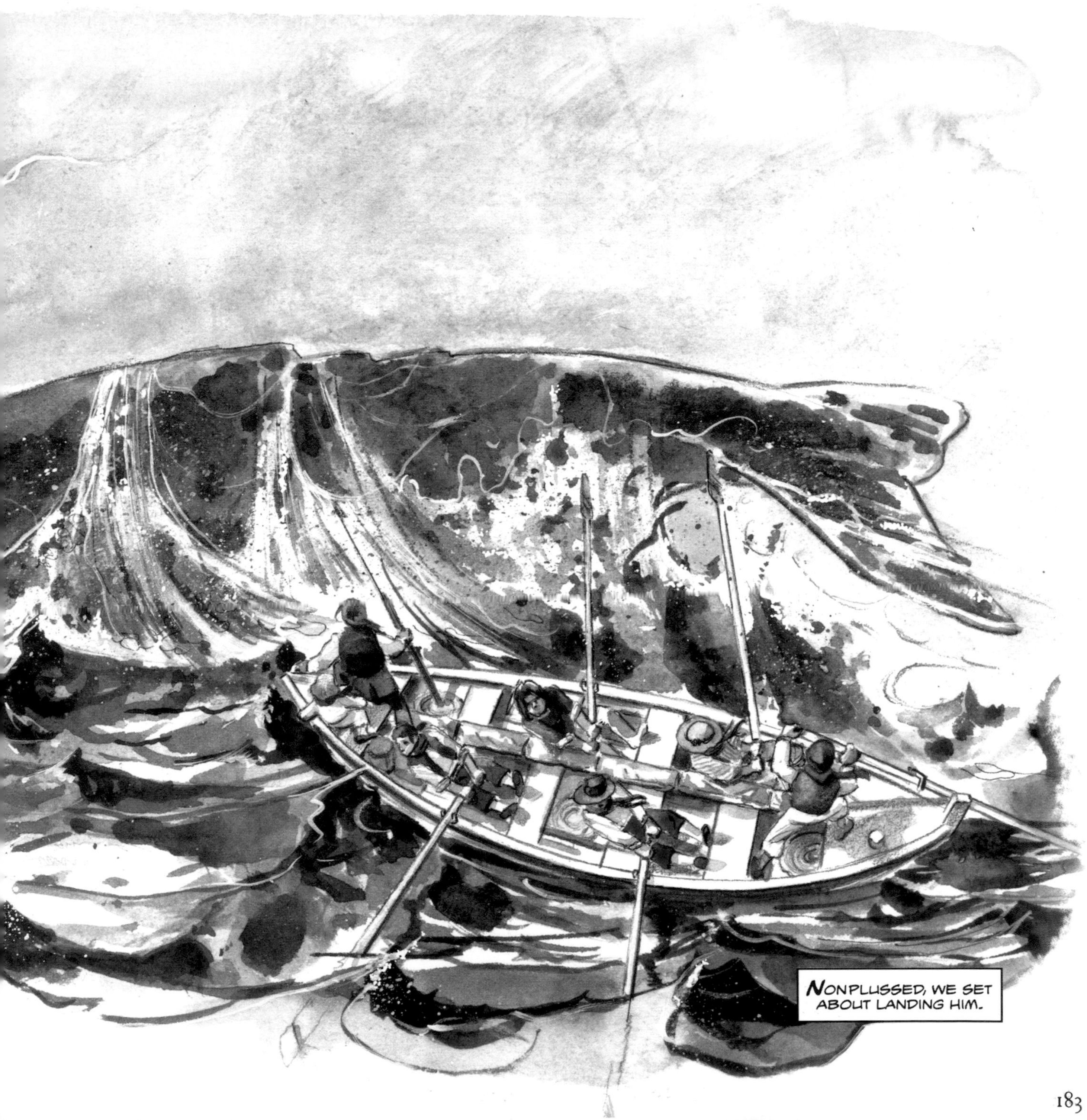
NONPLUSSED, WE SET ABOUT LANDING HIM.

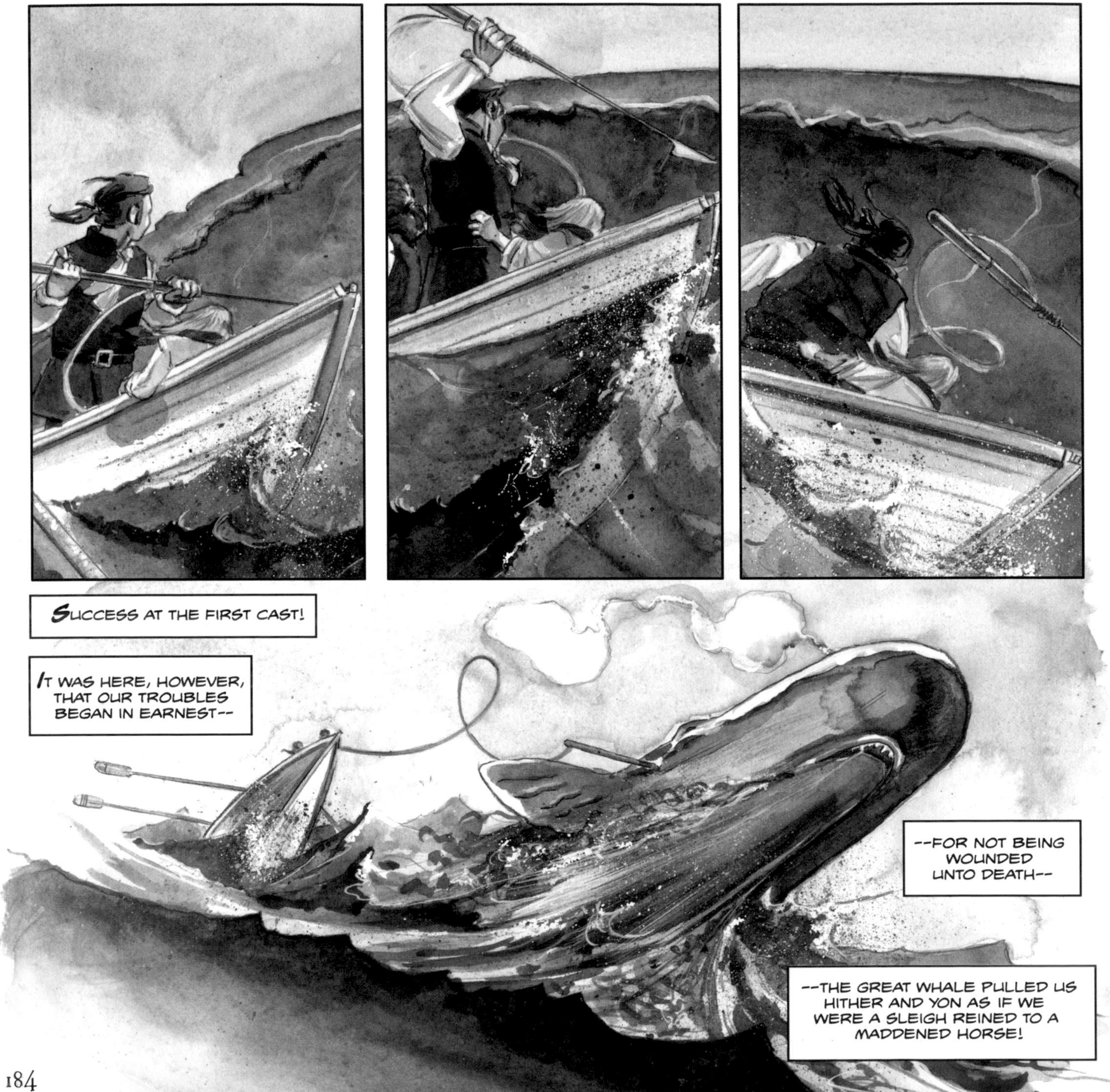
SUCCESS AT THE FIRST CAST!
IT WAS HERE, HOWEVER, THAT OUR TROUBLES BEGAN IN EARNEST--
--FOR NOT BEING WOUNDED UNTO DEATH--
--THE GREAT WHALE PULLED US HITHER AND YON AS IF WE WERE A SLEIGH REINED TO A MADDENED HORSE!

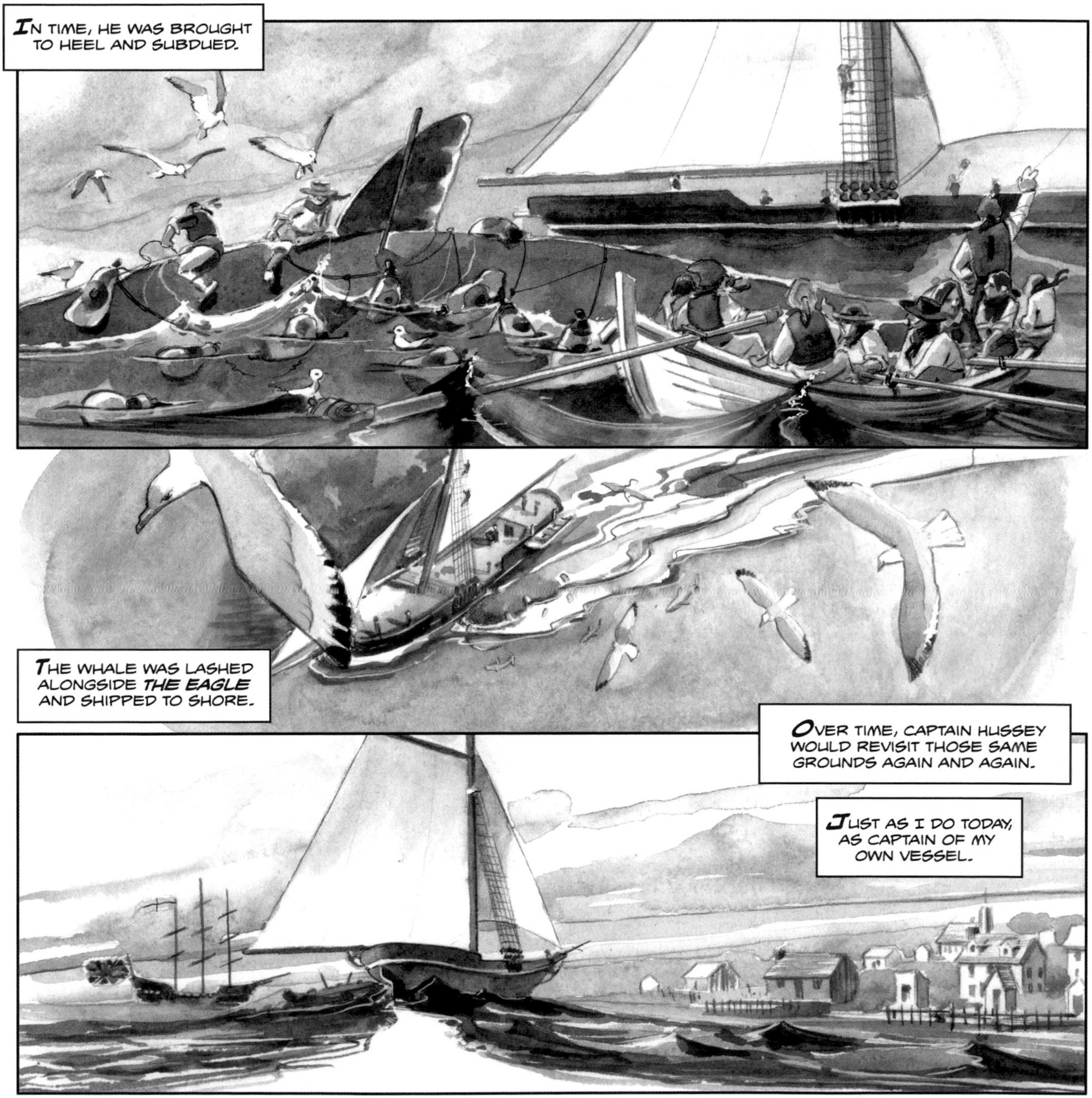
IN TIME, HE WAS BROUGHT TO HEEL AND SUBDUED.
THE WHALE WAS LASHED ALONGSIDE *THE EAGLE* AND SHIPPED TO SHORE.
OVER TIME, CAPTAIN HUSSEY WOULD REVISIT THOSE SAME GROUNDS AGAIN AND AGAIN.
JUST AS I DO TODAY, AS CAPTAIN OF MY OWN VESSEL.

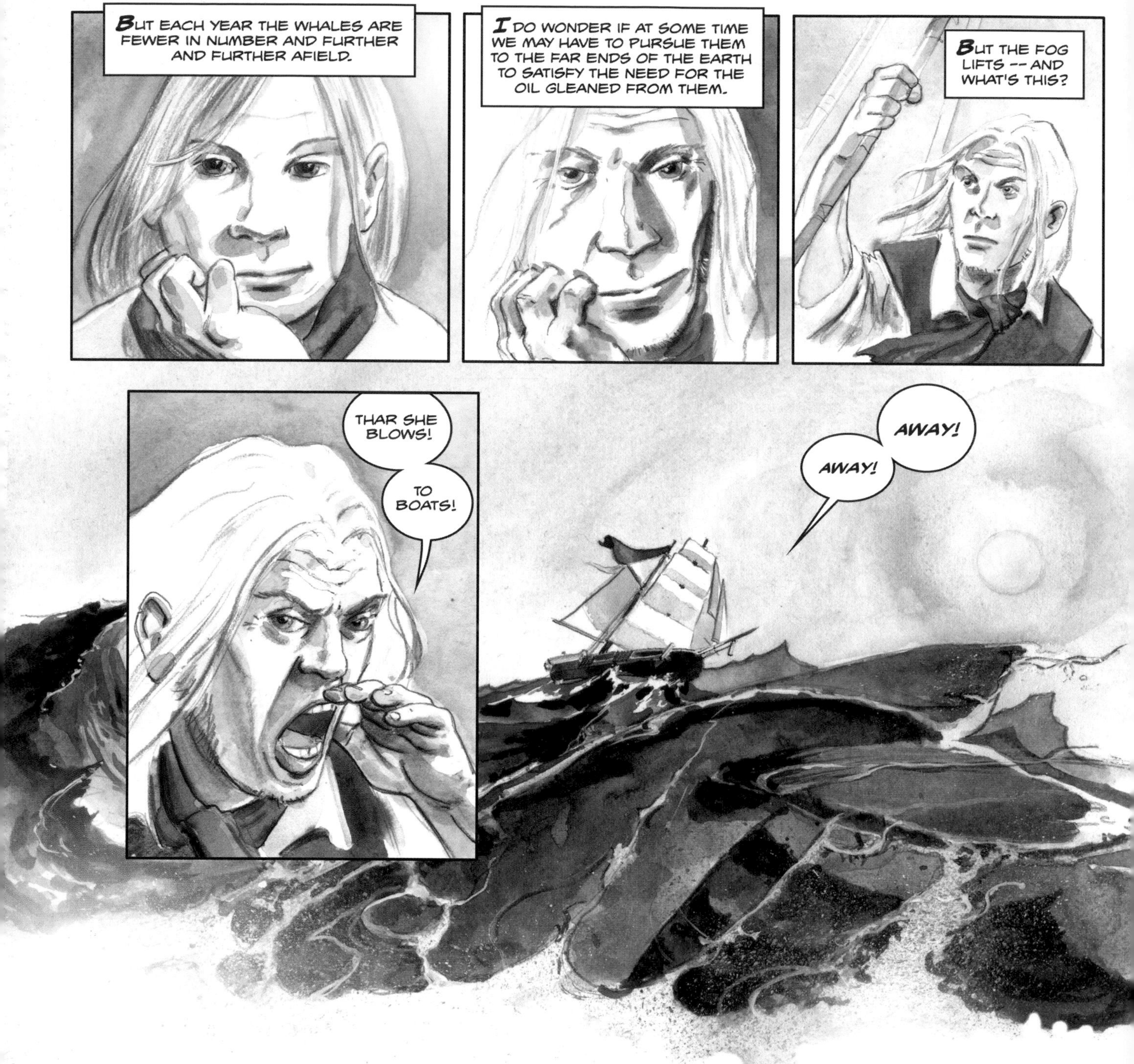
BUT EACH YEAR THE WHALES ARE FEWER IN NUMBER AND FURTHER AND FURTHER AFIELD.
I DO WONDER IF AT SOME TIME WE MAY HAVE TO PURSUE THEM TO THE FAR ENDS OF THE EARTH TO SATISFY THE NEED FOR THE OIL GLEANED FROM THEM.
BUT THE FOG LIFTS -- AND WHAT'S THIS?
THAR SHE BLOWS!
TO BOATS!
AWAY!
AWAY!

The End
of
COLONIAL COMICS: NEW ENGLAND, 1620-1750

The Journey Will Continue
in

COLONIAL

·QUI· MAL·Y· PENSE· ·HONI·SOIT·

COMICS

New England
1750-1775

Edited by Jason Rodriguez

Book Guide

The purpose of this book is to introduce readers to the underrepresented stories of colonial American history. When I was curating creators for this collection, I asked them to focus on stories that we normally don't read about in history books. I think they all did a fantastic job.

"The Press's Widow" (written by Erika Swyler and illustrated by Nœl Tuazon), for example, introduces us to Elizabeth Glover. By itself, it's a great story about a woman whose husband died and was left with nothing but a printing press, children, and two debtors who had to pay their passage to the New World. But this story, like all of the stories in this book, serves as a bridge to a larger story. Elizabeth Glover is just one person, but she represents so much more than that. Her story is about widows in Puritan society; about women who tried to open their own 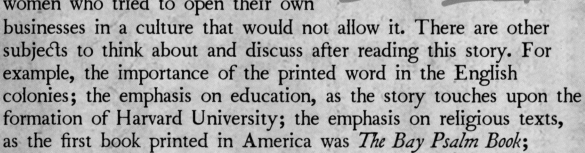 businesses in a culture that would not allow it. There are other subjects to think about and discuss after reading this story. For example, the importance of the printed word in the English colonies; the emphasis on education, as the story touches upon the formation of Harvard University; the emphasis on religious texts, as the first book printed in America was *The Bay Psalm Book*;

and the fact that many people couldn't afford passage to America, and were in debt to the people who paid their way.

These stories are launching points into bigger stories, and they help to paint a complete picture of the English colonies.

One of the first people I reached out to for this collection was Dr. Virginia DeJohn Anderson. She wrote a book called *Creatures of Empire,* which is about free-range animal husbandry and the role the practice played in English and Native American relations. When the colonists came to the New World, they brought livestock with them, which doesn't seem like that big of a deal to us now. However, there are two things that you need to understand in order to appreciate why this was important:

1. Native Americans did not domesticate animals. They farmed and hunted, but they did not keep cows or pigs for the purpose of food and labor.
2. Domesticated animals need a lot of room to graze.

I asked Dr. Anderson if we could do a story that emphasized how crucial livestock was to the tensions between these two societies and we set out to see how it could be done. The story in this book isn't an exact account—it's more an amalgamation of several stories, but it touches on the rising tensions in the following manner:

1. The colonists brought their livestock to the New World.
2. Needing room, the colonists would allow their livestock to graze outside of their farms.
3. The livestock found easy-to-get sources of food in Native American farms.
4. At first, the colonists tried to make reparations for any damages. Then they taught the Native Americans how to build fences. When the fences didn't work, the tendency was to blame the Native Americans.
5. As the Native Americans moved farther west to get away from the livestock, tensions began to grow.
6. These tensions eventually led to war... and the Native Americans did not win. They continued to move westward.

In Dr. Anderson's story (illustrated by Mike Sgier), we see three Native American men on trial. This was done to represent how Native Americans were forced out of their lands.

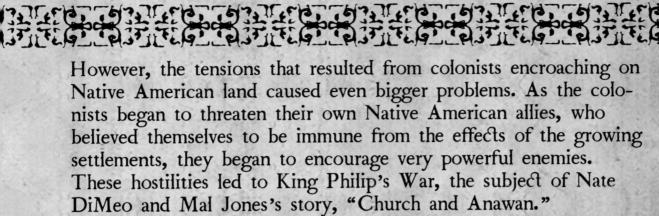

However, the tensions that resulted from colonists encroaching on Native American land caused even bigger problems. As the colonists began to threaten their own Native American allies, who believed themselves to be immune from the effects of the growing settlements, they began to encourage very powerful enemies. These hostilities led to King Philip's War, the subject of Nate DiMeo and Mal Jones's story, "Church and Anawan."

On the surface, Dr. Anderson's story is about a troublesome pig. But the story is really a collage, a connection of different stories that lead to war, and how a lot of it all started with a troublesome pig. That is a much bigger story and a much bigger discussion.

Because the book is laid out in chronological order, many of these stories lead directly to the next, even if the connections are not obviously stated. We are working to develop guides for the stories in this book, including guides that will help readers connect these stories for a full picture of colonial America. You will be able to find them on http://www.colonialcomics.com.

Sincerely,

Jason Rodriguez
Editor

Notes

A Note on Design

All maps were obtained from the Norman P. Leventhal Map Center. They were downloaded from http://maps.bpl.org/.

The squiggly design element that you see in this book, as well as in the text from the *The Bay Psalm Book* (including the misspellings), was re-created from the 1640 printing of the *The Bay Psalm Book*.

The re-creation of Ezekiel Cheever's *Latin Accidence* was taken from the 1838 printing.

The re-creation of the *Mamusse Wunneetupanatamwe Up-Biblum God* was taken from the 1685 printing.

Harried Out of the Land

This story is adapted from elements of Nick Bunker's book, *Making Haste from Babylon: The Mayflower Pilgrims and Their World: A New History*.

The introduction page map is *Europæ* by Abraham Ortelius and published by Aegidius Coppenius Diesth (1570).

Thomas Morton, Merry Mount's Lord of Misrule

The story was derived from several sources, listed alphabetically:

Cronon, William. *Changes in the Land: Indians, Colonists, and the Ecology of New England*. New York: Hill & Wang, 1938.

Dempsey, Jack, ed. *New English Canaan by Thomas Morton of "Merrymount," with Text, Notes, Biography & Criticism*. Scituate, MA: Digital Scanning, Inc., 1999.

Holly, H. Hobart. *Quincy's Legacy: Topics from Four Centuries of Massachusetts History*. Quincy, MA: Quincy Historical Society, 1998.

The Menotomy Journal, http://www.menotomyjournal.com/massachuset/.

Morison, Samuel Eliot, ed. *Of Plymouth Plantation, 1620–1647, by William Bradford, Sometime Governor Thereof*. New York: Alfred A. Knopf, 1970.

Peterson, Harold L. *Arms & Armor in Colonial America, 1526–1783*. New York: Bramhall House, 1956.

Winerock, Emily F. "Reformation and Revelry: The Practices and Politics of Dancing in Early Modern England, c. 1550–c. 1640." PhD diss., Department of History, University of Toronto, ON, Canada, 2012.

Grateful acknowledgments to Richard Pickering, Bob Charlebois, and Denise Lebica at Plimoth Plantation of Plymouth, Massachusetts, as well as to the Quincy (MA) Historical Society and the Massachusetts Historical Society. Thanks also to Emily Winerock, Lynn Nœl, Alexa Dickman, Brian Bixby, and Patrick Flaherty.

The introduction page map is *New France, New Englande, New Scotlande and New Foundlande* by William Alexander Stirling (1625).

TROUBLESOME SOWS
This story is adapted from elements of Virginia DeJohn Anderson's book, *Creatures of Empire.*

The introduction page map is *Carte de la Nouvelle-France, augmentée depuis la derniere, servant a la navigation faicte en son vray meridien* by Samuel de Champlain (1632).

GARDEN IN THE WILDERNESS
This story was derived from several sources, listed alphabetically:

Barry, John M. *Roger Williams and the Creation of the American Soul: Church, State, and the Birth of Liberty.* New York: Viking, 2012.

Bridenbaugh, Carl. *Fat Mutton and Liberty of Conscience: Society in Rhode Island, 1636–1690.* Providence, RI: Brown University Press, 1974.

Morgan, Edmund S. *Roger Williams: The Church and the State.* New York: Harcourt, Brace & World, 1967.

Wedgwood, C.V. *The King's War, 1641–1647.* New York: Macmillan, 1958.

Williams, Roger. *A Key into the Language of America.* Ed. John J. Teunissen and Evelyn J. Hinz. Detroit: Wayne State University Press, 1973.

Williams, Roger. *The Bloudy Tenent of Persecution.* Ed. Samuel L. Caldwell. Providence, RI: Narragansett Club, 1867. Accessed online via Google Books, books.google.com.

The introduction page map is *Nova Anglia, Novum Belgium et Virginia* by Jan Jansson and published by Hondius & Jansson (1636).

THE TRIAL OF ANNE HUTCHINSON
All dialogue for this story is paraphrased from court transcripts and the journals of John Winthrop. Some language and spelling have been modernized for clarity.

The Examination of Mrs Anne Hutchinson at the Court at Newton, 1637 (trial transcript). Accessed online.

Winthrop's Journal, "History of New England," 1630–1649, Volume 1, by John Winthrop. Accessed online via Google Books, books.google.com.

The introduction page map is *Plan of Boston showing existing ways and owners on December 25, 1635* by George Lamb (1635).

THE PRESS'S WIDOW: ELIZABETH GLOVER
The story was derived from several sources, listed alphabetically:

Biggs, Mary, "Neither Printer's Wife Nor Widow: American Women in Typesetting: 1830-1950." *The Library Quarterly,* Vol. 50, No. 4 (1980).

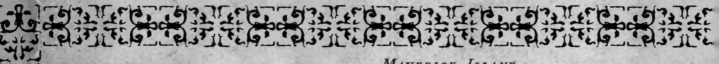

Hudak, Leona M. *Early American Women Printers and Publishers, 1639–1820.* Metuchen, NJ, and London: The Scarecrow Press, Inc., 1978.

Ingersoll, Ernest. "Our Earliest Printing-Press." *Art & Life,* Vol. 11, No. 3 (1919) 147–150.

Kimber, Sidney A. *The Story of an Old Press: An Account of the Hand-Press Known as the Stephen Daye Press, Upon Which Was Begun in 1638 the first Printing in British North America.* Cambridge, MA: University Press, 1937.

Littlefield, George Emery. *The Early Massachusetts Press, 1638–1711.* Boston: The Club of Odd Volumes, 1907.

Roden, Robert F. *Famous Presses. The Cambridge Press, 1638–1692. A History of the First Printing Press Established in English America, Together with a Bibliographical List of the Issues of the Press.* New York: Dodd & Mead, 1905.

Stephen Daye and His Successors. Cambridge, MA: The University Press, 1921.

Thomson, Ellen Mazur. "Alms for Oblivion: The History of Women in Early American Graphic Design." *Design Issues,* Vol. 10, No. 2 (1994), 27–48.

Winship, George Parker. *The Cambridge Press, 1638–1692.* Freeport, NY: Books for Libraries Press, 1968.

Introduction page map is *Plan of Boston showing existing ways and owners on December 25, 1638* by George Lamb (1638).

Maverick Island

This story was derived from several sources, listed alphabetically:

Adams, Catherine, and Elizabeth H. Pleck. *Love of Freedom: Black Women in Colonial and Revolutionary New England.* New York: Oxford University Press, 2009.

Josselyn, John. *An Account of Two Voyages to New-England.* London: Giles Widdowes, 1674.

Josselyn, John. *John Josselyn, Colonial Traveler: A Critical Edition of "Two Voyages to New-England."* Ed. Paul J. Lindholdt. Hanover, NH: University Press of New England, 1988.

Warren, Wendy Anne. "'The Cause of Her Grief': The Rape of a Slave in Early New England." *Journal of American History,* Vol. 93, No. 4 (March 2007), 1031–1049.

Introduction page map is *This harbour of Boston* by Philip Wells (1688), republished by the Massachusetts Historical Society (1893).

New Medicine

This story is adapted from elements of Walter W. Woodward's book, *Prospero's America: John Winthrop, Jr., Alchemy, and the Creation of New England Culture, 1606–1676.*

The introduction page map is *A map of New-England, being the first that ever was here cut, and done by the best pattern that could be had, which being in some places defective, it made the other less exact; yet does it sufficiently shew the scituation of*

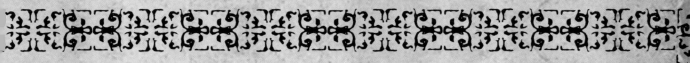

the country, and conveniently well the distance of places by John Foster (1677).

LOST TRIBE
This story was compiled from several sources, listed alphabetically:

Hoberman, M. *New Israel/New England: Jews and Puritans in Early America.* Amherst: University of Massachusetts, 2011.

Jewish Virtual Library, http://www.jewish virtuallibrary.org/jsource/vjw/rhode.html.

Touro Synagogue, http://www.touro synagogue.org/.

William and Mary Barrett Dyer. http://marybarrettdyer.blogspot.com/2012/06/jewish-settlement-of-newport-in-1658.html.

The introduction page map is *Tax list 1650, town papers 039, Providence, R.I.* by Henry R. Chace (1650).

THIS INDIAN WORK
This story was compiled from one primary source:

Winthrop, J., and J.K. Hosmer. (1908). *Winthrop's Journal, "History of New England," 1630–1649.* New York: C. Scribner's Sons.

The introduction page map is *A map of New-England, being the first that ever was here cut, and done by the best pattern that could be had, which being in some places defective, it made the other less exact; yet does it sufficiently shew the scituation of the country...* by John Foster (1677).

SUI GENERIS, A SHORT INTRODUCTION TO EZEKIEL CHEEVER
This story was compiled from several sources, listed alphabetically:

Cohen, Sheldon S. *A History of Colonial Education, 1607–1776.* Wiley: New York, 1974.

Gould, Elizabeth Porter. *Ezekiel Cheever, Schoolmaster.* Boston: The Palmer Company, 1904.

Hassam, John T. "Ezekiel Cheever and Some of His Descendants." *The New England Historical and Genealogical Register,* April 1879.

Johnson, Claudia Durst. *Daily Life in Colonial New England.* Westport, CT: Greenwood, 2002.

Parker, Franklin. "Ezekiel Cheever: New England Colonial Teacher." *Peabody Journal of Education,* Vol. 37, No. 6 (May 1960), 355–360.

Introduction page map is *The town of Boston in New England* by John Bonner and published by William Prince (1723).

CHURCH AND ANAWAN
This story was derived from one secondary source:

Sabin, Edwin L. *Boys' Book of Frontier Fighters.* Philadelphia: G.W. Jacobs & Co., 1919.

The introduction page map is *A map of New-England, being the first that ever was here cut...* by John Foster (1677)

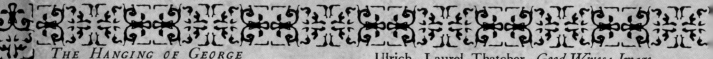

The Hanging of George Burroughs

This story was adapted from the research of Mary Beth Norton, including the seminal work, *In the Devil's Snare: The Salem Witchcraft Crisis of 1692* and her online essay, *The Refugee's Revenge.* For dramatic effect, Thomas Putnam's letter was adapted into a court scene.

The introduction page map is *A new mapp of New England and Annapolis and the countrys adjacent* by Christopher Brown (1690).

The Missing Cheese

This story was compiled from several sources, listed alphabetically:

Fischer-Yinon, Yochi. "The Original Bundlers: Boaz and Ruth, and Seventeenth-Century English Courtship Practices." *Journal of Social History,* Vol. 35 (2002), 683–705.

Huntress, Paul. "George Huntress of Bloody Point (Now Newington), New Hampshire and Some of His Descendants." Genealogical essay at rootsweb.ancestry.com.

New Hampshire Court Papers, 1674–77, New Hampshire State Archives.

Noyes, Sybil, Charles Thornton Libby, and Walter Goodwin Davis. *Genealogical Dictionary of Maine and New Hampshire.* Portland, ME: Southworth Press, 1928–39.

Rothman, Ellen K. *Hands and Hearts: A History of Courtship in America.* New York: Basic Books, 1950.

Ulrich, Laurel Thatcher. *Good Wives: Image and Reality in the Lives of Women in Northern New England, 1650–1750.* New York: Alfred A. Knopf, 1982.

The introduction page map is *A correct plan of the province of New Hampshire...* by Anonymous (1730).

Captives: The Stories of Eunice and John Williams

Demos, John. *The Unredeemed Captive: A Family Story from Early America.* New York: Alfred A. Knopf, 1994.

Hæfeli, Evan, and Kevin Sweeney. *Captors and Captives: The 1704 French and Indian Raid on Deerfield.* Amherst and Boston: University of Massachusetts Press, 2003.

Harrington, M.R. *The Indians of New Jersey: Dickon Among the Lenapes.* New Brunswick, NJ: Rutgers University Press, 1966. First published 1938.

Kamensky, Jane. *The Colonial Mosaic: American Women, 1600–1760.* New York: Oxford University Press, 1995.

Lenski, Lois. *Indian Captive: The Story of Mary Jemison.* New York: HarperCollins, 1995. First published 1941.

Williams, John. *The Redeemed Captive Returning to Zion.* Boston, 1707. Reprinted 1853 by Thomas Dickman. Greenfield, MA, accessed online via https://archive.org/details/redeemedcaptive01willgoog.

The introduction page map is *A map of New England, New York, New Jersey and Pensilvania* by Herman Moll (1756).

GLOOSCAP AND THE NEW MEN
This story is an adaptation of the Algonquin legend "How Glooscap Found the Summer."

The introduction page map is *A map of the coast of New England, from Staten Island to the island of Breton* by Cyprian Southack and published by Jno. & Tho. Page Mount (1737).

CHASING MONSTERS
This story uses the Nantucket Historical Association's article exploring the myth of Captain Hussey's first whale hunt as a starting point, accessed on the web via http://www.nha.org/history/hn/HNsimons-hussey.htm

Imagery was used from photo references taken at the New Bedford Whaling Museum.

The introduction page map is *Nantucket Island and the eastern half of Martha's Vineyard* by Joseph F.W. Des Barres (1776).

CREATOR BIOS

Tara Alexander is combining history and comics, two of her favorite things. She has a BS in history from Oklahoma Wesleyan University and her first published comics story appeared in *Once Upon a Time Machine*, an anthology from Dark Horse Comics/Locust Moon Press.

Virginia DeJohn Anderson is a professor of early American history at the University of Colorado, Boulder, where she has taught since 1985. Her area of specialization is the history of Colonial and Revolutionary America. Her latest book, *Creatures of Empire: How Domestic Animals Transformed Early America*, received the Phi Alpha Theta Best Subsequent Book Award in 2005.

Jason E. Axtell is an educator and illustrator from Virginia. His credits include the comic adaptation of *Family Guy*, and colorist for Matt Dembicki's *Mr. Big* and *Wild Ocean*. He self-published *The Strange Fungus in Mr. Winslow*, and *Strays' N Gates*, a collection of the serialized comic strip. Find him online at axtellustration.com.

E.J. Barnes is a comic writer and artist as well as gag and political cartoonist, illustrator, and animator. Her comics have appeared in anthologies such as *The Friends of Lulu's Girls' Guide to Guys' Stuff*, *Gauntlet: Exploring the Limits of Free Expression*, the Boston Comics Roundtable's *Hellbound 1* and *2* and *Inbound 5: Food*, and *The Greatest of All Time*

Comics Anthology. Her self-published comic books, historical and otherwise, can be found at www.drownedtownpress.com. She lives and works in Cambridge, Massachusetts.

J.L. Bell is a Massachusetts writer specializing in New England history, especially the Revolutionary period. He has written a book-length report for the National Park Service about General George Washington's Cambridge headquarters, lectured at numerous historic sites around Boston, and consulted on two episodes of *History Detectives*. Bell has also scripted comics printed in the anthologies *Minimum Paige*, *Hellbound*, *Oziana*, and *The Greatest of All Time*. Visit his website of "history, analysis, and unabashed gossip about Revolutionary New England" at http://boston1775.net.

Matt Bœhm is an animator working in the video game industry. As an avid reader of both history and comics he enjoys any opportunity to combine the two. His first collaboration with his wife, Ellen Crenshaw, was "Littery Men," a comic about Mark Twain, published in *Inbound 4: A Comic-Book History of Boston*.

Nick Bunker is the author of *Making Haste from Babylon, a History of the Mayflower Pilgrims*, described by the *Washington Post* as "a remarkable success." His most recent work is *An Empire on the Edge: How Britain Came to Fight America*. He now lives in Lincolnshire, England.

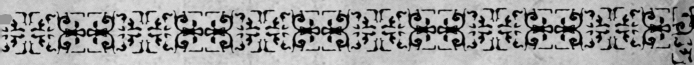

James Comey a graduate of the Maryland Institute College of Art, is a cartoonist living and working in Philadelphia, Pennsylvania. Along with his various self-published limited edition mini-comix, his work has appeared in the Locust Moon Press anthologies *Little Nemo: Dream Another Dream*, *Once Upon a Time Machine*, and *Quarter Moon*. James also has an amazing mustache and paints a lot of murals (comey2.tumblr.com).

Ellen T. Crenshaw is a California-based artist and avid comic book reader. When she's not freelancing in illustration, she makes comics, both self-published and distributed by publishers such as IDW, Ninth Art Press, River Bird Studios, and Draw More Inc. This is her second collaboration with her husband, Matt Bœhm; their first comic together, "Littery Men," can be found in *Inbound 4: A Comic-Book History of Boston*. Ellen is online at www.etcillustration.com.

Alexander Danner is co-author of *Comics: A Global History, 1968 to the Present*. He teaches online courses in comics literature and comics writing for Emerson College. He also writes comics, including the graphic novel *Gingerbread Houses*, and the formalist series *Two for No*, which can be found online at TwentySevenLetters.com and TwoForNo.net. He is also president of The Writers' Room of Boston, a nonprofit organization providing secure, affordable workspace for writers in the Boston area.

Matt Dembicki is a cartoonist workin' and livin' in the DMV (District-Maryland-Virginia area). He previously edited and contributed to the Eisner-nominated and Aesop Prize–winning *Trickster* and *District Comics*, which the *Washington Post* included in its top books of 2012. He recently edited the anthology *Wild Ocean*, which explores the adventures of twelve iconic endangered sea animals. Matt's other comics projects include the nature-based graphic novels *Xoc: The Journey of a Great White* and *Mr. Big: A Tale of Pond Life*.

Nate DiMeo is the creator of *The Memory Palace*, a podcast and public radio segment. He's the author of *Pawnee: the Greatest Town in America*. He lives is Los Angeles.

Charles Fetherolf has been drawing since he was old enough to hold a pencil. Through his imprint, Giant Earth Press, he has self-published *Giants in the Earth* and *Sons of Cain*. More recently, Charles has contributed to *District Comics* (Fulcrum Publishing, 2012), the Harvey-nominated *Once Upon a Time Machine* (Dark Horse, 2012), and the forthcoming *Little Nemo, Dream Another Dream* (Locust Moon Press). He lives in New Paltz, New York, with his wife, two children, and several annoying neighbors.

Jœl Christian Gill is the associate dean of student affairs at the New Hampshire Institute of Art. He wrote the words and drew the pictures in *Strange Fruit: Uncelebrated Narratives from Black History* and *Bass Reeves: Tales of the Talented Tenth*. The allegations that he ghostwrote *Hamlet*, *The Voynich Manuscript*, and started the Chicago Fire are completely unfounded. To learn more about Jœl Christian Gill, see the beginning of this paragraph.

Jason "Jaco" Hanley was born in Miramichi, New Brunswick, Canada, and, despite being Canadian, isn't a professional hockey player and doesn't live in an igloo. His love of comics began at a very early age. He started to create comic books in elementary school, and continues to do so today, nearly thirty years later. Although he has traveled the world, he still loves New Brunswick and resides there with his partner, Carrie, and their menagerie of animals.

Steve Harrison hails from a small town in California where he learned to illustrate comics and develop software. He migrated to a small town in Ohio with his wife and son, finding time during the long winters to draw comics, play banjo, and design games. Steve has self-published several science-fiction comics, including *Fabricari* and *Parity*. He has collaborated on a handful of short stories, including "Lending Can Openers," written by Alexander Danner and published by the Boston Comics Roundtable. He has recently released two iPhone games into the wild: *Dangerous Garden* and *Bacon Slider*. You can follow his work on his website (www.fabricari.com).

Mal Jones is an illustrator and designer based in Alexandria, Virginia, who has been working in and out of comics for more than fifteen years. More of his work can be found at maljones.com and rocketkoi.com.

A. David Lewis was born and raised in Massachusetts, earning his PhD in religious studies from Boston University. He is the co-editor of *Graven Images: Religion in Comic Books and Graphic Novels*, author of *American Comics, Literary Theory, and Religion: The Superhero Afterlife*, and collaborator with artist mpMann on *The Lone and Level Sands* and *Some New Kind of Slaughter* graphic novels.

Dan Mazur writes and draws comics, and is a co-founder of the Boston Comics Roundtable and the Massachusetts Independent Comics Expo. His comics have appeared in anthologies including *I Saw You, Minimum Paige, Inbound, Outbound, In a Single Bound*, and *Hellbound*. He co-wrote, with Alexander Danner, *Comics: A Global History from 1968 to the Present*.

Josh O'Neill is a writer, editor, critic, and comics publisher. He co-owns and operates Locust Moon Comics, a comic shop and small press in West Philadelphia. He has contributed to the Dark Horse anthology *Once Upon a Time Machine*, Rob Woods's

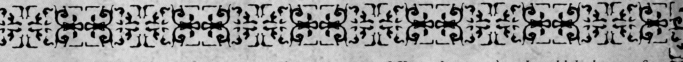

collection *36 Lessons in Self-Destruction*, and the upcoming Winsor McCay tribute project *Little Nemo: Dream Another Dream*. He talks about himself exclusively in the third person.

Chris Piers is a writer and illustrator living in Seattle, Washington, with his fiancée, painter Krissy Downing, and their four cats. He has contributed to several comics projects including anthology titles by the DC Conspiracy artist collaborative group and *Trickster: Native American Tales*, also by Fulcrum Publishing. He regularly writes for website therobotspajamas.com.

Dale Rawlings is a freelance illustrator and cartoonist living in the D.C. area. Some of his comics work includes *District Comics: An Unconventional History of Washington, DC*, *Magic Bullet*, and *Down and Out on Planet Earth*. He has also drawn comic strips for the FAA's employee website, illustrated magazine covers, and created conceptual illustrations for the National Holocaust Museum.

Matthew James Rawson is an artist residing in the Washington, D.C., area. His previous comics work has appeared in *Magic Bullet*. He has also done concept art and poster illustration/design for several independent horror films. His work can be seen online at www.glassicreative.com.

Christina Rice is the author of *Ann Dvorak: Hollywood's Forgotten Rebel* (University Press of Kentucky, 2013) and multiple issues of the *My Little Pony* comic book series (IDW Publishing). She oversees the photo collection of the Los Angeles Public Library and lives with her husband, writer Joshua Hale Fialkov; their daughter; two dogs; and a disgruntled cat.

Rafer Roberts is the man behind the comic book *Plastic Farm* and the comic strip *Nightmare the Rat*. His art has been seen in *X-O Manowar* and *Harbinger* (Valiant Comics), *Little Nemo: Dream Another Dream* (Locust Moon Press), *Henry and Glenn Forever and Ever* (Microcosm), and *Oxymoron* (ComixTribe). He currently lives in western Maryland with his wife and muse, and their hoard of cats.

Jason Rodriguez is an Eisner- and Harvey-nominated editor of comics and graphic novels. He writes, on occasion, and his first short story collection, *Try Looking Ahead*, is forthcoming from Rosarium Publishing. He currently lives in Arlington, Virginia, with his wife and many, many pets.

Arsia Rozegar first broke into the comic book industry professionally as a digital colorist for Todd McFarlane Productions, working on titles such as *Spawn: Dark Ages* and *KISS: Psycho Circus*. Shortly after, he was a colorist for Marvel Comics for several different series, while also enjoying extended stints on flagship Marvel titles such as *The Incredible Hulk* and *Iron Man*. He currently colors comics as well as creating his own digital art. To see his most recent projects, visit arsiarozegar.com.

Sarah Winifred Searle makes comics and pets cats from her secret lair based somewhere in spooky New England. She has produced historically inspired work at the Boston Public Library, Harvard University, and more, all of which you can learn about at swinsea.com.

Mike Sgier is a cartoonist and printmaker in Philadelphia, Pennsylvania. His first artistic inspirations were found in comics like *Teenage Mutant Ninja Turtles* and Jeff Smith's *Bone*, but grew to include such artists and writers as Lynd Ward, Stephen Alcorn, Neil Gaiman, and Joseph Campbell. His work has appeared in such publications as the *Philadelphia City Paper*, the comic anthologies *Secret Prison* and *Suspect Device*, and books published by Locust Moon Press.

Erika Swyler is an author, essayist, and comic lover. Her work can be found in *WomenArts Quarterly Journal*, *Litro*, Anderbo.com, *100 Entertainers Who Changed America: An Encyclopedia of Pop Culture Luminaries*, and elsewhere. Her illustrated debut novel, *The Book of Speculation*, is forthcoming from St. Martin's Press. She lives in New York, and can beat nearly anyone at Whac-A-Mole.

Nœl Tuazon hails from Toronto and works full time at the Nelvana Animation Studio revising storyboards. In his spare time he draws comics and, sometimes, the odd children's book or magazine. You can find his most current work in author Eric Hobbs's graphic novel, *Family Ties from NBM*, and *OSSM Comics's Foster* with writer Brian Buccellato. Unlike Erika Swyler, Nœl has yet to play Whac-A-Mole.

JT Waldman is a bicentennial baby based in Philadelphia. His first graphic novel was a biblical adaptation entitled *Megillat Esther*. His second book, *Not the Israel My Parents Promised Me*, was in collaboration with Harvey Pekar. His next project involves bourbon balabustas in early twentieth-century Kentucky.

Scott White is an illustrator and comic artist who lives in northern Virginia. His work can be viewed at theinkspill.blogspot.com

Walter W. Woodward is the state historian of Connecticut and an assistant professor of history at the University of Connecticut. He is the fifth person to hold the position of state historian, which was created in the 1930s in preparation for Connecticut's 300th anniversary. Woodward is a scholar of early American and Atlantic world history, specializing in New England and Connecticut. He has written numerous articles on subjects ranging from witchcraft in Connecticut, to the use of music by missionaries on the colonial frontier. His book *Prospero's America: John Winthrop, Jr., Alchemy, and the Creation of New England Culture, 1606–1676* was published by the University of North Carolina Press.

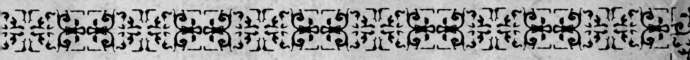

Acknowledgments

A book like this doesn't come together without the help of many people and institutions, and I'd like to apologize in advance if I've forgotten anyone.

First and foremost are the people at Fulcrum Publishing. Sam Scinta, who originally brought this project to me; Rebecca McEwen and Alison Auch for editorial support; and Melanie Roth and Jessica Townsend for marketing and promotion support. I couldn't have asked for a more patient and supportive publisher, so thank you all.

Then there are the institutions who met with us throughout the development of this book. They include all of the wonderful staff members at the Massachusetts Historical Society, the Concord Museum, Plimoth Plantation and the Wampanoag Homesite, the *Mayflower II*, the New Bedford Whaling Museum, the Massachusetts Archives, and the Boston Public Library.

Next are some of the folks who put in the extra effort. My assistant editors, J.L. Bell and A. David Lewis, who provided tremendous editorial support in fact-checking stories, offering advice, and gathering photo references for the illustrators when needed. A special thanks goes to Dan Mazur for introducing me to the folks at the Boston Roundtable and E.J. Barnes for helping J.L. Bell with outreach to institutions. Finally, Matt Dembicki who introduced me to the people at Fulcrum Publishing and helped me navigate the culture over there.

Of course, there are the creators who contributed to this book, often dealing with a scattered schedule and some last-minute changes to artwork, which, as any artist will tell you, is incredibly frustrating. Thank you all so much for your wonderful work—we don't have a book without you.

And, finally, thank you to all of the people who personally helped me as the book was coming together. Scott White and Mal Jones who reviewed the design aspects of the book over several trips to Bonchon Chicken. The attendees of the American Library Association's annual convention (especially John Sheblaski) who gave me advice on how to position the book. Chris Stevens of Locust Moon Comics for being one of my oldest friends in comics and recommending several illustrators to me. Marcello Illarmo for housing me while in Boston. My parents and my sister for their continued support, and my in-laws, the Castoldi family, for their support and for housing me in Framingham when necessary.

And last but not least, my wife and soul mate, the most wonderful woman I ever met, Robin Castoldi. I can't do it without you, my love. Well, you and the pets. The pets really help as well.

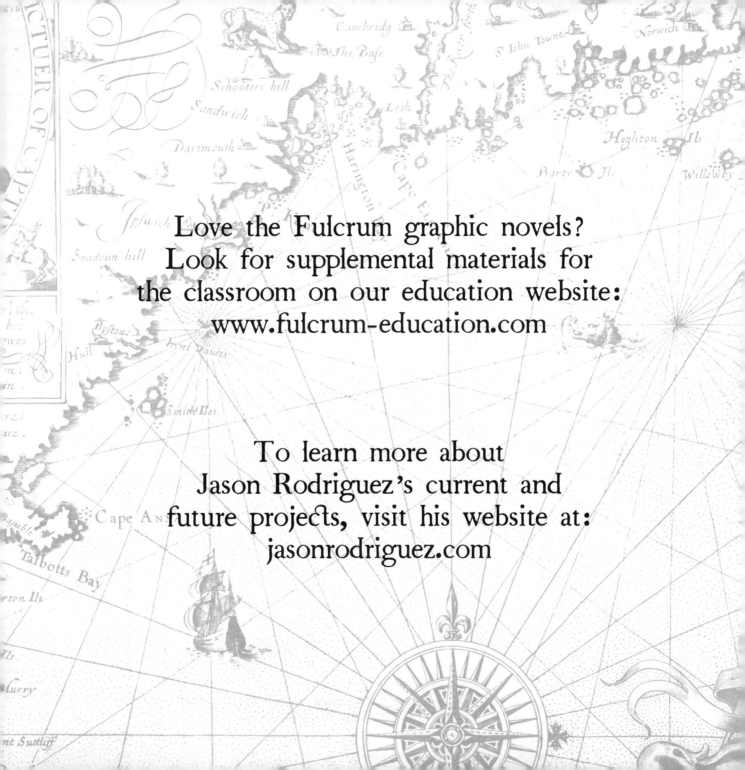

Love the Fulcrum graphic novels?
Look for supplemental materials for
the classroom on our education website:
www.fulcrum-education.com

To learn more about
Jason Rodriguez's current and
future projects, visit his website at:
jasonrodriguez.com

"This book is smart, surprising, fun, and educational. Each story has its own visual and verbal style but all will delight, intrigue, and enlighten both novice and expert alike."

James David Moran
Director of Outreach
American Antiquarian Society

"Jason Rodriguez has edited a visually attractive book that will encourage young readers to acquire a more meaningful understanding of Colonial America's history by helping make the stories come alive."

Julian L. Lapides
Past President
Baltimore Heritage, Inc.

"This collection of stories about early New England will appeal to kids of all ages. These fascinating stories concern both well-known and little-known New Englanders, including settlers, slaves, and Native Americans. We meet everyone from Anne Hutchinson to Yankee whalers. These engaging tales are beautifully illustrated and grounded in the latest scholarship. Highly recommended!"

Dr. Frank Cogliano
Professor of American History
University of Edinburgh